Schweizer Anglistische Arbeiten
Swiss Studies in English

Begründet von Bernhard Fehr
Herausgegeben von Andreas Fischer (Zürich), Henri Petter (Zürich),
Werner Senn (Bern)

Band 126

David Stamm

A Pathway to Reality

Visual and Aural Concepts in Dorothy Richardson's "Pilgrimage"

francke verlag

Cover picture: Helen Dahm (1878-1968), Paradiestraum, 1961, Öl auf Leinwand, 100/100,5 cm, Kunstmuseum des Kantons Thurgau, Kartause Ittingen

Die Deutsche Bibliothek – Cataloguing in Publication Data

Stamm, David:
A pathway to reality: visual and aural concepts in Dorothy Richardson's "Pilgrimage" / David Stamm. – Tübingen ; Basel : Francke, 2000
(Schweizer Anglistische Arbeiten; Bd. 126)
Zugl.: Zürich, Univ., Diss., 1998
ISBN 3-7720-2438-6

This thesis was accepted as a doctoral dissertation by the Faculty of Arts of the University of Zürich in the winter semester 1998/99 on the recommendation of Professor Dr. Henri Petter.

Dischingerweg 5 · D-72070 Tübingen

Printed by Müller + Bass, Tübingen
Bound by Gogl, Reutlingen
Printed in Germany

ISSN 0080-7214
ISBN 3-7720-2438-6

Table of Contents

Acknowledgements

I wish to express my deepest gratitude to the many people who have helped me to complete this book. I should particularly like to thank my supervisor, Professor Dr. Henri Petter, for his inspiring advice and critical guidance in my research. I am deeply appreciative of his patience and friendly encouragement as well as of his academic acumen, which were given most generously during the long time I spent writing on Dorothy Richardson.

I am also grateful to Professor Dr. Elizabeth Bronfen, my co-examiner, for her kind interest in my study. Her work on Dorothy Richardson has greatly informed and stimulated my own.

I am furthermore indebted to Vanessa Julie Holmes and Paul Kelly, who read, corrected and commented on my manuscript with the utmost care and efficiency.

Moreover, I wish to thank my piano teacher, Hans Brian, whose musical impulses and interpretative suggestions often started a fruitful train of thought, especially in our discussions on Beethoven.

I should also like to express my thanks to my fellow students at Zurich University, particularly Yvonne Studer and Michael Prusse, for truly motivating discussions, for their most useful tips and moral support in times of lonely research.

Special thanks are due to Marlies Pfister and Muriel Checksfield for highly stimulating discussions on modernist literature as well as for their personal reminiscences of early 20th-century London.

I am also obliged to Regula and Konrad Witzig, who in a most unbureaucratic way gave permission to reproduce the cover picture, Helen Dahm's 'Paradiestraum', as well as to Markus Landert of the Kunstmuseum des Kantons Thurgau, who made this picture accessible to me.

My warmest thanks go to my family: to my parents, Georg and Irene, whose love and encouragement accompanied me throughout my studies; to my brother Christoph, who often rescued me from the intricacies of word processing and made the printing of my study possible within reasonable time; to my mother-in-law, Susanna Fuchs, who time and again kept my door closed; and, above all, I should like to thank my wife Karin as well as our sons Lukas and Matthias, whose keen interest and belief in my work was an unfailing source of motivation, and whose love, understanding and (im-) patience helped me to accomplish this study.

David Stamm,
Autumn 1999

Abbreviations

1. *Pilgrimage*

All the quotations from *Pilgrimage* refer to the four-volume edition:
Richardson, Dorothy. *Pilgrimage*. London: Virago, 1979.
They appear in the text with the following abbreviations and page numbers:

PR	*Pointed Roofs*	(Volume I, pp. 13 - 186)
BW	*Backwater*	(Volume I, pp. 187 - 346)
HC	*Honeycomb*	(Volume I, pp. 347 - 490)
TU	*The Tunnel*	(Volume II, pp. 11 - 288)
IN	*Interim*	(Volume II, pp. 289 - 453)
DL	*Deadlock*	(Volume III, pp.11 - 230)
RL	*Revolving Lights*	(Volume III, pp. 231 - 396)
TR	*The Trap*	(Volume III, pp. 397 - 509)
O	*Oberland*	(Volume IV, pp. 11 - 128)
DLH	*Dawn's Left Hand*	(Volume IV, pp. 129 - 268)
CH	*Clear Horizon*	(Volume IV, pp. 269 - 400)
DH	*Dimple Hill*	(Volume IV, pp. 401 - 552)
MM	*March Moonlight*	(Volume IV, pp. 553 - 658)

2. Other Works by Dorothy Richardson

GGF *Gleanings from the Works of George Fox*. London: Headley Brothers, 1915.

JP *Journey to Paradise (Short Stories)*. London: Virago, 1989.

QPP *The Quakers Past and Present*. London: Constable, 1914.

WM *Windows on Modernism. Selected Letters*, ed. by Gloria G. Fromm. Athens, Georgia, and London: University of Georgia Press, 1995.

3. Further References

GM *The Gender of Modernism*. Ed. Bonnie Kime Scott. Bloomington: Indiana University Press, 1990.

OBEV *The Oxford Book of English Verse 1250 - 1918 (New Edition)*. Ed. Arthur Quiller-Couch. Oxford: Clarendon Press, 1939.

OED *The Oxford English Dictionary*. 2nd Edition. Oxford: Clarendon Press, 1989.

Introduction

> The eye is not satisfied with seeing nor the ear filled with hearing. (Eccl. 1,8)

> The highest and most profitable reading is the true knowledge and consideration of ourselves.
> (Thomas à Kempis, *Of the Imitation of Christ* 5)

> 'What?' she said suddenly, turning full round. Something had thrilled the air about her, bringing the whole evening to a head.
> 'Haldane's *Pathway to Reality*,' repeated the woman as their eyes met. Miriam was held by the intense radiance of the blue eyes. Light, strangely cool and pure, flowed from the still face. She was beautiful, with a curious impersonal glowless beauty. The light that came from her was the light of something she saw, habitually.
> 'But I ought not to recommend you to read. You ought to spend all your free time in the open air. Moreover, it's very stiff reading.'
> Miriam rose, beleaguered and flinching. How did people find out about books? Where did they get them from? This woman could not afford to buy big expensive volumes. . . . Why did her quick mind assume that the difficulty of the book would be a barrier, and not see that it was the one book she was waiting for, even if it were the stiffest and dryest in the world? . . . But the title was unforgettable; one day she would come across the book somewhere and get at its meaning in her own way (*DL*, 163).

Throughout *Pilgrimage* Miriam Henderson, Dorothy Richardson's fictional 'alter ego', expresses her deep dissatisfaction with most of the books she has read. An 'endless fuss about nothing' (*DL*, 45), a 'highly flavoured drug' and 'as much an abstraction as metaphysics' (*TR*, 426), fiction to her leaves 'life so small that it seems worthless' (*RL*, 276). Most novels to her are mere collections of incidents and sentiments, excluding what in her opinion is central: what does reality, i.e., the *individual* world of experience, mean to a character? In what way does his or her perception of their surroundings directly influence their life? Or, as Dorothy Richardson writes:

> Generally the surroundings were described separately, the background on which presently the characters began to fuss. But they were never sufficiently shown as they were to the people when there was no fussing; *what the floods of sunshine and beauty indoors and out meant to these people as single individuals,* whether they were aware of it or not. The 'fine' characters in the books, acting on

> principle, having thoughts, and sometimes, the less likeable of them, even ideas, were not shown as being made strong partly by endless floods of sunshine and beauty (*RL*, 243; emphasis added).

Out of this sense of dissatisfaction, missing the 'left out' material,[1] the not-yet-presented, Dorothy Richardson, in 1912, embarked on a project that was to occupy her for the rest of her life. It was her aim in writing to get at reality by rendering in a new form of fiction the immediate impressions and reactions of one single individual in all their manifold facets. What lent itself better to describing this undistorted reality than her own life, beginning with the experiences of a 17-year-old girl setting out on a long 'pilgrimage' to become a writer at last? By rigidly limiting the writer's point of view to the young girl's, or as Dorothy Richardson says, by describing 'her by the original contents of her mind [, h]er own images; what she sees and thinks' (*RL*, 285) she aimed at expressing in fiction what was absolutely crucial to her own thinking: the *'joy of life at first hand'* (*MM*, 569; emphasis added).

Applying this idea to her thirteen novel-chapters which eventually make up *Pilgrimage*, Dorothy Richardson created the method that to her great dismay was to be called 'stream of consciousness.'[2] Neubert's 'Wirklichkeitserlebnis' (97), a direct experience of reality, rather than 'Wirklichkeitserkenntnis', an abstract knowledge of reality, lies at the core of her writing, for to her all knowledge is 'bought only by experience. All else is hearsay.'[3]

The realization of this central notion of 'life as experience' can best be observed in Dorothy Richardson's consistent way of depicting the minutiae of the world as Miriam perceives it, of rendering her sensory perceptions and ensuing mental reactions in a superabundance of details. Thus, her experience of her surroundings is primarily an experience of the senses. What she sees, hears, and feels to a large extent determines her knowledge of the world. It is Miriam's eye and ear above all that perceive outer reality and transform these objective facts into her subjective impressions. It is her intense sensory perception, too, that both feeds and expresses her continuous, often overbrimming joy and wonder at the existence of life at all,[4] forming the vital

[1] cf. *DLH*, 239: 'The torment of *all* novels is what is left out. The moment you are aware of it, there is torment in them. Bang, bang, bang, on they go, these men's books, like an L.C.C. tram, yet unable to make you forget them, the authors, for a moment. It worries me to think of novels.'

[2] cf. letter to Bryher 1.1.1949: 'the death-dealing metaphor: stream of consciousness;' and letter to Henry Savage (26.1.1949): 'that lamentably meaningless metaphor "The Shroud (!) of Consciousness" borrowed some thirty years ago, by May Sinclair from the epistemologists (who have long since abandoned it) to describe my work, & still in lit.crit. pursuing its inane career' (*WM*, 597-600).

[3] quoted in Rosenberg 25.

[4] e.g. *HC*, 458; *DL*, 165; *DLH*, 137, 182; *CH*, 333.

basis of her mental conception of reality. Our discussion shall therefore focus on Miriam's visual and acoustic awareness. Starting from her direct sense impressions - what does she see and hear? - we shall examine the exterior conditions of context - what makes her see and hear them at this point? - as well as the consequences of these impressions on her inner life: what associations, memories, ideas and thoughts do they trigger off? In what sense are these impressions decisive for her idea of Life?

On the one hand, this analysis of Dorothy Richardson's extremely detailed description of Miriam's mind in motion from pure sensual awareness to thoughtful reflections as well as of her less conscious processes should yield a thorough character study. The long text presents its heroine and her world from an unprecedentedly consistent point of view, Miriam's consciousness; the absence of a commenting narrator creates an immediacy of Miriam's experiences, which, giving the reader an impression of 'unvermitteltes Erleben' (Bronfen 330), are not always easy to follow. This consistent method of perceiving and reflecting on the world exclusively through the mind of her heroine must necessarily include not only the beautiful vibrations and intensities, but also the incoherence, the triviality, the tenuousness of life in its often contradictory diversity. Dorothy Richardson aims at depicting *all* the 'different sets of realities' (*CH*, 309) that constitute a subjective life. In her narrative, which is an intense contemplation of Miriam's life, she thus would not merely *record* reality, but rather *discover* it in its subjective singularity (cf. Pykett 89): 'Contemplation is adventure into discovery; reality' (*MM*, 657). Though the literary result of her discovery is, as she herself concedes, in parts 'I.R.' ('imperfectly realized') (*WM*, 303), thin, superficial or dull (as life can be), she in her most intense passages achieves a sense of reality that not only draws us readers to the fascinating act of perception itself, but makes us, in Woolf's words, 'feel ourselves seated at the centre of another mind' ('Dorothy Richardson' 71), makes us follow Miriam on her way 'down and down to the centre of being' (*MM*, 609).

Dorothy Richardson's great literary attempt at the representation of consciousness at work thus distinguishes her as an innovative naturalist as well as a contemplative writer; in the presentation of Miriam's extremely subjective experiences she achieves an impressively profound form of realism, for, as William James writes, '*as soon as we deal with private and personal phenomena as such, we deal with realities in the completest sense of the term*' (1985:393; emphasis original).

On the other hand, in all its life-like realism, rendering the immediate contents of Miriam's mind, *Pilgrimage* is more than a means of self-expression. Contrary to other views,[5] I maintain that as a work of art it shows textual organisation both in micro-structural units of sentences, paragraphs and single chapters and on the macro-structural level of the whole text. Thus I want to examine Dorothy Richardson's use of sense impressions as poetic devices that importantly contribute to shaping her text. On this structural level we shall look at her use of visual and acoustic imagery and symbols, of echoes, repetitions and leitmotifs as formal elements in a text that at first sight lacks coherence.

While Dorothy Richardson is mainly remembered as an innovative writer breaking 'the sequence' by creating a new style of writing, I want to emphasize that she is, to quote Virginia Woolf, 'an *inheritor* as well as an originator' (*Room* 178; emphasis added), owing much of her writing to 19th-century thinking. In many of her views - on nature, music, silence - she takes up the Romantic tradition; the Bible and the Christian tradition are constant points of reference in personal, moral and social questions in *Pilgrimage*.

This investigation will focus on four central features to Miriam's experience: the journey, the garden, music, and silence, representing dynamic and static aspects of visual and acoustic awareness. Miriam's reflections based on her sensual perception will then be put in relation to the traditions Dorothy Richardson takes up and continues in her writing.

Pilgrimage as a metaphor for a journey of self-development, a quest for an identity, a pilgrimage through life towards Miriam's true self, has been much commented on. The novel-sequence, representing the 'inner voyage, the drama of the alienated consciousness' seeking its real being as a characteristic theme of 20th-century literature (Stubbs 234), can thus be positioned in the tradition of autobiographical or quasi-autobiographical writing (e.g. Augustine's *Confessions*, Brontë's *Villette*) or of allegorical writing such as Bunyan's *Pilgrim's Progress*, which is repeatedly referred to in the first novel-chapters. Yet, what makes Miriam's pilgrimage a pilgrimage? What are her concrete experiences of the *journey* itself? In our first chapter, a scrutiny of the three most important journeys in Miriam's life, the way Dorothy Richardson renders Miriam's direct impressions as well as the crucial impact of memory on Miriam's perception and reflection will be at the centre of our discussion. For both Miriam, the explorer, and Dorothy Richardson, the writer, looking *back* becomes as important as looking.

If the journey implies an extravert, dynamic process of 'becoming', the garden as a refuge suggests rest, stasis, interiority and 'being'. Thc themes of the journey and the garden represent what Lawrence (1936:457) calls 'the goal of the male' and 'female impulse,' which are at work together in

[5] e.g. Watts 7: She sees *Pilgrimage* as 'an accumulation of material, half-unworked, part unconscious, registered, but not [...] synthesized.'

Miriam's conception of life.[6] As she is highly aware of this duality in herself, her pilgrimage is determined by her search for an integration of such diverging aspects of life. In our detailed close reading of central scenes in their chronological order we shall examine the significance of Miriam's visual awareness both for the immediate moment and for her growth as an individual and thus highlight the development of these two 'impulses' in the text.

Our second chapter will focus on Miriam's garden experiences as reflectors of her mental state. The garden represents a refuge for solitary contemplation, the ideal place for Miriam to keep what is 'sacred' to her, 'the integrity of [her] own mind' (Emerson, 'Self-Reliance' 1983:26), a mind that is, to quote Virginia Woolf again, 'tuned to nature and reflection' (*Room* 96). Perception and reflection, body and soul, are inextricably linked; seeing with and through Miriam's eyes, we recognize Dorothy Richardson's notions of perception and conception both in the darkened or absent garden views after the death of Miriam's mother and in the most intense awareness of the beauty of gardens in moments of happiness. Miriam's visual perception plays a paramount part in her recurrent visions of paradise, which will be discussed in the last part of the chapter. Just as for her Romantic ancestors, paradise is set in childhood; reading her in this tradition, her bee-memory, her coming to consciousness in the garden of her childhood, assumes a deep symbolic significance, emphasizing the continual presence of paradise in Miriam's mind, both as a place of original happiness and of never-ending bliss to come.

If Miriam, at a first reading, seems to prefer her visual sense, we gradually come to recognize that her ear in fact plays as big a role in her perception as her eye. Not only does she register all sorts of sounds in minute details, but these sounds very often provide meaning to her perception of the world, as can be seen in her seismographic awareness of all shades of expression in other people's voices. The third chapter of this study will be concerned with the role of music, both as Miriam's second voice to express herself non-verbally and as the form of art that causes the strongest reactions in Miriam's being. We shall pay particular attention to the evocative power of the music Miriam plays or listens to and to the way immediate perception, reflection and subliminal feelings influence each other and make for her intense awareness of musical sounds. On a textual level, the continuous presence of music in *Pilgrimage* suggests musical structures in at least some parts of the text; they are to be exemplified in a structural reading of *Revolving Lights* in

[6] Lawrence writes: 'The goal of the male impulse is the announcement of motion, endless motion, endless diversity, endless change. The goal of the female impulse is the announcement of infinite oneness, of infinite stability. When the two are working in combination, as they must in life, there is, as it were, a dual motion, centrifugal for the male, fleeing abroad, away from the centre, outward to infinite vibration, and centripetal for the female, fleeing in to the eternal "centre of rest"' (*Phoenix* 457).

terms of Beethoven's 7th Symphony, which is played in the middle of this novel-chapter. Finally, I shall expand my view onto the meaning of music in Miriam's direct experience and as a binding element of the whole text by interpreting two opera scenes Miriam watches and listens to as representing crucial aspects of Miriam's relationships with men: art thus mirrors life.

The fourth chapter of this study will illustrate how *Pilgrimage* is more than a representation of Miriam's sensory awareness of exterior reality. There is more to life than what eyes and ears can perceive, as Miriam must have read in Thomas à Kempis (3; cf. *HC*, 458). Opening her ear and her mind to silence, the absence of sounds, Miriam, supported by her reading of Emerson and Maeterlinck and influenced by her Quaker host family, learns in solitude to listen to her inner voice, to come to terms with her own self, and in (female) society to find a non-verbal form of communication that leads to a feeling of intersubjective community. This treatment of silence raises fundamental questions about Miriam's attitude towards religion. It is one aim of the chapter to throw a clearer light on her religious experience as based on her affinity to mysticism. All in all, silence becomes a vital part of the whole, a constituent part of narration, as Dorothy Richardson traces the patterns of the mind and its relations to Miriam's ways of knowing and being.

To sum up our discussion of Dorothy Richardson's visual and acoustic concepts, the last chapter will be devoted to her use of polysensory perception and synaesthesia as a special form of perception. In the text the synchronized sensation of sound and vision appears at points of extreme perceptory intensity that make her lose the conceptual hold on reality, make her see and feel 'a reality that thought could neither touch nor express' (*CH*, 281). She then recognizes such moments of 'unearthly brilliance' as 'the real certain thing; the one real certain happy thing' (*TU*, 107). Beyond this splashing over of impressions from one sense modality to another Dorothy Richardson, as we shall see, uses the fluidity of synaesthetic metaphor as a poetic means to express the complexity of Miriam's outer and inner reality.

Like Haldane's *Pathway to Reality*, a series of lectures giving a compressed view of the history of philosophy, making, in Lucie Duclaux's words, for 'stiff reading' (*DL*, 163), *Pilgrimage* is not an easy book to read. It presents Dorothy Richardson's personal philosophy of life in terms of Miriam's individual seeking of her own 'pathway to reality.' As her subjectivity appears as the 'sole point of origin of all principles of order in the novel' (Würzbach 299), our understanding of the novel stands and falls with a compelling presentation of the subject's own construction of reality. In order 'to get at its meaning in [our] own way' (*DL*, 163) we have to read in detail, re-read, and develop a sense both for Miriam's astute perceptivity and for her powerful memory in relation to people and things. 'Il faut relire, il faut,' as Bachelard says (38), 'mener la lecture dans le double intérêt de l'homme et des choses, en ne négligeant rien du tissu anthropo-cosmique d'une vie humaine.' Each renewed reading of *Pilgrimage* then, not only makes us experience the plurality of the text - 'le texte pluriel: même et nouveau' (Barthes 1970:23), - but it also (re-)opens our eyes for the richness and diversity, as well as the unity and continuity of human life, and it may eventually take us closer to 'the heart of reality' (*QPP*, 35).

When the first volumes of *Pilgrimage* appeared, Dorothy Richardson's development of a new technique made her quite well known as one of the modern female writers, her name often being linked with those of Woolf and Mansfield. However, as the novel-sequence grew, the interest in her work decreased rapidly as each new novel-chapter written in the same subjective style seemed to add nothing but a further slice of Miriam's not too dramatic life. The short reviews of single novel-chapters of *Pilgrimage* by her fellow-writers Sinclair, Woolf, and Mansfield illustrate the critical attitude of her contemporary readers, pinpointing essential highlights, but even more the weaknesses of the text. Neither a first, highly approving book about her work, published by her friend J.C.Powys in 1931, nor the (to her) rather irk-some publication of her 12 volumes as the complete edition of *Pilgrimage* in 1938 could stop her sinking into oblivion. She died in 1957, still 'abominably unknown,' as Ford Madox Ford (773) had put it, leaving behind an unfinished last chapter, *March Moonlight*, which was first published in 1967.

Only after her death did interest in her work begin to rise, starting with a study of her life by Caesar Blake (1960). In a number of articles published in the early 1970s Shirley Rose focused on some central issues of *Pilgrimage*, emphasizing what she calls the 'unmoving center', Miriam's consciousness, as the stable seat of experience. Her psychological insights help to understand the working of Miriam's mind and have not lost their importance. John Rosenberg's centenary biography (1973) celebrates the 'genius they forgot', giving a traditional outline of her life and an evaluation of her work that sets her off as far more realistic than her 'romantic' contemporaries Joyce, Woolf, and Proust. Rosenberg and Thomas Staley, whose very readable biography was published in 1976, give a lively general portrait of the novelist who lived for her work. They both analyse *Pilgrimage* in terms of Dorothy Richardson's life and thus put her work in the tradition of autobiographical writing. While I do not agree with Rosenberg's denial of romantic elements, I appreciate Staley's interpretation of each novel-chapter as a representation of a stage of Dorothy Richardson's own life, but in his short book he evades the more complex issues of Miriam's life-story.

Gloria Fromm is *the* authority on Dorothy Richardson's life. Her biography (1977) is not only the most comprehensive to date, including photos and a detailed bibliography of Dorothy Richardson's forgotten writings for magazines and newspapers, it is also an invaluable sourcebook for details about her and her companions' lives and times; reading *Pilgrimage* in terms of autobiography thus sheds a clearer light on many problematic relationships in her life. After the publication of Fromm's biography, critical interest changed its focus. Fromm emphasizes Dorothy Richardson's role as a *woman* in the society of her times and thus supports the feminist readers and writers who claim Dorothy Richardson as one of their early representatives. The paperback edition of *Pilgrimage* (1979), published by the feminist Virago Press, then made the novels accessible again for a wider public. Thus, what has been at the centre of critical interest for the last 20 years is Miriam's spiritual pilgrimage read as her striving for an independent life as a woman, as her individual quest for her own *female* self.

An outstanding study in this respect is Gillian Hanscombe's book (1982), which examines 'the central role conflict between the demands made upon [Dorothy Richardson] as a woman, first by life, and secondly, by art' (27). One of the first to give up a chronological analysis of Miriam's life, Hanscombe evaluates the importance of Miriam's relationships to men and women in her self-finding; she inspired my own - more 'romantic' - reading of Miriam's friendships and love affairs as determining factors of her life.

Taking up this feminist reading, Penny Brown (1992) puts Dorothy Richardson in the larger context of female writers who gave women a voice of their own early in the century. Though Brown does not compare texts directly, her convincing presentation invited me to take an occasional glance at other women writers of the period - Woolf, Mansfield, Sinclair - , so as to show Dorothy Richardson's similar concerns and her unique voice in expressing them. Short articles and book chapters by Kaplan (1975), Henke (1978), Showalter (1978), Thorn (1978), Hanscombe (1987), Friedman (1988), Levy (1991), Loeffelholtz (1992) and Watts (1992) underline Miriam's feminist traits, most of them putting Dorothy Richardson in a socio-historical context and admiring her for her independent thinking.

Urs Bucher's dissertation (1981) does not follow this main stream of interest. He juxtaposes Dorothy Richardson and James Joyce as two influential practitioners of the 'stream-of-consciousness' technique and emphasizes the importance of the senses for Miriam's consciousness as well as her subjective awareness of time and space. While he summarizes Miriam's way of perceiving the world around her in a straightforward way, he restricts his analysis to *Backwater* and *Dimple Hill* only; though giving a convincing image of the inexperienced girl and the mature woman respectively, he eventually neglects major aspects of Miriam's experience of life.

Elisabeth Bronfen's long and complex study of space in *Pilgrimage* (1986, in German) gives a comprehensive analysis of the whole novel sequence based on a theory of space. Her reading starts from a detailed description of Miriam's awareness of actual rooms, which in their atmospheres act as seismographs of Miriam's inner moods. She then interprets the metaphorical aspects of *Pilgrimage* as a mental journey through different 'worlds', which is shown as a process to gain knowledge and thus to construct her identity. Bronfen sees space as a formative structural element of *Pilgrimage* and she develops a theory of spatial textuality that understands the text as a spatial construction rather than a chronological process. Bronfen's notions about the simultaneity of existence and the spiral, repetitive character of *Pilgrimage* support my reading of Miriam's subjective transgressions of time boundaries, especially of her experience of the past as an immediate reality in the context of her visual and acoustic awareness.

Jean Radford's *Dorothy Richardson* (1991), perhaps the best short introduction to the author and her work to date, presents some of the major issues of *Pilgrimage* in a clear, concise way. She reads Miriam's pilgrimage as a modern *Pilgrim's Progress*, analyses the difficult role that Miriam's reflections and recollections assign to her mother, and, within the framework of feminist criticism, reads Dorothy Richardson as a precursor of *écriture féminine*. Radford's reading of Miriam's first remembered moment, the 'bee-memory', as the 'beginning of the subject as a separate being' (119) gave impulses for my reading of the garden as an Edenic place of self-finding.

While Radford convinces as a general introduction, Watts's book (1995), published in the series 'Writers and their Work' and thus also addressed to a wide range of readers, does not really serve as an introductory book since Watts, reading *Pilgrimage* as an experience of modernity itself, presupposes the reader's acquaintance with Dorothy Richardson's life and time. However, she gives a very interesting interpretation of the record of Miriam's urban life and especially of her development out of Victorian constraints into the freedom of modernity. Furthermore, Watts's assessment of the author's lifelong interest in film and her cinematographic attempts in writing opens new aspects of reading *Pilgrimage* as a form of 'mobile impressionism' (82).

With this study I hope to further the discussion of Dorothy Richardson's use of sensual perception, particularly of vision and sound, as essential formative elements of *Pilgrimage*. It is one of my primary interests to analyse Miriam's attitude towards the world of phenomena and Dorothy Richardson's rendering of it, which becomes most obvious in the visual and acoustic concepts of the text. Looking at her in relation to some of her contemporary women writers, I shall show her role in modern feminine (feminist?) realism, but at the same time I want to underline the importance of her taking up and continuing older traditions and ideas (often explicitly referred to in the text) as crucial in her establishing her own view of life. Thus I maintain that as much as she breaks the sequence of literary traditions in her role as innovator of the novel, Dorothy Richardson partakes in it, enriching it with her 'opus magnum', *Pilgrimage*.

I.

THE EYE: VISUAL CONCEPTS IN *PILGRIMAGE*

1. Pictures of the Journey: Impressions of Change

1.1 'On Her Way to a Goal:' *Pilgrimage* as a Journey through Life

> Lift your eyes
> Where the roads dip and where the roads rise
> Seek only there
> Where the grey light meets the green air
> The hermit's chapel, the pilgrim's prayer.
> (T.S. Eliot, 'Usk', ll. 7-11; *Complete Poems and Plays* 140)

> One had the feeling of being on a journey that was both pathway and destination. (*DH*, 485)

When Dorothy Richardson had to decide on a title for her first novel, she wanted to name it *Pilgrimage*; however, as another book had just been published under this title, she had to change it to *Pointed Roofs*.[1] Thus, already at the beginning of what was to become her open-ended thirteen-volume life work *Pilgrimage*,[2] she conceived of her alter ego Miriam Henderson as a woman on a 'pilgrimage': the covering title of her work expresses two major aspects of her novels. According to the definitions of the *Oxford English Dictionary* a pilgrimage is a 'journey [...] made to some sacred place, as an act of religious devotion' as well as 'the course of mortal

---

[1] see 'Foreword', *Pilgrimage*, Volume I, 10: 'In 1915, the covering title being at the moment in use elsewhere, it was published as *Pointed Roofs*.' With her change of titles from the 'horizontal', progressive *Pilgrimage* to the 'vertical', static, architectural *Pointed Roofs* Dorothy Richardson turned from the general to the specific theme of this first novel-chapter, recalling John Ruskin, for whom the pointed arch was a signal of cultural difference: 'I know not any features which make the contrast between continental domestic architecture, and our own, more humiliatingly felt, or which *give so sudden a feeling of new life and delight* [...] as the quaint points and pinnacles of the roof gables.' (*The Stones of Venice* 403; emphasis added) This pleasure in the sight of the new and foreign is a central topic of Miriam's first voyage out. At the same time this new title shows us Miriam's indebtedness to 19th-century schools of thought (cf. Watts 1995:13).

[2] Volume 13, *March Moonlight*, was never completed and was first published only posthumously in the 1967 edition of *Pilgrimage*.

life figured as a journey.'[3] What that 'sacred place' of the first definition will be for Miriam shall be discussed later on; in this chapter we shall consider Dorothy Richardson's extensive use of this conventional image of the pilgrimage as a journey through life. By means of a discussion of Miriam's visual perception on her journeys, focusing on the protagonist's amazing eye, which registers in impressionist fashion the light, colour and movement of her natural surroundings, we shall aim at a deepened understanding of what these journeys mean to Miriam, both in their immediate experience of the 'Now' and in the overall development of her life. This 'mobile impressionism' of *Pilgrimage* (Watts 1995:82) subjects its world *and* Miriam's self to a form of optical testing. As we shall see, the perception of moving pictures serves as a 'catalyst for introspection' (Brown P. 208): Miriam recognizes as much about herself as about her surroundings, maintaining, as Dorothy Richardson writes elsewhere, 'a balance' between 'the thing perceived and herself perceiving' (*Close-Up* 3 [1928], 54).

Lukacs in his *Theory of the Novel* (77) states that 'outwardly the novel is essentially biographical', inwardly 'the novel has been understood as the process of the problematic individual's journeying towards himself, the road from dull captivity within a merely present reality - a reality that is heterogeneous in itself and meaningless to the individual - towards clear self-recognition' (80). This general definition can be adapted as a first definition of *Pilgrimage*: The highly autobiographical novel-sequence offers insight into Miriam's expanding self up to the point when her self-recognition allows her to start writing about her former life. It is the point where on her journey through life Miriam recognizes that the 'heterogeneous' realities of her past, inseparable parts of her being, have all helped her to become what she is:

> While I write, everything vanishes but what I contemplate. The whole of what is called 'the past' is with me, seen anew, vividly. No, Schiller, the past does not stand 'being still'. It moves, growing with one's growth. Contemplation is adventure into discovery; reality (*MM*, 657).

Pilgrimage, Miriam's journey towards herself, has been called 'a mystical journey to fulfillment and understanding of self' (Staley 62), the 'quest for the link between the subjective and objective reality made apprehensible through a literary work' (Rose, 1970:33), the 'quest for reality' (Radford 1991:78), 'an immensely personal pilgrimage towards an identity as well as a representation of the "flow of being"' (Brown P. 154); in all these descriptions the destination assumes a paramount importance. Miriam's 'pilgrimage' is understood as a teleological journey 'to a future state of rest or blessed-

---

[3] *Oxford English Dictionary*, 2nd edition, Volume XI. Oxford: Clarendon Press, 1989, 829. All subsequent references to this dictionary will be abbreviated to *OED*.

ness' (*OED XI*, 829), i. e. the 'blessedness' of being able to write about herself. When she does so, her quest ends: her 'search for both a particular quality of experience and the means to represent it' (Watts 56) has reached the last word of *Pilgrimage*: it has come to its 'fulfilment' (*MM*, 658).

However, if we bear in mind Miriam's reflection on life as being 'a journey that was both pathway and destination' (*DH*, 485), the immediate impact of the journey itself as a destination, which these critics tend to neglect, has to be focused on, too. In the first novel-chapters of *Pilgrimage* Dorothy Richardson explicitly refers to such diverse classical works of 'travel *literature*' as *Robinson Crusoe, The Pilgrim's Progress, The Voyage of the Beagle* or the *Divina Commedia*, which all emphasize the importance of the protagonist's changing places; the journey as a movement through space forms a central element in the textual body of these works. She thus puts her own text in a literary tradition that, using the topos of the journey as a means to an end - to account for the hero's progress through life towards some improved or 'redeemed' state - , at the same time underlines the importance of the means itself, the physical act of travelling.

The repeated hints at Miriam's going somewhere throughout *Pilgrimage* suggest the advisability of a close look at the accounts of her actual journeys, as these travel accounts most clearly represent her awareness of the interplay of change and stability both within and outside herself. Yearning for a stable resting place, for the 'home' she feels obliged to leave at the outset of her pilgrimage, Miriam's geographic removal, suggesting the thematic of exile, includes the flight *from* dissatisfactory circumstances and the escape *towards* an improvement of her reality. What Watts (1995:67) calls a 'compulsive pattern of escape and return' is the necessary consequence of her lifelong preoccupation with the two urges struggling inside herself: her wish to stay and to move on. This is her central dilemma between being and becoming:

> What am I doing here? [Miriam asks.] Though it sounded insistently, it held now a promise, as if of an appointment made towards which, though all her ways seemed blocked, she was invisibly moving. Always had been moving, driven on in the end, whenever she had for a moment thought herself arrived at her destination, by its warning cry. It had sounded everywhere, almost daily, at Banbury Park at Wimpole Street, at Flaxman's, in the houses of all her friends; everywhere. Except for a while amidst the loveliness of Newlands and, earlier, of Germany, where in the midst of suffering there had been that deep depth of happiness for whose sake she would have gone on enduring for ever (*DLH,* 166f.).

As none of these destinations can eventually hold her, as none of them appeals to the whole of her being, the life in-between becomes important; the 'train and its motion serve as a physical manifestation or model of the associative action of displacement and replacement by which Miriam's consciousness travels' (Gevirtz 141). The 'dialectical reflection of the worldly adventures of the novel's hero (the hero as Quixote) in the adventure of interiority (the hero in search of himself)', which Pecora (9) recognizes in the novel in general, is visible in *Pilgrimage* too, however unspectacular Miriam's worldly adventures might be. The journeys for all their surface impressions have their impact on her gradual expansion 'down through the layers of her surface being [...] nearer to the living centre' (*DH*, 498).

So the journey is its own destination as well as a pathway leading to an unknown aim, towards which she is driven by this vague 'promise, as if of an appointment made' (*DLH*, 167). As the outer destination is interdependently linked to her inner reaching of fulfilment, every journey, even if it leads to an irrelevant halt, can be the decisive step towards this promised target. The relevance of the details of the moment, which is so important throughout *Pilgrimage*, is evident in the treatment of Miriam's journeys, as every journey leaves its lasting impressions on her mind and helps to broaden her consciousness, to continuously form her self.[4] This aspect of the development of the self going along with her travelling activities outweighs the covering of measurable distances: 'There's more space within than without' (*DLH*, 168). Bronfen (96), claiming that Miriam increasingly prefers the experience of a dematerialised, imagined world to the concrete travelling impressions,[5] is right as far as the memory of her former journeys plays a more important part towards the end of *Pilgrimage*, eventually leading to the production of the text that - as a *text* - *is* a dematerialised recording of and reflection on original sense impressions. However, Miriam continues travelling even in *March Moonlight* we find her in trains heading towards unknown worlds; though trapped in 'windowless middle places' (*MM*, 647) that inhibit the view, she, here as much as when she was a young girl, in 'hilarious silence' enjoys 'this hour on *neutral* territory' (*MM*, 648; emphasis added) - in the most literal sense of the word[6] - as her personal space of freedom.

In most of the numerous short descriptions of Miriam's journeys, visual impressions predominate; it is her awareness of the phenomenal world which calls forth a reflective response in her consciousness. The account of a short tram ride on the South Coast illustrates this process in exceptional clarity:

---

[4] Staley (34) generalizes: 'All outward experience exerts a reciprocal pressure inward upon her innocence - this dialectic itself offering a gradual development of the character and her world.'

[5] Bronfen (96) sees in the whole text a 'Bewegung von der materiell gebundenen Welt zur entmaterialisierten, vorgestellten Welt der Kunst. [... Das] vorgestellte Erleben der entmaterialisierten Welt ist dem Reisen in der materiellen Welt vorzuziehen.'

[6] neutral = neither one nor the other, hence neither here nor there; cf. *OED X*, 355.

> When the tram moved off, the scenes framed by the windows grew beautiful in movement. The framing and the movement created them, gave them a life that was not the life of wild nature only. They lost their new pathos. Watching them, she was out in eternity, gliding along, adding this hour to the strange sum of her central being [...] (*DLH*, 265).

Miriam integrates the detached, objective world around her into the most subjective of all worlds, her own consciousness. The act of perceiving itself - 'watching' - is as important as the things perceived. The objects and scenes around her are collected in the focal lens, the eyes, which, by registering them as visual impressions, take them in, make them part of her inner world; the internalized scenes then initiate a subjective response. It is relatively rare, however, that this response is so directly and explicitly integrated in the narrative. Often Miriam's mental reaction to her sensory impressions can only be seen much later when she recalls some of these scenes. Then a filter of time leads to a new emotional response that is detached from the original observation. These 'recollections' appear in front of her 'inner eye' as fixed, idealized units of memory that play an essential part in her own affirmation of her stable self.[7]

In the descriptions of Miriam's travels the basic process of immediate integration and subjectification of external reality by means of intense visual perception can be seen time and again; the film-like, on-going change of scenes Miriam observes on her journeys most often has a positive effect on her mind. The moving pictures not only satisfy her eye, but they trigger off a series of happy, sometimes even ecstatic thoughts. This interrelation between surroundings and interior life is based on a more than sensory orientation of the consciousness towards the tangible world. Just as to Wordsworth

> living things, and things inanimate,
> Do speak [...] to eye and ear,
>
> ('Excursion' IV, p. 147, ll.1204ff.)

Miriam's feeling intellect in this same spirit 'communes with the forms of nature' so intensely that she experiences a rapturous joy.[8] In these rhapsodic illuminations Miriam's enthusiasm coupled with her sensitive eye for details mirrors the beauty of what she sees in such an impressive way that the reader senses this beauty almost physically.[9]

---

7 cf. Dorothy Richardson's use of leitmotifs in Chapter 3, 'Music'.

8 John Cowper Powys, one of Dorothy Richardson's friends and early admirers of her work, put her on the same level as Wordsworth as a 'philosophical inspirer' for his 'furtive cult of pure sensation' (letter to Dorothy Richardson, 5.8.1929, *WM*, 171).

9 Lawrence Hyde, an early critic of Dorothy Richardson, underlines Miriam's purely sensory surface perception but denies the reflective aspects in Dorothy Richardson's

It is in such passages of sensory perception that what Dorothy Richardson (*WM*, 68) calls her 'direct method' of writing, the method of rendering 'direct unmediated experience', is most purely presented. Contrasting the traditional novelistic 'method of statement, giving information', her method allows a 'sense of immediate experience' that forms *one* of the attractions for a reader tackling *Pilgrimage*. Yet she is also aware of the difficulty of her 'direct method': its pure use is hard to achieve as some external information has to be given for the text to remain readable:

> Information there must be, but the moment it's given as information, the sense of immediate experience is gone. [...] It is the great & abiding problem of all those who take the inward way, this business of getting something tremendously there as it were unawares. I haven't solved it. But a recognition of it all the time is necessary in order to avoid total wreckage of the sense of direct experience (letter to P. Beaumont Wadsworth, 30.4.1923; *WM*, 68).

In the at times long-winded descriptions of Miriam's impressions on her journeys Dorothy Richardson uses her 'direct method' most successfully to give such external information - the objective fact of changing place - by means of a description of the working of Miriam's perceptive mind. If Miriam's intense, but 'framed' views in movement convey the sense of her direct visual experience of outer reality as being limited, Dorothy Richardson allows the reader to take equally intense, direct, but limited views of Miriam's thoughts in movement, of her 'inward way' to experience and reflect reality. The fascinating 'slow-motion photography'[10] of Miriam's mind, which fully concentrates on short, discontinuous periods of time, finds its outer counterpart in these travel impressions. In the portrayals of both outer and inner reality Dorothy Richardson does not always succeed in finding the appropriate explicitness: losing herself in the account of minute details she at times bores the reader with endless, seemingly irrelevant and superficial explanations,[11] only to counterbalance them by taking for granted

---

portrayal of Miriam. To him, she fails to penetrate to a deeper truth, to 'plunge into life' (512) as a convincing fictional character:

'She serves principally as a delicate and efficient receiving instrument, a medium through whom we can look at life so surely and clearly that we forget that she is there between us and the pictures which are presented to us, forget that the pictures are ostensibly only there because of the effect which they had on *her*' (517).

To read *Pilgrimage* in such a way is to neglect some of the most interesting aspects of Dorothy Richardson's work: the interplay of the senses and the intellect, of perception and reflection, in a protagonist who has indeed taken this 'plunge into life.'

[10] cf. 'Foreword', 11.

[11] In her letters Dorothy Richardson repeatedly expresses her own awareness of and concern about her 'thin' texts: e. g. *WM*, 38: '[T]he rest [of *Interim*] I knew was thin and badly foreshortened.' *WM*, 142: 'I agree about "slightness" [of *Oberland*].' *WM*, 215 [on

important facts not yet - or only very obliquely - related.[12] Then she sometimes asks too much of the reader, to whom reading becomes exceedingly difficult. When finding the balance, however, she has us share Miriam's consciousness and she succeeds in conveying an impressive picture both of Miriam's constantly changing surroundings and of her inner growth.

Therefore, the examination of three crucial journeys on Miriam's way through life should help to cast some light on the development of her awareness of the outside world. The dominant role of the visual factor in these descriptions underlines Dorothy Richardson's impressionistic strength: the outer change of place implies a change of views and thus evokes a natural flow of impressions in Miriam's mind. Enjoying any sort of spatial movement, she registers the temporal motion connected with it; immersing herself completely in the rapidly changing, fleeting, *hic et nunc*, she often manages to grasp 'the unique quality of the passing moment' (*DLH*, 134) and to relish the immediate present.[13] At the same time, the journey as a time of transition frees her from all bounds. Neither here nor there, suspended in a spatial vacuum, she experiences her journeys as ideal places for contemplation, for self-contemplation. Watching the landscape passing by leads her, as Bronfen (74) observes, to an experience of the 'Essenzen des Seins.' In the perception of the beauty of nature combined with the experience of fairly fast motion Miriam becomes conscious of a heightened feeling of life, of a Bergsonian *élan vital*.[14]

Dawn's Left Hand]: '[T]he bad bits are uncollaborated. Superficial. Ghastly.' *WM*, 297 [on *Clear Horizon*]: 'The last few sections, having been written under difficulties, are rather scrappy & dim.'

[12] Some early critics comment emotionally on this tendency towards too great explicitness. Frank Swinnerton (403) wrote in 1935: 'If I am asked whether I consider such impressionism anything more than a marvellous feat of memory, or reproduction, I must answer there comes a moment in which one wishes that Miriam had died young, or that she had moved through life at a less even and ample pace.' G. B. Stern wrote to May Sinclair (15. 6. 1919) that 'of course the reason why she's so infinitely more wonderful than anything Dorothy Richardson has done is that Mary (Olivier) herself matters, and Miriam didn't - Heavens, how Miriam bored me!' (cf. Beauman 160.)

[13] This complete immersion in the physical experience of the present moment, a mixture of visual and acoustic impressions, is most impressively described in one of Dorothy Richardson's short stories, an account of her childhood journey to the sea:
'One could hear the faithful rumblings of the wheels, set now to hymn tunes sung quickly, and now, while the train sped rocking, and the telegraph wires, running together, refused to be counted, to a song of its own, *the wordless, exultant beating, it seemed, of life itself. And the great events of the day came in the silence to life between memory and anticipation*, blossomed in pictures upon the air vibrating to the song of the train.' ('Journey to Paradise,' *JP*, 127; emphasis added)

[14] e.g. the brake-drive in Germany (*PR*, 156f.), the 'boating' on the Thames (*BW*, 295f.), the toboggan rides in Oberland (*O*, 74, 84, 99). The *achtung* yelled from her

On Miriam's journey to Hanover in *Pointed Roofs* her senses are woken to a realization that there is a different life from the one known so far; the new experiences, mainly of her stay in - but already of her way to - Germany, will have a lasting impact on her life to come. Her second long journey, her break-away from London to Oberland, marks a turning point in her London career and depicts her as an enclosed city-dweller breaking free from her wonted way of life to be captivated in a new sense by the beauty of nature and the foreign atmosphere. Despite the limited period of time spent in the Swiss Alps the healing influence of the unknown beauties of the landscape is as important in *Oberland* as it is on her third journey, her way to and stay at Dimple Hill. Along with the change of place these three journeys entail a change of Miriam's mental attitude, they are decisive steps on her way to that inner stability that eventually enables her to start writing at Dimple Hill.

These three journeys lead to stays limited in time in hitherto unknown places within strange societies. In all three cases it is the outward journey that interests Dorothy Richardson far more than the return home. The journeys, all set at the beginnings of the respective novel-chapters, thus

---

toboggan in Oberland - 'seeming to be her very life sounding out into the far distances of this paradise, claiming them as long ago it had claimed the far distances surrounding outdoor games' (*O*, 85) - fills her with a juvenile joy in the intensity of the living moment.

In her experience of the relativity of speed and its impact on her perception of the landscape Miriam resembles the young Wordsworth delighting in winter pleasures: Like him, she feels her own real movements being reinforced by the apparent counter-motion of the landscape around her. While Miriam on her toboggan was 'careering down the first slope of the valley run with sky and landscape sweeping upwards, mountains gigantically sweeping upwards to the movement of her downward rush' (*O*, 85), Wordsworth skating along on ice feels this special 'gladness of swift movement' (*O*, 99) too:

> [...] and oftentimes,
> When we had given our bodies to the wind,
> And all the shadowy banks on either side
> Came sweeping through the darkness, spinning still
> The rapid line of motion, then at once
> Have I, reclining back upon my heels,
> Stopped short; yet still the solitary cliffs
> Wheeled by me - even as if the earth had rolled
> With visible motion her diurnal round!
> Behind me did they stretch in solemn train,
> Feebler and feebler, and I stood and watched
> Till all was tranquil as a dreamless sleep. (*The Prelude* I, 452-463)

While Wordsworth at the end of this swift movement still concentrates on his visual impressions, Miriam, who has not only an eye but also an ear for the beauty of her surroundings, 'stopped dead, [...] a motionless triumphantly throbbing atom of humanity in a stillness that at once kept her as motionless as itself, to listen to its unexpected voice: the clear, silvery tinkle, very far away, of water upon rock' (*O*, 85). The central role of silence and its sounds in Miriam's consciousness will be examined in Chapter 4.

symbolize Miriam's departure from an old, and movement towards a new society: they are *rites de passage* on her progress through life. In the detailed accounts of Miriam's perception the reader, being 'inside her thoughts and her skin' (Henke 52), is able to experience these phases of expectant transition together with Miriam. The return journeys do not lead to such new situations and therefore only play a minor role within the framework of the novel-chapters.[15] Miriam's heightened visual energies on her journeys seem to go together with an increased awareness of life, a sense of well-being that eventually leads to the lasting memory of experienced happiness. When in later volumes she recalls these journeys and their ensuing stays, they are associated with a dreamlike happiness that cannot be achieved in everyday life.[16] They thus stand out as emotional peaks in Miriam's memory and as such occupy a special position in *Pilgrimage*.

1.2 'Away from England-English People:' The Journey to Germany

As we rush, as we rush in the Train,
The trees and the houses go wheeling back,
But the starry heavens above the plain
Come flying on our track.

All the beautiful stars of the sky,
The silver doves of the forest of Night,
Over the dull earth swarm and fly,
Companions of our flight.

We will rush ever on without fear;
Let the goal be far, the flight be fleet!
For we carry the Heavens with us, dear,
While the earth slips from our feet!

(James Thomson, 'Sunday at Hampstead IX,' *Poems* 85)

---

[15] with the possible exception of her return from Oberland, described in the first chapter of *DLH* (131 - 135). Here Miriam's senses are dulled both by night and mist and by the uninspired conversation with an American spinster. Thus the awareness of motion, so strong and acute on her other journeys, here is very limited.

[16] Memory and anticipation of travelling can call forth the same feelings of happiness, as a day-dream during her work at Wimpole Street shows: 'Supposing I were able to go anywhere on this page [...] The breath of happiness poured in at the high window; all the places in the railway guide told over their charms; mountains and lakes and rivers, innumerable strips of coast, village streets to walk along for the first time, leading out . . . *going, somewhere, in a train.* Standing on tiptoe, she gazed her thoughts across the two garden spaces towards the grimed backs of the large brown houses. Why was one allowed to be so utterly happy? There it was . . . happily here and *happily going away . . . away*' (*TU*, 218; emphasis added).

> Away out here, the sense of imminent catastrophe that had shadowed all her life so far had disappeared. Even here in this dim carriage, with disgrace ahead, she felt that there was freedom somewhere at hand. (*PR*, 30)

Miriam's first journey in *Pilgrimage* is in some ways her most drastic and decisive one. It is not the type of holiday trip with a fixed return in view remembered from her childhood days and to be experienced several times later on in her life, nor is it a mere change from one place to another. Rather it is her consciously chosen escape from everybody and everything she has known in her life. Leaving behind a seemingly untouched world of 'silent sunny mornings', of piano-playing and tennis clubs (*PR*, 16), Miriam has made up her mind to become an independent adult. Her journey to Hanover physically reflects this passage from the world of her protected childhood to an open, unknown life of independent means.

Starting right in the middle of Miriam's journey to Germany at the beginning of chapter II, Dorothy Richardson establishes a method of narrating used very often in her later travelling accounts; she focuses on what seems most important to Miriam and provides the missing information only in the course of the following narration. Structurally speaking, Dorothy Richardson frequently uses the device of both external and internal 'analepses' (Genette 90), of flashbacks referring to times both before and after the story started. Generally, these analepses are used to fill the information gaps, in order to 'éclairer le lecteur sur l'antécédent' (90). However, Dorothy Richardson's strict method of fixed internal focalization does not always make the meaning of these enigmatic flashbacks clear. The text then appears in 'paraliptic' opaqueness,[17] which considerably impedes its accessibility. The reader experiences a distance to Miriam's mind as these retrospective allusions first appear unrelated to the main events. In the course of the chapter, however, this distance most often melts away until Miriam's pure consciousness emerges in an impressive, epiphanic moment.

In very few words Dorothy Richardson sets the scene in the opening sentences of this second chapter: 'The crossing was over. They were arriving' (*PR*, 26). What later on turns out to be physical relief from hours of sickness and despair, however does not relieve Miriam from her mental stress of leaving home, the farewell scene coming up again and again and thus pushing aside the immediate visual impact the unknown shore has on her: 'In her tired brain the grey river and the flat misty shores slid constantly into a vision of the gas-lit dining-room at home' (*PR*, 26). Although she wants 'to be free for the strange grey river' (*PR*, 26), wants to observe the unknown landscape, pictures of the recent past in her mind inhibit any deep sensory

[17] cf. Genette (211): 'paralipse' = 'moins d'info qu'il n'est en principe nécessaire'

awareness of her immediate surroundings.[18] The struggle between her inner, mental, vision of the past and her outer, sensory, view of the present, still won by the former, represents her struggle for detachment from her family, which she tries to achieve in the course of the journey. The physical presence of her father, who accompanies her through Holland to Hanover, will make this struggle all the harder. Yet, while travelling on, Miriam for a short time feels the appeal of the Dutch landscape:

> Presently they were in a train watching the Dutch landscape go by [...]. She looked at the dykes and the windmills with indifferent eyes, but her desire for the flat meadows grew (*PR*, 28).

The visual impression at once calls forth an emotional reaction: Not the manmade landmarks of Holland, but the solitary reunion with unspoilt nature, which later in her life will assume central importance, fascinates her: 'Miriam wanted to go out *alone* under the grey sky and walk over the flat fields shut in by poplars' (*PR*, 28; emphasis added). This single view of the Dutch landscape later on, in retrospect, induces a change in her behaviour. The sort of confidence she had scented 'everywhere in her hours in Holland' (*PR*, 30) fills her with a certainty of 'freedom somewhere at hand' (*PR*, 30). So, when the 'peaceful Dutch fields [come] into her mind again' (*PR*, 31) they suggest a new sincere freedom that would enable her to defeat her feelings of 'always lying and pretending and keeping up a show - never daring to tell anybody' (*PR*, 31) and promise a new happiness. The direct visual impression of nature and its memory shortly after is thus followed by a change in her whole attitude towards the future.

In this first section of her pilgrimage Miriam's sensory impressions do not yet possess the same direct imaginative impulse that plays such a central role on her later journeys. A 'cluster of "moments" which focus on exterior location' (Blake 98) describe the scene; on-coming night, then, inducing a visual void and solitude - her father being asleep - favour the turn of her consciousness from outside observation to inner contemplation, from perception to reflection: only what goes on within her mind irrespective of direct outer influences is important. During this passage to 'adulthood' Miriam looks back on moments of her past life with mixed feelings and imagines both nightmarish and promising possible situations in her immediate future. This shows her as deeply unsure about herself: though convinced of

---

[18] Although both the journey and the sea are important motifs in Dorothy Richardson's writings, she surprisingly never deals with sea voyages in any depth. It may be due to her negative boat experiences on crossing the Channel that boat trips are so insignificant compared to train journeys. Herein she shows a marked thematic contrast to Virginia Woolf's sea narratives (e.g. *The Voyage Out, To the Lighthouse*).

her coming failure in Germany,[19] she expects a liberating effect from her journey. She is determined to escape from her father's protection,[20] and she already feels free of 'the sense of imminent catastrophe that had shadowed all her life so far' (*PR*, 30). At the same time she still identifies with her father: 'I am a misanthrope. So's pater. He despises women and can't get on with men. We are different - it's us, him and me' (*PR*, 31). She is aware of his physical presence,[21] yet unable to communicate with him directly. But she recalls their common family history: in a short evocative sketch full of visual details (*PR*, 32f.) Miriam draws her personal biography of her father that reveals her basic admiration for his rather exclusive 'good taste' (*PR*, 33).

In this mixture of visualized scenes from Mr Henderson's early years before Miriam's birth to happy childhood memories, Miriam sums up her family past just to resolutely free herself from it soon after. What, as Parkin-Gounelas (17) writes, forms one central aim of the traditional *Bildungsroman*, the emancipation from personal (family) concerns, in *Pilgrimage* is the initial step of Miriam's entire development as a woman; the journey as an act of liberation forms part of the constitutive pattern of her self-finding. What ensues as a second goal of many *Bildungsromane*, the eventual integration into a new society, however, will be a lifelong problem for both Miriam and her creator. The series of details about Miriam's and her father's common past reveal the still existing family ties that, with her first journey abroad, are put to a first severe test. At the same time, from a textual point of view, this series of 'analepses externes', of retrospective associations referring to a time before the beginning of the story, provide a set of biographical hints that help the reader close some of the numerous information gaps about Miriam's past. The details described in the way they cross Miriam's mind still suggest scenes full of life.[22] The reader, who is now

---

[19] cf. *PR*, 29: 'It was a fool's errand . . . To undertake to go to the German school and teach . . . to be going there . . . with nothing to give;' *PR*, 30: 'she feared even the German servants would despise her;' *PR*, 30: 'with disgrace ahead;' *PR*, 31: 'with a false position ahead and, after a short space, disaster, she must get along.'

[20] cf. *PR*, 30: 'He had given her twenty-five shillings and there was her fare and his, and her return fare and her new trunk and all the things she had needed. It must be the end of taking money from him. She was grown up. She was the strong-minded one. She must manage.'

[21] cf. *PR*, 30: 'She glanced across at the pale face with its point of reddish beard, the long white hands laid one upon the other on the crossed knees.'

[22] In a letter to E.B.C. Jones (12.5.1921) Dorothy Richardson describes her problems in sticking to her 'direct' method of writing: 'It has been "horrible" to refrain from objective descriptions of her family (Sarah by the way just 24, Eve 23, M. & Harriett 17 & 16 respectively - & M. rather dumpy & *not* tall - about 5.4' - it was a short person who called her tall - but she did not observe that, only that somebody called her *tall*.) &

better able to visualize what she says between the lines, at last gets a picture of what Miriam has in front of her inner eye and can live with her what she relives.[23]

In this scene Miriam's thoughts flow without interruption. Her inner world of imagination and memory occupies her mind completely so that she is unaware of what is going on around her: In contrast to similar scenes in later novel-chapters there is no reference to outside reality, to the fact that Miriam is on a journey; exclusively foregrounding Miriam's consciousness, Dorothy Richardson creates the first of many illuminating scenes which cast light on her heroine's expanding mind. At the beginning of Miriam's development as an independent woman (and at the beginning of Dorothy Richardson's career as a novelist) the illumination is quite simple, reflecting the adolsescent's relative inarticulateness: it does not yet involve the fascinating interplay of thought and reality, of interior vision and exterior view that - for all its fragmentation - conveys the sense of an underlying unity and continuity of consciousness in the later novel-chapters. At this early stage concrete sense impressions recede completely in favour of an intense contemplation of Miriam's active mind. In its concentration on Miriam's inner world, however, the illumination reflects her semi-dormant state of mind, her thoughts circling around a childhood that appears in fragments of dreamlike clarity. These fragmentary associations convey the sense of a heightened inner awareness that can be experienced immediately before falling asleep. Such a moment of introspection, of exceptional intensity, however, is limited in time. The accumulation of related thoughts reaches its climax at the end of the chapter; any continuation would destroy the intensity of insight carefully built up. The dissatisfaction the reader of a realistic novel might experience when the account of Miriam's journey fizzles out in a childhood memory that eventually puts her to sleep, and when her arrival in Germany is never related, is turned into admiring understanding of what Dorothy Richardson is trying to achieve in rendering the minutiae of Miriam's experience: it is the direct insight into the working of Miriam's mind which draws the reader into the text and makes him or her step into her thoughts.

For the reader it is part of the fascination of *Pilgrimage* not only to share Miriam's perception of her environment visually and acoustically 'with extreme precision and subtlety, and experience it intensely' (Würzbach 297), but also to think with her, to see her grow intellectually from an immature adolescent to a philosophically-minded middle-aged writer. At the same time,

surroundings. The people & surroundings that come later are clearer because you see her seeing them, for the first time & share her impressions such as they are' (*WM*, 49f.).

[23] The three dots (. . .) joining her individual memories and thus typographically establishing the continuity of thought at the same time open up a space, which, unless filled by the reader's associative imagination, remains empty.

Dorothy Richardson's exclusive concentration on the protagonist as 'focalizer', however attractive it appears at the beginning, can tire out the reader, who in the long text is confronted with the description of the working of one single consciousness 'with nothing taken away from it - and nothing added' (Mansfield, 1919; *GM* 309).[24] However, any criticism confined to the highlighting of this flaw of narrative monotony does not do justice to those *additional* aspects of the text that make it a 'texte scriptible' (Barthes, *S/Z*, 10): in all its imperfection *Pilgrimage* is a text that demands of the reader an active, collaborative and productive role, offering us in turn something of the 'enchantement du signifiant', of the 'volupté de l'écriture' (ibd.) of the unfinished. It is therefore a central aim of our reading to interpret the text - and especially the accounts of the journeys with their drive towards arrival, completion and rest - with regard to the dichotomy of the Barthesian oppositions: not only to find the '*lisible*' aspects of 'finir, remplir, joindre, unifier' (112), the completive factors that satisfy our expectations, but also to recognize the '*scriptible*' parts of the text, to appreciate 'de quel pluriel il est fait' (11), and eventually to read this textual plurality as an apt representation of human life, which in its very plurality makes up a whole.

1.3 'Onwards through this Gladness of Light:' The Journey to Oberland

> In the mountains, there you feel free.
>
> (T.S.Eliot, 'The Waste Land', l. 17; *Complete Poems and Plays* 61)

> It was as if all her life she had travelled towards this radiance, and was now within it, clear of the past, at an ultimate destination.
>
> (*O*, 49)

One of the few obvious patterns of *Pilgrimage* is the nearly consistent reference to elements of Miriam's journeyings in the opening pages of each novel-chapter. While in some other openings this reference to travelling simply alludes to Miriam's lifelong pilgrimage,[25] in *Oberland* the whole of the first chapter is devoted to her longest journey ever. Dorothy Richardson's account of the journey from London to Grindelwald, Miriam's

---

[24] see also Mansfield, 'Dragonflies' (Review of *Interim*), *GM*, 310: 'Darting through life, quivering, hovering, exulting in the familiarity and the strangeness of all that comes within her tiny circle, she leaves us feeling, as before, that everything being of equal importance to her, it is impossible that everything should not be of equal unimportance.'

[25] *BW*, 189 / 192: the trams; *TU,* 11: the 'heavy bag;' *IN,* 291: her 'Gladstone bag;' *TR*, 399: her 'sense of arriving nowhere;' *MM*, 555f: the memory of her travelling to Les Lauriers.

'Oberland', is so impressive that Rachel Mary Roscorla later on speaks for the reader of this chapter when she tells Miriam: 'Your word-pictures make us all feel we have been in Switzerland' (*MM*, 585). *Oberland* (as well as *Dawn's Left Hand*) begins with a train journey to (and from) the mountains - 'as perhaps films should', Bryher (337f.) comments, emphasizing the visual, mobile impressionism of these openings. In *Oberland* the journey in its immediate sensory appeal not only creates a spatial distance to her life in the city, but through the experience of the foreign it also helps her to look at her situation afresh and thus to feel at a distance from her problems. At the ending of *The Trap*, immediately preceding *Oberland*, Miriam 'was left in a corner with death' (*TR*, 507) at the dismal flat at Flaxman's. In an 'impermeable' room, where life was 'being hated' (*TR*, 451), where everything 'spoke of death' (*TR*, 500), Miriam felt as if she was 'dying by inches' (*TR*, 508). Her desperate cry for escape: 'Away. Away . . .' (*TR*, 509), which finishes the novel-chapter, is answered in the opening of *Oberland*, where we find her in the middle of her journey.[26] This journey is a reaction against the growing and stifling isolation she felt when the relationship with Michael Shatov came to an end and when her best-loved sister Harriett and her family emigrated to Canada: In the very moment when their train was departing, they left her behind in the 'trap', made her feel that something was 'buried alive' within her (*TR*, 503). Thus, her journey to Oberland is an act of self-liberation from this corner of death; it is the necessary escape out of her sinister thoughts, out of her disillusioned, monotonous lethargy with Selina Holland into the width of the unknown; her movement against routine becomes an unprecedented ascension to the freedom of life, which Miriam's senses appreciate step by step on her way from London to the mountains.[27]

When the reader first meets her on the platform of the Paris station, Miriam's mental state is at its lowest. Tired and unsure of her destination she loathes the world around her as the petty problems of the solitary traveller threaten to overpower her. Still preoccupied with the London life she has just left, she feels unable to master her situation of being alone. The first

[26] Penny Brown (190) writes that *The Trap* 'ends on a triumphant note: Away. Away . . . ,' reading the scene with Miriam's Oberland experience in mind. However, at the moment of leaving Flaxman's, her only aim is to get away from this dismal place of loneliness and despair; at this point the triumphant beauty of Oberland is still hidden to her.

[27] The same idea of an escape to the Alps is found in Meredith's *The Egoist*, where Clara and Vernon eventually reach the wild freedom of nature (413/415/425), and in Lawrence's *Women in Love*, where Ursula and Birkin, Gudrun and Gerald, 'all four prepared for flight,' gladly set off on their journey to Tyrol. Gudrun, who 'could not rest any longer in London,' expresses Miriam's present attitude before leaving: 'I feel I could *never* see this foul town again - I couldn't *bear* to come back to it.' (429 & 435) Miriam, however, in the end *is* drawn back to London by its irresistible appeal.

paragraph with its abundance of negatively connoted adjectives underlines Miriam's subjective perception: 'brutishly pre-occupied' porters pass her by as in an 'evil' dream. Her 'miserable' handbags prevent her from running after them. The 'ill-mannered wilderness' would leave her 'helpless' on a journey 'that had held suffering enough' (*O*, 11). At the end of her first travelling day Miriam, without orientation, exhausted and at the end of her nerves, finds herself in the state she was in before leaving London, a state of darkness and mental pain.[28]

But she finds comfort in the visual presence of things and people known to her. The 'blessed outlines of a Burberry' - the epitome of Englishness - which she recognizes when 'the man was crossing a pool of lamplight' (*O*, 11) show her the way to the Oberland train as if in a flash of hope that strengthens her for the continuation of the trip. Light, Dorothy Richardson's most consistently used image for the positive sides of life, underlines Miriam's slow turn towards positive thinking. Torn between her inner opposing forces of death and life, of despair and hope, she experiences the journey as 'black and sudden gold' (*O,* 12). She lives it in the full intensity of individual impressions and feelings, which she denies the ordinary travellers to whom the journey supposedly 'was uniform grey' (*O*, 12). At the same time she envies these 'serene' travellers, who know their way round, and longs for their company, for their mere visually and aurally perceptible presence: 'The world deserting her just when she would have welcomed, for wordless communication of the joy of achievement, the *sight* and *sound* of human kind' (*O*, 14; emphasis added). She is therefore happy to find a seat in a nearly full compartment, where she feels 'at rest, escaped from nightmare voyaging amongst swaying shadows. The familiar world was about her again and she sat blessing the human kindliness of these sleeping forms, blessing the man who had first moved [...]' (*O*, 16). The mere *sight* of other English travellers thus helps her to overcome the insecurity that lies ahead, which at this stage of her journey is still negatively seen: 'Beyond Berne, somewhere in the far future of tomorrow afternoon, the terminus, the business of finding and bargaining for a sleigh - the last effort' (*O*, 14).

Her attitude towards the journey, however, changes in the middle of the night when the train reaches the French-Swiss border. From the very moment of her first contact with snow and winter Miriam sees things positively. All her senses register positive sensations: her ears perceive 'a far-off voice, but

---

[28] Her present lack of orientation reflects her situation, her uncertainty as to where to turn in her life, which she defines at the end of *The Trap*: 'I must create my life. Life is creation. Self and circumstances the raw material. But so many lives I can't create. And in going off to create my own I must leave behind uncreated lives. Lives set in motionless circumstances' (*TR*, 508). At the beginning of her journey to Oberland she undertakes a first attempt at creating her own life, which however still lacks a clear direction.

this time a jocund sound', she sees 'huddled forms emerging serene and bright-eyed from their hibernation' and feels the movement of air upon her skin 'of millions of infinitesimal needles, attacking. Mountain air, "like wine" [...] holding one up, feeding every nerve. [...] This air, that reached, it seemed, to her very spirit, would not let her feel anxious' (*O*, 18). In this scene, beautifully structured around a multiple turning point, the continuous interrelation between Miriam's senses and her responsive mind becomes obvious: her sensory experience affects her mind immediately, the touch of the cold air makes her mentally strong. The customs officer's simple questions about her 'whence' and 'whither' form the pivoting point of change, of leaving behind the old, known London world to turn to unknown regions, to Oberland:

> '*"Vous arrivez, madame?"*
> *"De Londres."*
> *"Et vous allez?"*
> *"A Oberland."*
> *"Vous n'avez qu'à monter dans le train"*'(*O*, 18).

A train, which - significantly - 'stood now emptied' (*O*, 18). The presently emptied train here represents her own mind. At this first moment of winter serenity Miriam can leave behind the oppressing thoughts, continue her journey with relieved senses: Her change of mood from the negative to the positive, from her clinging to old, dark spheres to her joyfully tackling the new situation finds its symbolic counterpart in her getting off and on the train that takes her out of the night into the light of the new day: 'She was at peace in morning light' (*O*, 20).

The first view of the mountains is the first in a series of ecstatic nature experiences in *Oberland*. While in other cases - such as at the *end* of the first chapter of *Oberland* - Dorothy Richardson builds up the moment of ecstasy through the development of carefully chosen images, here she starts *in medias res* and thus conveys Miriam's surprise at this unexpected view of beauty in a direct way. The intense experience of the unknown is expressed in words of both physical and mental immediacy, such as 'leap of recognition,' 'unheard-of unimagined tawny light', 'glad shock' as well as by an unusually active role of the landscape. It is not the train that moves but the mountains 'closed in', 'gliding by, the cliff throwing its light' (*O*, 21). They are even personified as people who 'knew, they smiled joyfully at the glad shock they were' (*O*, 21), at once establishing a personal relationship with their beholder. When the train moves on, for Miriam it is the landscape, the beautiful picture of lake and mountains that moves, 'soundlessly' receding, leaving her speechless. It is an instance that perfectly illustrates the relativity of movement: Miriam, as if watching a silent film, is the physically unmoving observer, through whom the landscape moves and who is moved by it.[29] Yet, unlike Mary Olivier's immediate experience of the relativity of motion that merely serves as a stimulus for philosophical contemplation,[30] Miriam's observations focus on the pure act of perception. In the sensory impression itself rather than in any intellectual reflection lies its central message: to perceive and be moved by the beauty of her surroundings.

As usual, Dorothy Richardson ends her description of intense beauty abruptly, starting a new paragraph on a new thought. She does not describe the on-going processes of Miriam's mind after this climax of visual experience, but endows this outstanding moment with special emphasis by placing it at the very end of the paragraph.

At first sight, and time and again during her whole stay in Oberland, Miriam is one of many British tourists exploring the Alps. Yet, as she is fully aware of her status as a tourist and of what is expected from her as a member of the tourist society, she treats the topic of tourist trips with sensitive irony, which shows her as an individual ready to both leave behind, and play with conventions. Even on the journey she nourishes her habitual belief that, in any society she might possibly belong to, she is an outsider who would neither fulfil the role suggested to her nor follow all the rules of the respective society. Thus, she wants to be excused for travelling with open windows letting in the cold air by explaining 'Je suis anglaise' (*O*, 21), assuming the role of a tourist. Very shortly after, however, she is glad to put a distance between the normal tourist and herself by not going to see the view of the Alps in Berne.[31] While 'she barely glimpsed' Paris (*O*, 13), she does not see Berne at all and thus experiences her journey from London to Oberland as a straightforward, upward movement not interrupted by any urban impressions.[32]

While on her early journey to Hanover, Miriam is torn between the past and the future, which reduces her capability of appreciating the present. She

---

29 cf. Mc Laurin 82. On the cinematic quality of *Oberland* see Fromm (1977) 210f.

30 Sinclair, *Mary Olivier. A Life* 136f:

'Green fields and trees rushing past now. Stop a tree and you'll change and feel the train moving. Plato. You can't trust your senses. The cave-dwellers didn't see the things that really moved, only the shadows of the images of the things. Is the world in your mind or your mind in the world? Which really moves? Perhaps the world stands still and you move on and on like the train. If both moved together that would feel like standing still.

Grass banks. Telegraph wires dipping and rising like sea-waves [...].'

31 For once, the overwhelming presence of visual sensitivity is given up in favour of one of the rare instances where Miriam's sense of taste evokes a mental reaction: The good continental breakfast ('tender-crusted rolls', 'life-giving coffee'; *O*, 22), reminding her of her time in Germany, makes her happy.

32 Schlanger (83) summarizes Dorothy Richardson's attitude to the continent: 'Elle a connu l'Europe britannique des voyages, faite de trains, de montagnes et de rencontres.'

does not seem to notice any fellow passengers apart from her father, who represents her past. Now, on her way to Oberland, having left behind her London past and living fully in the present moment,[33] she is *visually* aware of other people, who, however, still remain fragmentary 'impressions' of her journey rather than characters recognized as indivuduals she would get in personal contact with. When Miriam arrives at the terminus at Oberland, her journey from the highly civilized metropolis London to the 'wild' nature of Oberland is reflected in a convincing juxtaposition of people catching her eye. With her first visual impression these people are taxed and personally judged. The Croydon family she travelled with for the last part of her journey is seen as cultured and 'flowerlike:' 'Both the girls had the slender delicate fragility of flowers. And strength. Refined and gentle above a strength of which they were unaware' (*O*, 22). The sleigh drivers, on the other hand, 'fierce-looking men', first appear uncivilized and rude: Her driver is

> hot-eyed eagerness, yet off-hand. Brutish, yet making her phrases, that a London cabby would have received with deference, sound discourteous. In his queer German he agreed to the smaller sum and turned away to expectorate (*O*, 23).

Thus, the implicit comparison of the upper-class London girls and the barbarian Swiss driver is at once relativized as she attests the Swiss driver a certain nobility she would never expect from an Englishman in the same position. This ambivalent feeling towards the native people lasting throughout *Oberland*, shows Miriam at the same time as a 'normal' tourist looking down on natives and as a culturally interested individual registering the natives' idiosyncrasies.[34]

As in the other novel-chapters, the *outward* journey to Oberland is a journey into the unknown. But nowhere else is Miriam so full of expectations, so sure of happiness awaiting her. Thus, on her arrival at the terminus she feels a 'completeness of comfort' (*O*, 24) she has never experienced on English journeys. The 'intensity of welcoming shelter' (*O*, 24) at the station restaurant fills her with a feeling of well-being that provides a space for reflection: The immediate presence of 'unknown Oberland' (*O*, 24) reminds her of her first journey out alone, of the wonderful strangeness she had experienced there, a period 'perfect in pain and joy' and therefore worth remembering. The flash of memory of her stay in Brussels - structurally an external analepsis that, being unrelated to the rest of the plot, remains strangely enigmatic - is an incident emphasizing her momentary joy

---

[33] There is not a single reference to her former London life in this first chapter.

[34] Bronfen (43) emphasizes the social distance between the tourist Miriam and the natives when she remarks: the natives of *Oberland* 'werden wie die Natur betrachtet, üben aber keinen Einfluss auf die Touristen aus.'

of solitary watching, it is a 'swift glimpse' (*O*, 24) into her past which confirms Miriam's *credo* in remembering visual impressions as moments of happiness:

> And oh! that first glimpse that had begun it all, of Brussels in the twilight from the landing window. [...] In silence and alone; yet most people prefer to see everything in groups, collectively. They never lose themselves in strangeness and wake changed (*O*, 25).

It is this strange happiness 'that can be known only in solitude' (*O*, 24) Miriam is searching for in her coming holidays; hoping for a dreamlike immersion into the beauty of the unknown, she wants to 'wake' changed when returning to London, without the burdens she has left behind.

However, the vision of change, a recurrent notion throughout *Pilgrimage*, does not lead to happiness alone, but it even furthers her conflicting feelings of the outsider in a group: 'Usually in a party there is one who *is* alone. Harassed, yet quietly *seeing*' (*O*, 25; emphasis added). Here, Miriam's theoretical musings about groups and individuals become real, manifest themselves as part of her outer reality. In a double stream of consciousness of reflection and perception running parallel Miriam at the same time reflects on the position of the lonely observer and, by observing another tourist, *is* the lonely observer herself within the group of tourists. The continued reflection on her Brussels experience thus turns into a running comment on her present visual perception. Dorothy Richardson achieves a transition from the flash of memory back to Miriam's immediate reality at the terminus. Seeing herself as the observing outsider both in the past and the present, Miriam already fixes her position for the near future. For, when she identifies the object of her observation as a man of the Croydon party and thus as a member of the well-to-do class of sportsmen, she, in her constant fear of not living up to others' expectations, prefers to withdraw into solitude. This fear occupies her mind to such an extent that she momentarily abandons the hoped-for reunion with nature; the 'sunlit mountains of her desire' (*O*, 26) disappear from her inner eye and for a short time lose their charm. She sees herself resting on a balcony - the inactive outsider, 'harassed, yet quietly seeing.' But reality in Oberland will be quite different. She will soon make the acquaintance of Vereker and Guerini and other hotel guests. She will explore the region on walks and enjoy the fast toboggan runs. The absence of complete emotional and social commitment characteristic of a scratch holiday society will help her for once to perceive her lifelong role as a reflecting observer of her surroundings as thoroughly positive. The railway terminus becomes the last station of her self-pitying *via crucis* full of gnawing doubts, ambiguities and anxieties about the future; with her change to the sleigh the way opens up towards a new, deeply felt joy in life, an inspired appreciation of both man and nature.[35]

The account of Miriam's life is a set of innumerable, often fragmentary, yet carefully selected scenes, each of which reproduces some aspects of Miriam's experiences and consciousness. These scenes of widely varying length can take up a whole chapter, a few pages or only a few lines and then appear as mere impressionistic glimpses of her reality. They are very often juxtaposed without being linked, which makes coherent understanding difficult for, especially in shorter scenes, the context remains unsatisfyingly vague.

In conventional narratives of the period the contextual gaps between scenes are filled with explicit points of reference at the beginning of a new scene, thus forming what Genette (139) calls 'ellipses explicites'. Dorothy Richardson, however, in most cases uses implicit ellipses that either remain open - allowing the reader to draw his own conclusions - or are filled much later on by mere hints, so-called 'analepses internes complétives' (Genette 92), which help to maintain the basic coherence of the narrative and to establish the context. In order to follow Miriam's progress the reader would have to memorize each single scene and put it into relation to the overall context and thus come to a complete understanding of the meaning of the scene. Such a reading, however exciting it can be if restricted to a limited set of scenes such as we find them in short stories, becomes extremely hard if too little context can be detected or if the context remains too vague. Therefore, devices to link apparently unrelated scenes are more than welcome signposts on the reader's way through *Pilgrimage*; they help us to understand contexts and make our reading more rewarding.

Such linking devices are perhaps most convincingly used in *Oberland*, thus contributing to the unusual consistency and popularity that distinguishes this single novel-chapter. In some instances Miriam's new sensory impressions establish the context of a new scene. Similar to real life, it is an acoustic interruption - rather than a new visual imput - that induces a shift of attention and thus a natural progress from one incident to the next.[36] Therefore it is not the often found *visual* tensional climax or a mental resolution that brings the scene to an end, but the *acoustic* announcement of

[35] At its first American appearance *Oberland* was given an enthusiastic review in the New York Times. The reviewer was 'ecstatic' about *Oberland* because of its inspired and inspiring descriptions of nature: for anyone with an experience of Switzerland, or for that matter any of the northern mountains in winter, the book would be 'a perpetual joy' (*New York Times Book Review*, 11 March 1928,7; cf. Fromm [1977] 214).

[36] e.g. *PR*, 53: Fräulein's voice / *PR*, 145: Fräulein's voice / *O*, 95: someone calling from the house / *DLH*, 139: the gay undertone / *DH*, 438: a man's voice.

something new, which then leads to a flowing transgression into the new scene. Thus, the 'sudden jingling of sleighbells at the door near by' (*O*, 26) marks the smooth change from the inside static reflections to the outside dynamics of the continuation of the journey in a sleigh. This heralds one of the longest epiphanic rhapsodies at the end of a chapter, in which the intensity of the present moment is most convincingly expressed. The immediate sensory experience of the last part of her long journey is also captivating because of the rhythmically flowing language representing the sleigh's smooth movement: 'skimming along on hard snow to the note of the bells' that 'no driving on earth could compare to' (*O*, 27).

This chapter-ending is fascinating in its use of compelling pictures summoning up the beauty of the Alps; and it is significant as a marked counterpoint to the previous dark novel-chapter *The Trap*. The ecstatic joy of life makes Miriam forget her feelings of being outcast and out of place, she is all eyes and for once leaves behind her reflections.

Perhaps nowhere else in the whole of *Pilgrimage* is Miriam so totally immersed in nature, where everything seems miraculously sprinkled with beauty, and nowhere else does Dorothy Richardson describe the perceptions of Miriam's eye in such an abundance of colour terms, which, first seen in nature, reciprocally reflect and intensify the brightness of her emotions.[37] Miriam's enthusiastic eye thus, to quote Woolf, 'creates; it adorns; it enhances' ('Street Haunting,' *Collected Essays 4*, 160). Even Staley, who sees Miriam's Oberland experiences as not more than a 'lyrical reverie about surroundings' (103), as an irrelevant short halt on her true journey through life, concedes that in the dreamlike description of the mountains Dorothy Richardson achieves her 'most beautiful and powerful lyrical passages' (104). And Blake (132) recognizes that the 'sustained lyrical ecstasy' in Miriam's reactions is of 'crucial importance' in her changed 'attitude toward past life and future.' The actual immersion in the beauty of the Alps quickens her power of acute perceptiveness. She thus experiences a reality of pure impressions that essentially helps her battered self-esteem towards recovery, conversion, and health.

Comparing the account of this final part of her long journey, the sleigh ride, which Dorothy Richardson also published separately as a short story,[38] with a parallel scene out of Butler's travel diary *Alps and Sanctuaries*, the

---

[37] The colours Miriam sees in nature are: sungilt, gold, white, purest white, deepening blue, radiant white, gold, rose, ruby, rubied, soft greenish purple, mauve-green, green, deepening blue, smoky russet, amber, saffron-rose (*O*, 29-30).

[38] 'Sleigh Ride', *JP* 37-41; originally published in: *Outlook* 58 (1926), 588, some months before the publication of *Oberland*. The text of the short story, starting with 'The thin, penetrating mist promised increasing cold' (*O*, 28), deviates in minor details of single word omissions and punctuation from the *Oberland* version.

poetic qualities of Dorothy Richardson's text as well as her sense for both the overall atmosphere and visual details become obvious. Butler writes:

> It was delightful travelling in the sledge. The sky was of deep blue; there was not a single cloud either in sky or on mountain, but the snow was already deep, and had covered everything beneath its smooth and heaving bosom. There was no breath of air, but the cold was intense; presently the sun set upon all except the higher peaks, and the broad shadows stole upwards. Then there was a rich crimson flush upon the mountain tops, and after this a pallor cold and ghastly as death [...] (8).

In *Oberland* too, winter, the dead season, is for a short time associated with death, a form of dying imagined in sensory details (*O*, 28f.);[39] yet in Miriam's ecstatic sleigh-ride winter becomes the epitome of life full of colours and light. The dark sides of her London existence, which had put her into a corner of death, are eventually overcome and she revels in happiness. Juxtaposing Butler's purely descriptive passage to its corresponding parts in *Oberland* that are - at least in parts - literally the same, Dorothy Richardson's art of conveying the emotional response of the observer, of describing Miriam's mind being positively affected by the beauty of the scene, becomes apparent:

> [...] the sunlit mountain corridors still seemed to be saying watch, see, if you can believe it, what we can do [...] and still they turned and brought fresh vistas. [...] She still longed to glide forever onwards through this gladness of light.
>
> But the bright gold was withdrawing. Presently it stood only upon the higher ridges. The colour was going and the angular shadows, leaving a bleakness of white, leaving the mountains higher in their whiteness. The highest sloped more swiftly than the others from its lower mass and ended in a long cone of purest white with a flattened top sharply aslant against the deepening blue; as if walking upon it. It held her eyes, its solid thickness of snow, the way from its blunted tower it came broadening down unbroken by crag, radiant white until, far down, its pinewoods made a gentleness about its base. Up there on the quiet of its top-most angle it seemed there must be someone, minutely rejoicing in its line along the sky.

---

[39] 'The cold of a few moments ago, numbing her face, had brought a hint of how one might freeze quietly to death, numbed and if warmed by an intensity of cold; and that out amongst the mountains it would not be terrible. But this raw mist bringing pain in every bone it touched would send one aching to one's death, crushed to death by a biting increasing pain' (*O*, 28-29).

> A turn brought peaks whose gold had turned to rose. She had not eyes enough for seeing. Seeing was not enough. There was sound, if only one could hear it, in this still, signalling light.
>
> The last of it was ruby gathered departing upon the topmost crags, seeming, the moment before it left them, to be deeply wrought into the crinkled rock (*O*, 29f.).

While in Butler's factual description the beautiful mountain scenery can easily be visualized, his passage lacks the lyrical and personal quality of Dorothy Richardson's text. The precise description of Miriam's perception in both the reference to her senses - 'watch'; 'see'; 'eyes'; 'hear' - and the use of emotive words - 'longed'; 'gladness;' 'rejoicing', and later on 'marvel of colour', 'happiness possessed' (*O*, 30) - as well as her personification of the scene - 'there must be someone' - creates the ravished tone of enchantment that makes us see *and* feel what she sees and feels at the sight of the beauty of the Alps. It is a Romantic delight in the beauty of nature that reminds us again of Wordsworth, who described these very mountains:

> Or gazing from the mountain's silent brow
> Bright stars of ice and azure worlds of snow,
> Where needle peaks of granite shooting bare
> Tremble in ever-varying tints of air,
> Great joy by horror tam'd dilates his heart,
> And the near heav'ns their own delights impart.
>
> - When the Sun bids the gorgeous scene farewell,
> Alps overlooking Alps their state upswell;
> Huge Pikes of Darkness nam'd of Fear and Storms
> Lift, all serene, their still, illumin'd forms,
> In sea-like reach of prospect round him spread,
> Ting'd like an angel's smile all rosy red.
>
> (*Descriptive Sketches,* 1793, l. 556-567)

Miriam's Wordsworthian delight in the serene silence of the scene is enhanced by the driver's one interference with her solitary joy: '"*Schön, die letzte Glüh,*" he said quietly' (*O*, 30). Light, Dorothy Richardson's favourite leitmotif in all her novels, takes on a central importance. This one expression of beauty in direct speech on the whole sleigh ride serves as a catalyst to Miriam's awareness. In a kind of double-alienation from her direct, immediate experience - the *driver* expressing her thoughts in a *foreign* language - she learns to look at her surroundings in an even more intense way.

Her experience of reality features extraordinary qualities of something *more* and *different* that all indicate a moment of happiness. Blothner (62-70) lists these qualities as *harmony*, *power*, *support* and *vitality*:[40] Miriam is at one with her surroundings, the colours of the sky 'melting imperceptibly' into each other convey a deep sense of harmonious, almost transcendental, unity. Her 'living soul', like Wordsworth's,

> with an eye made quiet by the power
> of harmony and the deep power of joy

sees 'into the life of things' ('Tintern Abbey' l. 47-49). When she longs 'to glide forever onwards through this gladness of light', she gathers unknown energies and is filled by a power that makes her completely forget her tiredness after the long journey. At the same time she feels supported and protected both by the warmth of the sleigh and the seemingly familiar landscape enfolding her so completely that she can relax: 'She sat back released from intentness, seeing the scene as one who saw it daily' (*O*, 30). Finally, in this moment of wide attention she has sensory impressions of incomparable vividness; her experience of the massive beauty of snow and mountains goes beyond her faculty of seeing: 'She had not eyes enough for seeing. Seeing was not enough'; and it implies synaesthetic beauties hidden away: 'There was sound, if only one could hear it, in this still, signalling light.' In her intense perception of what appears to her as perfection, Miriam's state of mind comes up to Hoffmann's definition of happiness:

> Der Glückliche erlebt eine weitgehende Öffnung und Verfeinerung der Wahrnehmung für sonst Unbedeutendes und Flüchtiges im Zusammenhang mit erhöhter Wachheit und grosser Empfindlichkeit und Leistungsfähigkeit der Sinne: Farben, Geräusche, Gerüche usw. gewinnen starke Ausdruckskraft (169).

Dorothy Richardson summarizes this moment: 'The mountain lights were *happiness possessed*' (*O*, 30; emphasis added). Miriam's total devotion to the experience of the Now makes her see the ephemeral beauty of the skies as a culminating enchantment, a perfection 'never to return, begg[ing] for remembrance' (*O*, 30). When her attention is at its most alert, in this very moment of happiness, Miriam is aware of its end approaching; the only way to keep this experience is to store it as one of her treasures of memory to be recalled later on. Characteristically, the intensity of her real experience soon ebbs away, giving room to relaxed exhaustion: 'Drunk, she felt now, with sleep; dizzy with gazing' (*O*, 30).

The common sleigh-ride from the terminus to the hotel, which for the Croydon party - the average tourist - is a tiresome and cold journey to be endured, to Miriam thus fulfills the promise of the unknown, the 'angel's smile' on the mountains revealing a mystery of transcendence that surmounts

---

[40] Blothner uses the terms 'Harmonie', 'Kraft', 'Halt', 'Lebendigkeit'.

the mere sensory experience of beauty. In this upward movement, originally starting in the darkness of London and leading to the highest mountain peaks and from there on to the skies, there is a mystical ascension, an awakening towards an enhanced sensitivity that has a strong religious touch; Miriam's journey ends *beyond* the 'high snow-shrouded cone of a little church' (*O*, 31), the symbol of Christian religion, at a 'portico' symbolizing the gateway to a mystically happy life. Thus, her light-imbued Oberland may become Wordsworth's 'spot of holy ground,'

> Where from distress a refuge might be found,
> And solitude prepare the soul for heaven;
> Sure, nature's God that spot to man had given
> Where falls the purple morning far and wide
> In flakes of light upon the mountain-side.
>
> (William Wordsworth, *Descriptive Sketches (1836)* 39, ll.1-6)

1.4 'Into the Heart of Peace:' The Journey to Dimple Hill

> Away, away, from men and towns,
> To the wild wood and the downs -
> To the silent wilderness
> Where the soul need not repress
> Its music lest it should not find
> An echo in another's mind,
> While the touch of Nature's art
> Harmonizes heart to heart.
>
> (P. B. Shelley, 'To Jane:The Invitation', ll. 21ff., *Works* 668)

> Perhaps for life. Perhaps, this time, there need be no return? (*MM*, 606)

As we have seen, Miriam's journeys are at their core movements away from well-known surroundings that she wants to leave. The worlds 'from which one after another she had retreated' (*DH*, 424) are places no longer satisfying, places she cannot identify with as they do not allow her the freedom she needs for her own life. As a lifelong wanderer Miriam feels 'her need for escape from a stereotyped universe' (*DH*, 405) when things cease changing and some form of monotony sets in. Driven by her 'implacable life urge' (Powys 29), she moves away from her parents' home in *Pointed Roofs*, from the Pernes' school in *Honeycomb*, from her personal problems in *Oberland*. On each of these journeys of liberation she is aware of a new world expecting her, a world that is to have a lasting impact on her life:

> The moments passed, carrying her rapidly on. There was a life ahead that was going to enrich and change her as she had been enriched and changed by Hanover, but much more swiftly and intimately. She was changed already (*HC*, 351).

It is a question of being prepared for change, an act of will, which leads to her attempt to make the actual change of mind run parallel to her change of place. At Newlands, anticipating the world she is about to arrive at at the end of her journey, she wants to abbreviate the not very easy time of assimilation she had needed both in Hanover and at the Pernes' school. While this change towards the new situation is to a certain extent possible when arriving at the Corries', as her post as a governess in a rich household is defined by conventions, the situation is different at the beginning of *Dimple Hill*: In a 'general repudiation' (*CH*, 398) of everything and everyone she sets off upon the 'invisible path' (*CH*, 398) towards an undefined future.

At Miriam's 'gateway of her six months' freedom' (*DH*, 403) - as in all previous movements of escape - stand the twin ideas of leaving behind an old claustrophobic world of breakdown and isolation and of gaining new insights both into her exterior and interior realities by means of a journey. As Miriam does not know where to turn to, her journey first lacks clear direction: her short stays in-between the short trips reflect her wavering search for a new world, a new place to stay. Different from her frame of mind on her earlier journeys with fixed destinations - to Germany, where she mostly pondered on the past and the future, and to Oberland, where the immediacy of the moment was paramount - on this journey Miriam's searching consciousness moves constantly from visual awareness to reflections on her situation and back. Her glad expectation of the vague future, however, proves that she has overcome her thoughts of depression; her self-confidence on this piecemeal journey shows that she has matured.

At the beginning of Miriam's journey towards Dimple Hill Dorothy Richardson expresses the reach of this departure, her decisive turn away from the old towards the new within a few sentences. While for many years the home of the Brooms, her friends from Banbury Park, was 'a sudden incredible refuge' (*DH*, 405) from her everyday London life, this steady place of relaxed security now belongs to an 'enclosed world' (*DH*, 405) to be left behind; a radical new start has to be made: Florence and Grace

> became the symbols of all she was leaving, and when, as silently she gazed at the journeying landscape, that group of flaming poppies had darted by, she had commented on them in a phrase addressed to the consciousness of the young man, bringing his eyes across the carriage and, with them, a vision of the cathedral within whose twilit interior lived a stillness akin to that wherein spirits recognize

> each other, as she and the young man had recognized each other (*DH*, 403).

As in *Oberland*, the landscape as an active part leaves her in the role of the observer, but while in the earlier novel-chapter the accumulation of visual impressions fills her consciousness and leaves her happy in her solitary experience, here the single view of 'flaming poppies' subsequently leads to an inner vision of a possible future world of mutual spiritual recognition she has been craving for. It is important to note that Miriam does not experience this vision as her own, but that she externalises it into the eyes of the stranger; it is a spiritual world she herself for the time being has not yet found access to: 'she had precipitately assumed a vestment to which she had no right' (*DH*, 403).

Yet, in this visionary moment Miriam's spiritual search has found a direction: in order to retrieve the stillness of the cathedral Miriam has to break away from the Broom girls. As long as she behaves in the way Florence sees her, as a 'fickle, insincere, easy-going creature evading all issues' (*DH*, 409),[41] Miriam in their company cannot possibly find that inner stillness. She therefore chooses a place to stay alone. This first destination at Mrs Peebles', however, does not correspond to her inner vision, which would lead her from the anonymous bustle of London to the open country silence, and she soon decides to leave again. It is the visual impression of the place which leaves her dissatisfied because her preconceived image of peaceful countryside looks different:

> Here, in the lane, she had the illusion of being in suburbia with all the world at hand. Away behind, there could well be the ragged edges of building plots and, at the lane's end, a sophisticated village with a good service of buses to town. The birdless, flowerless hedges looked cowed; outskirt hedges accustomed to traffic and unable, in its intervals, to recover their wealth and assert their ancient power.
>
> No country scene could be more unlike the destination she had pictured herself reaching, by some unpondered route, immediately on leaving town. All these weeks it had accompanied her, filling every background, richly reflected into the inner twilight of her being: vast echoing woodlands, their green alleys and sunlit clearings traversed by streams and flower banks, and, in between, green open country unfenced and uninhabited, beneath high blue skies. Still, it was a lane, with its own little quality, however surrounded (*DH*, 413f.).

---

[41] one of the rare passages in *Pilgrimage* where the fixed internal focalization on Miriam's consciousness is broken by an outside glimpse at and comment on her.

This imaginary landscape forming distinctive visual contrasts to her London world of both spatial and personal confinement is unattainable on a real journey.[42] No real landscape can successfully compete with Miriam's fixed idea of her space of freedom; outer and inner reality, the objectively real and the subjectively imagined, as simultaneous presences in Miriam's consciousness seem to be irreconcilable contrasts. First, however, in spite of a gradual warming towards the place,[43] Miriam thinks that her search for 'the wooded distances of her first vision' (*DH*, 415), for a visual reality coming the closest possible to her mental image, to an agreement of view and vision, has to continue. Only later, when Miriam comes to know that her long-planned scheme of bringing together her best friends Amabel and Shatov has been fulfilled, does she realize that 'the open spaces of her first vision of freedom no longer attract' her (*DH*, 429). As soon as this last link with her London past has gone, the solitary, unlimited world has lost its charm. She realizes that the beauties of open nature, which she so much enjoyed on her previous journeys, were so attractive because travelling meant a contrastive progression *limited in time* not only from one world to another, but from one society with its imperfections to another. To be in a social vacuum for an indefinite time is too much to bear even for Miriam, for all her love of solitude.

After her separation from 'the two who had severally supplied her richest experience of human relationship' (*DH*, 429), her search changes direction. When Miriam accidentally finds Shatov's note with the address of a Quaker family somewhere in the country, again her inner eye sees a redefined perfect destination, now, to be noted, no longer an uninhabited, unlimited space, but female company in a clearly defined sheltering home:

> Far away within the twilit deeps of her innermost consciousness, she went up a pathway towards a farmhouse within whose doorway stood a little group of grey-clad Quaker women, smiling a gentle welcome. Michael's gift. A little Quaker stronghold at the heart of all she had first come forth to seek. Itself as remote as the deeps of country wherein it was set (*DH*, 430).

Mentally anticipating her new home, Miriam ceases to look back, she feels no longer the sense of leaving behind an unsatisfactory world, but a sense of reaching a state of perfection never experienced before. The passing landscape, on former journeys powerfully commenting on her concrete

[42] Miriam's idea of the Garden Eden is here enlarged to a whole landscape: the notions of light ('sunlit, high blue skies'), colours ('green, blue') and open space ('vast', 'clearings', 'open country', 'unfenced') are as consistent with her image of paradise as her wish to be there alone ('uninhabited'). See also Chapter 2.4.

[43] 'This magic angle at the edge of the world, seeming at first so desolate and so unknown, [...] was a cherished spot [...]' (*DH*, 415).

transition from one world to another, has lost much of its importance once she has set out on her journey to Dimple Hill. In the bus taking her to the farm she again looks out of the window 'as if, in the surrounding fields, there were something to be seen' (*DH*, 432), but what she perceives - the green hedge and the low fields - has no impact on her thoughts.

The traditional pilgrim's aim of his or her pilgrimage is to arrive at a sacred place of heightened religious radiance. This place is, in all its worldliness, an imitation of the celestial Jerusalem, a place of beauty and purity, the abode of eternal peace and happiness. The pilgrim hoping to leave behind his worldly troubles and to get closer to heaven even in this life at the same time seeks spiritual renewal as well as physical and mental rest from the journey and expects an unparalleled feeling of joy in the company of sympathetic fellow pilgrims.[44] The repeated references to Bunyan especially in the early novel-chapters of *Pilgrimage* support a reading of Miriam as a modern pilgrim.[45] And still now, approaching the final stage of her 'pilgrimage', Miriam in her thoughts follows this traditional pattern very closely. She imagines Dimple Hill to be her personal heaven, the Quaker women at the 'doorway' welcoming her to the completion of her search: 'On the way from solitude to perfect human association [...] she could now compose herself to arrive in heaven' (*DH*, 433). On the last stretch of her journey she seems to have left behind earthly heaviness and has mentally entered the inconceivable heavenly space where she experiences new feelings:

> Swift and invisible upon light, impalpable feet, her spirit already dancing within the nowhere and everywhere whither she was bound, whither days ago she had been translated; so that now, for the first time, life-obstructing speculation and excitement were excluded from the experience of arriving amongst strangers in a strange place (*DH*, 432).

---

[44] In Bunyan's *Pilgrim's Progress* (131) the Kings Trumpeters welcoming Christian and his brother promise the perfect company in the heavenly Jerusalem: They, 'by mixing their Musick, with looks and gestures, still signifie to *Christian* and his Brother, how welcome they were into their company, and with what gladness they came to meet them: And now were these two men, as 'twere, in Heaven, before they came at it; being swallowed up with the sight of Angels, and with hearing of their melodious notes. Here also they had the City itself in view, and they thought they heard all the Bells therein to ring, to welcome them thereto: but above all, the warm and joyful thoughts that they had about their own dwelling there, with such company, and that for ever and ever. Oh! by what tongue or pen can their glorious joy be expressed: and thus they came up to the Gate.' Visual and acoustic beauty and the mere idea of eternal rest transfigure them already on the hither side of paradise into an experience of unspeakable joy.

[45] cf. Powys 10: *Pilgrimage*, 'this modern *Pilgrim's Progress*.'

However, this certainty of reaching the perfect - literally 'utopian' - society of 'nowhere', her expectation of reaching an unlocatable place of light spirituality, is shatterėd in an illuminating moment of deep earthiness:

> Streaming from the misty rain-soaked meadows, visible whenever a gate passed by, [the air] poured into her being, describing those meadows, miles of them covering the earth in all directions, solitary, averted in the dim light, breathing out secretly, unnoticed, the evening fragrance of all that grew in them; claiming her, not as something added to the rest, but as her known companions, left behind long ago and now returned to and demanding forgetfulness of everything but themselves, for whom, they declared, she had mistaken the strangers at the top of the hill (*DH*, 433).

It is significant that here, on the verge of imaginable human paradise, the immediate sensory impression of concrete reality, conquers all her abstract constructs of the mind. Nature, to which she reverted on all her former journeys as a place of beauty and security, again assumes the role of her best companion; it is the place most worth striving for as it is something known since childhood,[46] an enriching part of her own consciousness, thus her true paradise. The visible world of her earlier journeys, however intensely perceived with her eyes, in the end always left her as an observer, passing but never staying in the beauty of nature. Now, at what she hopes will be the end of her pilgrimage, the strong fragrances of nature envelop her so completely that she, to the exclusion of everything else, achieves a union with nature.

It is this all-enfolding quality of certain smells Miriam felt around her on previous journeys which brings oblivion to everything else: through her nose Miriam experiences nature in the most complete way. In these earlier instances, however, Miriam's awareness of smells is no more than a pleasant, but unreflected upon breathing in through the nose. In *Pointed Roofs*, returning from the outing to the forest inn, 'the warm scents of the woods stood across the roadway. They breathed them in' (*PR*, 156). In *Backwater*, walking away with Max from the dance at her parents' home, Miriam registers the beauty of the night and notices: 'The freshening air streamed towards them from the meadows [...] The limes seemed heavily scented after their breath of the open' (*BW*, 219). On her journey to Oberland 'mountain air "like wine" [...] holding one up, feeding every nerve,' (*O*, 18) fills her with an unwonted freshness. In the continuing movement of her journey Miriam's senses register the various smells of nature as swiftly passing fragrances, as scarcely noticed parts of her surroundings, which have no lasting effect on her consciousness. The narrative in these earlier volumes

[46] cf. Chapter 2.4.2 on the 'bee memory.'

swiftly returns to the account of visual and acoustic impressions, which in their powerful descriptions clearly outweigh the perceptions of smells.

A much earlier scene in *Pilgrimage* anticipates Miriam's arrival at Dimple Hill: the opening lines of *Honeycomb* convey a similar dominance of her olfactory awareness, a total devotion to the impressions of her nose. Leaving the train near Newlands, her new place of working and living, Miriam first *smells* wet trees, which absorbs all her thoughts, causing her to enter and experience nature - 'reality' - in a most complete and satisfying way.

> When Miriam got out of the train into the darkness she knew that there were woods all about her. The moist air was rich with the smell of trees - wet bark and branches - moss and lichen, damp dead leaves. She stood on the dark platform snuffing the rich air. It was the end of her journey. *Anything that might follow would be unreal compared to this moment.* Little bulbs of yellow light further up the platform told her where she must turn to find the things she must go to meet. 'How lovely the air is here.' . . . The phrase repeated itself again and again, going with her up the platform towards the group of lights. It was all she could summon to meet the new situation. It satisfied her; *it made her happy*. It was enough; but no one would think it was enough (*HC*, 349; emphasis added).

Parallel to *Dimple Hill*, the scene, set in the evening towards the end of a journey to an unknown place, suggests in its moist, green, almost smellable atmosphere a rich moment of life, a deep inhalation of solitude before Miriam plunges herself into the - diametrically opposite - worlds of the Corries and the Roscorlas respectively. Thus, the smells of trees and flowers, 'her known companions, left behind long ago and now returned to' (*DH*, 433), if fully appreciated, provide unexpected and complete moments of relaxation. The harmonious unity with nature, the energy and support she gains from this swift physical immersion into the fragrances of her surroundings again suggest Blothner's qualities of happiness. These brief halts in nature are extraordinary moments of experience that have a strong effect on her subsequent, positive, first meetings with the two women who offer her a - temporary - home, Mrs Corrie and Miss Roscorla.

However promising this solitary reunion with nature seems to Miriam, it will not be the final destination of her journeys. They do not end under the trees of a suburban railway station or in the meadows of Sussex, but in the house and families of the worldly Corries and the spiritual Roscorlas. In *Honeycomb* Miriam approaches Newlands slowly, the drive in the brougham giving her time for reflection upon her situation, which is about to change. Textually, the detailed description of the last stretch of Miriam's journey and arrival is a slow tuning-in to the apparently rich, soft, warm world of the Corries, where everything at first sight seems to flow in 'soft' abundance. In

Dimple Hill, on the other hand, this move from nature to human society is represented in a typically abrupt shift of scene. The description switches from the rich smells of fragrant, open meadows over to a view of the bare, rather unwelcoming threshold and inner rooms of the farm, which suggests a life of hard discipline and frugality.

Miriam's sensory - mostly visual - impressions of rooms, objects and maidservants call forth a first assessment of her new situation. In both cases Miriam senses a certain discrepancy between the surfaces of her surroundings and the underlying reality of her own situation that retards her usual enthusiasm for a new place. While she is fascinated by the beauty and luxuries of Newlands, her own frightened look in the mirror leaves her 'disconcerted for a moment' (*HC*, 354) as she feels out of place in this house abounding with wealth, whereas the exaggerated piety seen in the 'look of conscious salvation' on the maid's face at Dimple Hill (*DH*, 434) does not fit her preconceived image of Quakerism. It reminds her of the rigid, lifeless atmosphere at her great-aunt *Stone's* [!], a memory which is rather 'disconcerting' (*DH*, 435).[47] But Miriam revises her negative first impression as soon as she meets Miss Roscorla: in the radiance of her presence Miriam immediately seems to have found a new home.

Has Miriam changed since her journey to Newlands? Is she still the same woman as the young governess-to-be? The question about her basic dilemma of 'Becoming' versus 'Being' presents itself. Functionally, the repeated descriptions of the outer, of concrete journeys as progress in time and space, make possible the revelation of the inner, of 'felt life' as being equally in progress (cf. Blake 93). Looking at her development as such a progress in time, Miriam has obviously *become* a different woman. Her outer

---

[47] The two contrasting arrivals are marked by notions of soft abundance and hard scantiness respectively: at Newlands 'a *soft golden* blaze' awaits her in a 'fire-lit, lamp-lit, *thickly carpeted* enclosure'; the lamplight fell upon a '*thick* pale greeny yellow *carpet*, the little settee with their *huge cushions*, and the strange-looking pictures set low on dull *gold* walls' (*HC*, 353). In her room she finds 'the mound of *soft* bath towel,' hot water 'sending up a great cloud of comforting steam,' 'the strange beautiful, beautiful long wide hang of the faintly patterny faintly blue curtains,' 'the blue-covered bed, the *frilled pillows*, high *silky-looking* bed curtains' (*HC*, 354; all emphases added).

At Dimple Hill she sees unadorned simplicity in front as well as inside the house and in the servant opening the door: 'a square plaster house, two-storied, *bleak*, an enclosed glass porch *nakedly* protruding, [...] a share of the ivy *sparsely* climbing the left side of the frontage' (*DH*, 433) ; 'a tall *lean* maidservant,' whose '*bony* form' is surmounted 'by an oblong strip of *starch-stiffened* cotton lace'; 'the *pallor* of the long *lean* face' is heightened by 'pale blue eyes' with a '*cold unseeing* gaze.' (*DH*, 434); 'a Philistine room, furnished without deference to shape and colour' contains a 'large *brass* bedstead', a simple washstand and a dressing-table (*DH*, 435; all emphases added).

The direct comparison of the maidservant at Dimple Hill to Wiggerson, Mrs Corrie's servant (*DH*, 434), suggests such a parallel reading of the two scenes.

circumstances have changed dramatically if we think about her mother's suicide, the splitting-up of her family, her active London years, which brought her great independence and many friends and acquaintances. Her emotional search has changed direction: accepting the post at Newlands, Miriam wanted to get away from the 'days of fear and isolation and helplessness in hard winter weather' (*HC*, 349) at her parents' home; she turned from enclosed family life to find satisfaction in the more open spaces of a professional life as a governess. Now, when coming to Dimple Hill, she has left behind the non-committing London society to find 'those to whom she belonged' (*DH*, 429). Her retreat into the intimacy of family life promises her personal satisfaction and happiness. Undoubtedly, her intellectual horizon has greatly widened since her days as a youthful governess. Her London relationships with Dr Hancock, Michael Shatov, Hypo Wilson and Dr Densley all contributed to the expansion of her intellectual understanding of the world. Miriam's life, indeed, can be read as an epitome of the 'spiritual growth of the human soul' (Powys 38), an ever-expanding movement towards a more complete understanding of life and a fuller realization of the self. And yet, despite these far-reaching changes in Miriam's life, her sensory awareness, her keen registration of her immediate surroundings with all her senses, basically remains the same. Her consciousness, the *locus* of impressions, is constant: the two scenes of arrival at Newlands and at Dimple Hill would be interchangeable as far as Miriam's senses are concerned. This subtle sensory awareness, her ability to recognize and appreciate within the world of everyday life the intensities of her subjective perception, is one of the stable factors of Miriam's core personality, of her own self (cf. Würzbach 297).The enormous power of her memory to register and recall experiences in their minute sensory details helps to perpetuate them, to integrate them as enriching parts of her unalterable 'centre of being'. As to the journeys, Miriam herself is sensitized to the futility of escape from herself, of *really* becoming someone different, in an exterior change of place; for all their mobile impressionism the accounts of Miriam's journeys in the end refer back to her own *being*, hinting at the existence of 'that self within herself who was more than her momentary self' (*DLH*, 222). Thus Miriam explains to Hypo:

> Of course there is actually no such thing as travel. So they say. There is nothing but a *Voyage autour de ma Chambre*, meaning *de tout ce que je suis*, even in a *tour du monde* (*DLH*, 167).

Reading the novel-sequence from an autobiographical focus, Dorothy Richardson's twin preoccupation with 'Being' and 'Becoming' has to be seen not as a treatment of excluding oppositions, but of complementary notions of what Miriam's - and, in parallel, Dorothy Richardson's own - life eventually is; though outwardly, in the fluidity of her consciousness, a continual process of *becoming*, the identity of her self is determined by her deep awareness of an underlying *being*. Thus, her development towards *becoming* a writer would not be possible without the persistent power of her sensory *being*. The sensory awareness of her immediate surroundings and present *being* will serve as a starting point when she begins writing at Dimple Hill; her intellectual awareness of her past circumstances and her own *becoming* what she is will eventually enable her to start retelling her own life at the very end of *Pilgrimage*. By putting down the memories of her personal pilgrimage, 'Dorothy-Miriam' then mentally sets off on her journeys again.[48]

1.5 'In True Perspective:' The Journeys Remembered

> These beauteous forms
> Through a long absence, have not been to me
> As is a landscape to a blind man's eye:
> But oft, in lonely rooms, and 'mid the din
> Of towns and cities, I have owed to them
> In hours of weariness, sensations sweet
> Felt in the blood, and felt along the heart;
> And passing even into my purer mind,
> With tranquil restoration: - feelings too
> Of unremembered pleasure [...]
> (William Wordsworth, 'Tintern Abbey' , l. 22-31)

> Can any one really know what they have really observed until they look back? (*CH*, 330)

Dorothy Richardson's immense retrospective strength enabled her to recreate her own youth in form of her heroine Miriam Henderson. Looking back is, in Radford's words,

> what *Pilgrimage* is all about. It looks back on a lifetime, to the acquisition of a woman's femininity, to the construction of her consciousness, to the pathways taken by the pilgrim in the course of her life's journey (1991:86).

Looking back on her earlier life, Dorothy Richardson in the activity of writing finds herself in the 'perpetual condition of reexperience,' (Rose 1970:33); her method of rendering the immediacy of these recalled impressions aims to make the reader see this to be Miriam's actual

---

[48] In the act of starting to write about her life the parallel between Dorothy Richardson, the author, and Miriam, the heroine, is completed: Dorothy becomes Miriam. Therefore Gregory's term 'Dorothy-Miriam' (4) expresses this completed identification.

experience. In this impressive achievement of memory, Miriam's life and experiences become the primary reality of the text of *Pilgrimage*.

The author's artistic and continual look back, which results in the complete novel-sequence, includes the heroine's own natural and sporadic looks back on her past. In the course of *Pilgrimage* there is an increasing number of retrospective glances, in which Miriam recalls told and untold scenes of her earlier life. Some of them refer to journeys, too. Her untold journeys to her childhood holidays at the seaside,[49] to Belgium (*O*, 24f.), and - in the longest look back of the whole novel-sequence - to Les Lauriers (*MM*, 556-577) form part of Miriam's hidden life-story and are only partly revealed in the indirection of these enigmatic flashbacks. As they do not appear as re-presentations of an immediate experience fully related at an earlier stage, the reader cannot relive these journey experiences. Structurally, they are mostly 'analepses externes', scarcely evocative, 'indecipherable' glimpses at moments of Miriam's past *before* her initial journey to Germany.

When Miriam, however, remembers some sensory impressions of those journeys explicitly described in the text at an earlier stage, there is still a sparkle of the first radiance, of the original impression. Still, in the reduction to some mere flashes of memory, Dorothy Richardson's complex stream-of-consciousness technique is illuminated. Thus, the actual moment of registering sensory impressions often seems to be part of a larger pattern of impressionistic perception, a mere detail in the dense fabric of Miriam's experience of the world. The 'unique quality of the passing moment' (*DLH*, 134) does not seem to ask to be recorded, but in its intensity of sensory impressions 'simply to be experienced' (Bucher 99). First of all, her delight in impressions of an everyday kind is there for its own sake. Unlike Miss Lonsdale in *March Moonlight*, who at the very moment of experiencing declares: 'I am going to *remember* the winter of '08-'09' (*MM*, 558), Miriam lets her momentary impressions sink into her consciousness to become part of her memory, unaware of any future significance. According to Miriam, *everything* is 'written in the book of consciousness. Written indelibly' (*TR*, 503), every impression can be a forming element of Miriam's expanding consciousness. Yet only in retrospection, once the original observation is sieved through the filter of temporal distance, may the most innocent and unconscious of details recollected assume greater significance in that they appear as 'sudden flashes of spiritual insight' (Henke 54), which hold together the disparate elements of life. With the odd exception, these memories are positive parts of Miriam's recorded past and thus have a positive impact on her present. As we shall see in Miriam's garden memories, her present state of mind depends very strongly upon the past when she says:

---

[49] cf. *PR*, 33. Such a journey is described in 'Journey to Paradise' (*JP*, 120-130).

'If the present brings up the happiness of the past, the present is happy' (*IN*, 402). Thus, the recurrent memory of 'the beauty, music and happiness of Germany' (*HC*, 351) makes her feel things rising 'warm and laughing and expanding';[50] 'in a single glance, the whole of the time in Germany was beautiful, golden happy light, and people happy in the golden light, garlands of music and the happy ringing certainty of voices. . .' (*TU*, 214) Her ecstatic praise of the past culminates in her affirmation that '*memory* was happiness, one happiness linked to the next' (*TU*, 214), a notion which is particularly true in the memory of her journeys to Germany and Oberland.

Looked at more closely, the reminiscences of her sensory impressions remain verbally indefinite, they are, in fact, catchwords on the surface of the text. Sharing Miriam's background of her earlier experiences told in the previous volumes, the reader's own reading memory is tasked: he or she has to imagine what exactly is being called forth in Miriam's mind when she recalls 'the beauty, music and happiness of Germany' or when she has 'a vision of Oberland before her eyes' (*CH*, 378). Her collective reminiscences of her past journeys - and of her sensory impressions in general, often summarized in a single sentence - can evoke highly varying images in the individual reader's mind. As the wonted explicitness of Miriam's thoughts turns amazingly vague, the reader recalls those details of Miriam's past he or she found most impressive in Dorothy Richardson's description. As long as these images correspond basically to Miriam's own remembered impression, we are able to follow her continuing thoughts. However, when her flashes of memory follow each other too quickly, or when past, present and future meet in one single thought in her mind, it will get exceedingly difficult for the reader to understand Miriam's mental proceedings, to decipher the heavily 'indicial' narrative and recognize the 'signified' referred to (Barthes 1977: 93). Miriam is herself aware of this problem of the individual's mind working infinitely faster than any communication can take place when she says: 'If only one could speak so quickly as one's thoughts flashed, and several thoughts together, all with a separate life of their own belonging, everybody would be understood' (*DL*, 218). Confronted with the near-simultaneity of thought, Dorothy Richardson's stream-of-consciousness technique reaches its limits: If only she could *write* so quickly as *Miriam*'s thoughts flashed . . . perhaps she would be understood completely. Yet Dorothy Richardson's verbal portrayal of Miriam's mind as a literary text does not aim at a complete recording of every single thread of thought to its tiniest detail; therefore Miriam's consciousness can never - and need not - be fully understood. For in this ultimate vagueness of description lies its literary

[50] see also *HC*, 470, remembering the Germans: 'Their mountains and woods and villages and towns were beautiful with joy. They were happy in their beautiful country in their own way. Germany . . . all washed with music and poetry and song.'

quality: the reader, having been given such an extraordinarily deep insight into the workings of Miriam's mind, eventually meets the mystery of the individual: at the 'motionless unchanging centre of her consciousness' Miriam feels 'bowed beneath the weight of incommunicable experience' (*CH*, 305). The secrets of her innermost being, which she aims to fathom for herself on her pilgrimage, in the end have to remain untold.[51]

As for her journeys, what has Miriam's larger self kept at her 'living centre' (*DH*, 498) that *can* be recalled from her past and be communicated to the reader? Considering her intense original travel impressions, it is surprisingly little. On her second journey to Dimple Hill, for example, she simply remembers the beauty of the woods perceived in 'breathless watching' (*MM*, 606) the year before; the people she meets on her journeys and their conversations hardly leave any memorable impressions. What is more, her own original thoughts 'convincing' though they were in the past, are no longer understandable. 'Picture after picture' may emerge from her past, but the 'deposits' of her thoughts, 'so long neglected, had lost their first lustre and become, save for a word here and a phrase there, *indecipherable*' (*DH*, 526f.; emphasis added). When Miriam later on also recognizes that 'the past, all our pasts, falling back into their places, will vanish from our midst' (*MM*, 611), she unexpectedly seems to deny the immediate power of past memories. It appears to contradict the basic theme of *Pilgrimage*, in which Dorothy Richardson recalls Miriam's, and thus her own, youth and describes it with an outstanding sense of immediacy.

However, once these images, though still existing in her memory, are *neglected*, they lose their meaning; they are not important for her conception of her developing self in a changing world. By way of contrast, the memories Miriam recalls again and again do not vanish but keep their 'lustre', become part of the present, as they are essential elements of her being. Dorothy Richardson describes this visual and mental process in one of her short stories:

> Whenever Weymouth is recalled to me it is not the seaside joys that return, but that first discovery of the sky. And each time more vividly than before. Just now, I felt the shock of it pass through me like an electric current. It is not memory. . . . Certain conditions, certain states of being, especially favour reentry into what we call 'past moments'? But they are not past ('Excursion,' *JP*, 101f.).

Thus, Miriam's Oberland impressions of beauty assume such an undying quality to be experienced time and again: The beauty of the mountains 'had

51 When Miriam starts writing in *March Moonlight*, she becomes aware of this problem of written communication: 'One after another the scenes passed before me, each with its unique claim. Impossible to choose. Impossible without special knowledge to convey. Flesh without bones . . .' (*MM*, 610).

entered into her for ever; its golden glow must surely somehow reveal itself' (*DLH*, 140). The powerful pictures of Oberland are still present: 'Oberland again; its golden light, and its way of making its outer world conform to its inner. Something of heaven [...]' (*DLH*, 157; see also *DLH*, 200; *DH*, 454).

When Dorothy Richardson succeeds in conveying Miriam's immediate experience of the moment, as she does in her journey account in *Oberland*, the later recall of such a moment assumes a meaningful function in the text. As the strong 'lustre' of the original visual impression has not faded, the memory of beauty is important both on the level of Miriam's consciousness as an emotional stimulus and on the narrative level as a cohesive means giving fresh impetus to the discourse. In her loving observation of nature and in her continuous endeavour to reproduce the most subtle sensations of Miriam's perception, Dorothy Richardson takes up the Romantic tradition; in fact, her attitude recalls Coleridge, who writes that

> bright colours in motion both make and leave the strongest impression on the eye. Nothing is more likely too than that a vivid image or visual spectrum thus originated may become the link of association in recalling the feelings and images that had accompanied the original impression (*Biographia Literaria* 258).

Providing a mental space of freedom from Miriam's wonted cloistered surroundings, the journeys in retrospect lose their ambiguous touch of insecurity, which, as we have seen, is strongly present when she is actually on the way. They are remembered as happy interludes of intense visual awareness, unburdened by the task of social responsibility of any sort. These visual memories, thus, to speak with Wordsworth,

> [...] flash upon that inward eye
> Which is the bliss of solitude;
> ('I Wander'd Lonely', ll. 21f.)

In numerous situations of Miriam's life they enrich and open up her 'innermost sphere of happy solitude' (*DLH*, 222) towards contemplation. These pictures are no longer bound to a chronological order of the past; but, belonging to Miriam's 'possessions, immortal, inexhaustible' ('Excursion,' *JP*, 102), they form part of her present consciousness. In 'Excursion', Dorothy Richardson describes this working of the individual mind:

> Life makes artists of us all? No longer seeing experience chronologically, we can compose it, after the manner of a picture, with all the parts in true perspective and relationship. Moving picture. For moments open out, reveal fresh contents every time we go back into them, grouping and regrouping themselves as we advance (*JP*, 103).

When Miriam gradually assumes such an artist's attitude towards her memories - not only - of her journeys, trying to find the 'true perspectives' of her past experiences, she approaches Dorothy Richardson's own point of view. Starting to write at the end of *March Moonlight*, Miriam takes the step from the travelling observer of Life to the unmoving contemplator of her own life, and embarks on a mental tour of the past. It is the awareness of the unlimited, enriching availability of her own - real - past, which forms the basis of her work of art: 'What is called "creation" imaginative transformation, fantasy, invention, is only based upon reality' (*MM*, 657).

Wordsworth's realization of the past may summarize her creative process:

> [...] he thence attained
> An active power to fasten images
> Upon his brain; and on their pictured lines
> Intensely brooded, even till they acquired
> The liveliness of dreams.
> ('Excursion' I, ll. 144-148)

Looking back, visualizing the reality of her own past in similar 'liveliness', she starts composing the moving picture, which, though never explicitly mentioned, will eventually turn out to become *Pilgrimage*. At last, Miriam Henderson, the open-eyed and reflecting traveller through time and space, has become Dorothy Richardson the artist, who, stepping beyond the temporal and spatial limits of real life, draws the picture of Miriam's life journey.

2. Garden Views and Visions: Reflections of the Self

> A garden is a perfect extension of your personality.
>
> (Letter to Peggy Kirkaldy, 23.11. 1936; *WM*, 322)

> It was odd, she thought, how it was alone, one leant to things, inanimate things; trees, streams, flowers; felt they expressed one; felt they became one; felt they knew one, in a sense were one; felt an irrational tenderness thus [...] as for oneself.
>
> (Virginia Woolf, *To the Lighthouse* 72)

Travelling through life, Miriam Henderson keeps a keen and interested eye on her constantly changing surroundings. She is intensely aware of the beauties of nature she passes by on her journeys, and the moving pictures seen from the train, sledge or omnibus have a positively restoring effect on her. These impressive travelling descriptions not only record Miriam's mere changes of place but moreover convey her inner journey away from one society - her family, Shatov, Wimpole Street, the Wilsons - towards an unknown new society - Hanover, the Corries, Oberland, the Roscorlas. Each time Miriam reaches yet another critical point of her gradual alienation from her wonted social surroundings, the same pattern occurs: she sets off on a journey in order to plunge herself into a social vacuum and thus to come to terms with her inner development. In the solitary communion with nature she finds a new understanding of her self: each journey thus marks a decisive step on Miriam's way towards becoming the woman she eventually will be.

If the dynamic, cinematic, experience of nature forms a 'macroscopic' liberating counterpoise to Miriam's often constrictive social involvement, Dorothy Richardson presents a complementary concept that allows Miriam 'microscopic' moments of escape from human society: the static, photographic views of gardens provide such moments of relief and insight. Throughout *Pilgrimage*, the longer contemplation, or sometimes even the mere glimpse, of a garden has an equally positive effect on her.

Hence, movement as the decisive factor of her experience of open nature on her journeys of *becoming* finds its counterpart in the stillness that provides stable views of enclosed, tamed, nature in gardens. These short instances of contemplative calm scattered over the thirteen volumes of *Pilgrimage* thus establish a pattern of specifically intense moments of *being*.

The experience of being is at the centre of *Pilgrimage*, perhaps best embodied in the presence of gardens. From these centres of contemplation the light of beauty emanates, expanding until it reaches the eye, which receives and transmits it on towards a depth where a different sense is reached, the most immaterial in the scale of senses assigned to the seizing of the real - memory. Though marking a passage towards the abstract, memory in its eidetic immediacy is present to Miriam's inner eye as a very concrete part of her reality. If Miriam loves the present, the direct sensory impression, it is because of the - often subliminal - presence of the past, specifically the garden of her childhood, where, as we shall see, years ago the world, revealing its beauty in 'flowers, bees and sunlight, a three-in-one,' first brought to her 'the sense of existing' (*JP*, 110f.), the experience of her self. In her later garden views she seeks this confirmation of the self, most gardens thus becoming Miriam's highly subjective locus of both passionate perception of outside beauty and intense introspection.

2.1 'Trying to See into the Garden:' The Limited View

> *As thinkers with emotional reaction, we give what seems to us a still higher degree of reality to whatever things we select and emphasize and turn to* WITH A WILL. These are our *living* realities; and not only these, but all the other things which are intimately connected with these. Reality, starting from our Ego, thus sheds itself from point to point - first upon all objects which have an immediate sting of interest for our Ego in them, and next, upon the objects most continuously related with these.
>
> (William James, 'The Perception of Reality,' *Psychology II* 925f.)

> The house and garden was nothing to [Gerald]. Just a house and garden. Harriett's house and garden, and he was going to take Harriett away. The house and garden did not matter.
> She glanced at the sunlit fruit trees, the thickets of the familiar kitchen garden, the rising grass bank at the near end of the distant lawn, the eloquent back of the large red house. He could not see all the things there were there, all the long years, or know what it was to have that cut away [...] (*BW*, 305f.).

In the wake of Darwin and still at the beginning of the twentieth century the problem of the perception and representation of nature was widely discussed. Darwin's 'perceptually limited eye' (Krasner 31), negating the Victorian narrator's supernatural completeness of perception, influenced many authors towards writing fragmentary descriptions of nature that would reflect the optical limitations of both characters and narrator. In order to come to terms with the abundance of natural forms perceptible to the human eye, the author had to select and arrange those specific forms relevant to the telling of his tale. Thomas Hardy for instance recognized that even if the artist wanted to represent nature in its minute details, 'the impossibility of reproducing in its entirety the phantasmagoria of experience with infinite and atomic truth, without shadow, relevancy or subordination' would thwart such a project.[1] Though his vision of a huge and desolate landscape would make man appear of marginal importance within nature, his narrator's close-up of a few highly selective objects show nature as controlled by man.[2] This zooming in on one single and simple form of nature allows the narrator to foreground man and humanity, and thus to shift his focal interest back from nature to man (cf. Krasner 107). Man's reaction to nature, his perception - vision, sound, smell, touch - of his surroundings rather than unfocused, unspecified nature *per se* lie at the core of Hardy's narrative.

The same holds for Dorothy Richardson's fiction, which aims at a precise representation of subjective experience, of Miriam's individual perception. Dorothy Richardson also accepts this impossibility of rendering the eye's perception in its completeness and selects her narrator's - and hence Miriam's - views of natural forms in order to foreground her protagonist's interactions with her surroundings. From the first the strictly applied technique of placing the narrator within Miriam's consciousness makes a mid-Victorian supernatural vision impossible. This photographic method of choosing a more or less small part of reality, of depicting only a limited number of natural forms at a time, is a direct rendering of Miriam's own limited view. As in large parts of *Pilgrimage* the narrator and the protagonist's consciousness coalesce into a single whole, the reader cannot directly see the surrounding objects themselves from the outside; for him or her a mediated, interior access is the only possible way to perceive her surroundings. Because of this basic perceptual 'limitation' of the narrator, this 'filtering' of the outer world through Miriam's consciousness, the focus of interest, in contrast to traditional, objective realism, eventually lies on Miriam's subjective reality, on her self '*perceiving*' rather than on the thing '*perceived*' (cf. Levine 218).

The world of nature then is no more a neutral territory, an objective background for the actions and reflections of the protagonist, but it bears the stamp of Miriam's individual perception. Throughout *Pilgrimage* this subjectively limited presentation of the outer world, which implicitly questions the existence of any form of objectively perceptible reality, reflects various parts of Miriam's inner world. Not only does this outer reality help

---

[1] 'Life and Art' 87, reprinted in Krasner 76.

[2] cf. Alcorn 6. Lodge (249) suggests that 'Hardy's methods can be readily analyzed in cinematic terms; long shots, close-up, wide-angle, telephoto, zoom etc.' Dorothy Richardson's static method of describing Miriam's garden perceptions can be seen in parallel terms of photography.

Miriam to understand her self,[3] but it also contributes to the *reader's* awareness of Miriam's being and thus forms an indispensable part of Dorothy Richardson's fiction.

Unlike 'naturist' writers, she does not see man (or woman) and nature as irreconcilable antagonists, as two opposing principles, but rather as partners in a life-enhancing harmonious union. She therefore hardly ever chooses naturist images of desolate and threatening nature,[4] but rather scenes of bright, often cultivated, 'man-made' landscapes.

Dorothy Richardson takes up the traditional notion of the garden as an antithesis to both unkempt wilderness on the one hand, and the denaturalized city on the other hand. Miriam, who 'had come to London and been shut out from garden summers' (*DH*, 463), misses the garden sights and smells of her youth, where she was still at one with nature, where perception and reflection were one. Once she has lost her innocence, however, her *reflections* on the garden get entangled in the network of dichotomies that make life difficult. Despite her rapturous sensory experience of the garden she sometimes senses the 'shadow of incompatibility; of the incompatibility of being at once bound and free. The garden breeds a longing for the wild, the wild a homesickness for the garden. Is there no way of life where the two can meet?' (*TR*, 453) As we shall see, it is one of Miriam's aims of her pilgrimage to find such a mediating way of life, to seek a place where the oppositions of life are overcome in a lasting harmonious unity, where she can feel both 'bound and free.' As for Miriam's immediate sensory *perceptions* of gardens in their highly appealing beauty, they reflect Dorothy Richardson's concept of the garden as a space of sheltered freedom and harmony, providing moments of rest and unity.[5] Critics who mention Dorothy Richardson's garden images describe her idea of the garden in the most general terms as 'a symbol of innocence and refuge' (Hanscombe 1982:80), as a 'metaphor for the secret joy of the inner self' (Brown P. 167), as one 'of her two life-long visions' contrasting the sea (Staley 15). Some have a closer look at Miriam's earliest childhood memory, where she establishes 'a rapturous and animistic compact with the natural world' (Watts 21), but it is only Radford who conceives of the garden as one of the central recurring images of *Pilgrimage*:

> The imagery of light and dark, of the baggage she must carry with her, of the 'well-known garden' which represents the enclosed

---

[3] cf. Staley 33; and Levine 218: 'All observation is ultimately observation of the self.'

[4] Both the untamed mountains of Oberland or the wild sea provide outstanding examples of positively experienced natural sceneries.

[5] e.g. From Sally's kitchen window she sees 'the little gate in the fence, *invitingly* open towards the hidden back garden, *a world apart*, its high trees already preparing summer *shelter* for that *refuge* from household tensions [...]' (*MM*, 588; emphasis added).

> spaces which call to her even as she leaves them, are repeated with variations in subsequent volumes (1991:28).[6]

That none of the critics, however, seems to be interested in Miriam's actual visual experience of gardens may be due to the fact that Dorothy Richardson limits her depictions to so few details that Miriam's swift glimpses may indeed appear to be of minor importance.

What, then, makes these gardens worth examining? What is there specific in the way Miriam sees 'her' gardens?

2.2 'Gardens Everywhere, Not Always Visible:' Impressions of Miriam's *Wanderjahre*

2.2.1 'Gazing out of the Window:' The Walled Garden in Hanover

> But wholly, at last, I wakened, opened wide
> The window and my soul, and let the airs
> And outdoor sights sweep gradual gospels in,
> Regenerating what I was [...]
> (Elizabeth Barrett Browning, *Aurora Leigh* 58, Book I, ll. 663-666)

> Miriam turned to the window. She looked down into a little square of high-walled garden. It was gravelled nearly all over. Not a blade of grass was to be seen. A narrow little border of bare brown mould joined the gravel to the high walls. In the centre was a little domed patch of earth and there a chestnut tree stood. Great bulging brown-varnished buds were shining whitely from each twig. (*PR*, 52f.)

On the eve of her departure for Germany Miriam looks down into the 'well-known garden' (*PR*, 15) at home, which, significantly, remains obscure. In the dusk she barely recognizes 'the outline of the round bed and the shapes of the may-trees on either side of the bend of the drive.' If it is, objectively, due to the lack of light that her view is at first limited, another glance into the garden on the 'bright morning' (*PR*, 22) of her departure shows that her obscured view directly reflects her blocked state of mind. When she at last glances 'fearfully out into the garden, seeing nothing' (*PR*, 25), her view of the present is completely blurred because of the haunting images of both past and future, the oppressive reality of her problem-ridden family life as well as the nightmarish dream-vision of her life at the German school (cf. *PR*, 21).

---

[6] The garden as representation of enclosed spaces, however, is a doubtful generalization. In many instances the opposite is true.

This 'experience of nothingness' forms a vital initial stage in the long process of Miriam's quest towards a deep awareness of her reality, her own self. Carol Christ, examining similar processes in a number of other modern literary heroines, considers this as an important preliminary experience for the *awakening* of a woman's soul to her self, for it is only in remembering the darkness left behind that the enlightenment of the consciousness is fully experienced. Thus, at the very outset of her independent life, Miriam's *visual* experience of literal nothingness, her non-view of the garden, summarizes her situation. Unwilling to bear the increasingly difficult situation at home, seeing her going away as a 'relief' (*PR*, 17), she yet visualizes her future life in the most negative light. Miriam is aware of an emotional vacuum forcing her onto her journey - a journey that will eventually lead to a deepened understanding of her self. However, this gradual awakening is not without relapses: Miriam later on is caught in similarly blocked situations, her inability to perceive a way out then is similarly reflected in a highly inhibited visual awareness of her garden surroundings.[7] Thus, what Christ (14) says, holds true for Miriam, too: 'as long as she lives [...] the experience of nothingness will reappear.' Her repeated blindness towards the beauties of nature especially in the early volumes of *Pilgrimage* then hints at some deeper-lying mental obstruction; in this 'dark night of the soul' (Christ 14, referring to St John of the Cross), her outer, sensory awareness is restricted, while she is struggling to find a new driving force, a new 'light of her own.' In each difficult situation the experience of nothingness has a catalysing effect on her, leading her on to some form of deepened self-knowledge.

Later, in Germany, her home garden in a rush of homesickness appears as a vision to Miriam, replacing the actual view of the little German garden. Her longing for home makes her see a garden of overbrimming yet unattainable beauty that by far outdoes the beauty of the chestnut tree in front of her:

---

[7] *BW*, 304: When Miriam learns that her mother is seriously ill, she in her despair looks out into the garden to find some comfort, but: 'The garden did not seem to be there. The tepid night air was like a wall, a black wall.'

HC, 388: Feminine worldliness meant 'pretence at the door of a hidden garden, a lovely hidden garden.' Worldly women pretend, they do not *see* the hidden garden and thus experience nothing.

DL, 148: The process of first growing aware of her blindness towards her natural surroundings in the London park and then responding to the beauty of nature exactly reflects her overall awakening from her 'sense of emptiness:' 'There were trees in the distance ahead, trees, *forgotten*. She was here to look at them. It was urgent, important. All this long time, and she had never once looked' (emphasis added).

Miriam supposes that other people can experience a similar visual inhibition because of a mental blockade; e.g. *HC*, 452: Gerald's friend, walking in the garden with Miriam, is not aware of its beauties. 'There was something between him and the little coloured garden,' something that does not allow him to see beyond his own self-pity.

> and there at home in the garden lilac was quietly coming out and syringa and gelder roses and May and laburnum and . . . everything . . . and she had run away, [...] (*PR*, 112).[8]

Time and again in later garden scenes the immediate reality, which Miriam might recognize in clear details, recedes in favour of a much stronger, though often rather vague, *mental* image. The concentrated intensity with which Miriam's inner eye visualizes a scene of her past or future makes it impossible for her to continue to perceive her real surroundings. The direct *view* of the *hic et nunc* is completely replaced by a *vision* of a non-existing or non-present situation, which by means of Miriam's imaginative power assumes an immediacy ousting the actual view. The garden thus becomes her 'locus of illusions and hallucinations' (Krasner 6), the place where her mind is most likely to leave behind outer reality in favour of the individual, inner reality of her visions. Miriam is fully aware of her tendency to foreground one thing exclusively when she says: 'One thing blots out another. You cannot have more than one thing intensely' (*TU*, 140). But for this intensity the reader would follow Miriam's often intricate ways of thinking and perceiving only with great difficulty; her concentration on one thing at a time helps him to enter Miriam's mind and glide with her from reality over to imagination, from outside to inside life, and back. In such intense moments, when Miriam's consciousness seems fully revealed in its working, Dorothy Richardson's fiction appears to be more moving than the traditional 'outside-in' novel, for the reader *is* the heroine, sharing her consciousness in exceptional inner liveliness (cf. Beauman 154).

This process of developing interior visions out of exterior views, her withdrawal from the reality of the world into the reality of the individual mind, forms an integral part of the exhaustive portrayal of Miriam's character and is repeated in numerous scenes throughout *Pilgrimage*. Thus, the sight of irises on the breakfast table in Hanover triggers the memory of another garden:

> She gazed at them, half-feeling the flummery petals against the palm of her hand. Fräulein seemed cancelled. There was no need to feel self-conscious. She was not thinking of any of them. Miriam found herself looking at high grey stone basins, with stems like wine-glasses and large square fluted pedestals, filled with geraniums and calceolarias. They had stood in the sunshine at the corners of the lawn in her grandmother's garden. She could remember nothing

---

[8] A simple linguistic device, the enumeration of plants linked by the repetitive 'and,' which culminates in the all-enfolding 'everything,' serves to enhance this vision of exuberant spring fullness.

> else but the scent of a greenhouse and its steamy panes over her head . . . lemon thyme and scented geranium (*PR*, 172).[9]

This momentary recollection in its one wide-angled view of the garden and its scent of the flowers is stronger than Miriam's visible, smellable, tactile reality. She actually re-experiences this past illuminated moment in such an intensity that it becomes part of the present, blotting out her sensory awareness of both people and objects around her.

Calling up the memory of one of her childhood gardens, Miriam achieves only a momentary escape from existential fears, from her self-doubting tendencies to define herself in terms of other people.[10] With such memories she creates a haven of freedom for her mind as a counterworld to the difficult reality, which, however, catches up with her before long. Throughout the following novel-chapters Miriam experiences an inner struggle between her emotional impulse to withdraw into her own self, to abide by her past recollections and visions, and the voice of reason that tells her to face reality even in oppressive human company. At this stage of her development Miriam simply suppresses the impulse of her memory: 'It was silly to forget all about [the worries of old age] and see granny's calceolarias in the sun . . . all that had to come to an end' (*PR*, 172). Only in the gradual development of her self will Miriam find the means to integrate the opposing voices of reason and emotion into a whole.

From the beginning of *Pilgrimage* there are not only visions but also views of real gardens that provide a space of emotional freedom. Among the numerous garden references in the early and late volumes, however, there are astonishingly few instances where Miriam experiences the garden from within. Most often she looks into a garden from a window or a door as an outside observer. And yet, even these distant views provide moments of respite from society, brief halts in solitude. Miriam thus continues a tradition of literary heroines who gather strength in the solitary, distant contemplation of a garden: seeing the beauty of nature, they experience an increased feeling of self-confidence.[11] Miriam's glances into the small Hanover garden, for

---

[9] In the late Victiorian age (the time when Miriam visited her grandmother's garden) certain flowers had certain social connotations. Geraniums and calceolarias, being fairly modern flowers, suggested a well-to-do household, which, however, lacked individuality. It is this middle-class conformity of his merchant parents that Miriam's father as an aspiring gentleman wanted to overcome when he planted a garden in Babington which contained within its walls fruit trees as well as a long, old-fashioned kitchen garden, and with these set signs of *upper-class* fashion of the 1870s and 1880s (cf. Waters 124).

[10] e.g. *PR*, 172, her identification with Fräulein: 'I shall be like that one day . . . an old teacher, and cancer coming.'

[11] e.g. James, Henry. *The Portrait of a Lady* 348:

instance, are temporary escapes from the environment of the school, which is, to quote Loeffelholtz, 'suffocatingly devoid of privacy' (59). Though in the constant company of the girls Miriam at times loses herself in the experience of intense shared happiness, she as often feels alienated from these school girls, to whom she as a foreign pupil-teacher only partly belongs. In need to counterbalance the often tumultuous school background and Fräulein Pfaff's inhibitive guardian eye, she tries to re-establish her sense of her own, separate self in repeated short contemplations of the garden.[12] The blooming gardens thus assume a thoroughly positive role in Miriam's development for the solitary beauty of these places has a restorative effect on her mind. At this early stage in her life the gardens of the past and present are *active* supporters of her mental balance; in their immediate appeal to the senses, and especially to her eye, they perfectly express her deep love of life.

The literary model for these early garden scenes is found in Charlotte Brontë's partly autobiographical novel *Villette*. Repeatedly referred to in *Pointed Roofs* and *Backwater*, *Villette* accompanies Miriam throughout her early years because she seems to see Lucy Snowe, the English girl teaching abroad, as a figure of identification. Therefore, not only do the features of the garden at Hanover resemble those of the Villette garden, but the contemplative, solitary silence of the two walled school gardens, shaded by trees, also has similar effects on the two young teachers, Miriam and Lucy:

> That old garden had its charms. On summer mornings I used to rise early, to enjoy them alone; on summer evenings, to linger solitary, to keep tryste with the rising moon, or taste one kiss of the evening breeze, or fancy rather than feel the freshness of dew descending. The turf was verdant, the gravelled walks were white; [...] there was a smaller, more sequestered bower, nestled in the vines which ran all along a high and gray wall.[...] Doubtless at high noon, in the broad, vulgar middle of the day, when Madame Beck's large school turned out rampant, and externes and pensionnaires were spread about [...], doubtless *then* the garden was a trite, trodden-down place enough.

'She was alone [...] The tall window was open, and though its green shutters were partly drawn the bright air of the garden had come in through a broad interstice and filled the room with warmth and perfume. Our young woman stood near it for some time, her hands clasped behind her; she gazed abroad with the vagueness of unrest.'

And 375: After Ralph declared his love for her, 'Isabel moved away and stood looking into the sunny stillness of the garden; but after a little she turned back to him.' So Isabel, too, needs these garden glances to dissociate herself from her immediate situation and human companionship.

See also: Browning, Elizabeth Barrett. *Aurora Leigh*, First Book 56, ll. 578 ff, and especially 58, ll. 663-666.

[12] *PR*, 52f: 'She looked down into a little square of high-walled garden. [...] The girls seemed to be gathering in the room behind her' (also *PR*, 92, 98, 112, 127, 140, 171).

> But at sunset or the hour of *salut*, when the externes were gone home, and the boarders quiet at their studies; pleasant was it then to stray down the peaceful alleys [...] (Brontë, *Villette* 131).

The garden scene is just one example of how Dorothy Richardson transposes Brontë's text into her own fiction. In Lucy's relationship to other girls of the school, in her admiration of M. Paul and her difficulties with Madame Beck, in the English lessons and in the school's outing further parallels to Miriam's experiences at Hanover could be traced. Her friendships with the German girls, her feelings for Pastor Lahmann, her problems with Fräulein Pfaff as well as her teaching or their excursion to Hoddenheim thus can be read as echoes of that former heroine's experiences (cf. Gregory 10f.). And yet, Dorothy Richardson creates a completely new character, who despite these parallels never appears as a mere imitation of Lucy Snowe, but remains an individual exploring her world on her own.

2.2.2 'The Shabby London Greenery:' The Gardens of North London

> Can we believe - by an effort
> comfort our hearts:
> it is not waste all this,
> not placed here in disgust,
> street after street,
> each patterned alike,
> no grace to lighten
> a single house of the hundred
> crowded into one garden-space.
>
> (H.D. 'Cities.' *Collected Poems* 39f.)

> This new secret was shabby, ugly and shabby. The half-perceived something persisted when the causeways and shops disappeared and long rows of houses streamed by, their close ranks broken only by an occasional cross-road. They were large, high, flat-fronted houses with flights of grey stone steps leading to their porchless doors. They had tiny railed-in front gardens crowded with shrubs. Here and there long narrow strips of garden pushed a row of houses back from the roadway. (*BW*, 195)

In the first three novel-chapters garden views are presented fairly consistently as moments in which Miriam hopes to find an oasis for her thoughts. In the view of the garden Miriam finds a mirror of her 'inner shrine of privacy' (Trickett 23), to which she tries to retreat from unsatisfactory experiences and encounters.[13] Not always, however, does the garden yield such a relief. Thus, the view of the small garden at Banbury Park only confirms her feelings of oppression. Squeezed in between a school for the deaf and dumb and the house of Polish Jews, the garden is seen as 'lying in deep shadow,' hedged in by 'the brownish backs of small old brick houses' (*BW*, 191). Miriam's sense of lifeless enclosure in the small garden, her 'ugly and shabby' secret (*BW*, 195), will be a formative experience for her whole stay in North London. The short impression 'coloured the whole of the district through which they had come' (*BW*, 195); thus the 'tiny railed-in front-gardens crowded with shrubs' are seen in the same uninspiring light. It is the very light in which, much later, Miriam will perceive her surroundings when travelling with Miss Szigmondy to North London: 'No touch of life or colour anywhere, hardly a sign of spring in the small parched shrub-filled front gardens, uniformly enclosed by dusty railings' (*TU*, 157). Colour and spring, Dorothy Richardson's two favourite images of life, are negated, the absence of open spaces - 'crowded, enclosed, shrub-filled' - delineates the suffocating atmosphere of her surroundings, which she cannot bring herself to accept. Her negative view of these gardens again directly reflects her present mood; she youthfully resists the demands of people whose authority in her eyes is questionable. Defying the physical and mental enclosure of the Pernes sisters as well as Miss Szigmondy's 'impudence' of stealing her free afternoon, Miriam finds her prevailing mood of opposition and dissatisfaction supported in her views of the gardens. Her visual awareness here is a *reactive* confirmation of her mental condition.

Such consistently unfavourable views of gardens, however, are rare. In most cases, the absence of appealing surroundings in the city evokes a substitute vision of beauty that gives rise to an increasingly positive mood in Miriam's consciousness. The very gardens of North London appear still as 'oppressing and darkening' (*IN*, 313) when Miriam visits the Brooms years later. She sees the 'colourless railed-in gardens' as parts of an unchanged - unchanging - reality, representing the dull, inhibited views on life of their owners, towards whom she develops ambiguous feelings of repudiation - they were 'banished and powerless' (*IN*, 314) - and secret affection - '*dear* north Londoners' (*IN*, 314). As already in Hanover and at Newlands, their fascination for her, which often turns into claustrophobic fears of human enclosure, fears of merging with the suburban mass that threaten her sense of

---

[13] A woman's retreat to a garden is a common topic in English literature. Not only Lucy Snowe, but also Sally Seton, Mrs Dalloway's old friend, seeks the balm of solitude in a garden: 'Despairing of human relationships (people were so difficult) she often went into her garden and got from her flowers a peace which men and women never gave her.' She achieves the same solitary happiness in nature that Miriam so often experiences too (cf. Woolf, *Mrs Dalloway* 217).

individuality, make her retreat into a solitary garden contemplation; in her mind Miriam creates a refuge that enables her to put herself at a distance from her surroundings. Since the tiny front gardens leave her unimpressed in this North London 'wilderness' of houses and roads (*IN*, 313),[14] the sight of 'little bushes of variegated laurel, grouped in railed-off oblongs along the gravelled pathway,' (*IN*, 314) a kind of miniature substitute garden, opens up a secret space, an imaginary large garden, where Miriam, within the despised surroundings, 'can possess herself' (Hanscombe 1982:80). Though the perceptible reality of North London is the same as it used to be, Miriam as a visitor is no longer emotionally involved. Her vision thus is stronger than her immediate reality. Textually, Dorothy Richardson underlines this in her verbal expression: first, the real view is rendered in an accumulation of *negatively* connoted words:

> She hurried along, feeling out towards them through *downcast* eyes. They glinted back at her *unsunned* by the sunlight, *rootless*, *sapless* surfaces set in *repellent* clay, spread out in *meaningless* air. To and fro her eyes slid upon the varnished leaves (*IN*, 315; emphasis added).

Yet as the real view is being superseded by an imaginary vision, her attitude turns increasingly *positive*:

> She saw them in a *park* set in amongst massed dark evergreens, *gleaming* out through afternoon mist, keeping the last of the *light* as the people drifted away, leaving the slopes and vistas *clear* . . . grey avenues and dewy slopes moved before her in the faint *light* of dawn, the grey growing pale and paler; the dew turned to a scatter of *jewels* and the sky soared up high above the growing *shimmer of sunlight green and gold*. Isolated morning figures hurried across the park, aware of its morning *freshness,* seeing it as their own *secret garden*, part of their secret day (*IN*, 315; emphasis added).

The view of the dull North London atmosphere - remembered as an 'indefinable psychic chill' (*CH*, 393) - recedes in favour of a visionary glimpse of light and beauty, which contains all the enchanting elements of the gardens of Germany and South England: sunlight, nature tinted in green and gold, an open vista and the absence of human interference. In her choice of words Dorothy Richardson subtly shows the impact of this vision on Miriam's mood. The transition from reality to imagination, from exterior to interior perception is accompanied by a radical lifting of Miriam's spirits so that her real surroundings look more appealing than before: 'She sauntered happily along through channels of sheltered sunlit silence' (*IN*, 315).

---

[14] Dorothy Richardson unites the poles of 'wilderness' and 'city' in order to emphasize the contrastive power of the beautiful orderliness of the subsequent garden image.

2.2.3 'Relief in the Deeps of the Gardens:' Moments of Privacy at Newlands

> To him who in the love of Nature holds
> Communion with her visible forms, she speaks
> A various language; for his gayer hours
> She has a voice of gladness, and a smile
> And eloquence of beauty, and she glides
> Into his darker musings, with a mild
> And healing sympathy, that steals away
> Their sharpness, ere he is aware.
> (William Cullen Bryant,'Thanatopsis,' l. 1-8. *Poems* 12)

> The roses were in bud. Every day she managed to visit them at least once, running out alone into the garden at twilight and coming back rich with the sense of the twilit green garden and the increasing stripes of colour between the tight shining green sheaths. (*HC*, 426f.)

Miriam's often observed transformed perception of her surroundings after she has seen a real or visionary garden is founded on a profound affinity of her soul to this natural space. The image of the garden, in fact, defines a space in Miriam's soul that contains a life-giving force of exceptional emotional intensity:[15]

> Deeper down was something cool and fresh - endless garden. In happiness it came up and made everything in the world into a garden. Sorrow blotted it over, but it was always there, waiting and looking on. It had looked on in Germany and had loved the music and the words and the happiness of the German girls; and at Banbury Park, giving her no peace until she got away (*HC*, 425).

Driven by her confidence in the continuity of her inner garden, her growing-space of happiness, Miriam watches out for outer corresponding gardens that would reveal their enchanting qualities. She conceives of this mental space as a garden while staying at Newlands; the real garden is almost omnipresent – almost 'everything in the world' there is strongly connected to this garden. In what Barthes calls 'transgressions topologiques' (1970:220), the outer and the inner, objective and subjective presentation, views and visions are intertwined: the blazing garden at Newlands is mirrored in Miriam's soul, while she experiences the garden as a re-presentation of her inner frame of mind.

[15] In Virginia Woolf's *Mrs Dalloway* (11), the heroine similarly conceives of the soul as a 'leaf-encumbered forest;' this image of natural peacefulness, however, is rather threatened by 'brutes' and'monsters' of hatred, and is thus - on this one day of her life at least - unable to spread the positive influence Miriam's inner garden most often does.

Like most other gardens in *Pilgrimage*, the outlines of the Corries' garden remain vague. At the beginning of *Honeycomb* it is introduced in one single, characteristic sentence: 'For a moment it seemed to Miriam that the large quiet room looking through two high windows on to a stretch of tree-shaded lawn [...was] all there for her appreciation alone' (*HC*, 363). In this one glance Miriam symbolically takes possession of her new surroundings before, shortly after, the powerful presence of spring both inside the house[16] and outdoors[17] suggests a large garden full of rich scents and colours that ask for a more intense sensory response. When Miriam manages to visit the roses every day 'at least once, running out *alone* into the garden at twilight' (*HC*, 426; emphasis added), she experiences the reunion of her inner vision and the actual view as a moment of solitary happiness: Her inner garden 'had come to the surface and was with her all the time' (*HC*, 426). The Newlands garden, with its two central qualities of light and solitude, thus becomes a place of retreat, where she can be her true self; the happy loneliness of the garden forms a counterworld to the turbulent social life of the house and her growing awareness of her socially confined life as a governess.

Not only to Miriam does this garden offer moments of self-affirmation. She sees that Mrs Corrie similarly needs this space as a refuge to 'compensate her for the emptiness of marriage' (Hanscombe 1982:80): it becomes a place of female sanctity suggesting an untouched innocence that is constantly threatened by male intrusion:

> Mrs Corrie sat and strolled about the garden, joyless, as if weighed down by some immovable oppression. If Mr Corrie were to come out and sit there too it would be worse. It was curious to think that the garden was his at all. He would come feebly out, looking ill, and they would all sit, uneasy and afraid. [...] It was intolerable to think of his coming (*HC*, 438).

Miriam recognizes that such a refuge of self-possession is destroyed by the presence of male company, by the 'hard brutal laughing complacent atmosphere of men's minds' (*HC*, 443). So Mrs Corrie 'had her garden. She would always have that, *when he was not there*' (*HC*, 439; emphasis added):

---

[16] *HC*, 369: 'She found spring in the house. The landing was bright with the light streaming through many open doors.[...]On a large tray on the landing table lay a mass of spring flowers and little flowered bowls of many shapes and sizes filled with fresh water.'

HC, 398: Flowers in the house 'blazed as if they were standing in a garden.'

[17] *HC*, 391f.: 'Spring; everywhere, inside and outside the house. The spring outside had a meaning here. It came in through the windows without obstruction and passed into everything. [...] You could not forget it for a moment; and it was a background for something more wonderful than itself; something that made it wonderful; something there were no words for.' This is an early instance of Miriam's transcendental consciousness within the intense presence of nature.

only in Mr Corrie's absence is the garden fully available. As the mere prospect of Mr Corrie's presence robs the garden of its innate happiness, Miriam is confirmed in her belief that happiness is most easily found in the *solitary* communion with nature. Later on, Hypo's presence will similarly keep her from experiencing this happy union and even at Dimple Hill the 'balm to the spirit afforded by the lovely gardens' is fully experienced in solitude only (cf. Brown P. 204).

Two pictures hanging in Harriett's new drawing room thus summarize Miriam's garden experiences so far.

> Square green garden scenes . . . There was relief in the deeps of the gardens and in under the huge spreading trees that nearly filled the sky. There were tiresome people fussing in the foreground . . . Marcus Stone people - having scenes - not noticing the garden; getting in the way of the garden. But the garden was there, blazing, filled with some particular time of day, always being filled with different times of day (*HC*, 449f.).[18]

The picture, as an artistic representation halfway between view and vision, epitomizes both Miriam's belief in the potential power of a garden and her lasting problematic attitude towards society. To her, conflicts in any form prevent a deeper communion with nature; only by evading human company can the unceasing impact of the garden be felt. The picture confirms the system of the interplay of views, visions and feelings of Miriam's comparatively carefree *Wanderjahre*. Since her childhood solitary garden views have often put her into a happy mood or triggered off a vision filling her with happiness; happiness on the other hand opens her eye to the beauty of nature. Only in the seemingly unending frustration and enclosure of North London does this mechanism fail. In most other cases the interplay of perception and emotion leads to a positive result. It is a system that allows Miriam to experience quasi-autistic, fragile moments of solitary happiness; in their repetitions they form one reliable basis for her positive attitude towards life. In these early garden scenes Dorothy Richardson's belief in the beauty of life, of the life of the individual's independent mind and body, manifests itself exceptionally well. It is - among others - because of these moments of illumination that to Miriam life appears as a 'chain of happy moments that cannot die' (*TU*, 215).

---

[18] Marcus Stone (1840-1921), a Victorian painter of, then, wide reputation, was famous for his paintings of human interest. He produced 'idyllic compositions full of tender expression - subtle domestic dramas in which love would always be found playing the leading part.' Portraying 'trivial quarrels' and little disagreements, he shows exactly those tendencies towards conflict inherent in all human company that Miriam in her pursuit of solitude and happiness wants to escape from (cf. Pratt, A.T.C., no pages).

2.3 'Echoes of the Tragedy:' The Long Shadows of Death

2.3.1 'Never Again in the Old Way:' Enigmatic Garden Views in Miriam's Early London Years

> Although the summer sunlight gild
> Cloudy leafage of the sky,
> Or wintry moonlight sink the field
> In storm-scattered intricacy,
> I cannot look thereon,
> Responsibility so weighs me down.
>
> Things said or done long years ago,
> Or things I did not do or say
> But thought that I might say or do,
> Weigh me down, and not a day
> But something is recalled,
> My conscience or my vanity appalled.
>
> (W. B. Yeats, 'Vacillation V.' *Poems* 301)

> In their midst lived the past and the thing that had ended it and plunged it into a darkness that still held that threat of destroying reason and life. Perhaps only thus could it be faced. Perhaps only in that way. What other way was there? Forgetfulness blotted it out and let one live on. But it was always there, impossible when one looked back. (*IN*, 316)

Dorothy Richardson was both in her life and her fiction extremely reticent about her most terrible experience of death; thus she gives only enigmatic information about Miriam's reaction to her mother's suicide. The fictional rendering of the brutal confrontation with death belongs to the more problematic parts of *Pilgrimage* as the scarce details do not add up to a coherent image of Miriam's true frame of mind. Fromm (96) points out that her mother's death was something Dorothy Richardson could hardly be brought to write about since it wrought upon her innermost feelings of guilt and sadness. As Hanscombe (1987:48) writes, 'the appalling trauma' had 'lasting effects on Dorothy's inner life' and led to a radical change in her outer circumstances, her move to London to earn her living in complete independence. While in her fiction she describes these outer changes extensively, Miriam's interior traumatic experience and its aftermaths are only very opaquely presented. And yet this very absence of an open confrontation with the horrifying tragedy throws its long shadows far into the middle novel-chapters of *Pilgrimage*. A number of vague hints at the unspeakable reveal Miriam's constant subconscious preoccupation with her mother's death. Feelings of remorse, which 'may be cleansing you' or may 'kill you outright' (*TU*, 94), accompany her incessantly. One clearly perceptible consequence of her loss is her changed attitude towards her natural surroundings - and towards the gardens in particular. These 'secret sacred places' of happiness (*IN*, 399) appear to Miriam's eyes and mind in a different light, emphasizing her mother's suicide as a turning point in Miriam's life. In the very long time of recovery from this shock her garden impressions are not only much rarer but mostly lack the intensity of her former garden views. In the gradual re-appearance of more intense, illuminated garden scenes her slow recovery from grief and sorrow manifests itself, but it is not until her holidays in Oberland that she looks upon herself as healed.

Let us then trace the few gardens Miriam sees under the influence of her mother's death in the middle novel-chapters of *Pilgrimage*: But for some occasional glances at nature, the first of which significantly take place at night (*TU*, 30, 127, 217), Miriam's exalted appreciation of gardens has come to a near-stop. Even when she sees 'the trees in Endsleigh Gardens [...] gently waving their budding branches in bright sunshine' (*TU*, 145), to her spring, epitome of flourishing life, 'was somewhere far away' (*TU*, 147). She cannot respond to the call of nature in her old way since the 'endless garden' (*HC*, 425) deep down within her, a resting place of her happiness, is covered with sorrow. As long as her inner world of the soul does not correspond to the outer world, the old moments of all-embracing happiness cannot be retrieved. Yet, first signs of a re-awakened response to the beauty of nature soon hint at Miriam's will to overcome her grief.

Thus, the Brooms' house and garden, where she spends many weekends in the shelter of her *ersatz* family, keeps a 'door of retreat' (*IN*, 316) open to her, providing a first haven. There she hopes to recover her - once strong - feelings for the seasons:

> You must be alone . . . or perhaps at the Brooms'. Perhaps next weekend at the Brooms' would be in time for the spring; in their back garden, the watered green lawn and the sweetbrier and the distant trees in the large garden beyond the fence. In London it was better not to think about the times of the year (*TU*, 147).

The vision of this oasis-like fertility, of an anti-urban place of beauty, serves Miriam as a refuge from her emotionally 'desiccated,' bleak city experiences. At one of her first Christmases after her mother's death, when she turns away from the reality of her overshadowed London life, a similar vision appears while watching the Brooms' garden from the conservatory door.[19] What she sees is not the real winter garden, but a vision of the garden

> in late summer fullness, the holidays over, their heights gleaming through long talks on the seat at the end of the garden, the answering glow of the great blossoms of purple clematis hiding the north London masonry of the little conservatory [...] (*IN*, 313).

This vision of the happy communion with other people in a garden is too much to bear. She, who believes that she has forfeited her chance of living in society by not preventing her mother's suicide, is filled with guilt that forbids her the feeling of happiness; afraid of being 'too happy', 'casting away sight and hearing' Miriam hurries 'thoughtlessly' out into the street (*IN*, 313). In order to stop this happy vision she does not feel entitled to she not only changes place but blocks off both her senses and her mind. Her conscience thus forcefully suppresses the feeling of happiness that time and again 'crops up before one can prevent it' (*IN*, 402).

This garden vision, guilt-ridden though it is, marks an important step towards her recovery. In her imagination at least she can conceive of a garden where communication may take place. A way out of her loneliness - a condition diametrically opposed to her self-elected solitude - seems to be possible. And yet, it is a vision that cannot last. Walking through the streets Miriam recognizes that though the little house of the Brooms 'brought forgetfulness and rest,' it cannot undo the terrible suicide. Talking obliquely about her mother's suicide - 'the thing that had ended' her past (*IN*,316) -, Miriam acknowledges the permanent power of this dark memory; although she believes in 'forgetfulness piling up within one into strength' (*IN*, 316), she only covers up the sadness within her, without really recovering from it.[20] At this stage of her search for a new life, to 'live on' is paramount. Her vision of this summer garden thus is a welcome means to gather strength for the continuation of her life.

---

[19] Waters (270) defines the conservatory in its imitation of Crystal Palace as an 'image of a delightful trouble-free world beyond the imperfect present' and 'within the here-and-now world' as an 'enchanted bubble appropriate to encounters of the more intimate kinds.' Dorothy Richardson casts an ironic glance at this Victorian meeting-place by accepting it as a place for visions beyond the present - triggered off by the immediate garden views - , but also denying Miriam the expected encounters: She 'sat sociably down in a low chair, her hands clasped upon her knees, topics racing through her mind in a voice thrilling with stored-up laughter.' But nobody joined her (*IN*, 312f).

[20] Later on she recognizes the limited influence of the Brooms' counter-world, where she finds an illusory easiness rather than a true liberation from grief: 'The many Christmases with the Brooms had been part of her long run of *escape* from the pain-shadowed family life; their house a *dream*-house in the unbroken dream of her own life in London, a shelter where agony was unknown, and lately a *forgetfulness*, for the long days of the holiday, of the challenge that lived in the walls of her room' (*DL*, 86; emphasis added).

Not only feelings of guilt at the past, but also oppressing thoughts about the present, about her complex relationship with Michael Shatov, inhibit Miriam's appreciating the beauty of gardens. On yet another visit to the Brooms, neither the company of Grace and Florence nor the view of 'the stricken garden' (*DL*, 206) offer consolation in her mental distress. Thus, similarly to her looking out for comfort in the home garden before leaving for Hanover (*PR*, 15), she now is looking into the garden, hoping to find a solution. But, though letting her eye roam through the garden, she cannot consciously perceive a single object in it; her view is completely blocked:

> She gazed at her problem in the garden. [...] She flushed towards the garden. [...] At last, still with her eyes on the garden, she told them, she must go and think in the open air [...]. She sat, driving from point to point in the garden the inexorable fact that she had reached a barrier she could not break down (*DL*, 206).

The garden assumes the role of the mirror of Miriam's mind: it is in the externalization of her thoughts into the spatiality of the garden that Miriam tries to keep her distance from them. She, however, fails not only here but also during the same visit at the Brooms' when she walks in solitude through a north London park. The first glance at it promises relief in an intense communion with nature:

> She reached the park at tea-time. Its vistas were mercifully empty. She breathed more freely in its greenery. Hidden somewhere here, was relief for the increasing numbness of her brain and the drag of her aching heart. The widening sky understood and would presently [...] offer itself in the old way, for companionship (*DL*, 207).

However, as this park vista does not offer her a solution in her difficult relationship, it even increases her dejection.

> She used her last strength to wrench herself away from the hopeless spectacle and wandered impatient and thoughtless in a feverish void. Far away from this barren north London, the chosen perfect stage for the last completion of a misery as wide as the world, was her own dream world at home in her room, her strange unfailing self (*DL*, 208).

Step by step Miriam recedes from the world towards isolation. Human company is abandoned for a solitary communion with nature, which in its turn is given up. Miriam would love to both physically and mentally retreat from the reality of north London to the illusion of her 'dream world', which she characterizes shortly after: 'There is no release save in madness; a suddenly descending merciful madness, blotting everything out' (*DL*, 209). This playing with the thought of an escape into insanity takes her down to the lowest point of her spiral of misery, where she at last is able to get out of the maddening whirl of thoughts: she recognizes the danger lurking behind by calling up the devastating effects of her mother's fatal disease, which Miriam repeatedly is afraid of having inherited herself (*TU*, 136); haunted by 'fear of a total collapse of self-meaning into madness' (Brown D. 81), she is eventually able to break through the imagined walls of self-isolation in a renewed perception of the natural beauties of her immediate surroundings and thus re-establish her own sense of self.

Actively supported by the view of the innocent 'cloudless blue' of the sky, her mind is filled with new energies that literally bring her back to earth: 'Something must be said; not to the sky, but to the world' (*DL*, 209). She eventually realizes that the 'deadlock' of her relationship with Shatov, which gives the whole novel-chapter its title, cannot be resolved by escapes into the darker realms of her mind, but only by fully facing her situation. Thus, yet another experience of nothingness leads her through the crisis to perceive a possible future:

> Tears sprang to her eyes, *blotting him out*, and with them she sprang forth into a *pathless darkness*, conscious far away behind her, soon to be obliterated on the *unknown* shores opening ahead, but there gladly in hand, of a debt, signed and to be honoured even against her will, by life, surprised once more *at this darkest moment*, smiling at her secretly, behind all she could gather of opposing reason and clamourous protests of unworthiness (*DL*, 212; emphasis added).

Rising out of complete darkness, this firm belief in the existence of a happier land beyond her present vale of tears, where life in its fullness will be possible again, eventually is stronger than guilt and remorse and helps her to see the immediate situation as only transitory. Even though for the moment the negative perception of nature and the dissatisfying conversation with Shatov leave her unhappy, this experience of nothingness at last triggers off a slow mental process towards facing her situation - not only in relation to Shatov, but to life in general - and opening herself to human society, to the 'world.'

2.3.2 'All the World, Waiting in the Happy Garden:' New Perspectives in Hypo's Garden

> Your garden sloped to the beach,
> myrtle overran the paths,
> honey and amber flecked each leaf,
> the citron-lily head -
> one among many -
> weighed there, over-sweet.
>
> The myrrh-hyacinth
> spread across low slopes,
> violets streaked black ridges
> through the grass.
> The house, too, was like this,
> over painted, over lovely -
> the world is like this.
>
> Sleepless nights,
> I remember the initiates,
> their gesture, their calm glance.
> I have heard how in rapt thought,
> in vision, they speak
> with another race,
> more beautiful, more intense than this.
> I could laugh -
> more beautiful, more intense?
>
> Perhaps that other life
> is contrast always to this.
>
> (H.D. 'The Gift', *Collected Poems* 17)

> Everything outside was sharp and near, but changed since yesterday. The flowers stood vivid in the sunlight; very still. The humming of the bees sounded careful and secret; not wishing to disturb. The sea sparkled to itself, refusing to call the eye. Yet outside there, as in the room, something called. She leaned out. Into the enlarged picture the sky poured down. The pure blue moved within itself as you looked, letting you through and up. An unbroken fabric of light, yet opening all over, taking you up into endless light. (*RL*, 345)

Throughout her early London years described in *The Tunnel*, *Interim* and *Deadlock*, Miriam represses the fact of her mother's suicide. Even when joining her family for Christmas there is not a single trace of a remark about the loss of their mother either in conversation or in Miriam's thoughts (*DL*, 88-103). This locking up of her innermost emotions has to be understood as a life-preserving mechanism that allows her to overcome her despair immediately after her mother's death and live on.[21] However, this suppression of emotions for the sake of mere survival seems to reduce Miriam's intense feelings at *both* ends of her emotional scale: utmost sadness *and* exalted happiness are equally repressed. It is under the shock of her mother's suicide that Miriam no longer feels the unreflected, all-enfolding bliss of the 'early golden years' (*TU*, 312). When, in spite of this, she experiences moments of happiness, they are a far cry from those early moments of innocent complete gladness, 'one long sin, piling up a bill' (*IN*, 402). Guilt and grief thus work within her against a basically unbroken positive attitude towards life. This inner conflict is also expressed in the rare positive garden impressions and in her yearning for summers that 'would never come again in the old way' (*IN*, 401). She defines summer as a happiness that would 'let her move about unhampered in the summers of the past' (*IN*, 401). These early London years, then, though they have brought Miriam a wealth of new friends and impressions, emotionally depend on her *past* feelings: 'The present can be judged by the part of the past it brings up. If the present brings up the happiness of the past, the present is happy' (*IN*, 402). But, and that is what Miriam wants to blot out, it is similarly true that if the present brings up the sadness, the despair of the past, the present is sad and unhappy. And it is this aspect of the power of memory that Miriam does not dare to face. In a few hints Dorothy Richardson makes clear that this darker side does exist within Miriam and would need some outlet in the present. The mere repression of things that in fact insistently still occupy her mind only hinder her development towards a more complete knowledge of the self, an integral view of life that consists of both happy and sad times.

A new, original and deeply rooted happiness is only within reach once the equally deeply rooted central feelings of guilt are brought to the surface and are consciously digested. Only then, when the inner gardens of her soul are open to self-contemplation, will Miriam be able to find full happiness in the calm beauty of physically existing gardens, as at that future point her outer and inner world will be reunited (cf. *DLH*, 157).[22] This slow act of mental liberation that eventually leads to her complete recovery is started off when,

---

[21] *HC*, 489: Immediately after her mother's death she had said: 'I shall not have any life. I can never have any life; all my days.'

[22] Gregory sees this process to be finished only at the very end of *Pilgrimage*: 'Her pilgrimage had begun in an aura of guilt - guilt for her mother's suicide, guilt for her sense of shame at her father's humiliation, guilt for her own "differentness." This aura had lingered throughout the course of her early life, throughout the span of years recounted in the first 12 sections of *Pilgrimage*. In *March Moonlight* the guilt is faced, articulated, and, in a sense, overcome' (82). And Dorothy Richardson writes: 'The past. Inexhaustible wealth. Inexhaustible remorse. [...] If one could fully forgive oneself, the energy it takes to screen off the memory of the past would be set free' (*MM*, 607).

on the brink of madness, Miriam faces the deadlock of her relation with Shatov and resolves to break free. In the Bonnycliff garden of the Wilsons', shortly after, she learns to recognize her original garden love again.

Miriam's gradual acceptance of her present state, starts with her first attempts at writing. Correcting a lecture for Mr Lahitte, a fellow-lodger at Mrs Bailey's, Miriam establishes a 'centre of life' in the 'paper-scattered lamplit circle' of her writing table (*DL*, 134). Drawing all her energy from this 'secret place,' she in the act of writing manages to release the tension of keeping her life shut up and at last to experience a 'new joy of going into life, the new beauty on everything' (*DL*, 136), that prepares her for a radiant future. Writing gives her a new direction in life, away from a passive endurance of the present and nostalgia for the past on to an awakening expectation of the future: 'It was mean to sit waiting for life to throw up things that would distract one for a while from the sense of emptiness' (*DL*, 148). Significantly, this awakening to a new life of activities is expressed in the first longer contemplation of a garden, a London park:

> Round the far-off lake were feathery green trees, not minding. She sat imagining their trunks, filmed over with the murk of London winters, but all the more beautiful now, standing out black amongst the clouds of green. There were trees in the distance ahead, trees, forgotten. She was here to look at them. It was urgent, important. All this long time, and she had never once looked. She lifted her eyes cautiously, without moving, to take in the wide belt beyond the stretch of grass. It was perfect. Full spring complete, prepared and set there, ungrudgingly, demanding nothing but love; embanked between the sky and the grass, a dense perfect shape of various pure colour, an effect, that would pass; but she had seen it. The sharp angle of its edge stood out against a farther, far-off belt of misty green, with here and there a dark maroon blot of copper beech (*DL*, 148).

Her own new beginning opens her eyes to the annual reawakening of nature. Her 'urgent, important' wish to look at the perfection of spring in the vast garden shows her longing for a confirmation in nature of life rediscovered in the happiness of writing. As we have seen in earlier scenes, it is in this direct, if possible solitary and silent, communion with nature that Miriam most completely reaches a sense of happiness. The beautiful park at last gives her back some of the confidence she had before her mother's death: the springs of Hanover and Newlands had filled her with a sense of ease and freedom, which she now happily recaptures and projects into the future: 'Whatever happens, as long as one lives, there is the spring. [...] I'm perfectly sure I shall always feel the spring; perhaps more and more' (*DL*, 148f.).

This illuminated moment of being, made possible by the hope for a satisfying future in writing, opens up the 'secret garden' of Miriam's self so that she can, however painfully, consciously tackle the deeply buried grief about her mother's suicide. In a discussion with Shatov she for the first time manages to speak about her dead mother: 'If there's a future life, all I care for is to meet *her*. If I could have her back for ten minutes I would gladly give up the rest of my life' (*DL*, 220). Though Miriam does not elaborate on her feelings, the barrier is broken; mentioning her loss explicitly she at once takes the first step to overcome her grief. Once the ineffable is put into words, she manages to conceive of this moment as a crucial moment of her life. She now sees this death as a continuing point of reference in her life, the 'cruel bitter destruction of her helpless youth' (*RL*, 245) as well as a chance for a happier future. She begins to accept the impossibility of a return beyond this point, which she unconsciously has always been striving for, standing 'fixed tearfully in the attitude of return' (*RL*, 245). In an act of self-insight Miriam recognizes that her longing for the 'spacious gentle surroundings' (*RL*, 244) of her early life, however beautiful they were, is vain. There are other ways of living, other forms of happiness in the future, which will be more rewarding than the attempt at the impossible. Her mother's death opened up a new dimension of unknown possibilities, which Miriam now considers, and she tries to see this tragedy even as a 'swift movement of her lucky star' (*RL*, 245).

Mrs Henderson's suicide only covered, but did not destroy Miriam's deep fondness for beauty. Her 'ease-and-beauty-loving soul' (*RL*, 244) thus rediscovers the need of beautiful surroundings for her own well-being. The intensity of her awareness of natural beauty directly influences the state of her innermost soul. Her enthusiasm for the magnificent natural scenery in Hanover and at Newlands thus had filled her with happiness, while the 'small ugliness and the empty crude suburban air' (*RL*, 244) of her first lodgings in London before moving to Tansley Street had made her ill. She attributes to the conscious awareness of beauty a healing effect so strong that it might even have saved her mother's life: 'If *she* had been able to escape into the beauty of outside things, it would not have happened' (*RL*, 244).

Facing this anti-climax of her life in such clarity and recognizing the direct interrelation between mental stability and the awareness of exterior, natural, beauty, Miriam takes an important step in her *Trauerarbeit* which she has suppressed for years. Once she has overcome her 'attempts to achieve misery by the process of reason' (*RL*, 245) and accepts a new, future life, she recovers her ability to appreciate natural beauty.

Thus, on one of her repeated visits to Bonnycliff, the Wilsons' house next to the sea, Miriam sees the garden in an enthusiasm reminiscent of her youthful responses. In the combination of garden and sea she experiences a reunion of the two areas of her strongest childhood memories, which reverberate with beauty and happiness:

> Rocky dryness and sea freshness mingled in the huge air. The little baked pathway ribboning the level grass, disappearing round the angle of the enclosing edge, the perfect sharp edge, irises feathering along it, sharp green spikes and deep blue hoods of filmy blossom patterned against the paler misty blueness of the sea. Perfect. [...] The sea glinting at your side between the leaf patterns of the creeper-covered pergola. The little roughstone shelter, trapping the sunblaze. The plain bench along the centre of a piece of pathway, looking straight out to the midmost sea; sun-baked gravel under your feet, clumps of flowers in sight. Somewhere the rockery, its face catching the full blaze of the light, green bosses clumped upon it, with small pure-toned flowers, mauvy pink and tender eastern blue. On the level just below it, a sudden little flat of grass, small-flowered shrubs at its edge towards the sea (*RL*, 338f.).

The reaction to the rapturous, breath-taking view is expressed in a series of ellipses and short sentences. In the staccato-like language Dorothy Richardson conveys the rapid flux of impressions that make up this illumination. The abundance of light, expressed in a great variety of colour terms,[23] once more is a decisive factor in Miriam's perception of natural beauty. Sunlight, solitude,[24] and silence, both outer and inner,[25] then form the basis for an illuminated moment of perfection (hence the repeated use of the word 'perfect'): 'There was no one to be seen. No sound. Nothing to break the perfect expressiveness' (*RL*, 339).

As Shirley Rose (1969:371) points out, such an epiphany, an extreme perception of the reality of the external world, is 'recognized as a result of our awareness of our own being,' of accepting the different sides within our selves. Miriam, who has learnt to accept the loss of her mother's death as part of her immutable being, is able to perceive nature's beneficent impact on her mind again 'through the mediation of the senses.'

In the structure of *Pilgrimage* this specific garden view at Bonnycliff plays a double function: It is a response to that other view of a seaside garden at the end of *Honeycomb* (482f.), where Miriam, in her mother's company and for a last time, had recognized the beauty of a garden. There, the threat of her mother's despair gave way to a hopeful glance into the future: 'Miriam felt that a new world might be opening' (*HC*, 483). Now, many years after her hopes were thwarted, the thread of this hope is

---

[23] e.g. green; deep blue; paler misty blueness; mauvy pink; tender eastern blue.

[24] cf. Miriam's Oberland experience: *O*, 65, English people on the slopes 'shutting out the scene;' *O*, 87: the skaters on the rink bring 'forgetfulness of the surrounding scene.'

[25] 'Mental liveliness *did* obliterate surroundings, stop their expressiveness' (*RL*, 344).

resumed; her wound seems to be healed to such an extent that in the intensity of the sunlit summer garden at the seaside she for the first time can see the possibility of a new world opening for her. The mere existence of such a future world is alluded to in the most general terms: 'All waiting for tomorrow, for endless tomorrows' (*RL*, 339). Thus, Miriam has to and will take an active part in finding this future world.

On the other hand this scene forms a magnificent counterpoint to that longest and most intense illumination Miriam will experience on her way to Oberland.[26] It is a brilliant foreshadowing of that complete immersion into the beauty of nature, equal in its colourful intensity, in its deep, mystical awareness of sunlight, parallel in its solitary view.[27] However, the marked contrast of the seasons - the 'sunbaked' summer heat of the garden (*RL*, 339) as opposed to the 'dry cold' winter evening in the mountains (*O*, 30) - underlines the differences between the two scenes.

In both scenes it is the open vista of wild, untamed nature - the sea or the mountains - that leads to Miriam's experience of rapturous happiness. While the *downward* glance towards the sea in its reminiscence of that earlier sea garden refers to the both geographically and mentally lowest point Miriam has ever reached, her *upward* glance towards mountain peaks and sky in a parallel way expresses not only her physical ascent, but also her mental exaltation accompanying it. The appreciation of natural beauty, which Miriam is able to see again in the short, *static*, 'unmoving picture' (*RL*, 345) of Hypo's garden, thus reaches its climax in the long, *dynamic*, film-like impressions of the mountains.

The garden scene at Hypo's, can be read as a sign of Miriam's having overcome her mother's death. While her blocked emotions used to inhibit her from seeing the beauty of her natural surroundings, her return to the sea, her retrieved understanding of nature, accelerates her mental healing process. So, shortly after this visit she notices that 'life flowed in a new way. Many of the old shadows were gone; apprehensions about the future had disappeared' (*TR*, 478).[28]

Miriam's stay in Oberland, where she inhales such enormous life-giving energies, makes her fully *conscious* of the fact that her mother's death lies

---

[26]cf. Chapter 1.3.

[27] On this visit Switzerland is first discussed as an ideal holiday place: 'She talked to them about Switzerland, where they had already been. It was for her the unattainable ideal of a holiday [...] She had suddenly remembered all she had heard about Swiss winters. Switzerland in summer was an oleograph. In winter an engraving' (*RL*, 363).

[28] In *The Trap* Miriam's regained, but still precarious positive garden experience finds its first figurative confirmation when she recognizes the hidden charm of Miss Holland, her rather difficult room-mate at Flaxman's: Her smile 'reached and touched like sunlight. Garden sunlight that had been missing through all the wandering years' (*TR*, 404).

behind her. Returning to London she is positive that her health - both physical and mental - 'was restored for evermore since she had seen the light on the mountains' (*DLH*, 149). She, therefore, is no longer afraid of facing her mother's death. Her response to the sign of Teetgen's Tea, so far provoking panic of madness and despair, appears as a paraphrase of St. Paul's words : 'O death, where is thy victory? O death, where is thy sting?'[29] Miriam sees

> the grimed gilt lettering that *forced me to gaze into the darkest moment of my life and to remember that I had forfeited my share in humanity for ever and must go quietly and alone until the end.*
> *And now their power has gone. They can bring back only the memory of a darkness and horror, to which, then, something has happened, begun to happen?*
> She glanced back over her shoulder at the letters now away behind her and rejoiced in freedom [...] (*DLH*, 155f.; emphasis original).

It is her Oberland experience which eventually shifts this large block from Miriam's soul: 'Oberland again; its golden light, and its way of making its outer world conform to its inner. Something of heaven, precarious, but temporarily closing the doors of hell' (*DLH*, 157), a hell she descended into at her mother's death and which she from then on has perceived as forming her everyday world: 'All of us who survive have things to learn down here in hell. Perhaps this is hell' (*TU*, 95).[30] In her long ascension to the heights of Oberland Miriam is leaving this place of 'darkness and horror' behind.

Years ago, when Miriam was attending a series of Dante lectures, she already felt closely akin to this seeker of spiritual light;[31] she transferred Dante's allegorical journey onto her own life and started to see it in terms of *purgatorio* - where redemption from evil is not impossible and where even 'moments of paradise' (*IN*, 402) are perceptible - rather than in terms of *inferno*, the site of eternal punishment. So, as it is the case in Dante's *purgatorio*, feelings of guilt and remorse, mixed with the faint hope of overcoming them for good, have prevailed. Now, however, keeping the medieval poet as one of her many explicitly named literary idols, Dorothy Richardson has Miriam experience the healing power of the heights; she follows Dante's way from the guilt-ridden *purgatorio* of the middle novel-chapters to a first glimpse of the outer circles of *paradiso*. Her fear of getting stuck in the shadows of moral weakness and impatience and of finding no

---

[29] 1 Corinthian 15, 55. When she quotes these very words much earlier (*TU*, 255), they appear as a defiant, yet powerless outcry against the force and horrors of death, which at that time still dominate her.

[30] cf. Fromm 128: In Mendizabal, the 'fascinating little devil' (*IN*, 430), she recognizes Miriam's guide through the 'hell' of London.

[31] cf. *IN*, 353-356; 402f.; 406. For more allusions to Dante see Fromm 128.

way out of self-accusations at last yields to a joy that promises not only momentary freedom and happiness, but exists beyond time and space: 'Joy is eternity. Eternity is joy' (*DLH*, 139). It is the 'golden eternity' of Oberland (*DLH*, 139), its overwhelming beauty, that induces this sense of lasting liberation.

Like Dante, who on the summit of Mount Purgatory drinks from the streams of Lethe and Eunoe - the oblivion of evil and the memory of good deeds, 'forgetfulness and sweet memory,' as Miriam calls them (*IN*, 402)[32] - in order to fulfil the necessary preconditions to get into paradise, she eventually manages to forget her feelings of guilt, imbibing with her eyes the beauties of nature. In Oberland she could 'walk and walk on [...] with thought shut off and being changed, coming back refreshed and changed and indifferent' (*O*, 72). And, as if she had drunk from Eunoe, she recalls only positive memories of her past, for instance of her months in Hanover. A piece of music, which she 'through all the years [...] had tried in vain to recall' and which now 'came, to welcome her, piling joy on joy' (*O*, 35) triggers off the memory of the 'high-walled' school garden at Waldstrasse, where Miriam in the sheltered contemplation of living nature, of 'trees and grass and clustering shrubs' had found an early understanding of her own self.

Similar to Dante's experience at the end of his *purgatorio*, where he feels restored by the waters of Eunoe,

> rifatto si come piante novelle
> rinovellate di novella fronda
> puro e disposto a salire a le stelle,
> (*Purgatorio* 372; 'Canto XXXIII,' ll. 143-145)

the catalytic cleansing of her mind when facing the mountain peaks eventually enables her to 'enter [...] paradise' (*O*, 74).[33] In her recurrent images of timelessness Dorothy Richardson seems to follow Dante into the higher realm of bright eternal bliss; but Miriam, a woman of the twentieth century, is aware of her precarious situation: the 'doors of hell' are but temporarily closed, a re-lapse into some form of self-doubt is still possible. In the end, at least, her experience of the 'heavenly' harmony of exterior and interior world in Oberland enables her to maintain her deepened positive awareness of both herself and her surroundings.

---

[32] cf. Alighieri, Dante. *The Divine Comedy: Purgatorio* 310-311 and 370-373 ('Canto XXVIII', ll. 121-133 and 'Canto XXXIII', ll. 127-145).

[33] In Oberland, 'this winter paradise' (*O*, 98), even the celestial city seems within reach: 'Far away in the haze beyond the visible distance a group of slender peaks showed faintly rose-misted pinnacles of a dream-city' (*O*, 102).

2.3.3 'Escape from Lifelessness?' Breaking Free (From Men)

> If I had had to choose seven years ago, before I knew, I'd have chosen Richard; I couldn't have helped myself. But if I had to choose now - knowing what reality is - between losing Richard in the way I have lost him, and losing reality, absolutely and for ever, my real self, knowing that I'd lost it? . . .
>
> (May Sinclair, *Mary Olivier. A Life* 379)

> To hold back and keep free . . . and real. Impossible to be real unless you were quite free. . . . Two married in one family was enough. (*HC*, 459)

When Miriam is confronted again with the everyday world of London, her newly-discovered self-confidence makes her think about a stable relationship with a man. Marriage, hinted at and rejected already before her 'golden life within her life' in Oberland (*DLH*, 136),[34] now could be the consequence of her feeling that the 'loneliness that during the past years had been moving away from her life' (*O*, 123) in fact no longer exists; the ways of communication she has found with Hypo, Densley and especially Shatov at times promise a lasting union with one or the other. Yet, anticipating that the inevitable role-playing in marriage would attack the integrity of her own identity, she at last cannot accept any of them (cf. Hanscombe 1982:96).

In our context of garden imagery, Dorothy Richardson's way of including short garden views into each of the decisive 'man-dismissing' scenes underlines Miriam's prevailing fear of commitment and subordination to male dominance,[35] which makes her keep her own independence, and her eventual withdrawal into her unbound self.

These three parallel scenes exemplify the three basic patterns of Miriam's garden views and visions. In the solitary, inspiring view of beautiful details, the garden has an *active*, positive impact on her; the direct visual impressions make her thoughts turn to enthusiastic, dreamlike visions, which fill her with vitalizing energy. Gardens which appear indifferent, uninspiring, lifeless, in a *reactive* way reflect her mostly negative frame of mind; the visual reality in

---

[34] cf. *TR*, 482: 'Marriage is no solution, only a postponement' - a putting-off of Miriam's central question of finding her own self. Shortly after, Miriam in a conversation with Dr Densley develops her bizarre ideas on marriage: 'Affairs not ending in marriage are even more objectionable than marriage. [...] Marriage, or sooner or later absurdity. Free-love is better than absurdity' (*TR*, 495).

[35] e.g. *PR*, 129: her refusal of Pastor Lahmann's advances; *HC*, 477: her shying away from Bob Greville.

its mirror-like function helps her to gain self-insight.[36] In some rare instances Miriam's garden contemplation shared with other people sheds light on social rather than visual aspects. What she feels towards the other onlooker is more relevant than what they actually perceive. Their sharing the garden view implies some form of mutual understanding, just as her awareness of their differences manifests itself in unshared, separate views. The garden in these scenes is no longer an 'interactive' partner, the literal *vis-à-vis* of Miriam's consciousness, but a *passive* object, important only as a common focalizer rather than as a consciously perceived individual space of natural beauty.

Visiting Densley shortly after her return from Oberland, Miriam longs to be gone as soon as he starts talking about his private life. Unwilling to enter into conversation, she glances out into the 'blinding light' of sunshine (*DLH*, 149), in which she has a vision of a spring park. She

> saw the several corridors of gold that broke across the long grey street and felt herself already escaped into its echoey stillness, going, as she had come, unspent, to meet the green mists of the park and find its new crocuses; find the close ranks of mauve and white hiding the grass of that little alley again, stand and look and again feel that cool English freshness as if touching her all over, as if she were unclothed (*DLH*, 149).

The visualization of crocuses, constant reminders of renewal,[37] together with the feeling of fresh nakedness, imply her longing for a change, for a re-birth into some kind of new life. Yet Densley's suggestion of the security of a conventional marriage, is not the right way. Just as in the real blinding sunlight there is, in optical terms, no way of seeing Densley, the promising 'strange new light within her' holds 'no personal thought of him' (*DLH*, 154). The *active* inspiration of this garden vision makes her withdraw into her independent self. Instead of intensely sharing the moment with her would-be bridegroom, she longs for a solitary communion with nature. The crocuses of her vision thus anticipate her answer to his proposal: in her new life there is no room for Densley.

The *reactive* garden view is exemplified in Miriam's decisive break from Hypo Wilson: though yielding to his sexual advances and, in true 'New-

---

[36] Würzbach (284) similarly writes: This 'influence of her immediate state of mind on her interpretation of the outside world, an influence of which Miriam is often not directly aware, can be observed throughout the novel: not only in her perception and judgement of people but also in her perception of her physical environment, in her thoughts about herself, about her past and about her expectations regarding the future.'

[37] cf. *TR*, 498; *CH*, 309; *MM*, 578.

Woman' fashion,[38] willingly spending the night with him at Bonnycliff, Miriam does not find any fulfilment - sexual or other - because the nightly adventure lacks the communion of the minds that is so important to Miriam's sense of an inspiring relationship. In the description of this night there is a host of words which all express Miriam's deep dissatisfaction and sexual frustration.[39] The first glance out of the window in the morning then confirms her feelings: the beauty of the garden does not appeal to her.

> Drawing back the curtain from the open lattice, she found in the outside scene no escape from the lifelessness of the room. The garden, sunlit beyond the shadow of the house, the blue sea behind the daffodils screening the edge of the downward slope; expressionless.
>
> The world was changed (*DLH*, 258).

Though various elements of visible beauty, which used to inspire her to a moment of illumination, are there - the garden, the sea, sunlight, flowers - Miriam's mind does not respond in the usual way. The uninspired garden view is the *reactive* result of her nightly experience; for the real garden here is the projection area of her own dissatisfied soul, reflecting with perfect clarity that perhaps 'this repellent bleakness was the truth lying beneath the bright surface' (*DLH*, 259) of what appears to be her brightly glistening relationship with Hypo. The blooming spring garden, symbol of overbrimming life, is inverted into a 'cold and lifeless' place, which, keeping the gloomy atmosphere of 'last night's lonely journey through uninhabited darkness' (*DLH*, 259), holds nothing but a view of a future 'dead world.'[40] At the height of her sexual intimacy with Hypo she experiences a nothingness that forms a starting point for her lasting liberation from this 'dead-seeming world' into a self-created reality, her independent life. Thus, when she observes in the mirror three birds flashing by 'in the form of an elongated

---

[38] cf. Luftig 95: The New Women believe 'that heterosexual friendship necessarily included sexual relations. [...] Friendship is no longer that which is not sex; sex indeed seems sometimes to inhere in "friendship", so the category in opposition to which friendship is defined is not sex but marriage and related social conventions.'

[39] *DLH*, 256-58: 'indignation;' 'alienated'; 'unwelcome adventure;' 'fathomless black darkness;' 'clenched and rigid form;' 'without thought or memory or any emotion;' 'obstructive clay'; 'more separated from him than in the unshared journeying'.

[40] Miriam remembers this journey 'through extended darkness' (*CH*, 306) as the point where she found a 'confirmation of her conviction of the inner vastness of space' (307), a vastness she wants to explore. Her experience of the 'flood-like darkness through which she had driven, face downwards, as if swimming' (306) fills her with a Freudian 'oceanic' feeling of total immersion into a space that goes far beyond her own self. According to Freud, this feeling, expressing a closeness with the outer world, forms the source of religiosity. Thus, the 'certainty that it was possible to float also in the outer vastness' (*CH*, 307) foreshadows her mystical experiences at Dimple Hill (cf. Freud 1974:191-270).

triangle' (*DLH*, 259), the arrow-like formation symbolically points at the existence of this future life: 'The sight of them as they passed had smitten through her as though she were transparent and left her thrilled from head to foot with the sense of having shared their swift and silent flight' (*DLH*, 259). The birds, images of a free spirit, transcending her physical and mental gravity, trigger the physical reaction she might have had the night before and fill her with the confidence of having reached a way of being that would find its own responses in the future. It is this prospect of a self-determined life-filled future that later on makes her eye turn back to her surroundings: 'Through the window, she watched the old, lost enchantment flow back into sea and sky and garden' (*DLH*, 262). In this retrieved, newly seen world there is no room for Hypo, a mere 'collector of virginities' (*CH*, 366), who would refuse to recognize a sharing of intimacies beyond the merely physical. Though Miriam is still fascinated by his intellectual brilliance, he cannot possibly be her partner for the future.

Neither can Michael Shatov, the most deeply fascinating of all her suitors: his Hebrew beauty, his intellectual interests and his personal charm keep attracting Miriam, but his strict religious ideas about marriage and family life, which form a strong contrast to Miriam's own point of view, make her withdraw. She, supposedly pregnant with Hypo's child, independent and enjoying her freedom, would experience the 'refuge' of marriage to a strict Jew as a 'permanent prison' (*CH*, 303). Therefore, Miriam hopes for Amabel's support in her decision not to marry Michael. Trying to free herself from her sense of guilt at his 'persistent helplessness' (*CH*, 284), and from her protecting mother instincts aroused by his childlike vulnerability to a strange world, Miriam expects Amabel's confirming comment after her first encounter with Michael. She anticipates a moment to 'share a perfection of silent incredulity. A mutual, dumb entranced contemplation of enormity' that would prove her feelings right. But Amabel reacts differently: 'Gone off alone, she stood at the far-off window, gazing out, very tall, posed against the upright of the window-frame, in her long flowing robe. Remote. Withdrawn [...]' (*CH*, 289). When Miriam looks down into the garden in order to join Amabel for a moment of communion, she has to recognize that Amabel 'was not with her. [...] She was not looking into the garden' (*CH*, 290).

Instead of sharing the view of the garden, *passively* lying in front of the window as a common focus of their sight, and thus suggesting the deeper common understanding Miriam longs for, Amabel in her averted look demonstrates that she is not going to share Miriam's point of view. The sense of unity with Amabel gives way to a 'fundamental separation' (*CH*, 292), which is confirmed in the continuing disparity of their glances. While Miriam 'moved impatiently away into the room' (*CH*, 291), Amabel stands 'averted there by her [!] window' (*CH*, 293) facing the garden. To Amabel the solitary glance into the garden means a moment of undisturbed rest from Miriam's society and it is to this space, or to herself rather than to Miriam, that she verbalizes her enthusiasm for Michael: '"He's wonderful," she breathed, "and so beautiful." And still *she did not turn*. [...] She was *set apart*, unable, while she still dwelt on [the recognition of his worth], to face one who was incompletely appreciative' (*CH*, 293; emphasis added).

Miriam's inability to share the view of the garden with Amabel reveals their emotional apartness that forbids a communion of the minds. Seen in a larger context, the garden showing no signs of individual beauty thus becomes an indicator of the degree of Miriam's and her present partner's emotional distance: the further apart they stand emotionally, the less likely a sharing of views is.[41] And this is what Miriam herself recognizes too: while she is determined to continue her life alone, Amabel stands 'protective at Michael's side' (*CH*, 291). Just as they cannot share the view of the garden, their different points of view on this issue cannot merge. Miriam therefore finds a solution which is satisfactory both for her, who is always reluctant to take on responsibility for others, and for Amabel, 'Michael's possible saviour' (*CH*, 294): 'Then marry him, my dear, yourself' (*CH*, 293). - Which Amabel eventually does.

The fact that Michael, the would-be husband who is of major importance in this affair, is absent in a scene that vitally concerns the future of all three of them, illustrates Miriam's inner detachment from him. After short moments of struggling with an emerging conscience she callously disposes of him, displaying a trait of her character that various people recognized in Dorothy Richardson herself. This 'inner aloofness,' holding back something 'that it seemed no one could really touch' (Hanscombe 1987:49), makes her appear cold, self-centred and obviously unable to embark on a lasting intimate relationship. Miriam had recognized this earlier on: 'The only sureness in things is the action of one's own spirit. Egoism? But egoism carried far enough. [...] There is not a soul I would sacrifice myself for. Not even Michael, in his helplessness' (*TR*, 465). This primary interest in her own affairs, the 'single-minded pursuit of the truthfulness and integrity of *her own existence*' (Hanscombe 1987:62; emphasis added), explains Miriam's repeated escapes from relationships with men that would entail some form of

[41] After her wedding, Amabel wants to talk confidentially about Miriam's situation, but now Miriam is reluctant to become too intimate: Amabel, 'speaking dreamily out into the barely visible little garden', 'leaning on arms propped upon the window-sill, so far out that one must lean, too, to hear' (*MM*, 601), almost physically draws her into a sharing of the garden view to get to know details about Miriam's relationship with Richard Roscorla. Miriam's non-response to the garden and her evasive answers, however, show the futility of Amabel's hope to renew their confidentiality.

responsibility. She has come to recognize that 'between men and women there can be no direct communication' (*DLH*, 223), that 'men and women are incompatible' (*DLH*, 246). This confirms her earlier observation of the basic differences of the sexes, which lead to a 'muddle of men and women with nothing in common' (*HC*, 376). She therefore rejects marriage and looks for a mystical communion not with people but rather with things, especially with the beauties of nature.[42]

Hypo's clever phrase of the 'homoeopathic doses of life' (*DLH*, 238) in lonely nature therefore falls on a receptive ground within Miriam's consciousness. His suggestion of a 'green solitude' (*DLH*, 238) has been out of her reach so far; but now it assumes a new meaning. Contemplating the idea helps her at last, who for years has not been able to make decisions, to see an aim in the not too distant future. Solitude in the inanimate, undisturbed world of plants now appears gainsworthy: it suggests a radical withdrawal from human society and its conflicts and it promises possibilities of reaching hidden zones of her inner self as well as of finding a way of self-expression in writing. The 'welcoming depths' (*CH*, 300) of her visionary shelter mirror the depths of her own soul that she wants to explore. Her vision of this imaginary place, filled with her spiritual search for integration and wholeness, thus far transcends Hypo's view of it as 'one of the amenities of civilized life' (*CH*, 300). Her vision of 'a little house whose little garden should lead down into a wood' (*DLH*, 238) is more than an idyllic image of beauty and rest, as she now includes in it her whole self, all her wishes and aspirations. The 'cool gardens and shadowy woods' (*DLH*, 238) of her vision are an unspecified conglomerate of her many garden views of the past, which, seen together, could in fact form her ideal garden of the future; it is an imaginary place where her outer and inner self, her conscious and subconscious fears and wishes, her views and visions, past and future would eventually be reconciled in her individual, solitary paradise.[43]

---

[42] cf. Kaplan 40-45. And Staley (68) writes: 'For the mystic, however, the experience of things is important.'

[43] The three men whose intimate companionship Miriam refuses in the end make her journey to paradise possible. Together with Dr Hancock, who grants her a generous 'holiday salary' (*CH*, 400), they help her to find her way there: Hypo by suggesting the idea of looking for a green solitude and mentally supporting her in her striving to break free; Densley by entitling her to take a long break for medical reasons; Michael by providing the place and leaving her the address of the Roscorla family. Miriam gladly accepts these signs of a looser form of friendship in which she can 'hold back and keep free . . . and real' (*HC*, 459); her innate concern about not losing her individuality makes her withdraw from their intimacies in order to find this lasting 'real' freedom for herself.

2.4 'Sunlit Endless Gardens:' Visions of Paradise

> Fair quiet have I found thee here,
> And Innocence thy Sister dear!
> Mistaken long, I sought you then
> In busie Companies of Men.
> Your sacred Plants, if here below,
> Only among the Plants will grow.
> Society is all but rude,
> To this delicious solitude.
>
> (Andrew Marvell, 'The Garden' II, *Poems* 48)

> Perfection. Rambling old Tudor house, ripe red walls, gables, wings, sloping floors, endless lattices, high-walled garden ablaze with all the right flowers, a peaked village in sight from the upper windows & woody hills all round.
>
> I'm much too tired to see anything - but its [*sic*] all here - I'm delighted to hear that no one ever goes beyond the garden.
>
> (Letter to Alan Odle, 1.6.1917; *WM*, 15)

In our scrutiny of the role of gardens in *Pilgrimage* we have been concerned with Miriam's direct visual perception, her appreciation of the beauty of her natural surroundings, as well as her reflections and visions arising from this direct sensory impulse. Her stable views are closely connected to her state of mind at the moment of looking into the garden, Seen as such, these garden scenes are mirror images of Miriam's soul that help herself to understand her situation.

At the same time, however, these gardens are parts of an underlying pattern that pervades the whole novel sequence; they give expression to a concept that both gives unity to the apparently loosely organized novel-chapters and illuminates a central issue of Dorothy Richardson's writing, her conviction of the 'indestructability' of the 'inner zones' of the self and its unchanging centre (*DL*, 153). This concept of an earthly paradise combines echoes of the Biblical Eden and its literary heritage, as perceived in Miriam's reading activities, with her personal experience of the world. It is a highly individualized paradise and, unlike the Victorian concept of a social paradise for a larger community, a place of *personal* fulfilment; here Dorothy Richardson takes up the Romantic notion of lost innocence and hoped-for salvation of the subjective soul. Similar to the Biblical idea of paradise, her paradise lies at both the beginning and the end of her time, in the irretrievable past of childhood as well as in an ideal world to come. Miriam's individual path through life thus resembles the Christian way of life, starting from a pre-lapsarian state of bliss through loss and dejection into a new, transformed state. But whereas the Biblical, heavenly paradise of the future is a place unattainable within life,[44] Miriam seeks a form of perfect happiness at an Edenic place of the here and now, in an earthly paradise.

So the gardens, as we have seen them, are reminders of the possible existence of another world beyond the immediately existing, of a place of perfect security and happiness. The abundance of flowers and trees in blossom in Hanover, at home in Barnes, at Newlands, in London, at the Brooms', at Bonnycliff and at Sally's create an Edenic atmosphere of rest and tranquillity just as much as the consistently warm spring or summer sunshine in which these gardens appear.[45] Protected against the negative influences of an evil world, some of the gardens - at Hanover, Banbury Park, her parents' brick villa, Sally's and St John's Wood - are walled; they provide a secure space for the unhampered movement of their inhabitants.

The happiness Miriam experiences when looking into these gardens is enhanced by the absence of social communication and conflicts. On the other hand, whenever she is in a garden in company, there is an element of sexual tension or some form of abuse of other people's confidence that clearly opposes the idea of a conflict-free and pre-sexual state of innocent bliss.[46] In these instances of social intercourse Miriam shows a significantly smaller interest in her garden surroundings than when she is alone. It is therefore only in the turn away from society towards solitude that Miriam fully registers the beauty of each individual garden.

These views of really existing, sensorily perceptible gardens express no more than an unconscious longing for a state of perfection, an evanescent visualization of the lasting happiness Miriam believes to have achieved time and again throughout *Pilgrimage*; on the other hand, Hypo's suggestion of a green solitude where Miriam in harmonious union with nature would be able to read and write brings to Miriam's consciousness an image of what she has been dreaming of for a long time: a solitary, protected place of nature, where her senses as well as her intellect would find satisfaction in the contemplation of natural beauty, would inspire her mind towards the experience of this lasting happiness.

---

[44] cf. Bible: Lk 23: 43; 2 Cor 12:3; Revel. 2:7.

[45] cf. *PR*, 52; *BW*, 200, 303, 305; *HC*, 405, 474, 482; *TU*, 147; *RL*, 334, 338; *MM*, 587f.

[46] When she is flirting with Max in her parents' garden at Barnes, Miriam - by ignoring her friend Ted - provokes Ted to end their relationship (*BW*, 222-224). When following the invitation of Alma, her old school-friend, to Bonnycliff, Miriam callously responds to Hypo's amorous advances, although his wife is nearby: 'Alma crossing the end of the lawn. There was not any feeling of guilt. Only the sense of her isolation. Companionship with her isolation' (*RL*, 393).

The vision of an earthly paradise to come forms a last and exceptional example of a long series of imagined garden scenes. Unlike other pictures of her mind these garden visions help Miriam to escape from the dissatisfying reality into an unreal world, whose enchantingly harmonious qualities, however, fade away as soon as some outer disturbance calls her mind back to the present. In Hanover, the two absurd prospects of marrying either Emma Bergmann's brother or Pastor Lahmann call up, though at once dismissed, images of perfection and harmony centred round a garden, in the one case 'a garden and German springs and summers and sunsets and strong kind arms and a shoulder,' where she 'would grow so happy' (*PR*, 167), and in the other 'a garden and fields, a firelit interior, a little woman smiling and busy and agreeable' (*PR*, 129).

At the Pernes', it is popular fiction which draws her into a world of perfect illusion. The 'blue and gold'[47] cover of *The Story of Adèle*, for instance, has an enchanting effect on her so that she completely loses herself in the fairy-tale world of Adèle, where the medieval *hortus conclusus*, epitome of an earthly paradise, provides a counterspace to the 'ugly, [...] coarse, [...] alien, [...] repellent' surroundings of North London (*BW*, 228). Yet again, the imagined paradise is an artificial refuge soon swamped by the facts of reality. The 'endless summer' (*BW*, 228), connoting the eternal bliss of paradise, turns into 'lines of black print' as soon as Miriam is unwillingly drawn out of her happy solitude of reading by the bell, announcing the ritual social gathering at tea-time.[48]

Rosa Nouchette Carey's books about 'good girls and happy marriages' (*BW*, 284)[49] and the innumerable volumes of Mrs Hungerford's novels - which are full of 'gabled country houses, the sunlit endless gardens, the deep orchards, the falling of the dew, the mists of the summer mornings, masses of flowers [...]' (*BW*, 284) - likewise promise Edenic abundance of natural beauty in an inaccessible world of peaceful affluence, forming a sharp contrast to her present 'sense of imprisonment' (*BW*, 232) at Banbury Park. Overwritten and as full of stereotypes as the 'daring' novels by Ouida she reads next, these books illustrate Miriam's uncritical appreciation of the

---

[47] Though the cover at first seems 'unpleasant', Miriam soon discovers 'some secret charm about the book' (*BW*, 227). Together with green, blue and gold are the colours Dorothy Richardson uses most consistently for Miriam's Edenic illuminations, expressing the perfect beauty of her surroundings (e.g. *BW*, 200: the 'gold and green' garden; *BW*, 303: the 'gold and blue' day; *RL*, 349, 366: 'blue and gold of the day').

[48] The book ends on a note of disappointment. The paradise-like atmosphere of Adèle's early years is destroyed by meaningless, unnecessary socializing: the discussions and 'fusses - all about nothing' soon destroy the sense of solitary happiness (*BW*, 232). This story within the story hints at Dorothy Richardson's critical attitude towards society, her love of solitude and her romantic concept of the lost childhood paradise.

[49] cf. Chapter 3.4.3.

popular taste of literature of the day. Her escapist reading allows her to identify with the heroines of an illusionary world of perfection, to find moments of *ersatz* happiness in a purely fictional paradise of romance.

Miriam's youthful indulgence in romantic fantasies continues at Newlands, when, despite the enchanting surroundings and the leisurely way of life of the Corries, she begins to realize that she is only 'a helpless dingy little governess' (*HC*, 396): she imagines she is being taken away by a lonely old gentleman to a large house and a 'large sunny garden with high walls,' where he, 'protecting her and keeping people off,' would shut her up.[50] In the garden abounding with the pleasures of singing, reading and playing she would at last die of happiness. This fantasy, which includes paradise features such as protecting walls, sunshine and consummate bliss, for the first time expresses a longing for an intense communion with another person: 'they would share the great secret.' In the superficial atmosphere of Newlands Miriam longs for some form of mutual, deeply-rooted trust and would be ready to give up her personal freedom and responsibility for herself and relish the protection of a much older man. Her wish for taking up the security and innocence of childhood and perpetuating it into her future adult life is to be understood as an immature yearning for an idealized father figure; in the person of Bob Greville, her elderly friend, such a paternal lover seems to become real. When reading his condescending letters, however, her vision of a love based on subordination evaporates. Though retaining him 'to decorate her breakfast tray with letters' (*HC*, 420), Miriam recedes when her fantasies threaten to become physically real, when Bob expresses his feelings for her; she recognizes that her vision of a paradisiac communion of the souls cannot so easily be transposed into her immediate reality.

At Newlands, in the unfamiliar world of the *nouveaux-riches*, new unthought-of possibilities are offered to her. Perhaps the most impressive one appears in connection with the most unorthodox vision of a paradise within *Pilgrimage*: Mrs Kronen, a weekend guest of the Corries', shows Miriam a radically different way of life that appears strangely attractive. She responds to this attraction with an impulsive vision of perfection, of a paradise not just earthly, but thoroughly worldly, revealing a momentary fascination with a looser lifestyle. Mrs Kronen is Dorothy Richardson's version of the great Tempter, a fascinating and at the same time repellent figure, a *fascinosum et tremendum*, who dominates and casts a spell on the whole household: 'She made everyone else seem cloudy and shrivelled and dim' (*HC*, 402). Neither Mr nor Mrs Corrie nor Miriam can escape the vulgar charm of this person, who, in spite of their similar social background, is shown as a strong contrast

---

[50] A garden perhaps reminiscent of Charlotte Brontë's high-walled garden at Thornfield, where Jane Eyre meets Mr Rochester, the much older man, who in this 'Eden-like' place proposes to her (Brontë, *Jane Eyre, Vol II*, 10 -22).

to the Corries: While Mrs Corrie, the 'sweetness of [whose] bones and [whose] thin voice of tears and laughter were of God' (*HC*, 404), represents the traditionally delicate, ignorant, but God-inspired wife and mother, Mrs Kronen is 'a sort of man' who is not easily perplexed and 'a woman too - because she was not mean and petty and fussy as men are' - as Mr Corrie in particular is (*HC*, 404f.). Showing characteristics of both sexes,[51] she appears as an oversexed being *and* as an androgynous 'thing' (*HC*, 400) who transcends sexuality.[52] With her lascivious French love songs she attracts men such as Mr Corrie, whose eyes, 'strange and hard with shadows' (*HC*, 405), lust for her, and fascinates women such as Miriam as a guide into unknown, forbidden worlds. She therefore becomes a figure of identification for Miriam's own slumbering bisexual tendencies: 'I'm a sort of horrid man' (*HC*, 404). The 'charme étrange' of her song lures Miriam into dreaming about following her into her world, which is empty of thought or feeling, a world of superficial beauty that would not know any sadness: 'Live, don't worry . . . I've always been worrying and bothering. I'm going to be like Mrs Kronen; but quite different, because she hasn't the least idea how beautiful things really are' (*HC*, 403). Miriam first recognizes the sham world of Mrs Kronen's pretended beauty that is based on 'something evil [that] was the price of her carelessness' (*HC*, 402), yet is tempted to strive for such a world: 'Now she knew that she wanted [...] a wilderness of beauty all round her all the time - at any cost.' The devil's disciple, a modern version of the Biblical serpent,[53] Mrs Kronen seems to have achieved her aim: Listening to her impressive, quite unmusical singing, Miriam yields to the temptation of defying God, whose sexual identity is questioned: 'Was God a woman? Was God really irritating? No one could endure God really . . .' (*HC*, 404).

When Mrs Kronen, the attractive, wild, seductive, but also dangerous *femme fatale* 'sings' her song 'Aime-moi et je t'aime,' she appears as a modern version of Keats' 'Belle Dame Sans Merci.'[54] Under the spell of this song Miriam has a vision of a paradisiac garden: The song

---

[51] *HC*, 400: 'She was not a woman, she was a *woman*. . .;' *HC*, 403: She is 'huge and strong' like a man; *HC*, 405: She has a 'strong baritone voice.'

[52] *HC*, 409: She thus is unable to have children, 'doesn't care, she doesn't want any. They're all like that, that sort [of women],' Mrs Corrie explains.

[53] The temptation scene of Genesis is alluded to in the handing round of a dish of fruit at table whereupon 'something illicit' *creeps* into the room (*HC*, 401). In many medieval paintings the serpent is shown with a human head, the mirror image of Eve, 'because like attracts like.' Miriam is similarly attracted to Mrs Kronen who she is 'going to be like' (*HC*, 403) (cf. O'Reilly, J. 'The Trees of Eden in Medieval Iconography,' in: Morris 168).

[54] 'For sidewise would she lean, and sing
A faery's song.
[...] And sure in language strange she said,
"I love thee true!"' (Keats 321f.)

> had brought her a moment when the flower-filled drawing room had seemed to be lit, from within herself, a sudden light that had kept her very still and made the bowls of roses blaze with deepening colours. In her mind she had seen garden beyond garden of roses, sunlit, brighter and brighter, and had made a rapturous prayer. She remembered the words . . . God. . . . I'm not afraid of you. Look at the gardens . . . and something had smiled through the lit garden exultantly, and Mrs Kronen's voice had raged through the room like a storm, 'Ai-me-moi! . . .' (*HC*, 405).

Exposed to Mrs Kronen's eloquent power, Miriam experiences a moment in which the 'paradise' of roses Mrs Kronen seems to promise is within reach. The short illumination of her mind culminates in a prayer that questions God's authority in this illusory world of perfect beauty. Miriam, who has repeatedly criticized Adam's and Eve's behaviour in Eden, thus seems to deny the impact of the Fall on humanity. For, as Milton suggests, the fear of God came into existence only with the first act of sin.[55] When Miriam under the 'evil', sinful influence of Mrs Kronen denies this fear, she suggests the existence of an immoral anti-Eden, where, similar to Adam's and Eve's pre-lapsarian innocence, living without the fear of God would be possible, for at that place God would have lost his (or her?) power.[56] What is it, then, that smiles through the garden? Is this 'something', this genderless being, God or the Devil? Is the garden a vision of Edenic perfection or is it as fake as Mrs Kronen's superficial song? In a world where only men, whose 'ideas were devilish' (*HC*, 404) know about the existence of 'gardens everywhere, not always visible' (*HC*, 405) this exultant smile appears as a devilish joy in Miriam's being tempted into another vision of a 'paradise'. The garden then is the image of a place of *pretended* perfection, temptingly close, indeed easily attainable by giving in to Mrs Kronen's powerful, vulgar charm.

This garden, containing flowers and sunlight as two of the recurrent elements of Miriam's paradise visions, forms the climax and turning point of her fascination with the life at Newlands. Her succumbing to the ease-and-beauty-loving upper-class world of sin and temptation is short-lived; her identification with Mrs Kronen's overpowering vulgarity does not last. She soon sees through the 'stifling atmosphere, the hard brutal laughing complacent atmosphere' (*HC*, 443) of Newlands and recognizes the falseness of such a 'paradise' of uncultured ignorance. It is a world so different from her own, that she perceives that she would never be at home there: 'I am the

---

[55] Thus, in *Paradise Lost*, Eve after having eaten from the forbidden fruit remembers times of innocence and asks: 'What fear I, then? Rather, what know to fear under this ignorance of good and evil [...]?' (Milton, John. 'Paradise Lost,' Book IX, ll. 773f, p.354)

[56] cf. 'Paradise Lost,' Book X, ll. 116 - 121 (Milton 369).

paid governess. You must not talk to me as you would to each other; I am an inferior and can never be an intimate' (*HC*, 430f.). Miriam recognizes the impossibility of finding happiness in a world that does not correspond to her own world view: 'At Newlands people might be dead, the women in bright hard deaths or deaths of cold, cruel deceitfulness, the men tiny insects of selfishness' (*HC*, 468) - the disillusioned comment of a girl who has to see thwarted all the expectations she had when arriving at this place. The experience of a *social* nothingness thus shows her that such a way of life eventually leads to a dead end. Behind the brightly glittering facades of social entertainment and small talk she recognizes the inability of these people to find a deeper understanding of each other and she grows aware of the utter emptiness of their lives. On her pilgrimage she therefore must search for other routes.

With her two sisters getting married and her mother's mental instability progressing, Miriam recognizes that her family, so far the reliable haven from her various explorations of the 'world', is falling apart. Home, this feeling of protecting, sometimes also confining security, though 'still there' (*HC*, 467) after the weddings, ceases to concern her and soon ceases to exist.[57] Her wish for the protective love of a man - 'because there would be somewhere then always to be, to rest and feel sure' (*HC*, 459f.) - is primarily her wish for a substitute home, 'lamplit rooms, gardens, a presence, understanding' (*HC*, 460). Just as in her dream-vision at Newlands (*HC*, 396), this wish shows Miriam's pining for security in a perfect world of house and garden. But reality looks different: none of the men she encounters around this time - Bob Greville, Mr Grove, Mr Tremayne - could possibly fulfil her wishes, marriage therefore has to be put off.

Before Mrs Henderson's increasingly dramatic mental decay, Miriam's repeated protestations of her belief in the beauty of life appear as eventually ineffective attempts at establishing a counterpoise of hope to her mother's despair.[58] She bravely plays and sings 'Freue dich des Lebens' (*HC*, 470) to cheer up her mother and does not abandon her hope for a better future even when she accompanies her on a trip to the seaside, which turns out to be Mrs Henderson's fatal journey. At the sea, sitting down to tea at the window of

57 Wherever Miriam goes in her later life, she tries to establish a *home*, a sheltered place she can rely on After the loss of her family life it is often a room rather than people she refers to as 'home' because a room appears more reliable: Returning to her first room in London she thinks 'of nothing but going home to Tansley Street' (*DLH*, 194), where she then feels 'the heart's ease of going home' (*DLH*, 201). Coming back to Dimple Hill for her second stay, she anticipates the joy of 'the promised weekend with Michael and Amabel and then - *home*. The place I found and where I belong [...]' (*MM*, 586).

58 e.g. *HC*, 468: 'One could go through [the day] in a drowse of strength, full of laughter . . . laughter to the brim, all one's limbs strong and heavy with laughter.'

the pension smoking-room, Miriam leaves the house and everything - including her sorrows about her mother's state - 'in another world' (*HC*, 482) to look out into the small garden, seeing it in rapturous intensity:

> A thick grey screen of sky must be there, above the trees, for the garden was an intensity of deep brilliance, deep bright green, and calceolarias and geraniums and lobelias, shining in a brilliant gloom. It was not a seaside garden . . . it was a garden . . . all gardens (*HC*, 482f).

In this triple intensification the garden assumes a symbolic significance that transcends the actual view: the basic colours yellow, red and blue of the flowers together with the 'deep bright green' convey an intense presence of fertile, *innocent* life, while the sheltering trees denote an atmosphere of security. *All* the gardens of Miriam's past are contained in this one view; her contemplation of the place thus rings with her memories of untroubled happiness: her childhood gardens at Babington and Barnes, her grandmother's garden with its calceolarias and geraniums, the Hanover and Newlands gardens as places of peaceful rest. Memory and immediate perception, past and present mingle in one culminating impression that even stretches out into the future. For a moment the limitations of time and place are cancelled and the small garden shutting out the 'real' world (*HC*, 483) appears as a paradisiac promise of life: 'Miriam felt that a new world might be opening.'[59]

Sharing this garden view with her mother, Miriam expects her mother to be equally seized by the all-enfolding rapturous beauty; she in fact seems to see in her mother some positive response, too: Mrs Henderson *eats*, and she even eats *serenely*, showing at least a basic interest in life. However, Miriam's hopes are short-lived. Their evening meal, their quiet 'feast' (*HC*, 483) in the blooming garden is their last supper. It is a last moment of relaxation, when everything is still possible, when even hope rather than despair, life rather than death seems to show up in the future. The seemingly cathartic effect of this evening in the garden does not touch Mrs Henderson, Miriam's impression of Edenic beauty and well-being is not taken up by her mother. On the following day her despair overcomes her. Under the impression that 'God has deserted me' (*HC*, 489) she puts an end to her life. This last act of her depression leaves Miriam motherless, hopeless, bereft of

---

[59] This promise of a turn to a better life is reinforced in Miriam's nightly reading of the Bible to her mother. During one of their last nights she reads Isaiah's great promise of Israel's return from the depressing slavery of Babylon to Jerusalem, thus to a new world of 'prosperity' and 'triumph': 'How beautiful upon the mountains are the feet of those who bring [good tidings]' (*HC*, 486). It is significant that the text breaks off before the 'good tidings', as they are no longer heard or understood by Mrs Henderson. She is beyond hope (cf. Isaiah 52, 7-14).

dreams and speech and throws her into a lifeless world 'full of perfect unanswering silence' (*HC*, 489).

The suicide, later remembered as a 'horror that had wrenched her life in twain' (*DLH*, 250), marks not only the crucial turning point in Miriam's circumstances and feelings but also finishes the time of her youthful visions of a paradise that has not much to do with her real life. While a reading of Miriam's outer life suggests her parting with childhood at the beginning of *Pointed Roofs*, when she leaves home for the first time, Fromm (1977:100) convincingly locates the end of Miriam's childhood as late as her mother's death. An abyss of horror and grief severs her from her early life for good. Miriam's fantasies of purely imagined places of perfection, her short would-be escapes into intrinsically unattainable dream worlds, her fleeting visions of paradise, come to an end. Day-dreaming in an atmosphere of childhood easiness is no longer possible. It is part of her development, of her growing awareness of her self as an individual, that from this point on her images of paradise are closely connected with her own real life: On the one hand Miriam is developing a more and more consistent vision of a future paradise that will grow organically out of her immediate life and will - so she hopes - be attainable some later day, on the other hand she discovers the power of memory, which, as Fromm (1977:82) points out, 'can not only venture everywhere and range through the past as though in the present, but can also retrieve the past and give it shape as well as permanence.' With this discovery time loses its limitations, the abyss of death can be bridged and former moments of happiness are mentally accessible again. Therefore, though the paradise of her childhood is already present in the first three novel-chapters in various recollections, to which Dorothy Richardson also attached significance (cf. Staley 40), it now assumes an even bigger importance in the unfolding of Miriam's individual identity. Though it is lost for ever according to the laws of exterior time, this paradise is present in the time-free spaces of memory; *because* it is lost, as Bachelard says, it can be relived all the more intensely on a more profound level of reality, forming an essential part of her being: 'Il faut perdre le paradis terrestre pour y vraiment vivre, pour le vivre dans la réalité des images, dans la sublimation absolue qui transcende toute passion' (47). In the continuous flux of life Miriam's childhood paradise becomes the lasting source for her awareness of the stable, unchanging existence of her innermost, individual self.

2.4.1 'The First Thing She Could Remember:' Miriam's Childhood Paradise

> The sun shone. The polished green blades of grass glittered. The gravel walk and the nasturtium bed together made a broad orange blaze. Specks like glass sparkled in the hot grey earth. On the grey flagstone the red poppy you picked yesterday was a black thread, a purple stain.
>
> She was happy sitting on the grass, drawing the fine sharp blades between her fingers, sniffing the smell of the mignorette that tingled like sweet pepper, opening and shutting the yellow mouths of the snap-dragon.
>
> The garden flowers stood still, straight up in the grey earth. They were as tall as you were. You could look at them for a long time without being tired.
>
> (May Sinclair, *Mary Olivier: A Life* 16)

> All the six years at Babington were that blazing alley of flowers without beginning or end, no winters, no times of day or changes to be seen. There were other memories [...], but all mixed with sadness and pain and bothers with people. They did not come first, or without thought. The blazing alley came first without thought or effort of memory (*TU*, 213f.).

Both Miriam's recurrent contemplation of real gardens and her fantasies about improbable paradises owe their strong appeal to the echoes they contain of what is possibly the most powerful and most consistent image in the whole of *Pilgrimage*: Miriam's childhood garden at Babington forms a reliable point of reference in all her later garden experiences. The concept of this garden, site of her earliest memory, pervades most novel chapters in explicit recallings of its beauty as well as implicit allusions and thus underlines the importance Dorothy Richardson attributes to childhood and its effect on later life.

As Ellen Moers (26) writes, 'childhood is where the self is created, in the female as in the male sex;' it is the formative period of life, in which the 'unchanging centre' of one's being evolves and is perceived as identity. Once this sense of the self has established itself, the individual as a being capable of thinking and organizing his or her sensory impressions is born. This 'beginning of the subject as a separate being' (Radford 1991:119), the 'birth' of consciousness from a pre-conscious life into the self, however, cannot at the time of its event be rationally grasped, just like the physical birth. Only later, when the sense of memory and the awareness of an individual past has developed, the individual on the search for his or her origin comes to a boundary, a point he or she fixes as the first moment of self-awareness. Hence, it is only in retrospective, in the searching of the memory, that this 'birth-date' is established. With Alice James we might ask ourselves:

> What determines the *selection* of memory, why does one childish experience or impression stand out as luminous and solid against the, for the most part, vague and misty background? The things we remember have a *first-timeness* about them which suggests that they may be the reason of their survival (127f.; emphasis added).

Why it is not possible to transcend this starting point of consciousness and retrace one's development right back to the physical birth is of less interest here than the question of how exactly this point evolved as the first memory of self-awareness. It seems to grow out of a subconscious clinging to one specific moment in early life, to some noteworthy incident, that later on is defined as the first one to remember.

Defining Miriam's solitary strolling through the parental garden, her awareness of herself in communion with nature as the starting point of her conscious life, Dorothy Richardson takes up the Wordsworthian tradition of cultivating the notion of a physically existing, natural childhood paradise:

> She tried to remember when the strange independent joy had begun, and thought she could trace it back to a morning in the garden at Babington, the first thing she could remember, when she had found herself toddling alone along the garden path between beds of flowers almost on a level with her head and blazing in the sunlight. Bees with large bodies were sailing heavily across the path from bed to bed, passing close by her head and making a loud humming in the air. She could see the flowers distinctly as she walked quickly back through the afternoon throng on the esplanade; they were sweet williams and 'everlasting' flowers, the sweet williams smelling very strongly sweet in her nostrils, and one sheeny brown everlasting flower that she had touched with her nose, smelling like hot paper (*BW*, 316f.).

In what we might call a primacy effect,[60] this first experience is present in an astonishingly clear set of visual, acoustic, olfactory and tactile impressions. Similar to Mary Olivier's direct sensory experience in her solitary garden of childhood, these first impressions of her natural surroundings initiate her not just to the world but to a world of fecund beauty.[61] The child's acts of

[60] Though there are a lot of other childhood memories scattered over the pages (e.g. *TU*, 213f), they never assume an intensity comparable to this first memory .

[61] Hanscombe (1982:80) sees this fecundity expanded to human sexuality when she recognizes the flowers and bees as 'stock sexual symbols of childhood;' the flowers possibly representing female receptivity, the bees male energy.

seeing, hearing and smelling, which the adult Miriam re-experiences in almost the same immediacy through the power of her memory, are remembered in details which Dorothy Richardson underlines in her choice of intensifying adjectives: flowers are *blazing*, the humming of the bees is *loud*, the sweet williams are *strongly sweet*. The paragraph thus reflects the little girl's keen sensory awareness of her surroundings, her complete immersion into one moment of being, as the necessary precondition and foundation of Miriam's later concept of a natural childhood paradise; the ability of the young adult's memory to recreate the opening scene of her self-awareness in such details then forms the second step on her way to a heightened sense of self-insight.[62]

Miriam's first memory thus resembles Wordsworth's recalled childhood scenes in *The Prelude* or in the 'Ode: Intimations of Immortality from the Recollections of Early Childhood.' What Wordsworth expressed so magnificently in his poems also forms the basis of Dorothy Richardson's prose: the awakening of a self-consciousness that in pure subjectivity explores its inner world as well as the outer, grows aware of herself, and then, consequently, of her surroundings. In the recollections of childhood Dorothy Richardson's *alter ego* Miriam enjoys herself and her observations of nature just as much as does Wordsworth's poetical 'I'. Sharing his belief

---

[62] Edna Pontellier, the heroine of Kate Chopin's *The Awakening*, remembers a very similar scene as the first point of her awareness of her individual self: 'The hot wind beating in my face made me think [...] of a summer day in Kentucky, of a meadow that seemed as big as an ocean to the very little girl walking through the grass, which was higher than the waist. [...] I was just walking diagonally across a big field. My sunbonnet obstructed the view. I could see only the stretch of green before me, and I felt as if I must walk on forever, without coming to the end of it. I don't remember whether I was frightened or pleased. I must have been entertained. [...] Sometimes I feel this summer as if I were walking through the green meadow again, idly, aimlessly, unthinking and unguided' (31f.).

Summer, nature, solitude and the feeling of unlimited walking fill both memories; for both women their recollections assume an almost physical presence in their mind as they form the foundation of their developing self-awareness. Telling other women (Amabel and Mme Ratignolle respectively) about their primary memory, both Miriam and Edna experience a gradual awakening and an ensuing liberation towards their true selves. However, depicting Edna's struggle with social constrictions, Chopin goes much further than Dorothy Richardson: The ultimate consequence of the complete acknowledgement of Edna's awakening to her self, which is incompatible with the demands of society, lies in death. On the point of drowning, this same childhood scene then accompanies Edna, organically completing the circle of her life: She was 'thinking of the blue grass meadow that she had traversed when a little child, believing that it had no beginning and no end. [...] There was the hum of bees, and the musky odor of pinks filled the air' (221). This childhood memory, pointedly present in its recollection of visual, auditory and olfactory sense impressions, fills Edna with a light serenity that lifts the fears and sorrows of life. Only at the moment of dying does she thus retrieve the 'unthinking' innocence of childhood, the once lost state of Edenic bliss.

in the 'restorative power of nature' (Legouis 100) as well as in the intense cultivation of the senses she expresses this idea throughout *Pilgrimage*.

The 'authentic' experience of her earliest childhood recollection,[63] the symbolical garden scene at Babington, is stored in Miriam's memory in an intensity that - after forming a first sense of self - defines her self as unvarying, whenever she recalls the scene. The child's absorption in a momentary situation has the same effect on her after-life as it has on Wordsworth's:

> But for those first affections,
> Those shadowy recollections,
> Which, be they what they may,
> Are yet the fountain light of all our day,
> And yet a master light of all our seeing.
> ('Ode: Intimations of Immortality,' ll. 149 - 153)

Every time Miriam recalls this 'bee moment,' this earliest communion with other creatures, she seems to draw water from this 'fountain,' finding an affirmation of her questioned self. Though a thing of the past, it becomes in Miriam's mind part of her immediate present: 'The moment she had just lived was the same, it was exactly the *same* as the first one she could remember' (*TU*, 213). The first memory thus becomes a constant point of reference, her infant power of experiencing nature becomes the ideal of all her later views and visions. Like Wordsworth's 'vanishings' ('Ode' l.144), the end of the perfect - because unrecognized - union of the self with nature, with the natural universe, and the beginning of an assertion of 'outward things' ('Ode' l.143; cf. Trilling 147f.), Miriam's first recollection marks the entry into the world of consciousness, which, however, bans her from the original paradise of innocence. The 'Heaven [that] lies about us in our infancy,' ('Ode' l.66) is lost as soon as it is perceived as such, only its beauty is remembered.

Miriam's memory of 'the morning sunlight, that smelt of the flowers and was one with them and me' (*DLH*, 243) calls up this perfect union with nature, from which, however, she is severed at the same time: 'the strange *independent* joy' of being began with this awareness of her immersion in nature in the Babington garden (*BW*, 316). Just as Wordsworth's loss of childhood paradise is balanced by a gain of understanding of the self,[64] so is

---

[63] cf. Hanscombe 1982:71. She calls it 'her first intense experience,' which is not quite adequate: it is her first experience *consciously remembered.*

[64] *The Prelude* (1850), 465: In Book 14, ll. 112-116, he talks about minds filled with poetic imagination:

> 'Such minds are truly from the Deity,
> For they are Powers; and hence the highest bliss
> That flesh can know is theirs - the consciousness
> Of Whom they are, habitually infused
> Through every image and through every thought[...].'

Miriam's loss of innocence turned into her individual 'fortunate fall' into a life of rich experience and deeper self-understanding.[65] Miriam's ideal of an earthly paradise after the loss of her childhood innocence is eventually perceived in those moments of insight and illumination when she experiences a profound happiness. They are moments that re-create the original feeling of being 'untouched by anything, free' to such perfection that they assume paradise qualities, too. Though she experiences the bliss of paradisal timelessness, she is also aware of its precariousness and grieves for its loss: as a child she thought 'that the world had just begun and would always be like that' but she also feared that this moment 'would be the last, and had clung to it with wide desperate staring eyes until tears came and she had turned away from some great open scene, with a strong conscious body flooded suddenly by a strong warm tide, to the sad dark world to live for the rest of her time upon a memory' (*TU*, 213).

Miriam's perception of a paradise within the mental spaces of her memory thus can be read as a literal interpretation of what Christ says about the kingdom of God, the eternal paradise: 'There will be no saying "Look, here it is!" or "there it is;" for in fact the Kingdom of God is within you' (Lk 17, 21). This Biblical word denies the localisation of a place of perfection in the world and asks for a mystical inward turn of the mind. It is not in the riches of the world nor in social recognition that this state of transcendental bliss can be found, but only in the full recognition of one's inner being. With the repetition of this Biblical verse throughout *Pilgrimage*, Dorothy Richardson underlines the religious, or spiritual, dimension of Miriam's paradise concept. Not only in the Romantic union with nature, but also in a mystical *inner* enlightenment can Miriam find her individual paradise. Hence, her pilgrimage through life is based both on her Romantic idea of an original childhood paradise stored in her memory and on her Bible-founded spiritual search for a future paradise that she would likewise reach within her life. The recurrent allusions to this Biblical paradise to come then are primarily to be understood as signposts towards a realm of personal bliss on this side of death, rather than as an orthodox Christian expectation of eternal happiness after death; for Miriam's mystical tendencies, her intense awareness of the passing moment and her profound love of life in its joy and beauty, are all directed towards the completion of a future paradise *on earth.*

Miriam's repeated recalling of the Babington garden helps her - and the reader - to keep this original paradise in mind. Although she knows that the

---

So, for him the highest bliss lies in the recognition of one's origins, inducing a heightened self-awareness.

[65] Whereas Milton's Fortunate Fall at the end of *Paradise Lost* leads to Man's search for a paradise within himself, Miriam follows Man's way on an extremely subjective, if not egotistical level. She in the end is only concerned with her own spiritual 'salvation.'

real moment in the garden belongs to the past for good,[66] she conceives of it as a lasting possession. This temporal paradox again recalls Wordsworth's idea, even in details of setting:

> Though nothing can bring back the hour
> Of splendour in the grass, of glory in the flower;
> We will grieve not, rather find
> Strength in what remains behind;
> In the primal sympathy
> Which having been must ever be. ('Ode' ll.178-183)

While Wordsworth manages to retain the positive nature experience and perpetuate it in his mind, Miriam does the same in constantly recalling her first memory, which then becomes part of and enriches her present situation. In her old age Dorothy Richardson expressed this belief in the indestructibility of one's earlier experience in a letter to John Cowper Powys:

> 'Tout passe, tout lasse, tout casse.' *No*, Mr neatly logical Frenchman and the wistfuller poets of all nations: Youthful confusion of brevity with disappearance. For these moments *announce*, even as they pass, their immortality. Pass into consciousness, never into nothingness. Are dividends paid out from invested capital, on which we may live when everything *seems* taken away (28. 6. 1948; *WM*, 586; emphasis original).

Miriam's memories provide a vital source of energy, too: the flowers and bees of her earliest childhood are not only *present* in her solitude, they also convey a vision of a 'marvellous scene' opening up 'beyond the world of daily life' (*DL*, 198). The power of the past, the strength of that 'primal sympathy' even transcends her immediate present and shows her the visionary 'bourne' of a future paradise.

> The open scene, that seemed at once without her and within, beckoned and claimed her, extending for ever, without horizons, bringing to her contemplating eye a moving expansion of sight ahead and ahead, earth and sky left behind, across flower-spread plains whose light was purer and brighter than the light of day. Here was the path of advance. But pursuing it, she must be always alone (*DL*, 198).

Transcending the limits of space, time and personality this grandiose vision, full of otherworldly qualities, seems, as Staley says, to be 'taking death aforehand' (30). However, seen as an expansion of her childhood memory, of a real event of her past, this heavenly abode, 'extending for ever' beyond

---

[66] cf. *DL*, 197: 'Far away in the distance [...] was the summer morning of her infancy.'

the border of death is to be read also as a 'memory' of a (far) future, an anticipation of an equally real scene in Miriam's earthly life.[67] The 'path of advance' should eventually lead to a mystical union with nature that even outdoes her immersion in it in the Babington garden.[68]

Flowers, images of innocence, which surrounded her in the childhood garden and fill her with happiness each time she recalls them,[69] accompany her vision of mystical fulfilment. Not seeing 'any end to being in the bright sun between the blazing flowers' (*TU*, 213) of Babington, she now equally sees the bright scene 'extending for ever.' In this vision of a hoped-for future happiness, which contains the characteristic images of her childhood memory, Miriam's longing, her *cri de coeur* for the innocence and happiness of childhood becomes obvious; the extension of her past experience onto a vision of a world to come expresses her nostalgia for the little world of perfection, 'which having been must ever be' - not only as a living memory but as a really existing, sensorily perceptible place. When Proust claims that 'le souvenir d'une certaine image n'est que le regret d'un certain instant, [parce que] la réalité que j'avais connue n'existait plus' (300f.), Dorothy Richardson at once transforms this regret about the lost past into a form of anticipated joy, the joy of retrieving it by means of her firm belief in the lasting existence of this early experience. That is why Miriam's 'bee memory' rings with untroubled happiness; it is eventually also the reason why Miriam on her pilgrimage through life never gives up her hope to reach some form of such a paradise again.[70]

---

67 In *Villette* we find this same - Bible-based - idea of an original state of bliss and a happiness to come: Yet Lucy's realism, so often a model for Miriam, appears as a sharp contrast to Miriam's mystical elation: facing the sobering voice of Reason in a similar situation, Lucy forces herself to stay on the ground of reality: 'My mind [...] made for itself some important rules, prohibiting under deadly penalties all weak retrospect of happiness past; commanding a patient journeying through the wilderness of the present [...] hushing the impulse to fond idolatry, checking the longing outlook for a far-off pro-mised land whose rivers are, perhaps, never to be reached save in dying dreams, whose sweet pastures are to be viewed but from the desolate and sepulchral summit of a Nebo' (292).

68 This original, clearly remembered 'unio mystica' of the child with nature is expressed in Miriam's disclosing her secret past to Amabel: 'I was back in the moment of seeing for the first time those flowerbeds and banks of flowers blazing in the morning sunlight, that smelt of the flowers *and was one with them and me*' (*DLH*, 243; emphasis added).

69 cf. *TU*, 214. 'The blazing alley came first without thought or effort of memory. The flowers all shining separate and distinct and all together, indistinct in a blaze. She gazed at them . . . sweet-williams of many hues, everlasting flowers, gold and yellow and brown and brownish purple, pinks and petunias and garden daisies white and deep crimson . . . then *memory* was happiness, one happiness linked to the next.'

70 When Dorothy Richardson suggests this retrievability of Miriam's childhood paradise through the power of memory and imagination, and the continuous existence of

2.4.2 'At the Edge of the World:' On the Way to Paradise

> Mean while the Mind, from pleasures less,
> Withdraws into its happiness:
> The Mind, that Ocean where each kind
> Does streight its own resemblance find;
> Yet it creates, transcending these,
> Far other Worlds, and other Seas;
> Annihilating all that's made
> To a green Thought in a green Shade.
> (Andrew Marvell, 'The Garden' VI, *Poems* 49f.)

> The mile of gently rising roadway leading to the Heath was overarched by huge trees. Shadowy orchards, and the silent sunlit outlying meadows and parkland of a large estate, streamed gently by them beyond the trees as they strode along through the cool leaf-scented air.They strode speechlessly ahead as if on a pilgrimage, keeping step. [...] The question of talk or no talk had definitely decided itself, the challenge of the light was silenced and the shaded roadway led on to paradise. Was there anyone anywhere who saw it as she did? (*BW*, 298)

The paradisiac freedom in nature that Miriam tasted in Oberland together with her resolution not to continue her intimate, but limiting male relationships and the feeling of having spent ten long years in a monotonous job turn her vague thoughts about a future green solitude into an urgent wish to be realized at all costs. When she sees her past as 'a long journey in a world of illusion' (*CH*, 296) and her present as 'life stripped bare before her and all its charm departed' (*CH*, 297), the 'discovery of some new way of being' (*CH*, 297) that would eventually make her happy becomes her primary task. In a visionary moment she experiences a spiritual re-birth, which Rose in a comparison of garden and womb aptly describes as 'the birth-thrust into the self' (1969:375). This deep self-realization shows to her 'opening inward eye' (*CH*, 299) the possibility of an inspired future: She caught a glimpse

---

it within the mind, she strongly differs from George Eliot, who - also working with the image of childhood paradise - sees Tom and Maggie Tulliver after their father's stroke entering 'the thorny wilderness, and the golden gates of childhood had for ever closed behind them' (*The Mill on the Floss* 270).

To George Eliot, who depicts life from a far less individual and more socio-realistic point of view than Dorothy Richardson, the outer influences of life, the drama of social involvement, forbid any longing for, or hoping to retrieve, a state of innocent perfection. Too much has been damaged in Maggie's life. Entering adult life with its moral and social weaknesses and failures, she cannot return to the paradisiac innocence of childhood.

> of a gap in a low hedge, between two dewy lawns, through which she could see the features of some forgotten scene, the last of a fading twilight upon the gloomy leaves of dark, clustered bushes and, further off, its friendly glimmer upon massive tree-trunks, and wondered, as the scene vanished, why the realization of a garden as a gatherer of growing darkness should be so deeply satisfying, and why these shadowy shrubs and trees should move her to imagine them as they would be in morning light (*CH*, 299).

The gap in the hedge, a natural gateway, allows Miriam in her literal 'profanity'[71] (*CH*, 299) to see her self evolve into a non-temporal sanctuary of natural beauty where a future 'morning' more brilliant than her present situation would receive her. The garden of her mind is such a strong image because it 'gathers' all the really existing gardens of the past, shows her 'some forgotten scene' lying in the near-darkness of the past. It is an image of her own soul, long ago defined as an 'endless garden' (*HC*,425), which she calls 'the changeless central zone of her being' (*CH*, 299): it expands out of its limitation to the present far into the past and into the future. Dorothy Richardson continues to play on her closely intertwined notions of exterior and interior reality, of view and vision, of world and self, one feeding the other and revealing its full meaning only in their complementary interplay; for this symbol of her soul, waking to the 'final unfolding of the consciousness,' (Rose 1969:375) shows traces of a realistic, seizable 'worldly' future too, that Miriam now strives to attain. It is the visionary glimpse of 'twilight, trees and flowers, the first inhabitants of a future into which, until this moment, she had cast no investigating glance' (*CH*, 300). Now Hypo's green solitude, a *real* lonely place in nature which would correspond to this *imagined* garden, becomes the focus of her thoughts about her future.[72]

Her decision to break away from her old friends, to give up her job and seek a personally satisfying future, however, is accompanied by the pain of parting and a growing sense of isolation: 'And now she was for ever excluded from that world [of Hypo], and the world she had entered was closing against her and the one she had inhabited with Amabel was breaking up. Ahead, nothing was visible' (*CH*, 365). The experience of nothingness, of the 'clear horizon' of the title that for the time being proposes no new target, marks another turning point in her life; it makes her aware of the social vacuum she has brought herself into and thus serves as a starting point for her renewed search for a spiritually and socially fulfilled life. Out of this 'spiritual panic' (*CH*, 366) Miriam creates a vision of an earthly paradise that should guide her to her place in solitary nature:

---

[71] profanum = literally: 'outside, in front of a temple or a sacred precinct' (cf. *OED* XII 570).

[72] cf. Chapter 2.3.3

> All these weeks [this image] had accompanied her, filling every background, richly reflected into the inner twilight of her being: vast echoing woodlands, their green alleys and sunlit clearings traversed by streams with flower banks and, in between, green open country, unfenced and uninhabited, beneath high blue skies (*DH*, 413f).

This 'green Thought' (Marvell 50), anticipating an 'ocean of beatitude' (*DH*, 408), is full of Edenic details: with sunlight, trees and the sky Dorothy Richardson combines the three 'paradise' colours gold, green and blue, and she sustains the idea of Eden with the presence of water and flowers and the absence of people.[73] Such a place, however, is hard to find in reality. Miriam's epiphanic happiness in the beauty of nature so far has come unasked. When she now tries to find a real equivalent to her mental image, she is met with the 'chastening realization' of a 'dismal' 'dulled' 'grey' landscape (*DH*, 414), in which she only gradually manages to perceive some Edenic features. In a first, promising communion with trees seen at a distance she opens 'the depths of her, [...] unchanged [...] since childhood' (*DH*, 413) for she is 'for the first time since childhood [...] alone with summer trees.' In contrasting these trees to the ordinary 'impersonal' London trees of all the past years Dorothy Richardson underlines Miriam's efforts to link the present with the enchanted past of her childhood where she understood the 'secrets' of the trees.[74] It is a 'magic angle at the edge of the world', very close to the much loved seaside of her childhood, that now provides some sort of

---

[73] These very colours are mentioned in a description of a summer excursion in *Revolving Lights*, where they are also associated with Edenic perfection: 'Before each pair of eyes, cleared of heat and dust by the balm of the evening air, the picture of the English summer, in blue and gold and green, stood clear within the outspread invisible distances.*That* was the harvest [...] that remained afterwards for ever' (*RL*, 271f.).

It is noteworthy that Charlotte Brontë presents a similar picture in *Villette,* which even uses the same colours to express Lucy Snowe's personal retrieval of happiness:

'Conceive a dell, deep-hollowed in forest secresy; it lies in dimness and mist: its turf is dank, its herbage pale and humid. A storm or an axe makes a wide gap amongst the oak-trees; the breeze sweeps in; the sun looks down; the sad, cold dell becomes a deep cup of lustre; high summer pours her blue glory and her golden light out of that beauteous sky, which till now the starved hollow never saw.

A new creed became mine - a belief in happiness.' (Vol. II, 1)

[74] In this communion with the trees on the horizon Miriam seems to anticipate a discovery soon to be made when reading about Emerson's relationship with nature: 'In the tranquil landscape, and especially in the distant line on the horizon, man be-holds somewhat as beautiful as his own nature. The greatest delight which the fields and woods minister, is the suggestion of an occult relation betweeen man and the vegetable. I am not alone and unacknowledged. They nod to me and I nod to them' ('Nature', 1983:10f.).

Miriam thus unconsciously paraphrases Emerson's idea *before* reading him; this accounts for her rapturous delight when actually reading his words and finding her own viewpoint so well expressed.

enchantment taking her from 'the other side of eternity' (*DH*, 415) into an apparently endless solitude - the August holiday makers being still a few weeks away.

Unlike her earlier illuminations, it is this feeling of solitude alone - amidst a landscape 'at first so desolate and so unknown' (*DH*, 415) - and not the impact of a *beautiful* landscape that inspires her to read in the open an unnamed book on Emerson. This reading triggers a mystical ecstasy, an unprecedented illumination of the mind that finds its perceptible counterpart in nature, in the radiant shadowless sunlight above the trees. It is an Emersonian intuitive perception of Christ's word 'within,' as in 'The Kingdom of Heaven is *within* you,' quoted and thought about much earlier in *Honeycomb* (458);[75] this is a word that 'in a context that had not prepared her for its coming' (*DH*, 420) Emerson uses in his 'Essay on Self-Reliance': 'for God is here within' (*Essays* 272).[76] Miriam's experience is a pure example of Emerson's transcendental thought, an asserting of her mind's ability to transcend the world of mere sense experience and objects and to become conscious of a higher, all-pervading spirit existing within her self.

Miriam's *mind* rather than her senses inspired by the 'familiar quotation' is first seized by this ecstasy as she understands this sentence at once, while her sensory awareness, her illuminated glance at 'the patch of bright colour in golden light' (*DH*, 420), is only the confirmation of her preceding mental experience. It is one of Dorothy Richardson's rare 're-active' nature illuminations in which the contemplation of the scenery confirms rather than causes an elevated moment of bliss.

At this moment she not only *understands* the idea of God's presence within her self, but in the flashlike perception she *experiences* with mind and body, with 'all she knew and was' (*DH*, 420), this central truth of her own being: the 'long[...]forgotten' Biblical quotation, the meaning of which she at that time did not fully grasp, expresses what she unconsciously has been feeling before. Reading the sentence she experiences its true mystical meaning and recognizes her own spiritual power. This is a crucial turn of

---

75 Lk 17,20. In *Honeycomb* the sentence expresses the focus of her attention when reading Thomas à Kempis *Of the Imitation of Christ*, a book she got from the pious Miss Perne and which leaves her basically untouched. At that time she does not understand its mystic meaning and therefore ridicules its 'fretfulness' (458), its incomprehensible suggestion of getting 'the sense of God' in one's individual life. This resuming of a long-forgotten topic reveals something of Miriam's character growth (cf. Thomas à Kempis, Book II, 70).

76 In the same essay Emerson favours a life in the here and now, an idea that Miriam tries to apply to her own life, too: 'Man postpones or remembers; he does not live in the present, but with reverted eye laments the past, or, heedless of the riches that surround him, stands on tiptoe to foresee the future. He cannot be happy and strong until he too lives *with nature in the present*, above time' (270; emphasis added).

mind towards spirituality, a turn significantly underscored by Miriam's (extremely short) experience of nothingness: the shock-like perception leaves her 'emptied being' open to be filled by the rapture of the sight of the golden light on the trees. In this moment of knowledge, of *self*-knowledge,[77] she not only experiences an exterior, sensory assertion of the purely mental process but also comes to understand her *earlier* illuminative experiences in nature as transcendental moments of insight. Having 'seen the smile of God' (*DH*, 420) Miriam has reached a *unio mystica*, an Edenic re-union with God, which she at the point of her mother's death feared to have forsaken for ever.[78] Her present joy thus takes up the memory of an earlier, untroubled happiness - based on the feeling of being filled with God's presence[79] - and strives to extend it into the future: She 'looked thence into her mind and found there, bathed in its full light the far-off forgotten world from which she had fled and, with a last glance at the sunlit trees, turned to run and seek it there' (*DH*, 421).

Past and present are thus inspired by the light of knowledge, the trees in their recent association with childhood allude to this lost paradise of early bliss that Miriam now *turns* to find somewhere in the exterior world of the future. After a 'final' break from her London life,[80] guided by a vision of a place to share with 'the first of the new, heaven-lit humanity' (*DH*, 421), she eventually finds her way to the farm at Dimple Hill, where her senses perceive the Edenic beauty of her natural surroundings and where her re-awakened spirit finds a home in the little Quaker community.

---

[77] expressed in her relieved outburst: 'I know . . . At last I *know*' (*DH*, 420; emphasis original).

[78] Miriam quotes St Mark (9, 48): 'I am in eternity . . . where their worm dieth not and their fire is not quenched' without mentioning the place of eternity St Mark specifies - hell. This again is an allusion to the very last sentence of Isaiah (66,24), which - just as *Honeycomb* - concludes on a warning to all those sinners who are excluded from the new heavens and the new earth, who are forbidden to enter a future paradise. The notion of everlasting damnation that has overshadowed Miriam's life after her mother's suicide is lifted at last: what awaits her now, after her spiritual re-birth, is a 'transfigured earthly life' (*DH*, 421), hence a form of this new, paradisiac earth.

[79] This belief in God's omnipresence and goodness is expressed before her mother's death in an allusion to Psalm 139 (7-8): 'Where can I escape from thy spirit? Where can I flee from thy presence? If I climb up to heaven, thou art there; if I make my bed in Sheol (=hell), again I find thee.' Dorothy Richardson writes in *Honeycomb*, 386: '. . . in hell; thou art there also [...] that shows there is no eternal punishment.' It is an early trust in redemption which she then lost in the 'conflict of ideas' (*DH*, 420) following her mother's death and which she now, in the 'sly' smile of God seems to rediscover.

[80] Miriam gave her 'joyous blessing' (*DH*, 428) to Amabel's and Michael's engagement: 'With an almost audible snap, the last link parted that had held her to the past. Released, she could seek those to whom she belonged' (*DH*, 429).

2.4.3 'Piercing the Sky:' Trees of Paradise

And while those lofty poplars gently wave
Their tops, between them comes and goes a sky
Bright as the glimpses of eternity,
To saints accorded in their mortal hour.
(William Wordsworth, 'A Parsonage in Oxfordshire,'
Poetical Works, Volume 3, 41)

The poplars say:
Les yeux gris
Vont au paradis. (*TR*, 446)

Before focusing on Dimple Hill, a glance at the function of trees in *Pilgrimage* might help us to a more complete understanding of Miriam's personal paradise. Trees are obvious and indispensable features of Dorothy Richardson's gardens; they are often the most specified elements in her garden descriptions. Appearing in great variety in the various gardens of Miriam's life, they are often simply prominent parts of domesticated nature catching her eye. The undefined trees at Banbury Park, Newlands, in Sussex and at St John's Wood[81] as well as the innumerable trees she sees in various London parks show her open-eyed awareness of nature.[82] The 'life-breath of the trees' in London, daily companions in her Tansley Street room (*DLH*, 201), furthermore sustains her belief in the beauty of everyday existence. In some cases Miriam names the trees *en passant,*[83] but in a few instances a specific tree is noted for some special qualities. Thus, when she smells rather than sees the lime trees in Hanover and at Barnes her joy in life is heightened to reckless daring; it is under these lime trees that she becomes unfaithful to Ted.[84] Or the fruit trees of Babington, Barnes and Dimple Hill,[85] the three places most strongly associated with paradise, are mentioned as obvious signs of fecundity, as elements of life in the rich beauty of these gardens.

None of Miriam's gardens exists without trees. It is not surprising that 'twilight, trees and flowers' (*CH*, 300) are her wished-for companions in a future world. Both light and flowers, however, play a more dominant role,

---

[81] cf. *BW*, 191; *HC*, 363, 430; *DH*, 413; *MM*, 630.

[82] e.g. *TU,* 30 / 145: the huge trees of Endsleigh Gardens; *TU*, 217: tree-shaded Bloomsbury gardens; *IN*, 402: the summer trees of the park; *TR*, 445: the heavy, tinted trees of London; *CH*, 309: the leafless trees in the park as signs of spring.

[83] e.g. *PR*, 15: the may trees at Barnes; *PR*, 92: the almond tree at Hanover; *HC*, 474: laburnum and may trees blooming in gardens on the way to Waterloo Station; *TU*, 130: the pines at Hypo's; *DL,* 148: the copper beech; *DH*, 438: larch trees; *DH*, 450: elm trees.

[84] cf. *PR*, 124; *BW*, 200 / 218.

[85] cf. *PR*, 32: the peach trees; *BW*, 305: the apple-trees; *DH*, 518: the peach trees in the greenhouse.

for only these have the the memorability that makes them most easily visible when she recalls garden scenes of the past. As memory excludes superficial particulars in order to recall the essential, we seldom find trees in her recollections, whereas her looks back abound with flowers and images of light.

As Rose points out, Dorothy Richardson seems to rely on 'the impressionistic value of images, which function organically in her novel' (1969:370). Her imagery in most cases directly reflects Miriam's sensory impressions, the perceptions of the beauty of nature; she does not seem to attach any deeper symbolic meaning to it. Hence Rose denies the existence of 'organizing symbols' (1969:370). Yet there *are* two trees that are named again and again: the poplars and the chestnut tree do grow into consistently expanding symbols in the overall context of *Pilgrimage*.

The poplars, whose tall, vertical shape suggests a direct link between the earth and the sky, appear as signposts to heaven, as gateways to an earthly paradise.[86] Dorothy Richardson uses this traditional image of a gate to another world, already found in the *Odyssey*,[87] as a symbol that expands out of an almost unnoticed detail of simple visual perception.

On her first visit to Banbury Park Miriam's view from the window ends 'at a row of Spanish poplars' (*BW,* 189). The 'distant row of poplars' thus forms the outskirts of the small, old-fashioned world of the Pernes and marks the borderline to the open, modern world beyond. Miriam's immediate impression of enclosure at this place 'shut in by the poplars' (*BW,* 189) is intensified when she later on actually lives there. Then, however, the poplars, still at the margin of her living space, are no longer barriers *against* the world, but gateways *towards* an unknown world beyond. When reading the *Story of Adèle*, Miriam unwillingly leaves the fictional paradise of endless summer to return to the real shabbiness of North London. The first thing she perceives directly is the sun, blazing

> just above the gap in the avenue of poplars. A bright yellow pathway led up through the green of the public cricket ground, pierced the avenue of poplars and disappeared through the further greenery in a curve that was the beginning of its encirclement of the park lake' (*BW*, 228).

---

[86] e.g. *TU*, 231: 'Poplars shot up, drawing her eyes to run up their feathered slimness, and sweep to the top of the pointed plumes piercing the sky.'

[87] cf. *Odyssey*: Poplars were growing at the entrance to Hades where Odysseus entered. Circe advised him in the following way: 'But when in thy ship thou hast now crossed the stream of Oceanus, where is a level shore and the groves of Persephone - tall poplars and willows that shed their fruit - there do thou beach thy ship by the deep eddying Oceanus, but go thyself to the dank house of Hades' (Homer, *Odyssey*, Vol. 1; Book X, ll. 510ff., p. 381).

A mere glimpse of a hot summer afternoon? A close description of the route of a path through a park to set the scene for Miss Jenny Perne's appearance? On a first reading it is not taken for more than its mere 'impressionistic value;' its deeper meaning is only revealed when we come across the same poplars later on again: Recalling the 'strange independent joy' (*BW*, 316) within herself, of her earliest childhood memory in the Babington garden, Miriam realizes that this secret of innermost happiness even at Banbury Park - where she lives in the 'backwater' of life - 'though it could never come out and surround her, [...] was never far off. It lurked just beyond the poplars in the park, at the end of the little empty garden at twilight [...]' (*BW*, 318). The trees are thus connected to her childhood paradise of happiness, whose secret still exists '*beyond the poplars*,' in a world she for the time being is separated from. It is a short first hint at this other, ideal, world; each time, however, Miriam comes across these poplars again, their importance increases as their symbolic meaning as gateways becomes more and more obvious. So she records her renewed encounter with the same trees:

> Les yeux gris vont au paradis. That was the two poplars, standing one each side of the little break in the railings, shooting up; the space between them shaped by their shapes, leading somewhere. I *must* have been through there; it's the park. I don't remember. It isn't. It's waiting. One day I will go through. Les yeux gris, vont au paradis (*TU*, 256).

Miriam's stream of thought starts at the automatically recalled little French verse, and then seems to shift haphazardly on to the visual impression of the trees and the park behind. At this point their meaning deepens as they appear as gates to an unknown future world. Their symbolic power, implicitly present already in the first poplar scene in the paradise tricolour - gold (of the sun), green (of the park), and blue (of the lake or sky) -, becomes explicit and finds its confirmation in the repetition of the verse at the end. When Miriam passes the same spot at the edge of the park years later, the trees themselves then speak the very words again, reminding her of this other world:

> But this opening, with its view of the short broad path, belongs to no one. The sight of it is always a stepping forward into nowhere with eyes on the low fence at the end, the gap, the two poplars pluming up on either side, making it a stately portal to the green expanses beyond.
>
> The poplars say:
>
> Les yeux gris
> Vont au paradis.
>
> And the picture remains after the high railings have come back again. Its message brings more light than there is into the thickets of

> shrubs and bushes, and takes the suggestion of sadness from the stretches of grass dulled even in sunlight by the thick autumn air.
> *Les yeux gris*; in spring and autumn (*TR*, 446).

The two poplars now not only form the explicit 'portal' to an unknown world but actively invite grey-eyed Miriam to enter a paradise suggesting light and happiness. Though the choice of words underlines the sensory act of seeing,[88] the concrete moment of perceiving this portal is short. What is more important is Miriam's own interpretation of this view, her idea of the promising existence of such a future place of bliss almost within her reach. The visible path on the other side of the gate suggests some form of progress 'into nowhere;' held in the trap of Miss Holland's stifling companionship, Miriam seems to recognize that another step into an experience of nothingness might reveal to her a lasting life of 'serenity' (*TR*, 445) on the other side. This portal of poplars belonging 'to no one' invites her *alone* to dare enter this new world. Miriam soon after translates this abstract idea into reality when travelling *alone* to Oberland to find her 'winter paradise' (*O*, 98).

As Humphrey points out, Dorothy Richardson's imagery at first sight is 'concrete, not abstract; and it is reflective, not dramatic' (78). Looking at Miriam's overall development, however, we perceive that often behind the concrete visual image an abstract meaning is hidden: the tall trees refer to a world transcending Miriam's immediate surroundings, a future world that is better than her present one. The image of the trees forming a natural portal becomes one of several symbols in *Pilgrimage* for the entrance to a paradise where a better life is promised.[89] Does Miriam ever go through this poplar gate? Does she ever enter this unknown world beyond the trees?

At Dimple Hill, in a world of its own, she will experience a profound happiness that indeed appears to be of another world. Entering through the unassuming, white five-barred gate (*DH*, 433) she thus finds herself within the unknown promised land. Exploring its grounds, Miriam soon discovers 'a row of Dutch poplars' standing 'on the edge of the wild [...] just within the fence' (*DH*, 465). As in the London park, the 'urbane' poplars mark the border-line between two worlds, the 'wild' outside world of topographical and spiritual flatness and the beautiful inner world abounding with fertile

[88] expressed in the words 'view,' 'sight,' 'eyes,' 'picture,' 'yeux,' 'sunlight.'

[89] 'Portals' as gateways to paradise appear in different forms throughout *Pilgrimage*, as metaphors of short-lived openings to a world she is, has been or will soon be excluded from: e.g. the 'secret sacred portal' of the gabled porch at Barnes brings her a 'moment in eternity' and makes her and Harriett realize the end of their childhood paradise 'as it slipped [...] away into the past, realizing that soon it would be inaccessible' (*MM*, 608). The portico of the Oberland hotel at the end of her long journey similarly suggests the gate to her winter paradise (*O*, 31), and the white gate at Dimple Hill opens up to admit her to a paradisiac summer world (*DH*, 433).

profusion. Now, however, she looks at these poplars from the inner side; her 'grey eyes' have reached her paradise, a 'temple undesecrated by the presence of the implements of toil,' a 'refreshing harbour of the mind' (*DH*, 464), an Edenic garden of well-tended order.[90]

Showing the trees from this other, inner, side as well, Dorothy Richardson confirms the increasing symbolic power of the poplar imagery. What first appeared as a casual impression accumulates meaning with each new occurrence. Thus, the image expands to a symbol that helps to give some structure to the overbulging text; though not always consistently worked out, it hints at some 'deeper', reflective meaning of Miriam's flow of thoughts.

The other tree to assume a deeper symbolic function in *Pilgrimage* is the chestnut tree. Unlike the poplars, which are set in pairs or rows, it always appears as a single tree with its individual attraction. In its blooming beauty and huge power it oozes with life, and, being planted at the centre of a garden, becomes the image of an Edenic Tree of Life.[91]

On her arrival at Hanover, Miriam perceives the chestnut tree as the only living object in the 'gravelled' garden of Waldstrasse (*PR*, 52): it is a plant whose 'great bulging brown-varnished buds [...] shining whitely from each twig' (*PR*, 53) announce the reawakened natural life of spring. Later, when she observes the change from 'the young chestnut leaves drooping in tight pleats from black twigs' (*PR*, 112) to the 'shadowy foliage' (*PR*, 140) of the

---

[90] cf. Boies 16: 'Eden is a garden of order. Outside is the thorn and the thistle. [...] Beyond Eden is an unweeded garden.'

[91] Although the chestnut tree never assumes the pervasive presence as a personal tree of life of the focal pear tree in Katherine Mansfield's short story 'Bliss', it might be interesting to juxtapose the two texts with regard to their tree imagery. Bertha, the heroine of 'Bliss', sees 'the lovely pear tree with its wide open blossoms as a symbol of her own life' (133), Miriam's chestnut similarly reflects the state of her own life; Miriam as well as Bertha find a refuge for their minds in the contemplation of the blooming tree; and just as Miriam perceives a deeper communion with other people in sharing the view of the garden and its trees, so does Bertha see her closeness to Miss Fulton confirmed when they together look out into the walled garden: 'And the two women stood side by side looking at the slender, flowering tree [...] How long did they stand there? Both, as it were, caught in that circle of unearthly light, understanding each other perfectly' (138).

Yet, despite these obvious thematic parallels, the two texts diverge to an extreme degree in structure, attitude, purpose and tone. In playful irony Katherine Mansfield keeps the tree symbol in its perfect peacefulness unchanged up to the last line of the story. Though Bertha's life has been shattered to its roots, though her rival, Miss Fulton, refers to the tree in trenchant callousness, the narrator calmly closes with: 'the pear tree was as lovely as ever and as full of flowers and as still' (141). She thus in an apparently light tone radically questions the self-defined identification of the heroine with her tree of life and foregrounds the fragility of 'bliss' as a state of the human soul, while Dorothy Richardson, lacking Katherine Mansfield's ironic detachment, uses the tree image as an unambiguous, straightforward element, solidly supporting Miriam's continual striving for happiness, for lasting 'bliss' (cf. 'Bliss', Mansfield 1991:129-141).

midsummer tree, the growth of its leaves not only comments on the progress of the year but also reflects Miriam's personal progress, her swift growth in life towards a first, though precarious, sense of independence and adulthood. The tree is constantly and reassuringly present in her life at Waldstrasse, visible or audible from table and from her bedroom (*PR*, 140 / 148); in its unobtrusive omnipresence it is her partner in nature. What in later novel-chapters assumes a more explicit importance is here at least hinted at: her tree of life is a first object of nature to form a protective and regenerative counterpoise to her often not very fulfilling social involvements. Thus, 'sitting about under the chestnut tree' (*PR*, 132), she recovers strength, enjoying her own private life in the shadowy stillness of hot summer days, which frees her from the - at times - burdensome task of conversing in English with the German girls.

Miriam experiences the same life-restoring force when she settles in a deckchair in the garden of Dimple Hill: the huge chestnut tree

> made of this corner of the lawn a retreat, its sturdy trunk between her and the backward immensity, its wide branches a roof beneath the towering heights of the sky and an irregular crescent of shadow upon the invading sunlight (*DH*, 442).

The tree, beneath which she spends 'a part of almost every morning' (*DH*, 535) conveys the feeling of protected solitude, providing a sheltering space as well as time to contemplate her life in the silence of the garden, where 'memory vanished and her lonely purpose [to write] filled all the future' (*DH*, 520). The chestnut temporarily becomes the centre of her life, the centre of her earthly paradise, hence her tree of life. Its huge greenness suggesting longevity and vitality furthermore hints at the notion of Edenic everlastingness. The impact of the chestnut, unrivalled even by the similarly huge sycamore and larch trees at Dimple Hill, thus is a decisive factor in Miriam's experience of the farm as her Garden of Eden.[92]

---

[92] We might, however less convincingly, identify the evergreen oak, standing opposite the chestnut on the front side of the house, this 'most queer tree' (*DH*, 531), as Miriam's tree of knowledge: After Richard explained to her the peculiarities of this tree Miriam feels entitled to live at Dimple Hill no longer as a paying guest, as this 'wealth of knowledge qualifying her to be [...] a faint shadow of the departed Richard' (*DH,* 532) seems to underline her position as a quasi-member of the Roscorla family. So, the knowledge about this tree initiates the closeness between Richard and Miriam that eventually leads to her 'expulsion' from paradise. Mrs Roscorla's wrath at their unauthorized tasting of the fruit of (purely platonic) intimacy grown after his explanatory tour of the garden makes her leave Dimple Hill. Yet even before Mrs Roscorla's verdict Miriam recognizes the incompatibility of an ongoing intimacy with Richard and a continued stay in the Quaker household. When Richard is away for a few days, Miriam's inner tension relaxes and she gets closest to the Quaker beliefs: 'Things had come so near. Even this dingy old evergreen oak, the least valued of her possessions, was

Even after leaving Dimple Hill, Miriam's ability to adjust to new surroundings is remarkable. The opening page of *March Moonlight* contains a further image of a chestnut tree in spring that in its 'varnished beauty' (*MM*, 555) suggests another new life opening to her. Here, Dorothy Richardson takes up the image of *Pointed Roofs*, where the budding tree promised a blooming life; recovering from flu at her sister Sally's, Miriam experiences the new start as a continuation of her stay in Switzerland with Jean, her new friend, who remains strangely enigmatic as she is consistently referred to in an indirect way only. Miriam seems to be establishing a new focus of interest that lies outside the here and now in the retrospective, written or visionary communion with Jean. Hence, her tree of life is at once connected with this non-present, mysterious reality of Jean's world:

> Now the chestnut tree has joined company, being a participant of mystery, with those bare larches opposite the *Lauriers* balcony where every afternoon I sat talking with Jean (*MM*, 556).

Her immediate life, represented by the growing chestnut tree, is more and more replaced by 'bare' recollections and recollections of recollections, almost unidentifiable hints and thoughts that empty the text of its life. The impressions of direct experience retreat as Miriam approaches the beginning of her writing career. Perhaps Dorothy Richardson's own difficulty as a writer is apparent here: living in a present that is very different from her past she tries to write about this past with the intensity of the immediate moment. Her successful concentration on the past time makes her neglect her present. Miriam's slow shift away from her present experience in *March Moonlight* thus marks a time of transition in her life. Though Dorothy Richardson argued for 'the desirability of substituting "life" direct, first-hand energizing experience, for interest in life, thinking and writing about life,'[93] she - and with her Miriam eventually as well - chose the indirect way of writing about life and thus to a large extent forsaking the immediacy of the *present* experience. If Dorothy Richardson in the first twelve volumes succeeded in conveying the sense of 'first-hand' experience, her last volume does not convince. Though there are still several impressions showing Miriam's awareness of the present,[94] their overall presentation lacks coherence and insight. Maybe Dorothy Richardson's death prevented a revision of the text that

---

individually beloved. Stretching up her arms to it in the last of the last twilight before his home-coming, she knew that she wished Richard would not return. Everything, since he left, had fallen to a new depth within her. Nothing disturbed this ceaseless communion' (*DH*, 539). The tree reveals to her her deeper wishes: Giving up Richard would entail an advancement in Quaker spirituality; it might grant her a lasting place at Dimple Hill; but as she still feels his strong appeal when he returns, she feels doomed to leave this place.

93 'Comments by a Layman,' reprinted in Hanscombe 1982:86.

94 e.g. her second stay at Dimple Hill: *MM*, 606-623.

would have filled it with more life. As we read *March Moonlight* now, Miriam's tree of life turned into the bare larches of Switzerland sees no other spring within the pages of *Pilgrimage*. Miriam the Writer's life has ceased to bloom.

2.4.4 'Perfection:' Paradise at Dimple Hill

> Not wholly in the busy world, nor quite
> Beyond it, blooms the garden that I love.
> (Alfred Lord Tennyson, 'The Gardener's Daughter,' l. 33f. *Poems I* 556)

> House, large garden, a unity, complete. (*DH*, 463)

When in 1938 *Dimple Hill* was published as the latest chapter of Dorothy Richardson's 12-volume *Pilgrimage*, it was commonly considered to be her last novel-chapter as it appeared in a first complete edition of this work.[95] Only in 1967, when *March Moonlight* was posthumously published, did it become clear to the reading public that Dorothy Richardson had intended to continue her life-work, to fill the gap in Miriam's life up to the point when she actually started writing about her own life, to bring the story full-circle. *March Moonlight* exists, a comparatively unpolished piece of writing, enigmatic, taking up and dropping all possible threads, but adding little to Miriam's inner and outer development. It underlines Dorothy Richardson's rejection of a linear narrative with a traditional conclusion and her concern with the continual flow of life rather than with 'the satisfaction of coming to an end' (Radford 1991:4). She in fact strongly declined to have *Pilgrimage* seen as completed: taking *Dimple Hill* for its last chapter would make it seem 'a *cul de sac* rather than a conclusion,' as too many things would not be resolved (Fromm 312); and yet the consistent quality of the twelve volumes published in her lifetime and various signs in *Dimple Hill* which express a certain finality might suggest that novel-chapter would have been a preferable conclusion to Miriam's life-tale.[96]

---

[95] *Dimple Hill* thus appeared in the new edition that was announced as 'the complete work of twelve parts, including one not hitherto published' (cf. Fromm 310).

[96] e.g. - *DH*, 546: 'Farewell, farewell to youth:' this important phase of her life, which started with her journey to Hanover comes to an end. The story of her youth is thus told.

- *DH*, 547: Michael and Amabel's wedding puts a definite and irrevocable end to Miriam's longstanding intimate relationship with both of them - and, indeed, they are but background figures in *March Moonlight*.

- *DH*, 549: Miriam sees Hypo for a last time on a train station - itself a place suggestive of finality and farewell - and ends their short conversation in a terminating 'Good-bye!' - Hypo is no longer actively present in *March Moonlight*.

Her retreat from the world of social and spatial enclosure in London, her successful escape into an Edenic place of freedom in nature would in a way echo more traditionally plotted novel endings, where the heroes turn away from the 'world' to a symbolic place of wisdom in order to find a final, all-enfolding communion with nature: Tess to Stonehenge, Stephen Wonham to Cadbury Rings, Birkin and Ursula to Sherwood Forest; Miriam to Dimple Hill? The places ringing with the presence of history and mythology give way to one that summarizes Miriam's personal history ringing with the completion of her individual nature experience.[97]

Bearing in mind that the novel-sequence does *not* end in the gardens of Dimple Hill but comes to a close in the city again, we can still read the garden and the outspreading landscape at Dimple Hill as the culmination of Miriam's garden experience; it is the place where many traits of earlier garden scenes are taken up and intensified and where the sheltered farmer community provides the stillness necessary for contemplation. It is also the place where her moments of illumination extend to an almost unbroken intense awareness of the beauty of her surroundings. Here her experiences of her childhood paradise are confirmed, here the never-ending beauty of the Garden of Eden, the equilibrium of protection and freedom in an atmosphere of pastoral fecundity appears as a reality. Dorothy Richardson's celebration of the agricultural life at the farm, where the Roscorlas' honest work is rewarded by abundant growth, hints at the tradition of Georgic literature that praises the Edenic simplicity of rural life (cf. McClung 48).[98] Giving them a hand now and then, Miriam actively participates in the farmers' life and sees this place with more inner involvement than a mere holiday-maker would.

Dimple Hill differs from other places of natural beauty also in that the appeal of the Quakers' spirituality exalts Miriam's own spirit, her mystical being rather than her intellectual awareness, to such a height that her sense of beauty is constantly stimulated. The spirit of reconciliation and unity of the Quaker household seems to spread out into the landscape so that the outer world of beauty expresses their inner state of harmony; the location of the house and gardens at the top of the hill open to all directions thus embodies their personal, social and religious freedom, which Miriam adopts at once.

---

[97] Dimple Hill itself is not without a historic-mythological background: In Richard Roscorla's allusion to Jack Cade, the local hero and rebel against the King, who walked on the ridge of the horizon 'nearly 500 years ago' (*DH*, 447; see also: 449, 484), the echo of the pride and fascination of the local population for their legendary hero is still audible.

[98] A case in point would be Richard Jefferies' *Amaryllis at the Fair* (first published 1887), a novel which not only lovingly describes life on a farm, but which in the person of Farmer Iden introduces a character not unlike Richard Roscorla in his strength, his love of work and especially in his careful tending of the beautiful walled garden 'with old English flowers and plants, herbs and trees. In summer time it was a glory to see: a place for a poet, a spot for a painter [...]' (104) - a place of almost Dimple Hill perfection.

As long as she senses the presence of an unspoken communion between her and the Roscorla family, 'a moment to moment building up of shared existence' (*MM*, 611) that might eventually make her a full member of this tiny society, Miriam sees her surroundings in Edenic beauty.

Each part of the garden contributes to this impression of an earthly paradise in displaying qualities known from earlier garden scenes or in recalling the Edenic gardens of her childhood. The little *walled* garden, seen in solitude on a Sunday, 'unthreatened today even by the passing footsteps of a worker, became one with the garden at Babington and the Barnes garden, both of them empty and, as they had always seemed on Sundays, a little aloof' (*DH*. 490). The enclosed, compact space providing a refuge from the everyday world of work opens her eyes to its otherworldly beauty and light:

> One saw the whole garden in a single eyeful and from all angles at once, because the part one was in, belonging to itself and seeming to throw one off, sent one's mind gliding over the whole, alighting nowhere. And it was at these times that all the different beauties were most apparent and most deeply bathed in unattainable light (*DH*, 490f.).

The 'ambivalent ontological status' (Waters 223) of this garden between the real and the other world becomes obvious in Miriam's awareness of the perfection of this picture-like scene: She expands her limited view of the exclusive 'here and now' into a realm existing beyond space and time. When Dorothy Richardson underlines this importance of the 'there and then,' of spatial and temporal *distance*, in the perception of the spiritual, unworldly qualities of the scene, she understands this distance only as a *means* to grasp these qualities, a means that does not *per se* possess any power of Romantic transfiguration:

> Distance does not *lend* enchantment. It shows where it is. In the thing as well as in the eye of the beholder. And I realized one of the Quaker secrets. Living always remote, drawn away into the depths of the spirit, they see, all the time, freshly. A perpetual Sunday (*DH*, 491).[99]

---

[99] This is her response to the opening of Thomas Campbell's 'Pleasures of Hope:'

> At summer eve, when Heaven's ethereal bow
> Spans with bright arch the glittering hills below,
> Why to yon mountain turns the musing eye,
> Whose sunbright summit mingles with the sky?
> Why do those cliffs of shadowy tint appear
> More sweet than all the landscape smiling near? -
> 'Tis distance lends enchantment to the view
> And robes the mountain in its azure hue. (*Works* 2)

Miriam finds this paradisiac idea of everlasting beauty and bliss, where sensual and spiritual pleasure abounds, confirmed in visual and audible forms of art: Fra Angelico's angels, the hymns with the expressive titles and perfectly fitting texts *Light's Abode, Jerusalem the Golden* and *O Paradise* (*DH*, 491) point to the same place of peace and perfection. The sanctity of the garden is further underlined in its allusion to the medieval *hortus conclusus*: high-walled like the garden in Hanover, flower-filled like her grandmother's garden, the '*cross*-shaped thinning amidst the dense masses and a glimpse of a rose-garlanded trellis' (*DH*, 441; emphasis added) faintly suggesting the religious connotation of the Virgin Mary's rose garden, which was traditionally seen as a second Eden of blooming innocence.[100]

If this walled rose-garden forms the centre of Dimple Hill, the most intimate part of the farm, the outer parts of the garden are at least as attractive to Miriam. Similar to the walls, the huge chestnut tree suggests Edenic protection from the world, whereas the parts opening up from the 'wide lawn' (*DH*, 463) provide a view of singular expansion that in its vastness alludes to a prelapsarian paradise of unlimited dimensions (cf. McClung 3): '"I never saw anything quite like your view," she said, "the way it spreads all round the horizon, and the huge distance across it to that green rim against the sky"' (*DH*, 446). Later on 'she found her eyes drawn up and up to measure the immense height, above the outspread scene, of pearl-blue sky' (*DH*, 462). With the 'clouds appearing in bright coppery gold in the

---

In *March Moonlight* this spatial dimension assumes temporal qualities, too: 'Why do they say distance *lends* enchantment? Distance in time or space does not *lend*. It reveals. Takes one into heaven, or into hell. From hell, heaven is inaccessible until one has forgiven oneself. So much, much more difficult than accepting forgiveness. [...] If one could fully forgive oneself, the energy it takes to screen off the memory of the past would be set free' (*MM*, 607). The central issue of the middle novel-chapters of *Pilgrimage* is taken up again: paradise was only attainable once Miriam had overcome the feelings of guilt that had accompanied her after her mother's death. Is this remark, then, *after* her leaving the heavenly place, a sign that she could not stay at Dimple Hill because she is tormented by guilt? While the hypothetical 'if one could fully forgive' suggests the impossibility of the act, her second return to Dimple Hill at the same time suggests a renewed attempt at reaching heaven. The everlasting conflict of her memory between 'inexhaustible wealth' and 'inexhaustible remorse' (*MM*, 607) cannot be solved. And it is the recognition of this dualism, eventually, which is revealed to her when contemplating her former life from a greater distance towards the end of *Pilgrimage*.

100 Thinking about the traditionally female domain of the garden - they 'inhabited gardens while most men [...] only visited them. Made them, and worked in them; for women. Men to make, and women to love that which is made' (*DH*, 464) - Miriam recognizes that she had 'wandered back into problems [...] that in this new world were without significance' (*DH*, 464). The question of the male-dominated creativity and authority of Eden (God the Creator, Adam the overlord) and the female 'uncreativeness' (*DH*, 464) becomes irrelevant when Miriam considers the existing beauty of her earthly paradise.

light of the hidden sun' (*DH*, 462), the paradisal tricolour of green-blue-gold is once more completed. If to a less inspired eye the huge view is at best remarkable for its openness and may appear rather monotonous in its absence of eye-catching sights, Miriam perceives in this expansion of the basic elements - earth, sea, sky - also a temporal openness: under the impression of the 'widespread ceaseless loveliness' of her surroundings she feels 'time cease. Her stretch of freedom [...] expanded now to infinity' (*DH*, 449).

In her enthusiasm for the place and its inhabitants she thus discovers Edenic perfection in all the aspects of the garden. The far-reaching view as well as the contemplation of details of nature fascinate her. The delphiniums in their '*many* blues' (*DH*, 485) appear as a form of 'ultimate beauty' (*DH*, 484), equalling even the 'bluest blue' (*DH*, 485) of her childhood lobelias. Juxtaposing the flowers of the past and present in this way, Miriam believes that her early paradise, the 'long-lost world whose gardens [...] were full of lovely growth' (*DH*, 484), is regained.

It is Richard Roscorla, who - like Dante's Beatrice - guides her through *his* paradise and who - like Adam - names animals and flowers, reveals hidden beauties and thus makes his world her own.[101] Miriam is sure that he is 'certainly alive to the beauties of their gardens,' that he would recognize it as 'a refreshing harbour of the mind' (*DH*, 464). When he reads the 'farmer's song of triumph,' Psalm 65, his 'simple, childlike' voice (*DH*, 475) moves her deeply and she senses a consummate spiritual perfection when their glances meet in a mystical communion at one of the Quakers' meetings: 'It was only for an instant that his eyes rested [...] For an eternity during which everything vanished, leaving us alone in space. In eternal life' (*DH*, 515).

Is Richard, the sensitive farmer, the 'naive' (*DH*, 475) yet deeply inspired Quaker, whose presence is 'all-pervading and comforting' (*DH*, 532) and who gives Miriam 'the marvellous sense of support and earthly security' (*DH*, 515)? Is he 'the unknown sharer of the transfigured earthly life' of her earlier vision, member of the 'new, heaven-lit humanity' (*DH*, 421), her new Adam in an eternal paradise?

Not only Miriam would like to believe in this. Rachel Mary, and with her all those readers expecting a conventional romantic ending of the novel with a wedding and never-ending happiness, would like 'to see thee [Miriam] in that gown' (*DH*, 543) to make her stay in the family for good.[102] But these expectations are thwarted, for the closer Miriam approaches the possibility of

---

[101] 'That's a *wren*,' he had said (*DH*, 478); 'those flowers newly met . . . *delphiniums* - but if he had not been there, they would still be nameless' (*DH*, 477; emphasis original). See also Genesis 2, 19-20.

[102] Only three pages later there is another wedding gown: To Miriam the wedding of Michael and Amabel becomes the substitute for her own, their son Paul will eventually also be a kind of substitute child for Miriam's maternal 'urgencies' (*MM*, 658).

conjugal, 'paradisiac' bliss in a union with Richard, the stronger Miriam's usual social behaviour shows through this picture of coming perfection: Her initial enthusiasm for a place *and* its inhabitants gradually gives way to a view sobered by some disappointing experiences and leads to a withdrawal from society to solitude. Though she may keep her sense for the *genius loci*, for the atmosphere of the place, she perceives human imperfections and eventually leaves the place in search of a better understanding of human society and herself. In her memory, however, the beauty of nature and the mostly positive experiences with people leave lasting impressions.[103]

The compelling beauty of Sussex in summer and the beneficent stillness of the Roscorla family life prolong Miriam's phase of unquestioning enthusiasm, of seeing the place as her paradise, to an unprecedented length. However, throughout *Dimple Hill*, Dorothy Richardson underlines the earthly, man-made, postlapsarian quality of this paradise. The greenhouses, artificially created climates for higher fertility, though normally hidden from view, 'announced themselves as the makers and keepers' of this world (*DH*, 463). Only the unrelenting 'labour' and 'toil' of the Roscorla family[104] - working 'with their own hands' (*DH*, 463), as Miriam stresses - guarantees the continuous blooming of this *hortus deliciarum*, this beautiful garden of delights.

Yet once she retreats into the solitude of writing, she recognizes this - and not the company of the family - as 'centre of her life' (*DH*, 523). She puts a distance between her and them by seeing them as 'strangers whose ways were not her ways' (*DH*, 524) and perceives the 'untellable number of days as level as the marshes' (*DH*, 529), the so far so positive notion of endlessness, as unremarkable, eventless, 'bleak.' Although she admires Richard, she comes to see that the hoped-for true and lasting communion of their minds is not possible. It is even Alfred, the neglected brother, rather than Richard, who would glimpse the 'depths in herself that Richard could never reach' (*DH*, 536). Happy in 'ceaseless communion' with each of the natural objects surrounding her, she even wishes 'Richard would not return' (*DH*, 539); so she tries to persuade herself that when she is not in his presence he is 'reduced to nothing. Indifferent. Apart from his surroundings, Richard is nothing to me?' (*DH*, 546)

The question mark, however, reveals Miriam's conviction as a defensive pose as she at least unconsciously feels that Richard, under the chastening influence of his hard and domineering mother, is to 'draw back' from her

---

[103] This pattern is best seen in Hanover, at Newlands and Oberland, to a lesser extent also in her short stays with family members or friends at the seaside.

[104] cf. *DH*, 440. 459, 461, 463, 511. See Genesis, 3, 17, after the Fall: 'Cursed is the ground because of you; in toil you shall eat of it all the days of your life.' See also 'Paradise Lost,' Book X, ll. 201-206.

(*DH*, 551).[105] The guardian angel of this little perfect family circle, Mrs Roscorla, who is here to 'watch and protect' (*DH*, 542), puts an end to Miriam's paradise. She is expelled from her Eden because of Mrs Roscorla's selfish clutch on her son. This forced end of her months of happiness is accompanied by 'autumn's first breath' (*DH*, 550), which shows her the transitoriness of her 'everlasting' summer paradise. She has to accept that her paradise is an earthly one, provisional and eventually exposed to the destructive forces of human companionship.

Dimple Hill thus ends on a note of unsettled agitation. Like Milton's first couple, Miriam descends from the hill of her Eden to the 'subjected plain' of normal life. Just as to Adam and Eve

> The world was all before them, where to choose
> Their place of rest, (*Paradise Lost,* Book XII, 441)

to Miriam a 'solitary way' into an unknown future opens. *March Moonlight* in its incessant changes of place then presents her numerous hapless attempts at 'choosing' her 'place of rest.' Her restlessness, however, which pervades the whole of this last novel-chapter, eventually reflects Man's pilgrimage on earth: driven forth from Paradise, she takes up her restless search for her true being. Starting to write about herself, she at last reaches that promised post-lapsarian 'paradise within thee, happier far,' (Milton, Book XII 439), which she already perceived when reading Emerson, a lasting state of time-transcending reality that gives her a final 'sense of fulfilment' (*MM*, 658).

Retrieving her past self in the act of writing about past times, Miriam's immediate present seems to lose importance. The natural, external paradise of Dimple Hill, which was temporarily open to all her senses, is replaced by an internal reality, the memory of her past experiences called to life again, 'resurrected', and living on in her mind as long as she lives. What Augustine in a theological context describes as the opposition of the Edenic to the resurrected state, of original perfection to final completion, could be transferred to Miriam's worldly existence. The *posse non mori*, the possibility of an unending bliss in the fragile existence of her Edenic Dimple Hill, is replaced by the *non posse mori* - the impossibility of coming to an end - of her recollections of the past, the secure, undamaged 'treasure' (*MM*, 655) and lasting companions of her mind.[106]

---

[105] This idea is repeated when Miriam returns to Dimple Hill after Mrs Roscorla's death: 'Apart from his surroundings, Richard is, for me, almost nothing' (*MM*, 620). Though the obstacle of Mrs Roscorla's presence has gone, they cannot find a deeper communion as each is too much bound up in their individual worlds: 'Nearer to him than I am, than I could ever be, is his inseparable companion, the ceaseless challenge of his labour' (*MM*, 620). His love of nature, his 'joy in hill and valley, in meadow and wood, in air and sea and sky' eventually outdoes his love of people, his interest in human affairs.

[106] cf. St Augustine, *The City of God* 406. See also McClung 17.

II.

THE EAR: AURAL CONCEPTS IN *PILGRIMAGE*

3. Sounds of Music: Patterns of Life

What, Peggy is Music? Where does it *go*, & we with it?
(Letter to Peggy Kirkaldy, 19.10.1946; *WM*, 549)

. . . you are the music
While the music lasts. . . .
(T.S. Eliot 'The Dry Salvages', *The Complete Poems and Plays* 190)

What is the function of music in *Pilgrimage*? Are the musical sounds pervading all thirteen novel-chapters mere audible details, more or less mimetic representations of Miriam's acoustic background? Is music merely one of the 'circling worlds of sound' (*DL*, 114) surrounding her, whose 'only apparent role in the text is that of denoting a concrete reality,' (Culler 193) thus producing nothing but what Barthes calls 'l'effet de réel'? (1970: 88) Is music with its innate temporality more than a reflection of Miriam's treasuring the 'unique quality of the passing moment' (*DLH*, 134), of her deep awareness of the flowing of time? Does music add to the meaning of the text by assuming thematic, symbolic or structural significance? If so, what does music mean to Miriam?

In *Pilgrimage* there seem to be many 'trivial', 'insignificant' or 'superfluous' musical instances, the tiniest mosaic stones in the rich web of Miriam's experiences; their function is purely referential, they do not lend themselves for further interpretation;[1] thus the 'tinkling melody' coming 'from a large glass-framed musical-box' in a restaurant in Hoddenheim *(PR*, 118) or the 'blare of the Salvation Army's band marching townwards' in London on a Sunday evening (*RL,* 209) convey nothing but a detailed, realistic impression of Miriam's acoustic environment. Radford (1989:30) insists that this 'mania of precision,' the repeated use of detailed physical description - not only in connection with music - ultimately does not aim at ensuring Barthes' reality effect but serves as a means to impel the reader on towards 'the ever-deferred point where its significance will become recognisable;' but she neglects another factor that makes *Pilgrimage* at once both hard to read *and* fascinating - Dorothy Richardson's individual realism *is* to some extent a pure, subjective, representation of reality, describing

[1] cf. Culler 193, where he defines characteristics of Barthes' reality effect.

sound for sound's sake, not even 'impelling the reader onward,' but making him stay, to experience the immediate presence of Miriam's impressions, and thus together with Miriam and Dorothy Richardson, 'feel astonishment over the fact [...] of there being anything, anywhere.'[2] This primary wonder at the existence of phenomena as mere phenomena thus accounts for the large number of seemingly irrelevant musical details in the text. In these background sounds Miriam, similar to Mrs Dalloway, perceives an underlying joy of life: in 'brass bands, barrel organs' and other street sounds 'was what she loved; life; London; this moment' (Woolf, *Mrs Dalloway* 2). This phenomenological aspect of sound, together with her awareness of the present moment, also forms an essential element of Miriam's musical understanding in the 'great' musical scenes to be analysed.

With regard to the communicative function of music, aspects of Miriam's awareness of other people play an important role in *Pilgrimage*. What we may call her *interpersonal* awareness becomes evident whenever her musical experience is determined by performers and listeners. Music as 'the one all-inclusive art'[3] carries a meaning, communicating 'a way of feeling, seeing and interpreting that the artist offers to other people in the hope that they will perceive at least part of his intentions' (Bigand 232). And Bujic says: Music, which is both 'expressive' and 'impressive,' 'must transmit experience' (261). In *Pilgrimage* this form of aural communication, non-verbal in the numerous instances of piano-playing, verbal with regard to the songs and hymns spread throughout the novel-chapters, can be read as an extended 'voice' delivering a message from the player to Miriam, from Miriam to her audience, from the narrator to the reader. The textual rendering of these acoustic impressions eventually helps to highlight Miriam's social sensitivity in her response to individual encounters.

As Sloboda (10) reminds us, the prime feature of music is its ability to evoke a rich and varied range of feelings and emotions: 'Somehow the human mind endows these sounds with significance. They become symbols for something other than pure sound.' It is this mental process of appropriation, the transformation of 'objective' sounds into 'subjective' feelings, thus into personal significance, that lies at the core of the most important musical scenes in *Pilgrimage*.

These *intrapersonal* aspects of listening involve different degrees of perception that may be classified and analyzed according to Gibson's theory of perceptual systems.[4] *Imposed perception* or exteroception thus means passive hearing of sounds, where the external stimulation is registered but

---

[2] Letter to Henry Savage, 18.10.1952, *WM*, 685.

[3] Letter to Bryher, 9.5. 1943, quoting Walter Pater, *WM*, 464.

[4] Gibson 44f. He considers not only aural perception but all senses.

does not cause any reaction in the listener. The numerous instances of background music in *Pilgrimage* belong to this class.[5] When the listener reacts directly and without reflecting to what he hears with some form of physical movement, Gibson speaks of *imposed proprioception*, which is rather an uncommon way of perception in *Pilgrimage*.[6]

Active perception, on the other hand, entails not only stimulation from the music, but also from the listener's own attentive actions and reactions (cf. Gibson 32). Thus, the field of *obtained perception* - active listening to obtain information concerning sound and form, to understand music and decode it into the language of the self, to integrate it into the framework of one's own personal experience - is closely and with gradual transitions linked to the field of *obtained proprioception*, where the individual aware of his perceptive activity becomes active and takes over the control of this (mental) activity. As the significance of the scenes of music in *Pilgrimage* largely depends on Miriam's *active* perception, the inquiry into these two latter fields will form one focus of this chapter.

As Ihde (44) points out, a pure auditory experience does not exist. Listening is always embedded in a background of 'global experience,' whose 'focal dimension' it can form. Given such an embedded listening, four zones of perception can be distinguished. The central object of attention forming a 'focal core' is surrounded by a 'peripheral fringe' of perception: an awareness of one's background of experience which is constantly present, though maybe not explicitly noted; an awareness that may engage any of the five senses, thus often unconsciously adding to the total experience of a situation. At the farthest extreme from ordinary focal attention a 'horizon' as the limit of the field of aural perception is very difficult to discern: Sound does not extend indefinitely; as soon as the absence of sound is perceived, however, the borderline of the horizon has been crossed and the fourth zone of perception, 'beyond the horizon', the rich realm of silence opens. Silence *is* 'the horizon of sound' and may form the basis of a new focal core of perception, be it aural or visual, or the background of a dematerialized experience of the mind.[7] Thus, beyond their exclusively aural aspects of perception even Miriam's most intense musical experiences have to be examined in the wider context of her 'global experience' of life itself. And it

---

[5] e.g. *BW*, 318: 'The town band played Anitra's Dance or the moon-song from the *Mikado*.' / *HC*, 395: 'A piano-organ broke into loud music in the street.' / *IN*, 340: When Mr Mendizabal is singing: 'a little melody sounded for an instant in a smooth swaying falsetto.' / *DLH*, 163: an army band playing march music below Densley's window.

[6] *RL*, 321: Miriam, remembering a Norwegian song, whistles the tune: 'Her limbs stirred to a dance. How *slowly* he had played that wild Norwegian tune [...]. She could not keep within the slow rhythm. Her feet flung off the clogs and flew about the room.'

[7] cf. Ihde 50, and later in chapter 4, 'Silence'.

is only in the combination of musical perception, imagination and reflection that the importance of music and its impact on Miriam's life is fully grasped.

Reflecting on music in a more abstract way, Miriam considers music as *the* means to express cultural identity, be it in terms of opposition such as the contrasts between England and Germany in *Pointed Roofs*, in terms of identification such as her impression of Mrs Kronen's singing in *Honeycomb*, or in terms of differentiation such as her reflections on Alma's playing Chopin. Personal, individual expression then represents the expression of a social class, of a country, of a whole culture.

While in the later novel-chapters of *Pilgrimage* there is a tendency to move away from the immediate experience and overwhelming presence of music, the importance of memory increases reciprocally. Triggered off by some acoustic stimulus, earlier musical memories crop up, subdued in their emotional power, filtered by time and oblivion, reduced to their essential message and therefore all the clearer to both Miriam's and the reader's understanding. This process of juxtaposing some scenes in their immediate perception and in their recalled 'simplification', may reveal traces of what makes up Miriam's unchanging being.

Music, like a language, consists of sound, form, and expression (cf. C.Pratt 1). Music in a text can likewise fulfill aural, structural, or semantic functions. When analysing Miriam's sensual awareness of music and her mental reaction to the sounds perceived, it is of little importance what specific piece she plays or listens to. Indeed, quite a number of the essential musical passages in *Pilgrimage* are not further specified. What 'brilliant piece' (*PR*, 43) is Clara Bergmann playing that evokes Miriam's childhood memory? What is this 'thing she disliked' (*HC*, 471) that ought to soothe Mrs Henderson's despair? When Miriam is waiting for a first lesson with Shatov (*DL*, 31), the music she is playing remains as vague as the music that prepares her for her unexpected first meeting with Amabel (*DLH*, 186). Even in one of the longest music scenes in *Pilgrimage*, the concert that ends with Michael's proposal to her and her clear recognition that they would go separate ways (*CH*, 295-308), it is some undefined music that enables Miriam's self to brood over itself and to think of a possible way into a future.

This very vagueness of the music described reflects what Reinold (292) calls 'pathetic' perception; it emphasizes Miriam's emotional reaction to pure sounds and perfectly renders the ambiguity and surprise of her deeply felt response; it also forms a contrast to the identifiable musical passages, where Reinold's 'gnostic' element (292), the intellectual recognition of and reflection on specific structures in a well-known piece of music, plays a dominant part. It is precisely this 'gnostic' perception in playing or in listening that makes up the 'historical' dimension of Miriam's understanding of music; for in the recognition of a concrete piece of music lies the effect of a *déjà-entendu* that links the past to the present. This sense of identity in contemplating the past as a living reality in the present and experiencing time as an organic whole, on a perceptive level helps Miriam to feel 'the unchanging presence' of her 'strange centre of being' (*DLH*, 186), to see the continuity of the 'changeless central zone of her being' (*CH*, 299; cf. Thorn 214); on a narrative level, references to real, identifiable pieces of music provide a structural basis which at least in parts helps to unify single parts of *Pilgrimage*. These passages make up what Scher (1982:234f.) calls 'verbal music,' plausible literary semblances of actual or fictitious music in a larger context, which is 'normally sustained by a network of anticipatory and retrospective allusions.' In this wider context, then, some musical scenes assume an extra-musical significance crucial for the understanding and interpretation of the corresponding parts of the text.

3.1 'Piling Joy on Joy:' The Sensual Beauty of Musical Sounds

> They were listening. Each note sounded pure and sweet as if it went out into an empty room. [...] Their eyes were soft and quiet like the music. [...] She was too happy to care. Nothing mattered so long as she could listen to herself playing the Moonlight Sonata.
>
> (May Sinclair. *Mary Olivier: A Life* 187)

> She was nothing but an ear. (*BW*, 205)

Playing the piano - together with learning French - formed a fixed part of education in the life of any Victorian girl growing up in the (upper-) middle class. Musical accomplishment was considered an essential social virtue for ladies-to-be, and it is therefore obvious that Mr Henderson - keen on fulfilling his role as a gentleman - had his daughters play the piano, too. Miriam, however, discovers more in it than mere social accomplishment: like other late-Victorian heroines such as Lucy Honeychurch, Mary Olivier or Rachel Vinrace, Miriam experiences her own piano-playing as a means of getting in touch with her innermost self and of giving some non-verbal shape to the expression of her feelings. The individual self-expression thus lies at the centre of all these heroines' playing. None of them, however, puts as much emphasis as Miriam does on the verbalization of these musical processes, none is as conscious as Miriam of what her piano-playing means to herself.

Whenever Miriam is aware of her listeners, her playing changes direction and loses its directness: she no longer plays in order to find a means of self-expression but rather to create emotional responses in her listeners' minds, to guide their feelings and to provide them with an image of her supposed emotions. Her playing becomes intentional, and is no longer true to her own self. Is it this increasing discrepancy between feeling and playing, is it the rupture from her surroundings at the first turning point of her life, or is it simply the replacement of music as *her* means of self-expression by something else that leads to her gradual abstinence from the piano? While the first three novel-chapters are full of music scenes with Miriam at the piano, they become rarer as Miriam progresses in life, but they do not altogether cease.[8]

From her arrival in Hanover Miriam, the piano-player, experiences the irreconcilable presence of both her interior and her exterior worlds in her music. Playing to herself, the material, the structure and the expression, the sensory, the formal and the emotional aspects of her music form a convincing unity. Listening to her own playing, she notices that the purely self-reflective quality of her music filling her with happiness and enhancing her emotional sensitivity is constantly challenged by her craving for a positive response from outside. She comes to believe that music only becomes complete and lively when a listener participates in the performative act through his or her attentive presence. This audience-oriented playing, however, not only inhibits the range of her expressiveness, but also the spontaneity and individuality necessary for a truly artistic performance. In this eagerness to please, in this anxiety to conform to some assumed expectations, Dorothy Richardson very convincingly depicts the immature, self-conscious character of the seventeen-year-old girl struggling for an independent musical voice of her own.

Thus, it is only in rare instances of supposed solitude that Miriam achieves a most profound form of self-expression: In Hanover she

> felt for the pedals, lifted her hands a span above the piano, as Clara had done, and came down, true and clean, on to the opening chord. The full rich tones of the piano echoed from all over the room; and some metal object far away from her hummed the dominant. She held the chord for its full term. . . . Should she play any more? . . . She had confessed herself . . . just that minor chord . . . any one hearing it would know more than she could ever tell them . . . her whole being beat out the rhythm as she waited for the end of the phrase to insist on what had already been said. [...] Grave and happy she sat with unseeing eyes, listening, for the first time (*PR*, 57).

Sound - 'the full rich tones,' 'that minor chord' - , form, and meaning - 'she had confessed herself' - harmonize: she realizes that she is in the mood to play.[9] Having thus found access to the highly admired, 'musical,' 'German'

---

[8] *PR* 34,41,45,56-58,66; *BW* 201,206,214,216f,297,317; *HC* 365,374,470f,485; *TU* 27f,72,131; *IN* 319,332-35,400; *DL* 30f; *RL* 264; *TR* -; *O* -; *DLH* 186f; *DH* 529; *MM* 638.

[9] This disposition to play is an essential condition for a musical performance, as Miriam soon learns in her musical growing up: 'She soon discovered she could not always "play" - even the things she knew perfectly - and she began to understand the fury

way of playing, she sees a way to overcome her youthful inhibitions in front of listeners: Her audience might 'hear her play *by accident*, and acknowledge the difference in her playing. Oh yes, besides seeing them all she wanted them to hear her play' (*PR*, 66; emphases added). To play no longer in the mechanical, insipid English way, but to perform music in front of a non-present audience might lead to a wished-for, unifying, musical communion.

Separated from her childhood world, Miriam tries to find a new cultural identity in her music: she puts away her English songs 'at the bottom of her Saratoga trunk' (*PR*, 58)[10] in order to get to know Schubert, Grieg and Brahms, and she juxtaposes the ways of playing of both the English and the German girls; and she concludes that the 'self-consciousness' of the English girls, who 'knew' how to play but 'did not dare' (*PR*, 44f.), obstructing the direct interplay between their selves and their music and thus diminishing the emotional intensity of their playing, reflects her own inhibitions when playing in front of an audience.[11] The expressive potentials of her inner being and of the music played on the piano so far have seemed to inhibit each other rather than to cooperate and to lead to a truly stirring performance; yet when she admires the deep German expressiveness of the Bergmann sisters, whose playing seizes her and transposes her into a state of rhapsodic elation, she discovers the simple liberating secret of good playing: the ability to listen.

Just to listen to her own music and to play out of an inner drive and thus to hear the essential power of music while oblivious of the presence of both her surroundings and the workings of her mind now becomes the core of her new understanding of music. Her preoccupation with music may have escapist tendencies, in that it repeatedly frees her from a consciousness of the difficulties of her present life;[12] whenever this complete presence of music is achieved, however, it at once penetrates her awareness, and takes her out of herself 'in a loss of self-awareness' (Ihde 70), in which the focal core of her

---

that had seized her when her mother and a woman here and there had taken for granted one should "play when asked," and coldly treated her refusal as showing lack of courtesy. "Ah!" she said aloud, as this realization came, "Women."

"Of course you can only 'play when you *can*,'" said she to herself, "like a bird singing"' (*PR*, 58).

[10] The Saratoga trunk, symbol of the journey, is an obvious reminder of her limited stay in Germany: although she now imbibes German culture, her English upper-middle class roots will accompany her on her journey through life, forming a solid basis for all further discussions on cultural identity.

[11] *PR*, 42: At home 'she had both played and sung, hoping each time afresh to be able to reproduce the effects which came so easily when she was alone or only with Eve. But she could not discover the secret of getting rid of her nervousness.'

[12] cf. *TU*, 28; *IN*, 400: 'I sit here . . . playing to hide myself from the Baileys'; *CH*, 301. Lucy Honeychurch in Forster's *A Room with a View* (27) expresses a similar escapist thought: 'I myself have worries, but I can generally forget them at the piano.'

perception expands to the horizon, completely filling the auditory space. Her perception then turns into what Ihde calls 'obtained proprioception', in which she experiences the - both mentally and physically stimulating - power of musical sound: her whole being, body and soul, behaves in accordance with the music. In other words, music - though the most time-bound of all arts - lifts her out of her temporality into a condition of timelessness that opens up the world of the unconscious, manifesting itself in visionary scenes of the past and of the future. In the intense awareness of music, sound and vision, time and space, past, present and future merge into a 'featureless freedom' (*PR*, 43), a 'total presentness' (Kaplan 42). In ecstatic moments, such as her playing Beethoven in the solitude of Mrs Bailey's drawing-room (*IN*, 334f.), the borderlines between the different dimensions of perception are dissolved.[13] Then Miriam experiences music not as an escape, but rather, in Pratt's words, as a 'fulfillment and a completion' (1968:XXXII) in her mystical awareness of 'the importance of the individual deep sense of being' (*DLH*, 167). Under the 'outbreak of her best reality' (*IN*, 334) she thus succeeds in discovering herself in her own sounds.

This deep power of music, which Miriam for the first time experiences at the *Vorspielen* in Hanover, fills her with an unforgettable happiness that spreads over her whole stay in Germany. Looking back on these five months, she in leitmotific repetition associates Germany with beauty, happiness and - above all - with music.[14] What Knapp, writing about Proust, calls the 'technique of involuntary recall' (113), a diving down into the world of pure perception and intuition, into memories stored in the unconscious where the rational domain of intelligence loses its power, is found in rare instances of Miriam's intense listening, as for instance during the *Vorspielen* in Hanover:

> There was a pause. Clara threw back her head, a faint smile flickered over her face, her hands fell gently and the music came again, *pianissimo*, swinging in an even rhythm. It flowed from those

[13] Bronfen (71), analysing the passage in *Interim* (335), says that the 'Auflösung der physisch begehbaren Raumgrenzen' leads to a 'Grenzerlebnis von erinnerten Räumen.' Physical and mental sensations, reality and memories, can no longer be clearly distinguished.

[14] *PR*, 82: 'And yet . . . German music, a line of German poetry, [...]' / *HC*, 351: 'the beauty and music and happiness of Germany [...]' / *HC*, 392: 'In Germany [spring] had brought music and wild joy.' / *HC*, 470: 'Germany . . . all washed with poetry and music and song.' / *TU*, 164: 'strong, cheerful, musical, tree-filled Germany' / *TU*, 214: 'In a single glance, the whole of the time in Germany was beautiful, golden happy light, and people happy in the golden light, garlands of music [...]' / *O*, 35: The sound of a piano takes her back to 'her Germany where life had been lived to music that had flowed over its miseries and made its happinesses hardly to be borne.' / *DLH*, 167: In Germany 'there had been that deep depth of happiness' [...] Her deep sense of being 'in Germany had its voice in music that drew even Fräulein into the magic circle and disarmed her.'

> clever hands, a half-indicated theme with a gentle, steady throbbing undertow. Miriam dropped her eyes - she seemed to have been listening long - that wonderful light was coming again - she had forgotten her sewing - when presently she saw, slowly circling, fading and clearing, first its edge, and then, for a moment the whole thing, dripping, dripping as it circled, a weed-grown mill-wheel. . . . She recognized it instantly. She had seen it somewhere as a child [...] Her heart filled. She felt a little tremor in her throat. All at once she knew that if she went on listening to that humming wheel and feeling the freshness of the air, she would cry. She pulled herself together, and for a while saw only a vague radiance in the room and the dim forms grouped about. She could not remember which was which. All seemed good and dear to her. The trumpet notes had come back, and in a few moments the music ceased (*PR*, 44).

Gradually leaving behind her sensory and perceptual awareness of sound and form being *performed* - Clara's hands, the music at *pianissimo*, the even rhythm - Miriam actually regresses into her childhood memory, experiencing this former time-period in her imagination as a living and present reality of visual, aural, olfactory and tactile perceptions. The musical stimulus functions here as a kind of catalytic agent leading away from reality - 'she had forgotten her sewing' - and also away from an active listening to the music. The music arouses emotion *through the mediation of these imaginings*, but it itself plays no controlling part in shaping or determining this experience - a typical case of involuntary recall (cf. Meyer 9 and 256). Miriam's trains of thought and inner images take up the emotional mood of the music to develop their own series of associations, largely independent of the musical succession itself, until her *ratio* - 'she pulled herself together' - leads her back to perceive the tonal and structural aspects of the music being performed: 'The trumpet notes had come back [...].'

In Mursell's terms (220), Miriam performs a change from 'listening' - 'attending to the musical form for its own sake' - to 'hearing' - attending to the suggestions and associations of music and gradually allowing an arousal of imagery within herself - and back to 'listening' again. This diving down and emerging out of different layers of her consciousness characterizes the working of Miriam's mind in connection with her reaction not only to music, but, on a wider scale, to sensual impulses in general. It is in music, however, that we can best identify the pattern of different 'intensities' of awareness.

In the passages that describe scenes of music, Miriam often translates the sounds perceived into technical terms or universally accepted images.[15] In

---

15 *PR*, 43: 'a prelude of unfinished phrases;' *PR*, 44: 'The music came again, *pianissimo*, swinging in an even rhythm [...] a half-indicated theme with a gentle, steady, throbbing undertow.'

this intellectual, 'formalist,' perception of music, Miriam concentrates on 'intrinsic factors,' i.e. volume, melody, harmony, rhythm and structure (Mursell 210-215).[16] This *analytic* perception, found in many passages throughout *Pilgrimage,* does not involve Miriam's emotions. From a narrative point of view, however, these technical details are an important factor in establishing a credible musical reality, a step towards conveying a sense of the music actually performed.

At this stage her awareness of the performer and of her surroundings often competes with her attentiveness towards music itself.[17] Miriam here establishes what Ihde (39) calls the 'peripheral fringe' of musical performance, momentarily foregrounding what is 'never absent' in music - the performer, the instrument(s) - what is always implied in but does not make up the 'focal core' of her musical awareness. On this most disinvolved, distant level of her perception of music, which still forms an important 'extrinsic factor' of her listening (Mursell 206), Miriam is well aware of her 'horizon' - the room, the audience - and demonstrates that 'pure auditory experience' is virtually impossible as it cannot be isolated from its situation, its embedment, its background of global experience (Ihde 44).

Setting out from this rather peripheral point of musical perception, which is concerned with the outer, surrounding world of phenomena involving *all* her senses, her whole body and mind, Miriam then concentrates on listening, making the auditory dimension of her perception stand out, and thus moving into a more 'subjective' realm of what might be called *imaginative* or *fully emotional* perception.[18] She assumes what Meyer calls an 'expressionist'

[16] Meyer (3) defines: For a formalist the 'meaning of music lies in the perception and understanding of musical relationships set forth in the work of art.'

[17] cf. *BW*, 344f. / *TU*, 28, 125 / *IN*, 370 / *RL*, 317, 365 / *O*, 36 / *DLH*, 260 / *MM*, 638.

[18] While Miriam's imaginative listening always implies emotionality to such a degree that imaginative perception *is* emotional perception too, Edna Pontellier in *The Awakening* makes a difference in her response to music between mere 'material pictures' and a profound stirring of her emotions which encompasses both body and soul:

'Musical strains, well rendered, had a way of evoking pictures in her mind. [...One] piece called to her mind a dainty young woman clad in an Empire gown [...]. Again, another reminded her of children at play, and still another of nothing on earth but a demure lady stroking a cat.

The very first chords which Mademoiselle Reisz struck upon the piano sent a keen tremor down Mrs Pontellier's spinal column. [...] She waited for the material pictures which she thought would gather and blaze before her imagination. She waited in vain. She saw no pictures of solitude, of hope, of longing, or of despair. But the very passions themselves were aroused within her soul, swaying it, lashing it, as the waves daily beat upon her splendid body. She trembled, she was choking, and the tears blinded her' (49f.).

Chopin thus combines this immediate emotional response with a strong form of 'obtained proprioception': Edna's mental reaction finds a physical outlet in the 'tremor', the 'choking', the 'tears.' Body and soul cooperate as parts of one undivided being.

attitude in that she wants the music to excite emotions in her, thus changing the mode of her perception from the passive, imposed mode to the active, obtained.[19] Intensely aware of the immediate presence of sounds and their effect on her, she experiences an epiphanic moment of being. At the same time the dynamic quality of music implies a constant 'becoming' which she as a listener takes up when she embarks on a kind of musical quest; leaving behind her fringe impressions, she is ready to follow the music and to be moved and guided by it into other spheres, aspiring to the condition of an 'ideal listener.'[20] When Dorothy Richardson puts forward the crucial question: 'What [...] is music? Where does it *go* and we with it?' she underlines the dynamic process of music, which like life itself contains both growth and decay, tension and release, beginning and end. As she shows throughout *Pilgrimage*, a generally approved answer is not even wished for, as long as there *is* movement both in music and life, as long as we *are* moved by it in some way as individuals with our *individual* ideas and responses.

Miriam appears as an ideal listener during Meg Wedderburn's performance at Barnes, where the text focuses upon her individual process of delving down through different intensities of awareness to an imaginative perception. Sitting in the drawing-room at home Miriam is keenly aware of both the performer and her audience, of the light inside, the darkness and stillness of the garden, before she starts concentrating on the music itself:

> 'Mm - and then the *Cavatina*,' murmured Miriam, as if half asleep, turning wholly towards the garden, as Eve went to collect the piano scores.
>
> She seemed to grow larger and stronger and easier as the thoughtful chords came musing out into the night and hovered amongst the dark trees. She found herself drawing easy breaths and relaxing completely against the support of the hard friendly sofa. How quietly every one was listening. . . .
>
> After a while, everything was dissolved, past and future and present and she was nothing but an ear, intent on the meditative harmony which stole out into the garden (*BW*, 205).

Miriam's visual awareness of the garden, the night and the audience, the tactile presence of the 'hard' sofa and the bodily awareness of herself give way to an auditory experience that expands in its intensity to the 'horizon' of her perception, encompassing her completely. In this way of listening she hears the voice of her own inwardness, 'that inwardness for which alone

---

[19] Meyer (3) defines somewhat vaguely: For an expressionist 'relationships in music are in some way capable of exciting feelings and emotions in the listener.'

[20] Copland (9) defines the 'ideal listener' as a person who 'above all else, possesses the ability to *lend himself* to the power of the music' (emphasis added).

music lives, far from the world of matter and space' (Brelèt 104). The sounds penetrating her ear open up an inner, timeless space where images created and memories triggered off by music expand to an *imaginative* perception of music. For shorter or longer moments the sounds of music, though still the focal core of her auditory experience, are complemented by these, mostly visual, pictures and memories of her inner self, her *imagination*, which Dorothy Richardson defines as 'holding an image in your mind. When it comes up of itself, or is summoned by something. Then it is not outside, but within you' (*MM*, 613).

In such a synaesthetic perception of real sound and imagined pictures Miriam experiences rare moments of ecstatic happiness in which she - 'standing outside her self' - reaches at the same time both a wholesome distance from everything and every one and a feeling of interior completeness.[21] There is a suggestion that the pleasure underlying her sensory experience is not just her subjective response, but moreover that it manifests an intrinsic characteristic of the sounds themselves, transcending mere exterior perception. Thus, the immediacy of the music engages not only her aural sense, but also fills up the auditory space in herself. This feeling of a Parmenidian expansive oneness of her listening self, comparable to the unending completeness of a sphere, the most perfect of all bodies, gives rise to joy, even to a musical ecstasy that forms a strong contrast to her objectifying, analytic listening mentioned above.[22]

When playing a Beethoven sonata in the solitude of Mrs Bailey's drawing-room she perceives that 'all round her was height and depth, a sense of vastness and grandeur beyond anything to be seen or heard, yet stretching back like a sheltering wing over the past to her earliest memories and forward ahead out of sight' (*IN*, 335). The focal core of her listening thus expands beyond the horizon of temporal or spatial dimensions, transferring her whole being into a state of perfection.[23] Whenever, during her own

---

[21] cf. Chapter 5.2.

[22] This positive impact of music on her inner life is felt by Edna Pontellier too: 'Edna did not at once read the letter [from her lover Robert]. She sat holding it in her hand, while the music penetrated her whole being like an effulgence, warming and brightening the dark places of her soul. It prepared her for joy and exultation' (*The Awakening* 154).

[23] Edna Pontellier has a similar experience of musical spatiality: Once more reading one of her lover's letters, she listens to Mademoiselle Reisz playing a Chopin Impromptu:

'The shadows deepened in the little room. The music grew strange and fantastic - turbulent, insistent, plaintive and soft with entreaty. The shadows grew deeper. The music filled the room. It floated out upon the night, over the housetops, the crescent of the river, losing itself in the silence of the upper air' (*The Awakening* 121f.).

This is a perfect passage where Ihde's idea of sound stretching out to its horizon can be taken literally: aural (silence) and visual (upper air) horizon are one. Edna synaesthetically perceives her surroundings to their utmost limits.

playing, her being expands in such a way, it is due to her questioning the female norm of playing the piano, due to her finding her individual voice in music, as Dorothy Richardson shows in various instances. She does not play in order to please her listeners, but by expressing her own self she subverts the traditional feminine role and takes up a masculine position. Still, as long as she observes herself playing, this role is somehow threatening: 'The dingy woman playing with the directness and decision of a man was like some strange beast in the room' (*IN*, 335). Only when she manages to lose her self-consciousness, giving herself up to unrestrained, unreflected listening in an act of complete immersion, does the music expand to its full expressive power. Therefore the 'triumphant echoes' filtering 'out into the quiet street, out and away into London' (*IN*, 335) carry more than Beethoven's sound: they reverberate with Miriam's self-assurance as she has regained 'a sense of control over her circumstances' (Brown, P.178): at least for this moment she is at one with her music, and at one with her self.

Only much later on will she hear such perfection again when Hypo is playing the first phrase of Beethoven's 7th Symphony:

> Back in her room she prepared swiftly to go out and meet the day in the open; all the world, waiting in the happy garden. Through the house-stillness sounded three single downward-stepping notes . . . the first phrase of the seventh symphony. Perfect. Eternity stating itself in the stillness [...] living in space alone, at one with everybody, as every one was, the moment life allowed. Beethoven's perfect expression of the perfection of life (*RL*, 365).

In this second scene her experience of perfection does not reach her inner self and fails to create an emotional, imaginative response. Influenced by Hypo's objectifying intellectualism, she listens to his music as a detached observer who, standing both physically and emotionally outside, analytically follows the forms and technical details rather than its emotional message. Yet Miriam recognizes the drawbacks of such a formalist way of listening:

> To watch a shape adds interest to listening. But something disappears in listening with the form put first. Hearing only form is a kind of perfect happiness. But in coming back there is a reproach; as if it had been a kind of truancy . . . People who care only for form think themselves superior. Then there is something wrong with them (*RL*, 365f.).[24]

---

[24] It is exactly this purely intellectual approach to music that E. M. Forster ridicules in his ironic portrayal of Tibby Schlegel in *Howards End*, who haughtily, 'untroubled by passions' (247) listens for the formal structures of the music and thus misses any emotional message. There is indeed much wrong with Tibby, who in his emotional sterility fails to establish any personal relationship and thus eventually misses life.

Despite the 'kind of perfect happiness' such listening can evoke, it is not Miriam's ideal way of listening to music, as 'something disappears.' However well-written the music may be, this 'something,' the individual expression and her emotional response, eventually forms the crucial element that to her makes any musical experience whole, perfect.

Comparing the scene above with Miriam's listening to a Chopin ballad in Oberland, where she, sitting in her room, is just as much physically separated from the source of sound, the difference between the two ways of listening becomes obvious:

> The familiar sound of tea pouring into a cup heightened the surrounding strangeness. In the stillness of the room it was like a voice announcing her installation, and immediately from downstairs there came as if in answer the sound of a piano, crisply and gently touched, seeming not so much to break the stillness as to reveal what lay within it.
>
> She set down the teapot and listened, and for a moment could have believed that the same theme was playing itself only in her mind, that it had come back to her because once again she was within the strange happiness of being abroad. Through all the years she had tried in vain to recall it, and now it came, to welcome her, piling joy on joy, setting its seal upon the days ahead and taking her back to her Germany where life had been lived to music that had flowed over its miseries and made its happinesses hardly to be borne. [...] She relived the first moment of knowing gladly and without feeling of disloyalty how far a Sommerabend outdoes a summer's evening, how the evening beauty was intensified by the deeps of poetry in the Germans all about her, and remembered her fear lest one of the English should sound an English voice and break the spell. And how presently Clara Bergmann, unasked, had retreated into the shadowy saal and played this ballad and just in this way, the way of slipping it into the stillness. [...] And this ballad was joy. Eternal Sommerabend; and now, to-morrow's Swiss sunlight (*O*, 35f).

This music is much more internalized, living in her own self; the sound of the piano growing organically out of silence seems to start within her: She 'could have believed that the theme was playing itself only in her mind.' The music fills her and evokes beautiful images of the past, of her stay in Germany where Clara Bergmann played the *same* ballade in the *same* way. The once experienced joy in the beauty of the music *and* of her surroundings is here again in synaesthetic intensity. She *hears* the sunlight of the past - 'warm light upon the garden' - as the same light of the future - 'to-morrow's Swiss sunlight.' Again music transgresses the boundaries of time and space, creating a timeless expansion of joy in Miriam, who 'was everywhere at once.'

This recall of the past as the immediate present forms an integral part of Miriam's most profound musical experience. According to Guetti (183), this nostalgia generated by music forms 'the most consistently felt but difficult to explicate property of aural experience.' The importance it assumes for Miriam's understanding of life is well expressed in Gabriel Marcel's words:

> Any true musical creation consists first of all in conjuring up in us a *certain past* [which] is rather the inner depths of oneself, inexplicable with respect to what the present not only arranges, but - again and most particularly - qualifies. These multiple pasts are really sentimental perspectives according to which life can be relived, not as a series of events, but to the extent that it is an indivisible unity which can only be apprehended as such through art (148f.).

In such moments of intense listening when the music corresponds to her mental state of being, when she can give herself up to it, 'breathing the atmosphere of music in its purest form' (de Selincourt 160), Miriam is taken back to the consciousness of her own existence. What Marcel (151) calls her 'remembrance' of herself, whether it is in an earlier period or disconnected from any representation of a real past event triggered off and sustained by music, strengthens her present self and helps her face the outer world anew.

The analysis of these few scenes of music has shown us Miriam's deep appreciation of this art and her individual response to it: moments of 'passive' exteroception are followed by 'active' analytical listening and rare instances of fully emotional, imaginative perception. However, in the majority of musical scenes in *Pilgrimage* the completion of Miriam's musical experience is not achieved at all. The fragile balance of exterior and interior perception is susceptible to any form of disturbance, both outer and inner: whether it is the overwhelming presence of the performer that gets between her and the music,[25] the performer's 'wrong' understanding of music,[26] the annoying presence of an audience,[27] the interruption of her own playing by

---

[25] e.g. *PR*, 143: Herr Bossenberger 'hammering and shouting [the song] out into the *saal*;' *HC*, 404: Mrs Kronen 'singing song after song to her own loud accompaniment' while all are 'waiting for her to stop getting between them and the music.'

[26] e.g. *TU*, 125: 'Alma followed with a morsel of Chopin. The performance drove Miriam into a rage. Mr Pinner half murdered his German ballad innocently, his little Oxford voice and his false vowels did not conceal the pleasure he took in singing his unimagined little song. Alma played her piece at her audience, every line of her face and body proclaiming it fine music, the right sort of music [...]. The Wilsons had discovered "good" music, as so many English people had, but they were all wrong about music; nearly all English people were.'

[27] e.g. *IN*, 371f: Miriam does not feel comfortable at Mr Bowdoin's party because of her fellow guests: 'Mr Bowdoin had probably thought she would talk to those women. But after talking to them how could one listen to music? Their very presence made it almost impossible. She was unable to lose herself in the Wagner overture. It sounded out thinly

an intruder from outside, her sudden awareness of the room that leads her back into the presence of time and space,[28] technical problems,[29] or mere inattention;[30] they are all 'accountable barriers' (*CH*, 298) between herself and the music, hampering her concentration on music and weakening or breaking off a deeply felt full emotional perception, the roundness of experience that might lead to moments of happiness. Thus, to use Ihde's terms, the interference of various parts of the peripheral fringe of her sensory attentiveness in these cases prevents the focal core from expanding.

Yet, the few scenes discussed above make a lasting impression on the reader in their precise rendering of the wide range of Miriam's perceptive qualities. Her deeply-rooted love for and understanding of music as an essential part of her self, as a partner speaking to her and evoking her response, makes her gladly accompany a piece of music on its way through time, moving with and being moved by it. What Bujic says, then, is - at least in these instances of complete musical perception - true for Miriam too:

> I find in music [...] my own ideal self, speaking to me from the notes or expressing itself in them, in their harmonies and sequences. I am this self, that is to say the self that has identified itself with the sounds - not only imagined self, but real, i.e. a self actually experienced, a self that experiences a fully-rounded interior history in the sound structures that occur in succession and form themselves into musical units. The essence of music lies in this interior history (304).

Music, influencing Miriam's behaviour in such an intense way, assumes a meaning that lies beyond the perception of sounds and phrases. As we shall see, this extra-musical function is not only important with regard to specific scenes, but plays its role in the narrative unfolding of the text as a whole.

---

into the room. [...] She began thinking secretly of the world waiting for her outside and felt she was affronting every one in the room; treacherously and not visibly as before. She had got away from them but they did not know it.'

[28] e.g. *DL*, 31: Sissie tells Miriam that Shatov would not come: 'She could not go on playing, the room was cold and black; horribly empty and still. [...] She played on zealously for a decent interval, closed the piano, and went downstairs.'

[29] e.g. *DL*, 97: the gramophone not running at the right speed.

[30] e.g. *IN*, 346: 'growing weary' of the sounds, Miriam 'had left off listening.'

3.2 'A Pattern Woven Continuously:' Musical Form in *Pilgrimage*

> A work of art [...] has internal order. It may have external form. That is how we recognize it.
>
> (E.M. Forster, *Two Cheers for Democracy* 88)

> How not be struck by the inside pattern of life? It is so obvious that everything is arranged. (*RL*, 282)

Unlike novels such as *A Passage to India* or *To the Lighthouse*, where the rigidly structured text in its 'classical' form-consciousness shows formal aspects comparable to sonata or symphony forms,[31] the open, unfinished character of *Pilgrimage* does not suggest such a formally coherent musical parallel. *Pilgrimage*, a 'symphony that swells into larger dimensions as it progresses through various movements' (Kumar 496), expands the scope of a closed, rounded-off structure, contrary to the expectations of some of its contemporary critics. Richard Church, for instance, believed that, the 'narrative coming full circle & the portrait of the heroine rounded off,' *Clear Horizon* would be Dorothy Richardson's last volume.[32] And when *Dimple Hill* appeared as part of the four-volume edition of *Pilgrimage,* presented, to Dorothy Richardson's 'helpless dismay and disgust,' as a *complete* work,[33] critics either passed over this 'cul-de-sac,' in silence or triumphantly claimed that 'this endless chronicle never was getting anywhere & now peters out.'[34] Any expectations of a traditionally satisfying conclusion in a well-plotted end were thus thwarted. Marriage, madness or death, are options available for women characters in many traditional novels, but not for Miriam.[35] Dorothy Richardson herself never aimed at such a precipitated conclusion of her narrative, as many of her letters show.[36] All the material of her life

---

[31] The three sections of *A Passage to India* have been compared to 'the three blocks of sounds of Beethoven's Fifth Symphony (Brown, E. K. 113); whereas the three parts of *To the Lighthouse* in their inner development of fast-slow-fast or their acoustic quality (voiced-quiet-voiced) suggest obvious parallels to Mozart's classical sonata form.

[32] Letter to Koteliansky, 18. 4. 1936, *WM*, 311.

[33] Letter to P. Beaumont Wadsworth, August 1938, *WM*, 350.

[34] Letter to P. Beaumont Wadsworth, 8. 12. 1938, *WM*, 357.

[35] In her autobiographical sketch 'Data for a Spanish publisher' Dorothy Richardson writes: 'I believed myself to be, even when most enchanted, intolerant of the romantic and the realist novel alike. Each, so it seemed to me, left out certain essentials and dramatised life misleadingly. Horizontally. Assembling their characters, the novelist developed situations, devised events, climax and conclusion. I could not accept their finalities' (*JP*, 139).

[36] e.g. Letter to Bryher, 2. 6. 1938: 'I cannot say I enjoy having the twelve chapters to date, wich [sic] have landed Miriam in Quakerism from whose insufficiencies I am now engaged in rescuing her, represented as the whole of Pilgrimage' (*WM*, 347).

'clamouring for expression' made her go on 'until the pen drops at last,'[37] causing an ever-growing accumulation of details, characters and events increasingly independent of any formal principle.[38] Even when, in *March Moonlight*, Miriam starts writing about her life, when the character is on the point of becoming her author, Dorothy Richardson avoids this rounded-off closure and, in Loeffelholtz's words (61), leaves the reader 'with the sense of having approached, if never quite arrived at, the point of art's dissolution into life.' *Pilgrimage* as a whole will obviously not be remembered for its formal coherence; traditional musical structures as we find them in the pieces Miriam plays are not conspicuous elements in the organisation of this text.

Yet there are some musical parallels to be discovered, however inconsistently drawn and truncated. As with a piece of music, such structural elements are essential parts of the narrative framework, but it is only in the composition as a whole, in the union of material, form and expression, that the full impact of a work of art can be grasped. Being aware of the structural devices in the text helps us to understand it in a more complete way. The sequence of thirteen (open-ended) novel-chapters can be read as a growing, open-ended set of variations upon the theme of self-discovery, whereby each of the variations - as in some Beethoven variations - not only plays with the *theme* in a new way but at the same time also varies material of previous *variations*. Thus, in reading this text in its web of allusions and recalls, of faintly remembered threads of thoughts and reappearing relationships as a set of variations, thematic forms become audible that can in points be identified and traced as structural elements before they are varied and transformed.

If we just think of the recurring elements of the journey in each novel-chapter, best symbolized by Miriam's indispensable Saratoga trunk and Gladstone bag, of Miriam's ambiguous love-rivalry relationship to other women[39] and more or less serious flirtations with men in most novel-

---

And letter to P. Beaumont Wadsworth, 8.12.1938: 'You know, I daresay, that Pilgrimage is not finished' (*WM*, 357).

37 Letter to Bryher, 1.6.1943, *WM*, 470. This urge to continue at all costs, however, is at once, in the same letter, endangered by her feeling that 'I don't care a hoot whether or no I ever write another word.' These contradictory attitudes grown out of a certain tiredness with the unending demands of her subject, may largely account for the erratic progress of writing of the eventually incomplete 'last' novel-chapter, *March Moonlight*.

38 Feminist critics, such as Friedman (357), emphasize the incompleteness and formal looseness of *Pilgrimage* as a central point of Dorothy Richardson's 'formulation of feminine narrative:' she 'created a revolutionary option for her female protagonist. Miriam simply goes on; she grows progressively wiser, more complex, more confident. Her fate is to live, not to die, not to be subsumed in marriage to a superior male as is Emma but to remain at the center of the narrative.'

39 e.g. to Fräulein Pfaff (*PR*), Julia Doyle (*BW*), Mrs Corrie (*HC*), Mag and Jan (*TU*), Amabel (*DLH*), Rachel Mary Roscorla (*DH*), Jean (*MM*).

chapters,[40] of her repeatedly changing rooms,[41] but also of Dorothy Richardson's consistent use of the garden, of music, of silence as means of self-finding, we can read them as thematic and motivic concepts being taken up and varied time and again throughout *Pilgrimage*. In each of the variations the rich theme, promisingly laid out as *Pointed Roofs*,[42] undergoes change, accumulates meaning and reaches its densest and at the same time most unorganized representation in *March Moonlight*, which abounds with allusions and repetitions of elements presented earlier.

Tracing overall musical patterns, the order of the single novel-chapters and their suggestive titles resemble an alternation of major and minor keys: the dynamic energy of *Pointed Roofs* expressing the happiness of Germany is followed by more stagnant school impressions in *Backwater*. Sweet *Honeycomb* depicting the leisurely life of the upper classes gives way to the abysses of sadness and feelings of disorientation and being stuck of *The Tunnel*, *Deadlock and The Trap* respectively. These abysses, however, are bridged by the relatively gayer tones of *Interim* and *Revolving Lights*, the latter of which heralding a new period of light. This is reached in the turning point of *Oberland*, whereupon the remaining novel-chapters already in their title images of light, clarity and height (*Dawn's Left Hand*, *Clear Horizon*, *Dimple Hill*, *March Moonlight*) perpetuate the major mode of the beginning without ever quite reaching its original unreflected happiness. The theme has obviously grown in the course of this set of variations.

Apart from such highly generalized parallels to music there are other musical devices providing the huge textual material with some rhythmical shape. The tapestry of Miriam's mental life as depicted in *Pilgrimage* can be read as a complex musical score, a music that rises and falls in slow rhythmic variation and counterpoint, a music flowing through time whose notes weave fine threads in the rich texture of the account of Miriam's pilgrimage. It is in 'listening' to these threads that the reader may grasp the underlying coherence of the text. In an abundant web of allusions, working with elements of repetition that assume leitmotivic strength, Dorothy Richardson thus seems to emphasize Miriam's quest for unity and wholeness on a textual level as well.

---

[40] e.g. with Pastor Lahmann (*PR*), Mr Parrow (*BW*), Bob Greville (*HC*), Hancock (*TU*), Michael Shatov (*DL, RL, TR*), Vereker (*O*), Hypo Wilson (*DLH, CH*), Richard Roscorla (*DH*), Charles Ducorroy (*MM*).

[41] in Hanover, at Wordsworth House, at Newlands, at Mrs Bailey's, at the Brooms', at Flaxman's, in Oberland, at Dimple Hill and in a fast succession in Vaud, at Sally's, at St John's Wood, at Amabel's and Michael's and finally in London at Mr Noble's place.

[42] According to Radford the main ideas of the theme are even presented in the very first paragraphs of *Pointed Roofs* (cf. Radford 1991:28).

3.2.1 'With Perfect Freshness:' Past into Present through Repetition

> Notre passé est [...] ce qui n'agit plus, mais pourrait agir, ce qui agira en s'insérant dans une sensation présente dont il empruntera la vitalité. Il est vrai qu'au moment où le souvenir s'actualise ainsi en agissant, il cesse d'être souvenir, il redevient perception.
>
> (Henri Bergson, 'Matière et Mémoire' 370)

> [...] this knitting together of past and present [...] (*MM*, 597)

The most significant example of repetition that establishes textual coherence is Chopin's ballade, which Miriam listens to in Germany (played by Clara Bergmann), in Oberland (played by Vereker), and eventually on her final return to London. It appears at crucial turning points in her life as a herald of better times promising joy and a temporary home. She experiences the joy 'when music sounded up through the house, of home-coming from long exile' (*O*, 47). The same music announces her first meeting with Mr Noble, the fictional portrait of Dorothy Richardson's husband Alan Odle: the '*final complete* crescendo of the Chopin ballade that welcomed me in Oberland' (*MM*, 654; emphasis added) promises a similar welcome and home-coming. Both her new start in Oberland and her attempt at finding a new home in Germany resonates in the sounds of this ballade, thus joining the end of her 'pilgrimage' to the beginning.[43] With each repetition the anaphoric quality of the ballade increases as more and more of Miriam's personal history is referred to. It expands in meaning, but remains the *same* music, thus reflecting a central issue of Dorothy Richardson's writing: to recognize in the continuously expanding dimension of *becoming* the underlying existence of an unchanging *being*. The structure of the music as Miriam hears it summarizes and reflects what lies at the centre of *Pilgrimage*: The charm of the ballade

> she now saw, coming to it afresh and with a deepened recognition, lay partly in the way it opened: *not beginning*, but *continuing* something gone before. It was a shape of tones caught from a pattern woven *continuously* and drawn, with its rhythm ready set, gleaming into sight (*O*, 36; emphasis added).

Does *Pilgrimage* not open in the same way, 'not beginning' the story of Miriam's life from scratch but 'continuing' the life of the 17-year-old girl?

---

[43] This is an important aspect of plot cohesion, as Brooks writes: 'Repetition, recall, symmetry, all these journeys back in the text, returns to and returns of [previous material ...] allow us to bind one textual moment to another in terms of similarity or substitution rather than mere contiguity' (92).

Does not each of the many new starts in fact take up and include what has 'gone before'? And what is the whole text but a 'continuously' woven pattern, a steadily flowing rhythm of one individual life, highlighting here and there certain aspects of this life? The single sounds of this specific piece of music as they are heard by Miriam on her pilgrimage thus assume a symbolic significance that unexchangeably link them to the text of *Pilgrimage*.

There are a few other pieces of music whose repetitions have a deictic purpose, adding to the coherence of longer parts of the text: Schubert's *Ave Maria*, played by Miriam to distract her mother in her eventually fatal despair (*HC*, 470), appears again not much later during Miriam's first visit at the Wilsons'. The shabby, stiff and stifling atmosphere of home has been replaced by the superficial 'easy' 'unconcerned' small-talk of a well-to-do society, where Miriam feels at ease and accepted as 'one of the Wilson kind of people' (*TU*, 131). She thus plays the 'quiet waves' of the 'lovely' accompaniment and listens to the 'sudden, jolly sentimental voice' of the singer in a mood of relaxed, but pretended, 'happiness' that is markedly different from the strained effort to keep up 'a sort of blaze of happy strength' (*HC*, 470) in the 'dreadful little room where despair was shut in' (*HC*, 471). And yet, the very repetition of this *Ave Maria* pointing back to Miriam's darkest and saddest period of life links the two scenes, hinting at her feelings of guilt and grief that underly her superficial happiness. Again: repetition of the same, which through the very act of repetition is not quite the same, in order both to describe contrast and to imply continuity?

Chopin's *Funeral March*, announced and performed by Julia Doyle in *Backwater*, gives this single novel-chapter some internal structure in that it marks the starting point and end of Miriam's strange relationship with Julia, the pupil-teacher who came from Ireland with the sole purpose 'to learn Chopang's Funeral March. It's all I think about' (*BW*, 275). Julia's unrefined, outgoing behaviour easily winning the girls' confidence forms an antipode to Miriam's refined, scrupulous detachment; Julia's manners, which raise in Miriam a curious mixture of feelings of envy, hatred, fear and hidden love, are presented in a number of episodes that dominate large parts of *Backwater*. And yet, this apparently happy, cheerful girl knows the 'night' side of life, too. Tortured by nightmares, she would speak passionately about her hatred of the sea, her horror of woods and trees - a sharp contrast to Miriam's preferences - but it is only in music that she eventually manages to give expression to her secret, unhappy self.

Though the way from the mere idea of Chopin's *Funeral March* to its completion in Julia's performance is not described, it is clear from the result that Julia has not only acquired the idiomatic language of music, but in a singular act of appropriation has made this music her own: The melancholic march full of pathos and pomp has become everything there is in Julia's secret self (or so it seems to Miriam): 'Desolation' and pain, loneliness, 'shadow-filled life' and death (*BW*, 345). So, the *Funeral March* assumes a symbolic function revealing, in Forster's terms, Julia's 'hidden life at its source' (*Aspects* 56). In the expressive *finale* Julia, rather a 'flat' character in *Pilgrimage*, thus gains unexpected roundness and welcome depth.

And there is Beethoven's music, which Miriam plays throughout *Pilgrimage* as a means to express herself, to reassure herself, to *be* her self in a confining, strange and superficial world. It is not one specific piece of music but rather the unique voice of Beethoven 'speaking to one person' (*IN*, 346), the personified expression of Miriam's thoughts that accompanies her through life. It is in this repeated representation of Beethoven's music, if anywhere in *Pilgrimage*, that leitmotific elements can be identified;[44] for in each of these Beethoven scenes similar connotations are evoked, the textual meaning is the same. Structure and meaning - together with the primary sensuous quality of sound - complement each other.

From the beginning, from her first impressions in Hanover, Beethoven's music appears as ideal:

> That was music . . . not playing things, but listening to Beethoven. . . . It must be Beethoven . . . Grieg was different . . . acquired . . . like those green figs pater had brought from Tarring . . . Beethoven had always been real (*PR*, 56).

His music, thus, is *not* acquired but innate, part of her own self, expressing her own emotions and thus making her happy: 'grave and happy she sat' (*PR*, 57), 'drawing easy breaths and relaxing completely'(*BW*, 205), she can 'see the steady shining of broad clear light' (*TU*, 28), sees the 'friendly light,' hears 'the triumphant echoes' of the room (*IN*, 335), expresses her happiness at Dimple Hill in the solitary living-room in loud 'thunderings of Beethoven' (*DH*, 529), and, playing the last movement of the 'Pathétique,' experiences rhapsodic delight in growing again aware of '*being*, of the fact of the existence, anywhere, of anything at all' (*MM*, 638). Her sensuous awareness of Beethoven's sound makes her see behind 'things' and see the real truth: Playing a largo movement she hears 'the great truth behind the fuss of things [...] the great truth that was bigger than anything. Beethoven' (*TU*, 28).

In this apotheotic revelation Miriam not only realizes that such fundamentally moving music *makes* her happy, but as her most personal music also *expresses* her own happiness to the - potential - listener, to the reader. The Beethoven scenes thus appear in a leitmotific way at important moments of happiness in Miriam's life; while Chopin's ballade is associated

---

[44] According to Calvin Brown (1948:211), a leitmotif serves by way of its repetition 'to link the context in which the repetition occurs with earlier contexts in which the motive [*sic*] has appeared,' and thus forms one means to establish textual unity.

with the moment of home-*coming*, Beethoven's music is strongly linked with the notion of *being at home* in a house, together with other people: Miriam plays Beethoven at the school in Hanover, back *home* at Barnes enjoying the long summer holidays before school life at Banbury Park, at Harriett's, where she has found a temporary '*home*' after the nightmarish disintegration of her family, at Mrs Bailey's, her *ersatz* mother, at the Roscorlas', where she for a short time feels like a member of the family, and at the YMCA in St John's Wood, where - again - she has found a makeshift *home*, having been driven from her paradise at Dimple Hill.[45]

Structurally, Beethoven's music in *Pilgrimage*, apart from its 'horizontal' quality of establishing links between the various novel-chapters, thus shows a marked 'vertical' axis too, since each musical scene adds to the meaning, makes the text deeper, enriches it with another colour. As in *A Room with a View* and *Mary Olivier*, Beethoven's music in *Pilgrimage* at the same time adds to the 'horizontal' coherence of the overall text by the mere repetition of its verbal representation and - by the 'vertical' accumulation of meaning with each repetition - underlines some essential truths about the heroine's secret life.[46] Recognizing the extra-musical meaning of their music all three, Lucy, Mary and Miriam, gain insight into their selves and then use their music to express important aspects of their inner lives.

In Beethoven - and in Chopin - Mary Olivier finds happiness and a liberating retreat, away from family and social restrictions, into her own self: 'She was *too happy* to care. Nothing mattered so long as she could listen to herself playing the moonlight sonata' (187; emphasis added).When the Vicar of Renton, offering her unwished for social tasks in his parish, had gone

> she opened the piano and played, and played. Through the window of the room Chopin's Fontana Polonaise went out after him, *joyous, triumphant and defiant*, driving him before it. She *exulted* in her power over the Polonaise. *Nothing could touch you, nothing could hurt you while you played*. If only you could go on playing for ever - (177; emphasis added).[47]

---

[45] The same holds true, though to a far lesser extent, at Bonnycliff where she *hears* Hypo playing Beethoven twice, but where she is not really moved by his playing.

[46] May Sinclair uses a 'Hungarian March' as a leitmotif to underline the increasingly difficult relationship between Mary and her domineering mother. In various scenes this march comments on Mary's emotional response towards her mother, which turns from admiration (69) to a mixture of rivalry and self-reproach (120) and eventually to a form of resigned distance (323). The string that is ripped up in this last scene dramatically symbolizes the breaking of an inner band between the two women. Mary's estrangement from her mother is paralleled by her estrangement from music: It is the last scene in the novel in which the piano is touched, in which music expresses something about Mary's life.

[47] cf. 124f: 'Nothing could take [*her hidden happiness*] away. Anything might bring it: the smell of the white dust on the road, the wind [...]; the five elm trees, stiff, ecstatic

It is this same feeling of secure inviolability that seizes Lucy Honeychurch when she withdraws from pension life to play Beethoven, coming to terms with her feelings:

> It so happened that Lucy, who found daily life rather chaotic, *entered a more solid world* when she opened the piano.[...] A very wet afternoon at the Bertolini permitted her to do the thing *she really liked*, and after lunch she opened the little draped piano. [...] She *took no notice* of Mr Emerson looking for his son, nor of Miss Bartlett looking for Miss Lavish, nor of Miss Lavish looking for her cigarette-case. Like every true performer, she was *intoxicated* by the mere feel of the notes; they were fingers caressing her own; and by touch, not by sound alone, did she *come to her desire* (Forster, *Room* 29f.; emphasis added).

And so does Miriam when leaving the bustle of the Hanover school, the busy life at Mrs Bailey's or the family engagements at Dimple Hill to find some musical expression for her feelings. The structural, 'syntactic', aspect of Beethoven's music as a leitmotif supports the 'semantic' aspect of Miriam's understanding of music and its significance in her life. If other leitmotific elements, such as the sound of a violin in the streets of London, emphasise Miriam's aural awareness, Beethoven's music is by far the most important in *Pilgrimage*. For in its representation sound, structure, and meaning ideally complement each other as parts of the persuasive language of music.

3.2.2 *Revolving Lights*: Dorothy Richardson's 7th Symphony

> Der formelle Kern der Symphonie steckt noch heute im dritten Satze derselben, dem Menuett oder Scherzo, wo er plötzlich in vollster Naivität hervortritt, gleichsam um das Geheimnis der Form aller Sätze offenbar zu machen. [...] Was sich aber in dieser Form ausdrücken liess, das sehen wir zum höchsten Entzücken in der Symphonie Beethovens, und gerade da am schönsten und befriedigendsten, wo er seinen Ausdruck ganz nach dieser Form stimmte.
> (Richard Wagner, 'Ueber Franz Liszts Symphonische Dichtungen' 307)

> [...] music that was once more the promise of joy [...] (*RL*, 366)

In the chapter structure of the thirteen novel-chapters of *Pilgrimage* two obviously stand out. Most parts of *Pilgrimage* are subdivided into 9 to 15

dancers, holding out the broken ladder pattern of their skirts; haunting rhymes, sudden cadences; the grave "*Ubique*" sounding through the Beethoven sonata.'

chapters each; in contrast, *The Tunnel* with its 33 short chapters, suggesting the 33 cantos of Dante's *Inferno* mentioned in the text, and *Revolving Lights* with its only 4 lengthy chapters show a special concern with form.

According to Dorothy Richardson, *Revolving Lights* is, 'I think, though not in its form, the best of the books;'[48] and yet it *is* its form too, its dense structural organisation, that places it among the most ambitious of her novel-chapters. It is the most musically composed, showing parallels to Beethoven's 7th Symphony - the performance of which lies at the centre of this *7th* volume of *Pilgrimage* - not only in the coincidence of the number 'seven' Fromm (1977:147) pointed out, but also, and much more impressively, in the four chapters corresponding to the four movements of the symphony, each of them highlighting one possible form of a 'love' relationship. The world of London offering anonymous protection on her walk in the first 'movement;' Michael's foreign world in the second and Hypo's bohemian world in the third movement; finally a strange oscillation between all these worlds, including her world of work at Wimpole Street, in the last movement: these are four massive blocks of text,[49] like Beethoven's four movements, discontinuous, separated by gaps, and yet held together by a unifying thread that provides overall coherence. In the music it is the unceasing and varied expression of a deep joy in life both in theme and mood, in the text it is basically Miriam's ever-renewed quest for her own world, a world that is eventually to be filled with a similar individual joy.[50]

London, 'this mighty lover, always receiving her back without words, engulfing and leaving her untouched, liberated and expanded to the whole range of her being' (*RL*, 272), is enthusiastically received in the long walk of the first 'movement', as it offers her life in all its aspects and gives her this ideal mixture of closeness and freedom, of uncommitted virginality that has to dread no consequences. The tune of this 'ambulatory meditation' (Fleishman 442), her walk home through the Westend to Tansley Street, is polyphonically enriched by the voices of different London worlds: 'the established, unchanging world of Wimpole Street' (*RL*, 233), the 'full and bright' (*RL*, 264) yet 'small isolated Tansley Street world' (*RL*, 233), the socialist world of the lecture she has just attended, the Russian

48 Letter to Bryher, 21. 6. 1946; *WM*, 540.

49 Chapters I and III being the two longest of *Pilgrimage* with 56 and 53 pages.

50 In Proust's later parts of *A la Recherche du Temps Perdu* Genette (128) similarly notices a tendency towards the creation of enormous scenes, 'séparées par d'immenses lacunes,' towards a narration 'de plus en plus massive, d'une brutalité beethovenienne.' Dorothy Richardson, however, later on gives up this discontinuity and massive expansion of scenes for a much more coherent 'flow' of action from one shorter chapter to the next, especially so in *The Trap* and *Oberland*, which she considered her best books from a formal point of view (cf. Letter to Bryher, 21.6.1946; *WM*, 540).

revolutionaries she is going to meet (*RL*, 239), Michael (*RL*, 239, 260f, 279, 284), her parents' different backgrounds of Puritans and West country yeomen, people 'she helplessly belonged to' (*RL*, 247), Hypo's intellectual circle, Tommy Babington as part of her lost childhood world, Eleanor Dear, Mrs Bailey - they all in turns occupy her consciousness, add to her critical self-examination and progressing perception of her inner reality, which is firmly held together by the framework of the outer reality of her nightly walk home through the brightly-lit streets of London - hence the double-meaning of the title of this novel-chapter.[51]

In Barthes' structuralist terms, the various references to the process of changing place from the lecture hall back home to Tansley Street make up the *cardinal function* or *nucleus* of the narrative, the chronological and logical line forming its 'hinge-points' (1977:93ff.). In the precise geographical data given 'on the way,' Dorothy Richardson underlines the consecutive and consequential aspect of walking home. These so-called 'informants' (Barthes 1977:96) serve to authenticate the reality of the scene - on a map of London Miriam's walk home could be followed for a large part.[52] Using a musical metaphor, this narrative basis of the chapter harmonizing the text can be seen as a form of a thorough-bass: though constantly present and giving the chapter its unity, it is rarely foregrounded; and yet it forms an essential part of the composition: if it were not for this underlying movement through real space, Miriam's wanderings of the mind would lack the basic coherence that make the text a readable narrative at all. In a different context Barthes (1970:35) stresses the importance of these 'séquences proairétiques', which are the actions that can be summarized in one term (here: walking home), when he compares them to 'le fond des cordes, [...] ce qui soutient, ce qui enchaîne régulièrement, ce qui harmonise le tout.' This basically musical concept of building up and keeping together the text is of central importance in the long first chapter of *Revolving Lights*.

---

[51] This unique panoramic unfolding of Miriam's past, present and future life in her consciousness, the purely subjective 'narration' of different aspects of Miriam's being typically changing from 3rd to 1st-person narration and back - would perfectly lend itself for a Genettian analysis of narrative chronology. An analysis of the subjective anachronies, both analeptic and proleptic, in this first chapter of *Revolving Lights* would reveal the immensely rich working of the individual mind so impressively rendered in Dorothy Richardson's language. Such an analysis, however, would go far beyond the scope of this chapter on *musical* structure (cf. Genette, 'Discours du Récit' 80 ff.).

[52] The reader is able to follow Miriam from the lecture hall into the street and via Oxford Street, Bond Street, Piccadilly, Piccadilly Circus, Shaftesbury Avenue further east towards her home in Tansley Street (*RL*, 233 - 289). Preceding Mrs Dalloway's famous walk through London by just two years, Dorothy Richardson's description does not achieve the elegant structural balance between outer and inner reality of Woolf's text.

What makes up the bulk of these fifty-odd pages are - to quote Barthes (1977:97) - 'expansions' of the 'nucleus', many-voiced excursions of Miriam's imagination into spaces of her own past, present or future. Her thoughts, memories, anticipations, digressions are to some extent 'indices' of Miriam's self, revealing in a particularly intensive and detailed way the working of her associative mind.[53] Whether it is men or women, being English or being a foreigner, silence or Sunday: what Fleishman (442) calls the entire 'urban network of associations,' like a set of brilliant variations upon a theme, eventually refers to her individual self.

Like the rhythmic element that determines the first movement of Beethoven's 7th Symphony, this insistence on Miriam's individual mind forms the thematic core of the first chapter of *Revolving Lights*, which - similar to Beethoven's music - opens with a slow movement, gradually increasing in depth, celebrating in a unique way the perfection of the passing moment. Her walk home, which fills her with the richness of life, thus finds its counterpart in Hypo's playing Beethoven's first movement: 'living in space alone, at one with everybody, as every one was, the moment life allowed. Beethoven's perfect expression of the perfection of life [...] He was revealing himself as he was when alone' (*RL*, 365), and so is Miriam: fully aware of the perfection of her solitary moment, of the spaces of London surrounding her and exposing her self to herself. Miriam thus is, to use Dorothy Richardson's words, living through 'whole strands of life' simultaneously, 'in current possession, from a single point of consciousness, of [her] whole experience intact,' 'onlooker at [her]self living.'[54] Both in music and text this first and longest dynamic 'movement' is formally and thematically the richest, determining to a large extent the unique character of the whole symphony and novel-chapter.

The pensiveness of Beethoven's *Allegretto*, in its mood taking the traditional position of the slow movement of a symphony, is reflected in the serious topic of the second chapter of *Revolving Lights*. Here Miriam realizes that her own and Michael's character are profoundly incompatible; their fundamental opposition thus resonates in the opposing voices of Beethoven's music too. Michael, who sees her as a 'proud English possession' (*RL*, 291), would like to get married 'at once' (*RL*, 301), - a thought Miriam recoils from as she perceives their unbridgeable separateness.[55] It is in the visit of the Lintoffs that this contrast between her

---

[53] Barthes, 1977:92f. I use the term 'indice' in the very broad sense of referring to something else paradigmatically.

[54] Dorothy Richardson's review on H.A.Foster's *Studies in Dreams*; cf. Fromm 173f.

[55] Michael's 'perpetual continental science,' his male rational 'enlightened' thinking 'had helped to kill their relationship. With him there could *never* be any *shared* discovery.' Miriam is '*no longer* passionately *attached* to him' (*RL*, 303f.; emphasis added).

and Michael appears all the more poignantly, for Lintoff, the Russian, and Madame Lintoff, the Jewess, represent the two alien sides in Michael that Miriam eventually cannot imagine ever becoming her own identity. In the 'quivering *alien* song that was singing itself in the spaces of the room' (*RL*, 297) she hears cultural and religious differences; furthermore, in the 'duet of *contrasting* voices' (*RL*, 311) she recognizes the abyss that separates them in their relationship: 'Of the actual life of the passing moment they felt no more than Michael. Itself, its uniqueness, the deep loop it made, did not exist for them' (*RL*, 314; emphases added). Due to the catalysing power of this meeting Miriam sees her break away from Michael as the inevitable consequence of their being so different. Still physically attracted to his 'glowing Hebrew beauty, [to] his kind, reverberating voice', (*RL*, 291), to the man who first threatened her self-imposed isolation, she struggles hard between opposing forces which tell her that solitude brings 'perfect happiness' (*RL*, 330) and warn her of the return of 'dreadful' loneliness (*RL*, 320).

While Beethoven juxtaposes the introvert, resigned beautiful songline in minor with some repeated glimmers of pervading joy, still subdued but more extravert passages in a major key equalling the intermittent emerging of an underlying joy, a 'hilarity against which *nothing* seemed to be able to prevail' (*RL*, 321), Dorothy Richardson in the second part of this chapter underlines the struggle between hope and resignation in the use of contrastive notions when Miriam sits in her room, contemplating her situation (*RL*, 320 - 330): silence and noise, warmth and cold, light and darkness, deeply felt religious communion and Miriam's solitary 'profanity;' all show her indecision, her feeling of 'looking with a hundred eyes, multitudinously seeing each thing from several points at once,' recognizing 'no goal' (*RL*, 324). In this fragmentation of her self she has momentarily lost orientation, resignedly accepting the feeling of her 'perfect social incompatibility' (*RL*, 315). Yet it is this fragmentation too, her feeling of emptiness, that - according to Hanscombe (70) - fuels her 'unceasing zeal for unity and lasting wholeness' of her self. Only in the final escape from all diverting outside influences 'into the tireless unchanging centre' does Miriam accept 'the certainty that she must remain alone' (*RL*, 330), a certainty which is also expressed in the confirming *forte* chords at the end of Beethoven's second movement.

The circling image of the title of this novel-chapter finds its best musico-structural equivalent in the 'round-and-round scherzo' of Beethoven's symphony (Canisius 191). The open dance form of this movement, full of repetitions and variations, contrastive elements of scherzo and trio, filled with a gay, rollicking inspiration corresponds to the dance-like constellations in the third chapter of *Revolving Lights*: Alma - Miriam; Alma - Hypo; Hypo - Miriam; Hypo - Edna; Edna - Miriam; these successive partners in conversation are all kept together by Hypo's witty, sometimes rollicking charm. Who but *Hypo*, focus of interest for all three women, should play Beethoven's symphony, at once casting his spell over them and causing feelings of rivalry in Miriam?

What Beethoven does in music, Hypo wants to do in relationships: to transgress the rules of convention, to open up established forms, to thwart expectations of traditional behaviour. As in Beethoven's *Scherzo* the traditional framework of scherzo-trio-scherzo is given up for a freer form, so Hypo, enchanting, fascinating, charming, leaves behind the conventional ideas of marriage for a freer form of love that allows him to be intimate with his wife, Edna, and Miriam *in turns*: He is casting a 'fascination that could not be defined; that drove its way through all the evidence against it. Married yet always seeming nearer and more sympathetic than other men' (*RL*, 341); 'married, but casting radiance' (*RL*, 345), he intermittently includes Miriam, Alma, and Edna in his bright 'revolving' light. Edna, talking to Hypo at dinner, is 'catching the light, expanding, expressing a secret joy' (*RL*, 346); Miriam, listening to his voice, watches 'the developing bright pattern' of his argumentation (*RL*, 350); his glance swept round to Miss Prout and 'flashed into admiration' (*RL*, 355); Miriam caught his eyes 'flashed upon her' (*RL*, 361); finally Hypo carries 'Alma off to the study with the bright eagerness he gave to an entertaining guest, but intimately' (*RL*, 362). This alternation of light and shadow falling on Miriam in Hypo's presence can be heard in the music of Beethoven's *Scherzo* too, where brighter and darker phrases repeatedly alternate - suggesting the 'revolving lights' of this novel-chapter.

It is, however, not easy for Miriam, who wishes to be 'the centre of [Hypo's] attention' (*RL,* 338), to accept the shadow of Edna's presence: 'There would be no expansive bright beginning [of her holidays], *alone* with Alma and Hypo, [...] the *centre* of their attention. "Who is Edna Prout?" she demanded *jealously* (*RL*, 338; emphasis added). Jealousy, weakly covered by condescending pity, becomes the driving force of Miriam's relationship to Edna.[56] Their shared interest in Hypo, the man, the writer, the piano-player, the would-be lover, creates a tense atmosphere of rivalry, which reaches its climax when Hypo plays Beethoven's 7th Symphony. The principal contrast of this chapter - bright vs dark - found in the settings of the scenes - outside vs inside, day vs night, garden vs house - seems to be reconciled in the 'perfect' music of Beethoven, but the inner tension culminates in Miriam's finding out that Hypo has played the symphony for Edna only.

---

[56] e.g. 'Poor Miss Prout with her short week-end' (340); 'My arrival was an interruption in a companionship that made conversation superfluous. What need for Miss Prout to talk when she could put into his hands, alive and finished, something that she had made?' (342) 'If Miss Prout was not enviable [...] then no one was enviable' (349). Edna's 'swift hot glance' suggests a corresponding feeling from her side (348). And Miriam is glad when Edna leaves: 'Evil had gone from the air, leaving it empty' (360).

Miriam, experimenting in relationships throughout *Revolving Lights*, feels the keen pang of disappointment when she realizes Hypo's preferences: not she, but Edna, her rival, is at the centre of his thoughts; she is both physically and metaphorically excluded from the 'promise of joy' of Hypo's Beethoven: 'The roomful of music was in another world' (*RL*, 366). Although the 'shock' of this discovery stops her direct, full-hearted participation in the dance of possibilities, the scherzo of her stay at Hypo's rolls on under a slightly changed maxim: 'To agree. That was the answer. Not to care' (*RL*, 366). In the ensuing conversation with Hypo the personal side of their relationship is hidden behind a witty, yet impersonal discussion of different forms of socialism. Only at the end of this third chapter is the original tone of the scherzo taken up: in the dance-like constellations of the tennis match new possibilities of friendships open up, the 'smooth young man' (*RL*, 381), the foreign giant, and Hypo attracting her in different ways each. Yet, as in the coda of the symphonic movement, the theme is only alluded to before the chapter closes: 'Now was the time for talk, exchange. [...] Perhaps the tall man . . . Alma had come forward and was saying her good nights, hurriedly. They were to go, just as everything was beginning. All chance of truth was caught, in a social trap.' Once more 'the door was closed' (*RL*, 383), shutting her out not only from the men's conversation, but from her own defence of truth, and from her finding her unified self again, which is left at the end of this scherzo shattered in 'three separate selves.'

The fourth movement, the shortest both in symphony and text, completes the central idea of the previous movements without adding many new aspects. When Miriam hears Hypo's interpretation of this movement, she perceives it in a rare instance of pure *analytic* listening. In contrast to the former movements she now, detached from the music and its performer, feels no emotional response, but is only aware of technical and formal details:

> But he liked best the slamming, hee-hawing rollick of the last movement. Because it did so much with a theme that was almost nothing. . . . *Bang*, toodle-oodle-oodle, *Bang*, toodle-*oodle*-oodle, *Bang*, toodle-oodle-oodle-*oo*. A lumpish phrase; a Clementi finger exercise played suddenly in startling fortissimo by an impatient schoolboy; smashed out with the full force of the orchestra, taken up, slammed here and there, up and down, by a leaping, plunging, heavy-hoofed pantaloon, approving each variation with loud guffaws. The sly swift dig-in-the-ribs of the sudden pianissimos (*RL*, 365).

This movement, accepting and expressing life in sounds of joyful, powerful energy, perhaps finds its best correspondence in the image of the tiger on the blue plaque in Mr Hancock's room, which opens chapter IV. The full force of this picture, 'inexhaustible, never looked at enough; always bringing the same joy' (*RL*, 384), resembles the direct powerful appeal of Beethoven's music. Sound and image, aural and visual works of art express the same *joy* of life that lies at the core of Miriam's present state of being. Despite her juxtaposing and rejecting different worlds in the hope of finding an ideal partnership and despite the continuously thwarted expectations, joy shines through everything in this last chapter, just as it does in Beethoven's music.[57]

It is here, then, that joy, 'the last deepest level of her being' (*RL*, 321), is revealed, admitted and confirmed in a powerful way. While Beethoven's last movement does 'so much with a theme that was almost nothing,' Miriam's joy, her underlying optimistic attitude, sees her through all obstacles, varying her life in all possible directions, approving of her own variations not with 'loud guffaws' but rather with a serene silence, 'almost nothing', yet in the end the only way of judging 'your relationship to a person' (*RL*, 389). It is in these joyful pianissimos that she hopes to find fulfilment.

Her own happiness as the only factor in establishing a lasting relationship, however, is not enough. As in her various earlier attempts at a complete integration and understanding of other people and their worlds she eventually fails here too. She sees herself and Hancock as 'foreigners in each other's world. Irreconcilable' (*RL*, 385). And with the Taylors 'she was incompletely in their world as in his.' She realizes that 'understanding speech she could never have with any one' (*RL*, 385), and she tells Hypo that she 'can't get on with anybody' (*RL*, 389). Though experiencing positive glimpses of unknown worlds in the visits of Mr Graham, with whom she feels a deep communion of souls, and of the fascinating, enchanting Grimshaws, she greatly enjoys the prospect 'of being once more single and clear, free of every one, homesick for London' (*RL*, 391). Beginning and end of the novel-chapter are thus linked: The joy of solitude in the big city is here again - stronger than in the first movement as she in the meantime has had her eye on different possibilities of love only to reject them all and concentrate on her own self. It is therefore a logical consequence that in the following novel-chapter, *The Trap,* Miriam leaves the well-known surroundings of Mrs Bailey's and hardly ever gets in touch with either Michael or Hypo. Miriam, who retreats to the 'nowhere' (*TR*, 399) of Flaxman's Court to enjoy once more the freedom of a new beginning, is accused by Hypo of living in 'a

---

[57] e.g. *RL*, 385: her joy of being with Hancock in silence / 386: the feeling of 'strong happiness' giving herself an extra day off / 386: the Grahams' 'marvellousness of life' made them 'both so serene. Everybody was lifted by being with them into that part of life that goes on behind the life that seems to be being lived.' / 390: 'The joy of being with [Hypo]' out of a feeling of being elected amongst women. / 394: 'The feeling of immense deliberate strength going forward, breaking out through life' when leaving Hypo. / 396: 'Joy had spoken first and left her no choice. Startling her with the revelation of the way her roots of her being still centred in [Hancock]. Joy deeper and more powerfully stirring than the joy of the past weeks.'

system of evasions' (*RL*, 387); and indeed, she evades all issues that would bear any consequences. As a contrast to her experiments in relationships in *Revolving Lights*, 'soaring freely within this new life' (*TR*, 406) thus is to become a primary experience of the first chapters of *The Trap*.

While we can read *Revolving Lights* in its clear four-chapter structure in terms of a musical composition, the situation is much more complex and unsatisfactory when looking at *Pilgrimage* as a whole. Just as with Wagner's musical dramas, the overlong text makes enormous demands on the listener, on the reader. In Dorothy Richardson's urge to write on, in her refusal to come to a rest, there results a huge middle with little or no end, or - musically speaking - a perpetual dissonance that is never resolved in the consonance of fulfilment, arrival and redemption. The progress from consonance to dissonance and eventually back to consonance characteristic of both 19th-century music and the conventions of the opening, middle, and end of 19th-century texts has no appeal to Dorothy Richardson; she seeks new, modern ways of meandering through dissonances and atonalities. Dissonances promising interest through tension are followed by new dissonances. This, however, becomes problematic, for if tension never relaxes, tension never really builds. There is, then, in M. Brown's words, 'little dramatic shape in the text' (1992:80f.). This is a point of justified criticism Katherine Mansfield, author of perfectly structured, economic *short* stories, makes when she writes about Dorothy Richardson: '[...]everything being of equal importance to her, it is impossible that everything should not be of equal unimportance' ('Dragonflies,' 64).

In the endless piling up of unresolved narrative dissonances Dorothy Richardson follows Wagner's concept of the 'infinite melody:' not only should there be unbroken continuity - Miriam's consciousness - but also significance in every detail; every note, every word should express something of practical relevance to the overall text that is inwardly linked to other moments. In order to accept this ceaseless 'becoming,' which abandons traditional structural emphases and meaningless formulae for the sake of a constantly expressive narrative, the reader is asked to enter into what Barthes (1977:163) calls 'practical collaboration.' He or she is asked to 'play' the text in the musical sense of the term, interpret it and denote those underlying structures that are relevant for the establishment of significance. Then the fascinating oscillation of the text sets in; a host of interpretive possibilities opens up calling the reader to a 'final approach to the Text, that of pleasure.' In this sense, the huge textual body of *Pilgrimage* allows innumerable interpretations, for it embodies, like every true work of art, a deeper significance than the original meaning the author may have intended.

Pursuing our analysis of the function of music in *Pilgrimage* we shall therefore examine the significance of some musical scenes with regard not only to Miriam's sensual impressions but also to their contextual setting in the development of *Pilgrimage* as a long novel.

3.3 'A Rapturous Message:' The Meaning of Music

> Music is something more than sounds and succession of sounds, melody, harmony, and rhythm. Like everything else that is beautiful, music is an expression of life.
>
> (Bojan Bujic, *Music in European Thought* 302)

> [...] the first phrase of the seventh symphony. Perfect. [...] Beethoven's perfect expression of the perfection of life. (*RL*, 365)

Whenever a piece of music is played, sound, form, and expression are present as its formative elements, ready for a listener to grasp. C.Pratt (205f.), defining the different types of listeners according to their listening experiences, makes the distinction between the 'autonomous' listener, who concentrates on music alone as a closed system - focusing his attention either on the *sensuous* experience of pure sound or on the more *analytic* perception of musical structure - and the 'heteronomous' listener, who insists on the power of music to transcend mere auditory form towards an extra-musical realm of thoughts. E. M. Forster characterizes these three main types most perfectly in the Schlegel family listening to Beethoven's 5th Symphony: Margaret, 'who can only see the music,' and Tibby, who is only interested in form, representing the two autonomous types of purely sensuous or analytical listening, Helen, who endows music with her personal, fixed, meaning, representing an extreme example of heteronomous understanding of music.[58]

However, what is shown time and again in *Pilgrimage*, in normal life listening preferences are not that stereotypical: they depend as much on the listener's personal situation, on his or her concentration or inattentiveness. Thus, the focus of listening not only varies from one performance to the next but can even change within one single piece of music. Attending a concert together with Michael Shatov, Miriam first listens to a piece of music in an emotionally detached way and thus appears as an *analytical* listener:

> [...] Though there was no gathering of the forces of her being in response to the music now advancing upon her and of which she was aware *only as a shape of tones, indifferently noting their pattern, the alternating prominence of the various groups of*

[58] Forster writes: 'The notes meant this and that to her, and they could have no other meaning, and life could have no other meaning' (*Howards End* 35). Music is here truly *hetero*nomous, naming something else, expressing her state of being.

> *instruments and the varieties of tempo and rhythm*, its presence was a relief. *The process of following the pattern* brought the movement of time once more into realizable being and, while she travelled along it, even to the accompaniment of *music stripped to its bones and robbed of its penetrating power by this chill preoccupation with its form alone*, she hoped that the fragment of courage with which, just now, she had urged herself forward, might be gathering force. [...] Once more she raised her eyes to glance, for reassurance, at Michael seated at her side. But before they could reach him, a single flute-phrase, emerging unaccompanied, dropped into her heart (*CH*, 298; emphasis added).

Yet the sensuous and emotional quality of this flute-phrase leads her away from analytical observation to an integrated, more intense *heteronomous* listening, in which this piece of music now has a meaning beyond the mere sounds: within its melody it conveys a crucial non-musical meaning.

> Oblivious of the continuing music, she repeated in her mind the little phrase that had spread coolness within her, refreshing as sipped water from a spring. A decorative fragment, separable, a mere nothing in the composition, it had yet come forth in the manner of *an independent statement* by an intruder awaiting his opportunity and thrusting in, between beat and beat of the larger rhythm, *his rapturous message*, abrupt and yet serenely confident, like the sudden brief song of a bird after dark; and so clear that it seemed as though, if she could turn her eyes, she would see it left suspended in the air in front of the orchestra, a small festoon of sound made visible.
>
> No longer a pattern whose development she watched with indifference, *the music now assailing her seemed to have borrowed from the rapturous intruder both depth and glow; and confidence in an inaccessible joy.* But she knew the change was in herself; that the little parenthesis, coming punctually as she turned to seek help from Michael who could not give it, had attained her because in that movement she had gone part of the way towards the changeless central zone of her being. The little phrase had caught her on the way (*CH,* 298f.; emphases added).

Beyond Miriam's awareness of all the technical details, this music becomes a medium for a deeper understanding of the subliminal existence of her being that is 'more than her momentary self' (*DLH,* 222), triggering 'an intensely apprehended revelation' of her innermost being (Rose 1969:373). The little phrase accompanying her on her self-discovery thus resembles Proust's little phrase of Vinteuil's sonata, which - at exactly the right moment - catches up with Swann's emotions, expresses his feelings and opens up a sphere of mythical interiority (Knapp 113). Unlike Proust, however, who attributes the little phrase with emblematic meaning and uses it later on in the text as a structural element, a signal to refer back to Swann's original love for Odette,[59] Dorothy Richardson mentions her little phrase only once: its only function is to open Miriam's inner 'barriers' (*CH*, 298). It is meaningful as a sign of Miriam's *intra*personal awareness only.

In other musical scenes, however, the wider narrative focus includes extra-musical, *inter*personal aspects, and music is used as a tool which carries meaning to express some aspects of Miriam's various relationships that remain unspoken or are only hinted at in the text. Beyond the mere phenomenological experience of sounds, music thus forms one of Dorothy Richardson's key figures that prompt some of Bronfen's queries.[60] Music can reflect Miriam's sensations of and emotions towards other people. In the text it thus fulfills what Mursell (17) calls 'the essential function of art' in general: 'to express and objectify emotion in design.' On this *inter*personal level of Miriam's awareness music, depending on its position in the text, carries important messages: of understanding and disagreement, of love and rivalry, of identification and contrast, of projections and disillusions. Let us just think of Miriam's original closeness to her younger sister Harriett, which finds its best expression in their playing duets (*BW*, 297), or of the occasional sense of intimacy with her elder sister Eve conveyed by music: 'Music, any music, would always make Eve real' (*DL*, 100). There is her difficult relationship with Gertrude Goldring in Hanover, which is best understood as soon as we 'collaborative readers' hear Gertrude's deeply unmusical singing (*PR*, 46f.); and there is the sense of an immediately felt communion of souls when Miriam plays to Amabel (*DLH*, 187). The rendering of Miriam's relationships by means of a musical setting is even more complex in the doubly removed music-dream reality of Lilla's piano-playing (*HC*, 484f.), which - as Radford (1991:95) shows - in its mixture of feelings of identity and contrast serves to describe hidden truths about Miriam's relationship to her mother.

In her relationships to men music carries similar interpersonal meaning: whether it is the implied communication of love in Ted's wish to hear 'Abide with me' before Miriam leaves for Germany (*PR*, 16), her disillusionment with Mr Tremayne's conventionality (*TU*, 27f), her projective listening to Hypo's Beethoven, which ends in rivalrous disappointment (*RL*, 366), her budding love for Shatov when playing and waiting for him (*DL*, 31), or her initial interest for Guerini, whom she supposes to be the Chopin player at Oberland (*O*, 40), music time and again takes up and expresses Miriam's

---

[59] Genette, 'Métonymie chez Proust.' *Figures III,* 58: 'La petite phrase de Vinteuil est devenue pour Swann et Odette "comme l'air national de leur amour:" autant dire son emblème.'

[60] Bronfen 176: 'Wie gestaltet [Dorothy Richardson] die phänomenologischen Empfindungen reflektierend? In welche *eigenen* Bilder ordnet sie sie sinnstiftend ein?'

attitudes towards men, conveying, on a narrative level, meaning that goes beyond intrinsic 'autonomous' *and* 'heteronomous' qualities of Miriam's immediate perception of the respective pieces of music.

In her repeated use of and allusions to vocal music Dorothy Richardson establishes a sub-text that gives decisive impulses for the understanding and interpretation of her text. It is *extra*personal, narrative significance that is implied in the unprinted texts of the many interspersed songs, hymns, operetta and opera scenes. What interests us most in these cases is not Miriam's awareness of such a musical text (though it does play some role), but rather Dorothy Richardson's use of the texts in the construction of her narrative. In what way does this vocal music underline explicit issues and throw them into relief? Where does it rather emphasize hidden or additional aspects and thus possibly qualify what is an apparent reality?

On the very first page of *Pilgrimage* music, the sound of the ballad 'Wearin' o' the green', not only triggers in Miriam some happy memories of the past - her intrapersonal reaction - but expresses an extrapersonal, narrative purpose: as Radford (1991:28) points out, the theme of exile and dispossession is introduced in its unspoken text, underlining the prevalent atmosphere of depressed leave-taking. Miriam's juxtaposition of English and German hymns in *Pointed Roofs* represents her continuous comparison of the two cultures and her highly favourable view of everything that is German.[61] At the same time their thoroughly Protestant texts emphasize the confidence and strong belief in authority that forms the backbone of Fräulein Pfaff's rigid school system.[62] Similarly, the strong notion of paradise pervading *Dimple Hill* is supported by the texts of the four hymns Miriam remembers on a Quaker Sunday, forming 'a class apart' (*DH*, 491). Though for Miriam the tunes rather than the words, 'whose meaning one had never considered' (*DH*, 491), make these hymns special, we recognize in these words the continual theme of the exiled pilgrim who seeks a home: the un-said words mark the subliminal presence of the idea of paradise in the text.[63]

---

[61] e.g. her comparison of the two versions of 'Nun danket alle Gott' (*PR*, 75), a hymn which reappears much later on (*RL*, 381), evoking Miriam's happy months in Germany.

[62] The hymn 'Lead kindly light' (*PR*, 72) expresses a belief in authority in the words, 'I loved to choose and see my path; but now lead Thou me on [...]' (*Hymns Ancient and Modern [=HAM]*, No. 266); or in the German hymn 'Ein feste Burg' the second verse includes these words: 'Mit unsrer Macht ist nichts getan / Wir sind gar bald verloren. / Es streit für uns der rechte Mann / Den Gott hat selbst erkoren.'

[63] cf. Chapter 2.4. Significant words are: 'Light's abode, *celestial Salem* [...] Mansion of the Highest King' (*HAM*, 232); 'O Paradise! O Paradise! / Who doth not crave for rest? / *Who would not seek the happy land* / Where they that loved are blessed? Now in the meanwhile, with hearts raised on high,/ *We for that country must yearn and must sigh;/ Seeking Jerusalem, dear native land,/ Through our long exile on Babylon's strand* (*HAM*, 234). The hymn *Jerusalem the Golden,* which expresses this happy belief in paradise in

The Schumann songs appearing in the first three novel-chapters likewise reinforce the atmosphere of their respective settings, reflecting Miriam's emotional state.[64] Especially in the early novel-chapters, there are other instances of narrative meaning in Miriam's music, such as the various pieces of *The Mikado*, the enormously popular operetta by Gilbert and Sullivan, or the volume of songs by Sterndale Bennett (*PR*, 58), whose main textual significance lie in their authentic, realistic rendering of middle-class taste of the period.[65]

While every piece of music performed in *Pilgrimage* can be seen as an external reference, a document of authenticity, we shall choose two cases of internal reference in the later volumes: Miriam's two visits to the opera show in an exemplary way Dorothy Richardson's establishing extra-musical, i.e. contextual meaning. Her choice of *Faust* and, above all, of *Der Fliegende Holländer* is not only interesting as they represent the French and German innovative opera of the 19th century, but it is also important in that their plots provide Dorothy Richardson's text with sub-texts and themes focusing on aspects of human relationships and emotions that correspond to Miriam's individual situation. Opera, 'the most complete and obvious nexus between music and extra-musical experience' (Mursell 268), flowing from and epitomizing life experience, turns out to be the appropriate comment on and congruous musical expression of such situations.

---

the most powerful way, even appears *expressis verbis* in a different context in *Pilgrimage*: on a bicycle ride through the countryside Miriam sings it as a direct expression of her happiness (*TU*, 229): 'Jerusalem the golden,/ With milk and honey blest, / Beneath thy contemplation / Sink heart and voice opprest. / I know not, oh, I know not / What joys await us there, / What radiancy of glory, / What bliss beyond compare. // They stand, those halls of Sion, / All jubilant with song, / And bright with many an Angel, / And all the Martyr throng. [...] O sweet and blessed country, / The home of God's elect! / O sweet and blessed country / That eager hearts expect! Jesu, in mercy bring us / To that dear land of rest; / Who art with God the FATHER / And SPIRIT, ever Blest. Amen' (*HAM,* 228).

64 cf. *PR*, 152f. Schumann's 'An den Sonnenschein,' op. 36. No 4. *PR,* 167: his 'Frauenliebe und Leben,' op.42, No 1. *BW*, 219: possibly his version of the *Lorelei, op.* 53, No.2. *HC*, 374: 'Ich grolle nicht.' *Dichterliebe*, op.48, No 7.

65 In such details, however, Dorothy Richardson shows great musical knowledge. Choosing Sterndale Bennett (1816-1875) of all her English composers as the only one worth playing in Germany, Miriam takes music that in its very essence is an ideal bridge between English and German culture: for Bennett, member of the 'Leipziger Schule' and founder of the London Bach Society, was greatly influenced by German composers and spent much of his time in Germany as a friend of Mendelssohn's. His living Romanticism was praised both in Germany and England by composers such as Schumann and Gade (cf. *Musik in Geschichte und Gegenwart*, I, 1662).

3.4 The 'Silent Significance:' Miriam and the Myth of Man's Redemption

3.4.1 Prelude: Gounod's *Faust*

> Almost the only elements of Goethe's *Faust*, Part 1, that are retained in Gounod's opera are the demoralized state of the hero and the tragic episode with Gretchen (who is called Marguerite in the opera). However, in its limited way, this facile example of Romanticism touched the hearts of the general public.
> (P. Brunel, *Companion to Literary Myths, Heroes and Archetypes,* 435)

> The sombre scene offered the consolation, suddenly insufficient, that she had found in the past in sliding idly into novels, the restful sense of vicarious life. She had heard of a wonderful philosophy in *Faust*, and wondered at Mr Shatov's claim for its charm. But there was, she felt, no space, on the stage, for philosophy. [...] The real meaning of it all was scenes, each with their separate, rich, silent significance. (*DL*, 199f.)

When Michael Shatov unexpectedly invites Miriam to see Gounod's *Faust*, which is for him 'perhaps the most beautiful and charming of all' operas (*DL*, 199), she for the first time receives a passionate love declaration encoded in the language of music. Unlike Goethe's play, Gounod's opera focuses on the emotional relationship between Faust and Marguerite; Shatov therefore understands it to be a perfect comment on his own relationship with Miriam, the philosopher's deep admiration of and love for the young girl epitomizing his own passion for Miriam. During the performance Shatov insists on 'a personal interpretation, surprising her in the midst of the garden scene' (*DL*, 200f.), the scene which, reflecting the protagonists' feelings, culminates in a deeply emotional union of the two. Watching this scene, his passion should be answered by Miriam's sincere feelings, which - parallel to the opera - would redeem their longing souls. But she does not respond to the unmistakable hints at the obvious parallels: She refuses to see any implied personal meaning in the opera that would go beyond the scenes actually played: 'The scenes were the story, the translation of the people, the actual picture of them as they were by themselves behind all the pother . . .' (*DL*, 200).

What counts for her, then, is the immediate appeal of the opera to her senses, which allows her to be 'bathed in music.' Already impressed by the 'strange appealing music of the overture' (*DL*, 199), one of the best things in the score, which - according to Harding (109) - alluringly invites the listener into Faust's world of mystery and world-weariness, Miriam is at once immersed in the German atmosphere of the scenes and leaves behind her thoughts about her relationship with Shatov for the time being: she is 'drifting *in solitude* away from the complications of the present' (*DL*, 200; emphasis added). At the same time Miriam is fully aware of Shatov's intentions, thwarting them very consciously: She first does 'not soften towards him' as 'it was too soon to let [the wonders of music] work, as an influence' (*DL*, 201). She likewise finds it absurd 'to try to invent life which did not come of itself,' to develop a relationship that is based on the 'weak' foundations of musical emotions. Miriam thus makes a clear distinction between the positive appeal of the opera - 'It *had* been a wonderful evening, opera *was* wonderful' (*DL*, 200) - and Michael's appeals to her heart, and she resists any temptations to yield to them: the 'sudden compunction,' the 'busy repentance' (*DL*, 201) she feels because of her cold-heartedness, even the sense of a 'strange radiance', 'some essential irrecoverable glory' (*DL*, 202) in being together with him, cannot induce her to an avowal of her happiness. As she does with all other men, Miriam shies away from close spiritual and physical intimacy. It is Marguerite's intimacy with Faust, after all, that leads to her destruction and death.

In the opera, in a climactic and archetypal scene, Marguerite first retreats, 'chaste innocence' (Gounod II, xi, 88), into the sanctuary of her pavilion, only to open her window and her heart again to have physical contact with Faust,[66] and finally to let him enter the room. For a short moment when Miriam and Shatov reach her home at the end of the evening, the 'vicarious life' (*DL*, 200) of the opera seems to have its effects upon reality:

> On the doorstep, side by side with his renewed silent appeal, she turned and met, *standing free*, his gentle tremulous salutation.
> For a moment the dark silent house blazed into light before her. She moved forward, as he opened the door, as into a brightness of light where she should stand visible to them both, in a simplicity of golden womanhood, no longer herself, but *his Marguerite*, yet so differently fated, so differently identified with him in his new simplicity, *going forward together*, his thoughts and visions as simple as her own in the life now just begun, from which their past dropped away grey and cold, the irrelevant experience of strangers (*DL*, 201; emphasis added).

On the verge of a new, shared life Miriam refuses the significance of the opera as implied by Shatov and, 'standing free', she once more keeps the sanctuary of her being to herself in a chaste retreat to the privacy of her room and of her untouched thoughts:[67]

---

66 Faust 'saisissant la main de Marguerite', elle 'laisse tomber sa tête sur l'épaule de Faust' (Acte II, Scène XIII, 90).

67 Shortly before this scene (*DL*, 193), immediately after Shatov's marvellous kiss, Miriam 'bade him a gentle good night and reached her room, unpursued by thought [...].'

> If he were to touch her now, they would again be separated for longer than before, for always. 'Good night,' she said, brushing his sleeve with the tips of her fingers, 'dear, funny little man.'
> He followed her closely but she was soon away up the familiar stairs in the darkness, in her small close room [...] while within the stifling air the breath of sunlit open spaces moved about her (*DL*, 202).

The parallels between opera and life as suggested by Shatov no longer count; in her bodily and mental retreat to her room and to the freedom of imagination Miriam wants to keep her relationship with Shatov on a purely spiritual level. In this episode it has become clear that musical meaning can go beyond its intra-musical quality of conveying the composer's aesthetic, emotional or philosophical message to an audience. The opera as an artwork combining music, text and movement in a dramatic concept is far more explicit in mediating ideas than instrumental music. With all kinds of music, however, the listener's mental activity is crucial: the listener's imagination is the starting point for any understanding of the meaning of music (Bujic 262). The centre of attention is switched from music to the individual mind and extra-musical aspects play an important part. In our context, in Shatov's 'personal interpretation' (*DL*, 200) - whose implications Miriam rejects as simply 'absurd' (*DL*, 201) - the opera has assumed an extra-musical *situational significance* that gives this music its very special position, especially in Shatov's life. Inasmuch as Miriam *understands* this situational significance of the garden scene in Shatov's mind, the opera - from Shatov's point of view - has worked as a catalyser, but not quite successfully, since Miriam does not *accept* its implied consequences.

Beyond all musical and personal, ambiguous aspects, the opera also shows some *textual significance* in the framework of *Pilgrimage*. At a crucial point in the development of the relationship between Miriam and Shatov, Dorothy Richardson uses this episode to highlight Shatov's point of view, his wishes, urges and disappointments. In this situation music, embedded in an account of a woman's mind, thus serves as one, however restricted, means of rendering Man's point of view and, to quote Goethe (526), his obsessive fascination with 'das Ewigweibliche.'

The image of intact seclusion is also there when, after hearing of Shatov's former women, Miriam escapes into the compartment of the departing train, where she is 'left untouched' (204), and in her fear of being touched by him when meeting again: 'For pity's sake don't touch me,' she cried involuntarily and walked on, accompanied, examining her outcry. It was right. It had a secret *knowledge*' (*DL*,210; emphasis original).

3.4.2 Theme: Wagner's *Der Fliegende Holländer*

> [Wagners] Verhältnis zur Musik war nicht rein musikalisch, sondern dichterisch auf die Weise, dass das Geistige, die Symbolik der Musik, ihr Bedeutungsreiz, ihr Erinnerungswert und Beziehungszauber dies Verhältnis entscheidend bestimmten. Sein musikalisches Dichtertum war es ja gewesen, was ihn zum allmählichen Fallenlassen der hergebrachten Opernformen geführt und ihm seine neue thematisch-motivische Gewebstechnik eingegeben hatte, - neu insofern, als sie in dieser beziehungsvollen Ausdehnung über das ganze Drama nie zuvor angewandt worden war. Das hatte mit dem 'Holländer' begonnen, dessen musikalischer Kern und Keim die Ballade der Senta im zweiten Akt gewesen war: das verdichtete Bild des Dramas, dessen Thematik sich dann als ein vollständiges Gewebe über das ganze Werk ausbreitete.
> (Thomas Mann, 'Richard Wagner und der Ring der Nibelungen,' 520)

> The emotions rising in her as she heard the massed music roll by and saw in her mind's eye the little figures on the stage whose voices boomed or yelled against the orchestral din, now reaching through, now lost in it altogether, were not those he intended. (*DLH*, 172)

What *Faust* is to Michael Shatov, *Der Fliegende Holländer* is to Hypo Wilson: the dramatic and highly emotional presentation of an ancient myth of love and death, of damnation and salvation, expressing in the overpowering sounds of music a masculine philosophy of life in general and their own immediate - male - urges in particular.

Returning from Oberland, Miriam is invited by Alma and Hypo to a performance of this Wagner opera. While to her the social aspects of opera-going initially outweigh her interest in the music itself, Hypo, the 'Archseducer' (Fromm 128), like Shatov hopes that the impact of the musical drama will work on Miriam's emotions and thus help him to win her heart. Just as Shatov, in his lonesome philosophical quest not unlike his operatic hero, tries to win Miriam's love, a love Marguerite grants so easily in the opera, Hypo, the uprooted, sexually unfulfilled man, 'wanders' from woman to woman to find fulfilment, seeming to aspire to the Flying Dutchman's condition; he, an 'alien [...] to any woman ever born' (*DLH*, 263), cursed by the gods to wander through the world and to 'fly' from one amorous relationship to the next, seeks redemption in the embrace (and lasting love) of a woman. And Miriam *understands* Hypo's sexual intentions. She realizes that he invites her, his 'lover elect', to this opera with its power of 'rousing and blessing his emotions and the emotions of the young lady at his side' (*DLH*, 171) just to tune her in for his further plans of seduction.

H. G. Wells, Hypo's *alter ego*, confirms such a reading in a strikingly parallel scene in *Ann Veronica*, where Ramage, the elderly would-be lover, attempts to seduce the heroine at the same place, a box at Covent Garden, by means of Wagner's music.[68] In Wells's text everything is louder, much more direct and brutal. Ramage's understanding of that opera - *Tristan and Isolde* - is forced upon Ann Veronica and the reader so directly that it crushes alternative interpretations. In his explicit account of the plot of the opera Wells firmly establishes the theme of 'love' and 'redemption'. The sounds of this 'love-sick' (142) music itself seem to support Ramage's seductive intentions: he immediately starts attacking Ann Veronica so that her original 'passionate and deepening interest' (138) in the opera turns into a shocked repulsion of his lust. In Wells's novel the male plan of conquering his object of sexual desire by means of the aphrodisiac of Wagner's sensual music is bound to die of lack of male sensitivity.

And Hypo's plan? When Miriam refuses to be carried away by his purposeful 'bath of music' (*DLH*, 171), when she hears the music as 'yell,' 'din', 'ado,' and 'fury' (*DLH*, 172) she 'in her detached coolness' (*DLH*, 172) not only refuses Wagner's powerful sounds but also the intrinsic meaning of the opera, Wagner's male-centred idea of redemption through love, which Hypo cherishes: 'The music swept by and left her incompletely attained. [...] She could feel no sympathy with the *planful tinkering with the hidden shape of things* implied in his conscious, deliberate submitting of himself and her to a bath of music' (*DLH*, 171; emphasis added). Rejecting the situational significance of the opera Hypo suggests, Miriam thwarts Hypo's plan of using music as an emotional 'solvent' in order to convey his individual message.

Once and for all? In the second act, at the very centre of this male-centred, massive and turbulent musical drama, Wagner changes the dramatic point of view to suggest female longing in Senta's soft, haunting introvert singing. In the dream-like assurance of the ballad sung at the spinning wheel Senta's feminine psyche lies open, revealing her growth from an innocent girl to a woman who can express her desires, who emancipates herself from her prescribed role as a daughter and fiancée. Senta, who, like Miriam, is 'about to take a lover' (*DLH*, 178) shows an unparalleled determination to be an instrument of salvation in order to find fulfilment and redemption too (which Wagner grants her in the final scene where the Dutchman and Senta are shown, transfigured in death, happily locked in embrace). This crucial scene,

[68] Wells 137 - 142. Published in 1908, it predates *Dawn's Left Hand* (1931) by many years; but as it was written only shortly after H.G. Wells's short affair with Dorothy Richardson, the parallels are more than coincidences (cf. Heath 129; see also footnote 87).

- Act II, scene 1 - according to Wagner the thematic germ of the whole opera (Martin 66), is a sudden, quiet 'outburst' of a feminine personality, a happy awakening of a woman towards her true destiny; it is the only scene of the opera whose unfolding on stage interests Miriam:

> Turning to the stage, she saw golden light, the warm gold of stage sunlight, long-haired maidens in full, bright skirts and dark velvet bodices laced across brief triangles of white muslin, Senta at her wheel in the midst: long-haired, a thicker rope of plaited golden hair distinguishing her as the chosen representative of girlish felicity. Singing to herself over her wheel. Singing her sunlight and her being and her happiness. 'Tragically brief.' . . . Indestructible (*DLH*, 172f.).

Sunlight - being - happiness: These key words reverberate with Miriam's idea of paradise as well as with her experience of Oberland, which in its sublime, peaceful rest was in so many ways an awakening towards her true destiny.[69] When seeing Senta's idyll as a pause before 'the din and fury of life' (*DLH*, 172) seizes her, when listening to her singing, Miriam recognizes the 'truth' about 'life's perfection' (*DLH*, 172), which she also felt during her stay in Oberland. At this point Senta, the *chosen* one amidst 'lots of little Miriams' (*DLH*, 172) - as Hypo significantly tells her - and Miriam, 'lover elect' (*DLH*, 171), experience the same deep insight into the nature of being; Hypo's wished-for complete immersion into and identification with the operatic plot, his idea of submitting her 'in the best possible circumstances, to the emotional solvent of music' (*DLH*, 171) seems to work at last: after the opera, once more recalling music of the immediate past, Miriam 'found that the music heard and the few scenes, seen so unsatisfactorily sideways, had yet reached to the depths of her being [...]' (*DLH*, 173).

But in recognizing the parallels between Senta's and her own position in life, Miriam perceives a situational significance of the opera which is quite different from Hypo's implicitly sexual interpretation. For Miriam, Senta's happy awakening towards her own individuality is far more interesting than the overall message of the music or Hypo's suggested implications. What is shown in this scene is perhaps true for the understanding of all art: whenever the listener or beholder manages to establish links between a work of art and his or her personal experience and situation, its immediate appeal to the observer will be greatly enhanced. For Miriam's appreciation of the opera her own mental activity, switching from an impersonal listening of the music to

---

[69] *O*, 123: 'For the first time, she was seeing London as people whose secret had revealed itself during this [*sic*] last two weeks, and *was at this moment beginning consistently to live her life there as in future it would be lived*, as she had lived it, but unconsciously and only intermittently, during the past year' (emphasis added). See also *O*, 127.

an understanding of the spinning scene as reflective of her own experience, is crucial; thus the music supports and emphasizes Miriam's own situation.

3.4.3 Variations: Miriam's Other Dutchmen

> . . . nicht Liebe, Sehnsucht nach dem Heil . . .
>
> (Wagner, *Der Fliegende Holländer* 23)

> Salvation. He wanted salvation - for himself. (*HC*, 455)

Beyond the situational significance for Miriam, Wagner's musical drama as a whole assumes a *textual significance*, which changes the focus of interest. *Der Fliegende Holländer* unifies and gives voice to a pattern that permeates *Pilgrimage* in various guises: Many of Miriam's relationships can be read as allusions to and variations of Man's - the Flying Dutchman's - yearning for faithful love, rest and redemption and Woman's - Senta's - spontaneous self-sacrifice born out of her fascination with the unknown, pale stranger and her wish to grant him salvation. In leitmotivic insistence the variations comment on Miriam's complex idea(l)s and realities in her relationships with men.

However, in each of these constellations which allude to the Wagnerian topos of love and redemption, Wagner's patriarchally straightforward '*ideal*' solution, woman's free but unconditional subordination to man's will, is questioned and dismantled as soon as Miriam finds herself confronted with establishing a *real* relationship with a man. This, of course, does not prevent Miriam from enjoying her fascination with the other, unknown, sex, dreaming of happy, more or less conventional partnerships. But even in these fantasies she withdraws towards her solitary self, at the latest when her own, female, self-sacrifice is asked for.[70]

As early as her time in Hanover, when Miriam hears 'Solveig's Song' out of *Peer Gynt* sung at a concert, she soon realizes that the words of this song were 'wrong' (*PR*, 142) as they clash with her own idea of woman's position in a partnership.[71] In these words, which continue to haunt her even in her

---

[70] In some ways Miriam thus resembles Joyce's Eveline, who, Senta-like, wants to follow her sailor on his ship: 'Escape! She must escape! Frank would save her. He would give her life, perhaps love, too. But she wanted to live. Why should she be unhappy? She had a right to happiness. Frank would take her in his arms, fold her in his arms. He would save her.' In the crucial moment of departure, however, Eveline fails to join him, fearing Senta's fate of drowning. She withdraws into her solitary, isolated self, too: 'Her eyes gave him no sign of love or farewell or recognition' ('Eveline.' *Dubliners*, 41-43).

[71] Like Senta, and Marguerite in *Faust*, Solveig sings her song, '*spinning* in the sun:'

'Winter may go, and spring appear, / Next summer pass, and all the year. / And yet a time there *will* be, when / My love is in my arms again. // God bless you in your

sleep,[72] Miriam, still single and unattached, recognizes that the Penelope-like role of faithful Solveig, who waits for the return and redeeming embrace of her lover, cannot be hers. The incongruity of life and the message of this song, which 'was not what she meant' (*PR*, 143), as well as the ignorance of its singer, annoy Miriam. It is obvious for her that the reality of a relationship with a man would have to be *different*.

But how? Miriam's instinctive refusal of such a role becomes explicit in her day-dreaming about Emma's brother, a man whom she - just like Senta - has never met, but who she imagines as her version of the Dutchman,

> *alone and sad* . . . despising his family . . . *needing her.* He loved forests and music. He had a great strong, solid voice and was strong and sure about everything and *she need never worry any more.*
>
> Seit ich ihn gesehen
> Glaub' ich blind zu sein.
>
> There would be a garden [...] and strong kind arms and a shoulder. She would grow so happy. No one would recognize her as the same person [...] No good. She could never get out to that. Never. *She could not pretend long enough.* Everything would be at an end before there was any chance of her turning into a happy German woman (*PR*, 167; emphasis added).[73]

---

journeying, / And to his peace your spirit bring. / Here shall I wait until my end, / Or meet with you in heaven, friend' (Ibsen, 360).

72 *PR*, 145: 'There was not a sound. "I shall never be able to sleep down here, it's too awful," she murmured and puffed and shifted her head on the pillow.

The winter may-pass. . . . The win-ter . . . may pass. The winter may . . . pass. The Academy . . . a picture in very bright colours . . . a woman sitting by the roadside with a shawl round her shoulders and a red skirt and red cheeks and bright green country behind her . . . [...]'

73 In *Mary Olivier: A Life* we find similar, yet completely unreflected day-dreaming of a naive, adolescent girl: Mary's fascination with strangers who intrude into the seclusion of her family life is not unlike Senta's. White-faced Mr Ponsonby is cursed to wander the world and eventually spend his life away in Australia, yet Mary promises faithfulness to him, who with his kiss and embrace has woken her to an awareness of life outside her family: 'I shall always love you just the same' (95). Later she feels attracted to Maurice Jourdain, the wild 'sallowish' (131) foreigner, outcast and despised by his family for his godlessness; as his 'immaterial' beauty charms her, she is lost in a reverie about a happy life together with him, offering him redemption: 'He was ill and she nursed him, [...] He was poor and she worked for him. He was in danger and she saved him. [...] It made her sad to think how unlikely it was that any of these things would ever happen' (134).

While adolescent Miriam, similarly prone to such day-dreaming, develops into a mature woman who seeks and defends her own individual self, May Sinclair tells us the tragic life of a Senta who, hearing the Dutchman's call, does not dare free herself and follow it: out of a sense of filial duty she bans man's love to 'her real secret life' of imagination (314) and sacrifices her active life to her mother's will. Neither Senta's unconditional love for a man and the happiness linked with it nor Miriam's independence

Miriam's romantic vision embodies Senta's blind love for the unknown, lonely stranger, and the comfort she offers in order to find a transformed identity and with it her own lasting happiness in his embrace. The quotation of the opening lines of Chamisso's then highly popular poem 'Frauen-Liebe und Leben', which Miriam probably got to know in the shortened musical form of Schumann's song, evokes the picture of the ideal woman as seen by the (male) bourgeois society of the 19th century: the adoring, subservient woman who would sacrifice everything in endless, selfless love for her hero. Looking at the hidden text of the poem, we see how closely Senta corresponds to Chamisso's ideal protagonist:

> Seit ich ihn gesehen, (1)
> Glaub ich blind zu sein;
> Wo ich hin nur blicke,
> Seh ich ihn allein;
> Wie im wachen Traume
> Schwebt sein Bild mir vor
> Taucht aus tiefstem Dunkel
> Heller nur empor. [...]
> O lass im Traum mich sterben (3)
> Gewieget an seiner Brust,
> Den seligsten Tod mich schlürfen
> In Tränen unendlicher Lust. [...]
> Ich werd' ihm dienen, ihm leben, (4)
> Ihm angehören ganz,
> Hin selber mich geben und finden
> Verklärt mich in seinem Glanz.[74]

Yet again, Miriam at once exposes the falseness of such a stance, which, as she clearly recognizes, would be built on insincerity. Her reality *does* look different: 'Certainly with a German man she would be angry at once. She thought of the men she had seen. [...] They had all offended her at once. Something in their bearing and manner. . . . Blind and impudent' (*PR*, 167). In Miriam's reality Wagner's ideal union of the sexes, his promised consummation of passion, is replaced by a sharp sense of division; unwilling to accept her expected role as a wife (and possibly mother),[75] she repudiates

---

will become realities in Mary's life. Her unlived attempts at a life of her own, however, stay with her as unforgotten memories until the end of her life.

[74] Chamisso 149-151. Schumann put the first two verses into music: (Schumann, Robert. 'Seit ich ihn gesehen', 'Frauenliebe und Leben op.42.' *Sämtliche Lieder, I*, 84f.)

[75] Thus she ridicules the traditional roles of the active, yet absent man and the waiting woman at home when she, remembering some books at home, has a vision of '*Iliad* and *Odyssey* . . . people going over the sea in boats and someone doing embroidery . . . that

men as sexual beings and establishes a basic attitude of isolation not to be overcome for a long time. There are - to quote Hanscombe (1982:66) - 'abortive attachments' to Mr Parrow, Dr Hancock, Dr Densley or Richard Roscorla, which, despite mutual attraction, Miriam gives up as soon as the question of marriage and what it entails is raised. Whether it is, as Hanscombe (1982:67) claims, 'her feminism [that] proscribes any commitment,' whether it is, at least in the latter cases, her artist's attitude that strives for detachment, or whether it is her ongoing subliminal wish to find an ideal, Dutchman-like partner, that eventually drives her away from 'her' men, Miriam, unlike Senta, cannot overcome her rationalist fear of sacrificing herself, of losing her individual identity - eventually her life - to help a man find redemption.[76] Man's attractiveness thus loses its glamour: Life is too dear for Miriam to strive for the exclusive redemption that Wagner grants his lovers only in the transfiguration of death.

So, whenever *real* men - Tremayne, Grove, Shatov, Max Sonnenheim - play some variation of the Dutchman's part in Miriam's mind and life, she stops short of Senta's self-sacrificing conclusions in order to continue her free, independent life, to be 'alone' but truly 'alive' (*BW*, 284). In life there is the promising encounter with Mr Tremayne, a 'marrying man' (*HC*, 446), who wants to be engaged to her at once, 'before the year is out.'

> 'What abominable cheek,' said Miriam flushing with delight. Then she had taken the right line. How easy. This was how things happened. [...]
> Miriam caught at a vision of the well-appointed man, a year . . . a home full of fresh new things, no more need to make money; a stylish, contented, devoted sort of man, who knew nothing about one [!]. It would be a fraud, unfair to him . . . so easy to pretend to admire him . . . well, there it was . . . an offer of freedom . . . that was admirable, in almost any man, the power to lift one out into

---

little picture of Hector and Andromache in the corner of a page . . . he in armour . . . she, in a trailing dress, holding up her baby. Both, silly . . .' (*PR*, 168).

[76] In rare moments of escape from some present misery, Miriam toys with the idea of redemption through the love of unknown men. In Rosa Nouchette Carey's books, for instance, Miriam discovers the potential of such an escape: 'Life might suddenly develop into the thing the writer described. From somewhere would come an adoring man who believed in heaven and eternal life. One would grow very good' (*BW*, 284). Yet the mere presence of other - rivalrous - women would destroy this state of perfection: 'I never thought of all the awful women in such a life. I only thought of myself and the house and the garden and the man. What an escape! Good God in heaven, what an escape! Far better to be alone and suffering and miserable here in the school, alive [...]' (*BW*, 284).

The separation between husband and wife, the impossibility to meet completely is also textually implied: 'house and garden', protective walls and spaces of solitary selfhood, are set between herself and 'the man', thus emphasizing the essential division between them.

> freedom. He wanted to lift her out - her, not any other woman. It was rather wonderful and appealing. She hung over his moment of certainty in pride and triumph. But there was something wrong somewhere (*HC*, 451f.).

This impersonal vision of a man - 'almost any man' - offering salvation from family and financial problems, however appealing it sounds, would again be based upon false pretences. Life with him, despite its outer shine, would never be genuine. Surprisingly enough, Miriam feels the same fascination with him when they meet again years later:

> She felt herself [...] the ideal wife and mother and he was a bad fast man who wanted to be saved. It was such an easy part to play. She could go on playing it to the end of her life, if he went on in business and made enough money [...] (*TU*, 27).

This is certainly a wrong Dutchman landed at her home; the fake 'redemption', which her husband would literally 'buy back' with his money, obviously cannot become real. As Miriam cannot establish any deeper, spiritual, communion with him, the gulf between them would eventually remain unbridged. Miriam gets this message across to Tremayne with the help of music: in her wild, unrestrained playing of a Beethoven sonata she honestly points out this abyss, destroying all possible illusions on his side; he therefore leaves her and is not heard of again.

At Harriett's there is yet another stranger, counterpart to Tremayne's outgoing attractiveness: the haunting presence of 'sallow' Mr Grove (*HC*, 450) rouses feelings in Miriam that, again, are not unlike Senta's. Recognizing a certain spiritual kinship with this man who desperately craves salvation, Miriam does not want to lose him and conjures up a vision of finding redemption together with him in death:

> If some cleansing fire could come and consume them both . . . flaring into the garden and consuming them both, together. Neither of them were wanted in the world. No one would ever want either of them. Then why could they not want each other? He did not wish it. Salvation. He wanted salvation - for himself (*HC*, 455).

However, as soon as she discovers his selfish, almost autistic attitude, she reacts in a similar retreat to her own needs, which makes a union impossible. When he expresses his feelings for her, she withdraws. What Senta seems to achieve without hesitation, to let go all self-centred concerns, to be 'caught in something' (*HC*, 456) by the strange fascination of the unknown and to give herself completely up to the stranger, is too big an obstacle for Miriam. Trapped in their solitary egoism, neither Mr Grove nor Miriam is able to come forward towards a redemptive union of their souls.

While these early attempts at and visions of shared life lead nowhere, Miriam later recognizes a pattern of male fascination in the quasi-Dutchman-esque 'attractive, *ultimately unsatisfactory* Tansley Street *foreigner*' (*O*, 48; emphases added), some wandering stranger who crosses her path offering and looking for salvation in the union of marriage.[77] Michael Shatov, the Wandering Jew, with his restlessness, his attractiveness for Miriam and his former experiences with women, his urge to find lasting happiness in marriage, perhaps comes closest to the image of Wagner's Flying Dutchman. In Miriam's imagination, the fellow-guest Guerini in Oberland as well, the 'piteous' stranger (*O*, 40) who is 'wistfully alone; attractive' (*O*, 45), possibly 'a refugee' (*O*, 75), 'a simpler Michael' (*O*, 92), assumes traits of the Dutchman who leads Senta towards mutual salvation. Yet Miriam realizes that this foreigner, soon reduced to a 'common and ordinary' businessman (*O*, 122), cannot offer true redemption: He too was

> lonely, had an empty life, in the busy businessman's way of having an empty life: no centre and a lonely leisure. And he was more than half bent on offering her the chance that so often in the past had been at her elbow, of pretending herself into a single settled existence, a single world, safe. Even now it was a temptation (*O*, 123).

What Wagner presents as the redemptive solution, is once more revealed as 'pretending.' Senta's decision to leave behind lover, family and friends, and with them her whole past in order to put an end to the lonely, aimless, 'empty' voyages of the Dutchman and to find a new, common, 'centre' in the safe embrace of love does appeal to Miriam: 'it was a temptation'; but she knows perfectly well that her independent self cannot find fulfilment in the traditional union and female subordination of marriage. Seen in the harsh light of reality this temptation thus turns out to be 'absurd' (*O*, 123).

The theme of the Flying Dutchman is varied in a most interesting way in the description of the Barnes dance in *Backwater*. In this scene not only do Miriam's thoughts and visions allude to Wagner's opera, but her very behaviour resembles Senta's - at least in the first two acts of the opera.[78]

---

[77] Throughout *Pilgrimage* the 'charm of strangeness' (*TR*, 488) is alluring to Miriam. What she summarizes as 'exogamy' (*TR*, 488), the marriage outside one's own tribe, is a recurrent idea in her fleeting attachments to foreigners such as Lahmann, van Heber, Mendizabal, Bowdoin or Ducorroy, as well as in her relationships to men belonging to the class she 'had been flung out' of (*O*, 77) such as Hancock or Densley. Yet the anticipated role-playing as a wife, which Miriam feels must attack the integrity of her self, makes her realize that men and their world represent a dead end (cf. Hanscombe 1982:92 and 96).

[78] In a kind of prelude Dorothy Richardson combines the notions of love and destruction with Wagner's water imagery by quoting a phrase out of Byron's poem 'The Dream': immediately before the dance scene Gerald writes into Miriam's album:

Like Senta, Miriam happily enjoys the sheltered atmosphere of life at home with her family, friends and her suitor Ted - Senta's Erik. Just as in the opera it is the arrival of a 'stranger',[79] whose '*white* handsome face' (*BW*, 217; emphasis added) immediately attracts her, that disturbs the domestic peace:[80] Max Sonnenheim, epitome of the Wandering Jew who restlessly travels through the world - Germany, England, Paris, New York - arouses an irresistible fascination in Miriam which is similar to Senta's fatal attraction to the Dutchman. Senta in an intuitive act of self-sacrifice leaves behind her furious suitor Erik to find the perfection of the Dutchman's redeeming embrace; Miriam, who wants to be together with Max, similarly neglects Ted, which leaves him 'hurt and angry' (*BW*, 225):

> If they stood here much longer, Ted, who had not been dancing, would join them. *She did not want that.* She would put off her dance with Ted until later. The next dance she would play herself and then perhaps dance again with Max. Once more from the strange security of his strongly swinging arms she would meet Ted's eyes, watching and waiting. She must dance once more with Max. *She had never really danced before* (*BW*, 218; emphases added).

Because of this feeling of initiation into the attractive, hitherto unknown, protective company of a man - which is so decisive in Senta's behaviour too - Miriam cannot escape Max's appeal. He, like the Dutchman, seems to be the wished-for man: 'Her mood expanded. He had come just at the right moment. [...] He was like a big ship towing the little barque of her life to its harbour' (*BW*, 219). So she joins him for a stroll round the garden. What follows is perhaps the most romantic scene in *Pilgrimage*, full of images of

---

'She was his life,
The ocean to the river of his thoughts -
Which terminated all.' (*BW*, 217; cf. Byron, *Works IV*, 24)

- thus introducing the theme of man's fatal attraction to woman. Byron's poem about unrequited love forms a counterpoint to Wagner's easy solution: the woman turns a cold heart to the man and does not grant him the salvation he wishes. In this respect, Byron expresses what many of Miriam's suitors must have felt: Ted, Mr Green, Bob Greville, Michael Shatov, Dr Densley - they all find their call of love unanswered by Miriam.

[79] In the stereotypical use of the word 'strange', which is used throughout the scene to characterize Max, Dorothy Richardson skilfully underlines Miriam's change of feelings towards him: the very unknown which initially looks so attractive (*BW*, 218: his 'familiar strangeness;' the 'strange security' of his arms; 219: 'this strange man;' 220: 'this stranger;') loses its appeal when Miriam recognizes differences she is unwilling (and unable) to bridge: Max's 'strange eyes [...] knew *all* about a big business,' while Miriam 'knew *nothing*' about the 'strange places' he would visit (*BW*, 224). A union of their different worlds remains impossible.

[80] Max's white face thus corresponds to the almost formulaic repetition of the phrase 'bleicher Mann' in Wagner's text (cf. *Der Fliegende Holländer*, Act II, Scene 1).

longing and seduction, of love and death, culminating in Max's words that summarize the focal idea of the myth of the Flying Dutchman:[81]

> 'Wie süss,' murmured Max, 'ist treue Liebe.'
> 'How dear,' she translated mentally, 'is true love.' Yes, that was it, that was true, the German phrase (*BW*, 220).

Faithful love, which Senta gives to the stranger and which Max expects of Miriam too, however, is too much for Miriam to promise. Her continuous concern with Ted's feelings and reactions causes very mixed emotions in her whenever she feels the touch of Max's embrace. At the same time 'horrified' and 'cradled' in his arms (*BW*, 220), she is fascinated with and somehow afraid of his straightforward action and amorous words, singling her out:

> 'I feel that there is no poison in you. I have not felt that before with a woman. [...] You are not as the women one meets. You have a soul serene and innocent. With you it should be well with a man.'
> 'I don't know,' responded Miriam. 'Is he telling me I am a fool?' she thought. 'It's true, but no one has the courage to tell me.'
> 'It is most strange. I talk to you here as I will. It is simple and fatal': the supporting arm became a gentle encirclement and Miriam's heart beat softly in her ears. 'I go tomorrow to Paris to the branch of my father's business that is managed there by my brother. And I go then to New York to establish a branch there. I shall be away then, perhaps a year. Shall I find you here?' (*BW*, 223)

Max's words remind us of the Dutchman and his redeeming companion: the innocent, happy woman who would faithfully, Penelope-like, await his return to join him for good. Just as in Wagner's opera, his physical presence has the catalysing power to wake her into another form of life, and yet Miriam leaves the final - crucial - question unanswered. It is on the one hand remorse for having neglected Ted (who in fact will leave her after her 'outrageous' behaviour), on the other hand her continuous questioning of a woman's

---

[81] The starlit sky, their solitude, the scent of the lime-trees and the nightly silence evoke a highly stylized romantic atmosphere, the coffin and Max's singing Heine's song of the *Lorelei* add some element of mystery and death to the scene. Thematically the *Lorelei* forms a counter-variation to the myth of the Flying Dutchman. Wagner's notion of female redemption goes hand in hand with destruction: Senta takes away his curse and thus ends his life. In their transfigured embrace of the final scene the lovers are united, eternal love triumphs. In Heine's poem, on the other hand, female attractiveness and the charm of music, brings only death and destruction to the man. Woman, the distant and unknown sex, is a *fascinosum et tremendum*, attractive and dangerous at the same time; once man is caught in the trap, there is no escape for him and no redemption in death. Miriam, whose beautiful hair is praised several times in *Pilgrimage*, playing the piano when Max first sees her, casts such a spell on him: his fascination with her is thus expressed in his song, music here once more assumes extra-musical, situational meaning.

traditional role that makes her refuse an answer. Senta's decisive step, her complete self-sacrifice for the sake of a man's happiness and salvation is not what Miriam eventually wants. Though she repeatedly takes such a role into consideration, Wagner's masculine point of view goes very much against her feminine quest for an independent, satisfying identity as a woman. And still, even though salvation together with Max is not achieved, even though she will not see him again - he shortly after dies of influenza in New York[82] - Max is an important character on her quest for selfhood: showing her unknown aspects of life that lie outside her wonted circle of 'home',[83] he opens her eyes to the perception of a new, liberating, and fulfilling way of living 'out and out *to a life of her own*' (*BW*, 224; emphasis added).

One of the main issues of Miriam's life is already pointed out: woman can and should find an individual way of life which is not exclusively defined by her relationship to a man. Yes, there might be a romantic attachment to a man; there might even be marriage - as the presence of Mr Noble, the fictional portrait of Dorothy Richardson's husband Alan Odle, at the end of *March Moonlight* suggests - but, as Dorothy Richardson emphasizes elsewhere (*RL*, 270ff.), there is more in a woman's life and there should be other forms of discourse between the sexes than those accepted by the standards of English 19th-century society. Man *is* a Flying Dutchman, 'puzzled, astray, [...] lonely and terrified in his universe of chaotic forces [...] pitiful. The chaos that torments him is his own rootless self' (*RL*, 280). For Miriam, this, however, does *not* mean that Woman has to be Senta, who lives up to patriarchal expectations by literally losing the chance of a *life* of her own and by giving herself up for the sake of a man's self-fulfilment and salvation.

At the same time, Miriam seems to fulfill these very expectations, she in fact confirms Wagner's vision of redemptive love when, just a few weeks after listening to *Der Fliegende Holländer* together with Hypo, she *does* give herself up to him in a sexual embrace. Has he, after all, achieved his aim to seduce her with the help of Wagner's suggestive music? What for Hypo - in his blunt view of Miriam as 'an object of desire' (*DLH*, 231) resembling Ramage in his seduction of Ann Veronica - and Miriam, still untouched in her sexual experience, should become the highlight of their friendship turns out to be an anti-climax, leading to a considerable cooling down of their relationship. Mr Duffy's words in Joyce's 'A Painful Case' (1991: 125) seem to be true for Hypo and Miriam as well: 'Friendship between man and woman is impossible because there must be sexual intercourse.'

[82] This is the only account of a male death in the whole of *Pilgrimage*; Miriam tells Miss Haddie rather light-heartedly about it (*BW*, 277).

[83] This is hinted at in Max's taking Miriam out of the protected, walled, home garden to a view of the open starlit sky representing the infinite possibilities of life (*BW*, 219).

Hypo's incapability of recognizing Miriam as a woman in all her aspects, his 'constricted, biological way of seeing sex that kept him blind' (*DLH*, 231), takes away what is left of her enthusiasm. Their awkward, mutually disappointing embrace not only destroys their present lust but radically does away with Wagner's idea of the lovers' transfiguration. While she assumes a stoic, 'madonna'-like attitude towards Hypo, showing a 'curious maternal solicitude' (Henke 59), he becomes her 'little babe, just born' (*DLH*, 232), resembling Bloom in Molly's bed, the weary traveller embarking on his quasi-foetal sleep;[84] but what for Penelope,[85] Senta, and Molly is the climax and end of fulfilled expectations, for Miriam becomes a moment of intense embarrassment. Blushing self-consciously in the embrace of her 'Dutchman', she feels completely out of place: instead of seeing him as a manly hero and desirable lover, she perceives behind Hypo's 'certainties' his all too human, 'pathetic' helplessness (*DLH*, 232); instead of romantic or sexual ecstasy she experiences an acute sense of failure.[86] In the account of this 'unwelcome adventure' (*DLH,* 257) into physical clay, in this 'ironic portrayal of Wellsian free love' (Watts 1995:69), Dorothy Richardson thus establishes a sober counterpoint to Wagner's sensuous music oozing with sexual overtones.[87]

---

[84] Joyce, *Ulysses* 606: 'Narrator: reclined laterally, left, with right and left legs flexed, the indexfinger and thumb of the right hand resting on the bridge of his nose, [...] the childman weary, the manchild in the womb. / Womb? Weary? / He rests. He has travelled.'

[85] Overjoyed at their unexpected reunion, Penelope, similar to Senta, 'could in no wise let her white arms go' from Odysseus' neck; she eventually led him to their couch to have 'their fill of the joy of love,' and to find 'lulled now by sweet slumber' their 'joy of rest.' (Homer. *Odyssey*, Book XXIII, ll. 239 - 301; 391-395)

[86] This is underlined with negative adjectives and adverbs: 'unsuitable,' 'unsatisfactorily,' 'inappropriate,' 'unwelcome,' 'ineffectual,' 'unsuitable,' (*DLH*, 232).

[87] In *H.G. Wells in Love*, Wells describes his view of his numerous 'amours': 'All these women I have kissed, solicited, embraced and lived with, have never entered intimately and deeply into my emotional life. I have liked them, found them pretty, exciting, amusing, flattering to the secret rakish braggart in my composition' (61).

A few pages later on he is more explicit about the 'special grave interest' he and Dorothy Richardson took in each other: 'For me it was a sensuous affair, for Dorothy was then a glowing blonde. But, as her book shows, she wanted some complex intellectual relationship, and I have never been able to talk to Dorothy. She wanted me to explore her soul with wonder and delight. But a vein of evasive ego-centred mysticism in her has always made her mentally irritating to me; she seemed to promise the jolliest intimate friendship; she had an adorable dimple in her smile; she was most interestingly hairy on her body, with fine golden hairs, and then - she would begin intoning the dull clever things that filled that shapely, rather large, flaxen head of hers; she would lecture me on philology and the lingering vestiges of my Cockney accent, while there was not a stitch between us. The adventurous student who cares to turn up her *Dawn's Left Hand* may confirm these statements' (64). In the world of reality their brief affair for him is thus not

In spite of its attractiveness and allusive power *Der Fliegende Holländer* eventually does not provide a model for Miriam's development as a woman. She dissociates herself from Wagner's patriarchal ideology, and she is aesthetically dissatisfied with his music: Listening back to Wagner's opera itself, we recognize that, with the exception of Senta's crucial song, Miriam resists the overpowering sounds and keeps a sober distance by recalling music that forms a big contrast to Wagner's. The 'tremendous ado' just increases her awareness of 'all that is left unsaid, all that is said by the music of Bach - which would have been quite unsuited to [Hypo's] purpose: stillness, dailiness, the quiet, blissful insight whose price is composure' (*DLH*, 172).

Noise and silence, outside and inside, Wagner, 'writing down the world in sound' (*IN*, 346), and Bach, showing the 'close pattern of life from within' (*RL*, 347), are juxtaposed: Bach's music tending towards silence, Ihde's 'horizon of sound' (50), strongly contrasts with Wagner's incessant drowning of his horizon in sound. It is not in Wagner's amassing of notes, in the hyper-sensuous dramatic power of the opera with all its implied messages but rather in the 'clean, cool poise' of Bach's music, in its 'secret joy' pouring through everything (*RL*, 347), that Miriam becomes aware of the 'deep quiet sense of *being*' (*DLH*, 172) lying at the core of everything. The freshness she hears in Hypo's playing Bach's music, which breathes in human dimensions,[88] convinces her of 'life's perfection' (*DLH*, 172): If you 'liked Bach, how not believe in people? How not be certain of God?' (*RL*, 347)

More than any words do, Bach's music conveys this sense of an 'inner serenity' (Trickett 24), which Miriam hopes to achieve in moments of harmony with the world and her self. The central notion of music as an audible, non-verbal expression of an inner life of the soul, of 'one's own deep sense of being' (*DLH*, 167), thus implies that music with its immediate expressive appeal is, finally, even superior to language.[89] Such an understanding of music harmonizes both with Miriam's growing awareness of the importance of what is left unsaid and with her deeply-rooted appreciation of silence.

---

more than one of his 'first wanderings of my desires' (61); for him Dorothy's asexual intellectual affectation wrecks all her latent, Senta-like, feminine redemptive qualities.

[88] *RL*, 347: 'The close pattern of life going on for ever, the end in the first small phrase, every phrase a fresh end and a beginning.' Wagner's music is a 'tide of sound,' 'massed music', having 'sheer size and strength' as its main quality (*DLH*, 171f.).

Gurney would understand Miriam's preferences as based in nature: 'The one condition we attach to the scope of the imaginative work is one which, as it happens, we find to hold in the organisms of Nature [...]; namely that it shall not be too vast, nor the relations of its parts too complicated, for the sense and the mind to apprehend' (Bujic 265).

[89] cf. Steiner 62. In *Pilgrimage* music, like silence, often exceeds words in force, as for instance when in Germany it draws 'even Fräulein into the magic circle and disarm[s] her' (*DLH*, 167). Fräulein loses her power when being taken in by music.

4. Silence: In Quest of Truth

Elected Silence, sing to me
And beat upon my whorled ear,
Pipe me to pastures still and be
The music that I care to hear.
(Gerald Manley Hopkins, 'The Habit of Perfection,' ll. 1-4; *Poetical Works* 112)

She heard life in the silence. (*IN*, 453)

In all music, sound draws attention to itself. To Miriam, the listener, the sounding of music is first of all an auditory event, a dense embodied presence of sounds that fill her with a sensuous immediacy and thus penetrate her awareness. For her, to listen to music, therefore, is to be engaged in a bodily listening that seizes her mind and calls forth a response. Her intellect, her memory or her imagination thus infuse the music with meaning and help establish it as a core experience of her consciousness. If the sound-meaning of wordless music is relatively opaque, as no standardized, objective means of expression are used, meaning seems to be even more undefined, subjective, when Miriam listens to silence. As with music, the atmospheric, sensual bodily experience of silence for her comes first. Yet the acoustic phenomenon of absolute silence *per se* hardly exists in Miriam's auditory experience: she almost always registers silence as a counterpart to sound, as a complement that engages her aural sense just as much as the most impressive sound penetrating her ear; as such it may - and often does - form a new core of experience.

In exceptional moments of contemplative introspection Miriam, like the very young Stephen Dedalus, who 'shut and opened the flaps of his ears' (Joyce, *Portrait* 11) to keep away and let in the surrounding noises, 'constructs' silence as an *exclusion* of sound.[1] As a rule, however, Miriam strives for a more embracing attitude of listening: her ears are open to seek the sound that is always, as a possibility, present within silence as well as its complement, silence inherent within sound (cf. Laurence 204). Melting into the ambient sounds, smells and sights of nature,[2] creating a soft atmosphere

---

[1] e.g. *DL*, 114: 'She dropped away from the circling worlds of sound, and sat thoughtless, gazing inward along the bright kaleidoscopic vistas that came unfailing and unchanged whenever she was moving, alone and still, against the moving tide of London.'

[2] e.g. *TU*, 216: 'A soft land-breeze was coming across the common carrying the scent of gorse; the silence of the sea reminded her of its presence beyond the cliffs; her own gorse-scented breeze, and silent sea and sunlit cliffs.' This experience is quite similar to

of unity, silence is set against the hard sounds of the city.[3] While the noise pollution of urban progress and technology is regarded as worse than pain, as 'annihilating' (*BW*, 326),[4] she 'feels' the influence of silence that surrounds her as peaceful, liberating, illuminating. Silence, therefore, is most often associated not with darkness but with light. In a synaesthetic intensity light appears as the fulfillment of silence; with its 'glimmering eyes' - to use Blake's image[5] - silence captivates Miriam's mind as it conveys a sense of the 'other', of the hidden side of things. Whenever she listens to these 'things speaking silently' (*RL*, 233) she shows a radiant consciousness of her surroundings together with a mystic awareness of her own self. Her reverence for silence is 'as determined in *March Moonlight* as it was in *Pointed Roofs*' (Hanscombe 1982:128); it even increases with the development of her consciousness: It is a lifelong delight in the special quality of quiet moments that illuminate her, make her see 'the inside pattern of life' (*RL*, 282).

To listen to silence for Miriam thus means to reach out for a phenomenological perception of being; it means to *be* silent, to delve 'down in the innermost sphere of happy solitude' in search of 'that self within herself who was more than her momentary self' (*DLH*, 222). Silence transcends the borderline of outer and inner life, it is a catalyst that helps her on her way from the external, characterized by action, noise, and - often - frustration, towards that internal, still richness of experience that provides lasting satisfaction.

If Miriam's repeated retreats into solitary silence can be regarded as a - mostly successful - strategy of self-defence,[6] silence reaches its most profound intensity when shared with somebody else. Self-reflective and self-centred thoughts widen into a deep appreciation of the power of personal

---

Stephen Dedalus's, who as a mature young man interiorizes his sensory awareness of external silence as a peace-giving mental source of energy. He 'felt in his heart the soft peace of silent spaces of fading tenuous sky above the waters, of oceanic silence, of swallows flying through the seadusk over the flowing waters' (Joyce, *Portrait* 283).

[3] e.g. *BW*, 298f: 'In the north of London there were all those harsh street voices infesting the trees and the parks. No! they did not exist. There was no North London. Let them die. They did not know the meaning of far-reaching meadows, park-land, deer, the great silent Heath, the silent shoulders of the windmill against the far-off softness of the sky. Harsh streetiness . . .'

[4] see also *DLH*, 206, where the sound of 'the jingle-jingle, plock-plock of the soulless north London trams' irritate her a great deal.

[5] Blake, William. 'To the Evening Star.' *Blake's Writings Volume II,* 753: 'Speak silence with thy glimmering eyes.'

[6] e.g. *DL*, 204. Leaving Shatov, Miriam relaxes in the train:
'Never again should her voice sound. [...] She had taken the first step into the featureless darkness where, alone, she was to wait, in a merciful silence, for ever. [...] A way opened narrowly ahead, attainable by one rending effort, into a silence, within which the grey light filtering through the dingy windows on to the grime-greyed floor offered itself with a promise of reassurance.'

relationships. As when listening to music in company, Miriam feels a communion of souls with people she is in tune with, a bond based on mutual understanding that in its essence lies beyond the power of verbal communication. Silence thus speaks the language of truth, confronting Miriam with the reality of her relationships more directly than any words: 'The test of absolutely everything in life is the quality of the in-between silences. It's only in silence that you can judge of a relationship with a person' (*RL*, 389). There are moments in which the shared silence appears as oppressive, as 'dreadful' (*RL*, 320), 'awful' (*RL*, 337), 'dead' (*TR*, 432) because the embarrassment, the incongruity or the gaping void in her more problematic relationships are unsparingly revealed; yet, as we shall see later, in the majority of encounters Miriam's positive attitude towards other people is enhanced once she has spent some time in silence together with her partners. The experience of the Dantean 'silenzio ne' concordi numi'[7] forms one of Miriam's 'moments of being', in which she finds the other, discovering an intensity of shared life that leaves her literally speechless.[8]

Miriam's increasing affinity to the mystic, her growing awareness of the inner side of life,[9] makes her receptive not only to the thoughts of Emerson and Maeterlinck, who are constant points of reference in the middle chapters of *Pilgrimage*, but also to the ideas of the Quaker faith. Especially in the Quakers' 'language' of silence as their expression of shared experience Miriam, who is 'only at the alphabet' (*DH*, 551), recognizes 'what makes life worth living' (*DH*, 551): In their practical reticence, in their acknowledgment of the ineffable in daily life as well as in divine inspiration Miriam observes a certain reservation about the power of language that resembles her own - and Dorothy Richardson's: In Miriam's strong pre- and non-verbal awareness Dorothy Richardson expresses her own highly ambiguous attitude towards language. She as a modernist writer is fully aware of the limits of language as a means of expression: 'Nothing' - at least nothing that is of lasting importance to Miriam's consciousness - 'can ever be expressed in words' (*TR*, 463). Does that mean that this huge accumulation of *words* is the wrong medium to convey the 'incommunicable blissfulnesses' of life (*RL*, 304)? Is this rich product of *language* a failed attempt at coming to terms with the wordless, the hidden, the absent? Or is it rather that in questioning the logocentrism of intellectual reflection Dorothy Richardson leads the reader towards an awareness of the immense presence of the tacit dimension in her text and thus to an understanding of non-rational, non-verbalized modes of

---

[7] 'the silence among the concordant souls.' Dante, *Paradiso* (Canto XIII, l. 31) 142.

[8] e.g. *IN*, 392: '"It's all too sacred for *words*." There was no choice in all that; only secret and sacred beauty; unity with all women who had felt in the same way.'

[9] A mystic is, first of all, to keep silence; see *OED*, X, 175: The Greek word μυειν means to close (the lips or eyes), hence to be silent.

being? In acknowledging this power of the non-verbal she in fact presents silence as the epiphany of what defies any verbal representation. Due to its complementary state silence thus becomes the necessary precondition to speech, to a *good* use of language: 'Real speech can only come from complete silence' (*RL*, 389).

Lexical,[10] syntactical,[11] and metaphorical[12] embodiments of silence help to establish this notion as a constitutive element of Dorothy Richardson's work.[13] Psychologically, *Pilgrimage* aims at presenting the silent, unarticulated underside of the mind, too; the text abounds with instances of the '*unsaid*', the '*unspoken*' and the '*unsayable*', as Laurence (1) defines three textual modes of silence:

The *unsaid* is what Miriam might have felt or experienced but what Dorothy Richardson does not describe. Both the author and the protagonist find 'no way of telling' certain 'untold scenes' (*IN*, 422). The unsaid, not being an active presence in the text thus remains infinitely potent. However, these gaps in the narrative provide a space for the cooperative reader in which to observe, to think, to create his or her own response to the text. It is, in Barthes' terms (1977:152), in the recognition of the 'inaudible', of the 'lack' of explicitness, that the readers will find a new significance - 'writing' the text anew in their own, individual way when reading, thus making it real. For, as Barthes claims, the text as a whole is '*experienced only in an activity of production*' (1977:156; emphasis original).

The *unspoken* - what is expressed by other means than the direct or spoken word and what is just implied in the context - and the *unsayable* - what is ineffable, 'impossible to explain' (*DL*, 70), ecstatic or religious experiences of life that go beyond the scope of language - are 'present'

---

[10] e.g. Dorothy Richardson's use of words in the semantic field of 'silence' during the Quaker service (*DH*, 495-505): still (7x); stillness (5x); silence (4x); quiet (2x); silent, tranquil, mute, voice ceasing, whisper etc.

[11] e.g. Dorothy Richardson's use of ellipsis to represent Miriam's often erratic working of the mind but also to hint at what cannot be talked about - the unsayable.

[12] In a feminist reading silence becomes a metaphor for femininity, representing 'the synthetic principle of human life' as opposed to man's rational, verbose, mechanical loudness. Man's 'mental tendency to departmentalize, to analyze, to separate' strongly contrasts the female non-verbal, intuitive awareness of the whole. Dorothy Richardson repeatedly refers to these different points of view as gender-based (cf. 'Comments', *Dental Record* XXXVI (10), 2 Oct 1916, 541).

[13] cf. Radford's psychological interpretation of silence in the text (1991:69f.):
'The words on the page (the representation of consciousness) are supplemented by a range of typographical devices: ellipses, italics, segmented passages, gaps and spaces in the text. These devices represent the repressions and gaps in consciousness, or that which is left unsaid or is unsayable. [...T]here are actually *printed silences* to register the activities of the unconscious which neither speech nor writing can reach. These blank spaces signal, more eloquently than any words, the blind spots of language and consciousness.'

silences that appear in the text by way of various devices of indirection. These silences are part of what Powys (21) calls the 'organic' 'obscurity' of Dorothy Richardson's style. Starting with a discussion of Miriam's sensory and mental perception of both solitary and shared silence, it will be a major aim of this chapter to reflect these different forms of the unheard in the light of their context and finally to show the importance of the ineffable in the growth of Miriam's consciousness.

These manifestations of silence as a *presence* on all levels of the text form the antithetical answer to the obvious power of the word in Dorothy Richardson's literary creation. Eventually it is in the synthesis of sound and stillness, in the integration of both silence and language as 'twin houses of being' (Laurence 213) in her narration that Dorothy Richardson hopes to convey to the reader what makes up Miriam's reality.

4.1 'The Quiet Sense of Life at First Hand:' The Silence of Solitude

> Fly the tumultuousness of the world as much as thou canst.
>
> (Thomas à Kempis 16)

> Miriam left the gaslit hall and went slowly upstairs. The March twilight lay upon the landings, but the staircase was almost dark. The top landing was quite dark and silent. There was no one about. It would be quiet in her room. She could sit by the fire and be quiet and think things over until Eve and Harriett came back with the parcels. She would have time to think about the journey and decide what she was going to say to Fräulein. (*PR*, 15)

In this opening paragraph of *Pilgrimage* silence appears as a crucial element of Miriam's experience of both her exterior surroundings and interior self. Withdrawing into the solitary silence of her room, she finds the inner tranquillity as well as the time to contemplate her present situation. The special position of this contemplative moment in solitude at the beginning of what was to become a long novel sequence, preceding any description of her active life and social involvement, underlines the importance of a theme that appears as a recurrent pattern throughout the novel: stillness, contemplation, and introspection form an accentuated contrast to what Miriam comes to know as a world bustling with movement, action, and sound.

Her own room - each of her many rooms throughout *Pilgrimage* - is the 'Ort kontemplativen Sammelns' (Bronfen 124) *par excellence*. It is an intimate space, which Bachelard (17) calls an 'espace heureux, [qui] concentre de l'être à l'intérieur des limites qui protègent'; thus it often offers Miriam the wished-for seclusion to start on a movement inward to her 'being far away within' (*DLH*, 225). Like Stephen Dedalus, who goes up to his room 'in order to be alone with his soul' (Joyce, *Portrait* 169), Miriam chooses the solitary stillness of her room to reach a contemplative stance, in which she can experience the concentrated fullness of a Woolfian 'moment of being.' Though silence is commonly understood as an *absence* of sound, though it is often associated with a strong notion of loss, in such solitary scenes as the opening scene of *Pilgrimage* it quite contrarily suggests a *presence* of insight and thought, actually restoring to Miriam a deep sense of being, a feeling of freedom emerging out of the surf of a noisy sea of every-day demands and activities. In this self-imposed 'harbour of solitude' (*DL*, 163) Miriam - for all their differences - feels like Mrs Ramsay, who 'could be herself, by herself. And that was what now she often felt the need of - to think; well not even to think. To be silent; to be alone' (*Lighthouse* 72).

'To think; well not even to think': It is this duality of conceptual reflection and intuitive perception that these rare moments of solitary silence offer to Miriam as well. On the one hand, the stillness allows her to embark on an intellectual process that aims at a deeper, conscious, understanding of her self and the world around her. On the other hand, the silence filling inner and outer space reduces her reflective perception, leading to what Bachelard (130) calls the 'silence des pensées'. In this intellectual silence her immediate, unreflected sensory awareness of herself is increased, which manifests itself consistently in an intense feeling of physical well-being.[14] Thus, in Hanover, she enjoys 'the great wide stillness' (*PR*, 149) spreading through her room immediately after waking up:

> She could feel the shape and weight of each limb [...] She felt that her short sleep must have been perfect, that it had carried her down and down into the heart of tranquillity where she still lay awake, and drinking as if at a source. [...] She stirred; her hands seemed warm and her cool chest and the warmth of her body sent up a faint pleasant sense of personality. 'It's me,' she said, and smiled (*PR*, 149f.).

In such moments of unreflected being Miriam's usually critical self-examination gives way to a conciliatory stance of acceptance; she feels contented both with her *self* and with the 'world', which expresses itself in her exalted wish for a harmonious global unity: 'She wanted to have the whole world in and be reconciled' (*PR*, 150). This same dream of a macrocosm merging with her own microcosm determines her nightly experiences at the Pernes' school: 'The plain room gave her encouragement.

---

[14] cf. Bachelard 30: 'Tous les espaces d'intimité se désignent par une attraction. Répétons une fois de plus que leur être est *bien-être*' (emphasis added).

It became the scene of adventure. She tip-toed about it in her night-gown. All the world would come to her there' (*BW*, 267). The silent room thus becomes the centre of her 'adventure in self-discovery,'[15] where she can retrieve the sense of her underlying, unchanging living being:

> She found when the house was still and the trams had ceased jingling up and down outside that she grew steady and cool and that she rediscovered the self she had known at home, where the refuge of silence and books was always open [...] It was herself, the nearest most intimate self she had known. And the discovery that it was not dead [...] brought her warm moments of reassurance. It was not perhaps a 'good' self, but it was herself, her own familiar secretly happy and rejoicing self - not dead (*BW*, 282).

Similarly, her room at Newlands, where 'no sound came in', 'so far away from everything, trams and people and noise - [...] in the centre of beautiful exciting life; perfectly still and secure' (*HC*, 360), becomes a refreshing oasis, revealing to her her deeper self that is likely to be stifled in the attractive yet disappointingly shallow suburban world of weekend guests and gossip. What may be read as an anti-social, solipsistic pull, is a survival strategy of Miriam's struggle for selfhood. Withdrawing from the masquerades and light conversations of Newlands to the nearest room of solitude available, she finds herself in Mr Corrie's study 'protected from the whole world in the deeps of his study chair - all the worry and the noise and the fussing people shut away' (*HC*, 366). Within these 'limites qui protègent' Miriam experiences silence as a beneficent absence: absence of thought, of sound, of people. In this solitary moment, in a mental, sensory and social void, emptied of all sorts of obstructions, she finds time for contemplation, time which she in her youthful naiveté fills with a daydream of hearing the 'understanding' voice of absent Mr Corrie. Despite his imaginary presence he would leave her 'undisturbed' (*HC*, 367), thus protecting her refuge.

When Miriam moves to London, driven out of her self-contained world of adolescent dreams into both the freedom and insecurity of the metropolis, the same atmosphere prevails in the quiet sanctuary of her room at Tansley Street. Staley (69) claims that after the big family disaster Miriam's reactions to sense impressions in her moments of illumination have 'become less euphoric'; yet her awareness of Sunday morning silence in *Tunnel* calls forth a response as enthusiastic as it was in the earlier novel-chapters:

> [...] at seven o'clock in the silence, with the air coming in from the squares smelling like the country, is bliss. [...] I *am* frantically,

[15] sub-title of Horace Gregory's biography: *Dorothy Richardson: An Adventure in Self-Discovery*. New York: Holt, Rinehart and Winston, 1967.

> frantically happy. I'm up here alone, frantically happy. [...] The only thing to do is to be silent or make cheerful noises (*TU*, 211).

The silence of the room at Mrs Bailey's, attenuating Miriam's preoccupation with her visual and acoustic surroundings, makes her increasingly aware of the other senses: both her tactile and olfactory senses grow more intense and give rise to that well-known feeling of physical well-being:

> The air smelt moist. She leaned out into the chill of it. Her body was full of sleep and strength; all one strength from head to feet. She heard life in the silence, and went through her getting up as quickly as possible, listening all the time to the fresh silence (*IN*, 453).

In each of her rooms, at Flaxman's, where she feels the 'strength' and 'joy' of light, 'silent and understanding' (*TR*, 403), in Oberland, at Dimple Hill, and finally in her London room where she starts writing, Miriam invariably enjoys her quiet solitude as highly welcome moments of both physical and mental relaxation. While in the final chapters of *Pilgrimage* Dorothy Richardson emphasises reflective and mystic aspects of Miriam's silent introspection, *Oberland*, a hymn to the beauty of winter, once more expresses her rhapsodic delight in her sensory impressions: deeply aware of the silence of the mountains she perceives the overwhelming presence of light in immediate synaesthetic intensity.

Thus when Miriam arrives at an 'ultimate destination' (*O*, 49) in the sunlit silence of her bedroom, she has reached a state of near-perfection echoing Dante's seventh sphere of Heaven, where for mortal ears movement and sound seem to cease altogether in the presence of an overpowering light:[16] Sound had 'become the inaudible edge of a sound infinitely far away. Brilliant light, urgently describing the outdoor scene. But she was unwilling to stir and break the radiant stillness' (*O*, 49). Her little bedroom, though 'merely a refuge off-stage' (*O*, 47), thus becomes an important space for regeneration, a counterpoint to the activities of both hotel society and outdoor life. While her delight in 'this Swiss stillness' (*O*, 78) is part of Miriam's ecstatic Oberland experience, even back in London sunlight and silence still occasionally call forth an inner serenity, a happiness which she cannot find in society. Having returned to her room at the top of Mrs Bailey's house, to her 'recently restored freedom' (*CH*, 309), she on a 'heavenly morning' draws energy from both sunlight and stillness to reach an inner 'reality' that cannot be heard in the noise of her everyday world:

---

[16] Dante, *Paradiso* (Canto XXI, lines 58-60) 236f:

'E dì perché si tace in questa rota	And tell me why in this wheel
La dolce sinfonia di paradiso	the sweet symphony of Paradise is silent,
Che giù per l'altre suona sì divota.'	which below through the others so devoutly sounds.

> No sound in house and street. Away in the square, the small song of a bird, measuring the height there of unimpeded air. And within this light and this stillness was the reality that disappeared in the din of the drama. Yet almost no one seemed to desire the stillness in which alone it could be breathed and felt (*CH*, 310).

Miriam's heightened intuitive perception as well as her sense of security in the solitary silence of her room are revealed time and again. Yet her intellectual and analytical faculties at work often obscure the light of intuition, dissipate her spontaneous perception of the present moment and thus restrain the full experience of her own essential nature, of 'reality'. Thought and reflection, in Shirley Rose's words, 'interrupt the process of self-realization, they inhibit immediate action and divert ordinary attention' (1974:167). Deeply involved in this process of self-realization, Miriam sometimes succeeds in banning thought for what Rose (1974:166) calls a 'moment privilégié', a literally 'illuminated' moment of self-insight, an unobstructed experience of the Now. This realization of her innermost being, however, 'takes time and solitude' (*DLH*, 238), as Miriam remarks, two criteria that are met only in rare instances such as the following:

> Once more her room held quietude secure and the old in-pouring influence that could so rarely and so precariously be shared. Here, in the midst of it everything seemed immeasurably far off and even thought seemed to exist and to express itself in another world, into which she could move, or refrain from moving. Her being sank, perceptibly, back and back into a centre wherein it was held poised and sensitive to every sound and scent, and to the play of light on any and every object in the room. Turning gently in the midst of her recovered wealth, in the companionship that brought, even with movement, a deepening stillness, she saw upon the end wall the subdued reflection of London light, signalling the vast quiet movement of light about the world. It held a secret for whose full revelation she felt she could wait for ever, knowing that it would come (*CH*, 363).

The experience of silence thus is more than a happy moment of rest in the flux of time, it is a realization of the mystery of her consciousness that moves her deeply. In this moment of inexplicable joy and release, of breaking through the dimension of ordinary life, Miriam in fact experiences a form of pseudo-religious mysticism that T. S. Eliot, a fellow-mystic and contemporary of Dorothy Richardson, calls 'psychological', as it 'seeks contact with the sources of supernatural power, divorced from religion and theology' (1937:23). Waiting for the 'full revelation' of the secret of light, her search for inner meaning might eventually lead to a contact with absolute Reality, revealing an existence that transcends everyday life.

Quietly contemplating the 'perfection of this clear light' (*CH*, 364) which moves around her, she, like Eliot, has reached the 'still point of the turning world' ('Four Quartets: Burnt Norton,' 1969:173), the silent core of her self or, as Dorothy Richardson named it earlier on, 'the *motionless* unchanging centre of her consciousness' (*CH*, 305; emphasis added). At this 'centre' she has a moment of mystical insight that resembles Eliot's poetic image of the hub of the wheel, where he experiences

> The inner freedom from the practical desire,
> The release from action and suffering, release from the inner
> And the outer compulsion, yet surrounded
> By a grace of sense, a white light still and moving,
> *Erhebung* without motion, concentration
> Without elimination, both a new world
> And the old made explicit, understood
> In the completion of its partial ecstasy.[17]
> ('Burnt Norton' 173)

Eliot's vision is a *religious* ecstasy, bearing the stamp of conversional illumination; his abstract light is the climax of his communion with the Divine that follows his depression, which expresses itself in the preliminary experience of the 'dark night of the soul.'[18] Excluding any sensual and intellectual awareness of the outer world, he experiences a spiritual 'concentration' that takes him closer to God.

Miriam's visionary moment, on the other hand, is first of all an intense experience of the senses, the concrete light of London triggering a deeper understanding of herself and the world. In this 'temporary crystallization of the mind' the light reflected on the wall, the 'signal', the representative of the huge world around her, becomes the projected vision of her own

---

[17] In *Interim* Miriam's insight into the depths of her self reads like a prose version of this passage of Eliot's poem starting with the lines:

> 'At the still point, there the dance is,
> But neither arrest nor movement. And do not call it fixity,
> Where past and future are gathered' [...] (173)

In Dorothy Richardson's words:

'Life danced and sang within her; shreds of song; the sense of the singing of the wind; clear bright light streaming through large houses, quickening on walls and stairways and across wide rooms. Along clear avenues of light radiating from the future, pouring from behind her into the inner channels of her eyes and ears, came unknown forms moving in a brilliance, casting a brilliance across the visible past, warming its shadows, bathing its bright levels in sparkling gold' (*IN*, 318).

[18] The spiritual vacuum as a preliminary stage for the reception of God's grace, for illumination, as put into words in the work of St. John of the Cross is an idea similarly expressed in Miriam's experience of nothingness (cf. Chapter 2.4: 'Paradise').

For a detailed analysis of St. John's influence on Eliot see: Bergsten 68, 113ff, 183ff.

illumination. The vastness of space outside suggesting the 'inner expansibility of space' (*CH*, 307) points at an immense expansion of the innermost zones of her self; the universe is, to quote Emerson, 'the externisation of the soul' ('The Poet', *Essays* 453). Eventually, this central sphere lies beyond cognitive observation and conceptual thought and therefore defies any form of verbal description: 'even thought seemed to exist and to express itself *in another world*' (*CH* 363, emphasis added). In Miriam's vision of what Bachelard (168f.) calls 'l'immensité intime' that is 'en nous', the exterior light therefore reflects the 'secret' of her innermost self. Miriam's process of introversion also corresponds to the description of inner expansion by Luhmann and Fuchs:

> Wer nach innen geht, erlebt, dass es keine Grenzen des Innen gibt. Je *tiefer* man steigt, desto tiefer wird die Tiefe. [...] Subtilere Selbstbeobachtung wird nicht nur die innere (temporale) Unendlichkeit des psychischen Systems registrieren. Sie wird (zumindest ahnungsweise) [...] eine Zone der Nichtbeobachtbarkeit spüren können, jenen Gedankenquellpunkt, um klassisch zu sprechen, den zu beobachten bedeutete: Nichtbeobachten oder Nicht-denken' (77).

In surmising this 'Gedankenquellpunkt', this 'still point', all opposites seem to gather in absolute equilibrium: sensory awareness and introverted contemplation become one. The duality of existence between the two poles of the dynamic principle, of time and becoming, on the one hand and of the static principle, of eternity and being, on the other hand might at last be unified and reconciled in a state of perfection, a state of 'pure consciousness' (Kalamaras 155), that allows such conceptual paradoxes as 'movement that is perfect rest' (*CH*, 282) or 'the endlessness of the passing moment' (*DL*, 196). This existential duality, which can also be expressed in terms of 'self' and 'other', of subject and object, is effaced in the light accompanying her in her intuitive vision.

This light, unlike Eliot's white light of redemption which will be shining as the aim and *end* of his religious quest, becomes the supporting guide on her *pathway* to the mystical perception of the secret of life. In the full revelation of this secret Miriam the perceiver will eventually identify with Miriam the perceived; she then might - rather intuitively than intellectually - grasp what Coleridge describes as a 'principle' of self-experience. This

> is to be found [...] neither in object nor subject taken separately, and consequently, as no other third is conceivable, it must be found in that which is neither subject nor object exclusively, but which is the identity of both. [...] This principle, and so characterized, manifests itself in the SUM or I AM, which I shall hereafter indiscriminately express by the words spirit, self and self-consciousness (*Biographia Literaria* 151).

Such a momentary perception of Miriam's own self, affirmation of her lifelong quest for identity, is only possible in the silent privacy of her room, as all her experience of essential knowledge needs this atmosphere of quiet intimacy. She seeks a condition of solitary stillness in which alone self-realization is possible: 'Nothing could be known except in solitude' (*DL*, 63). This exterior and interior stillness, encompassing her whole world, in the end resembles the 'wise silence' of Emerson's 'Over-Soul':

> We live in succession, in division, in parts, in particles. Meantime within man is the soul of the whole; the wise silence; the universal beauty, to which every part and particle is equally related; the eternal ONE. And this deep power in which we exist, and whose beatitude is all accessible to us, is not only self-sufficing and perfect in every hour, but the act of seeing and the thing seen, the seer and the spectacle, the subject and the object, are one (*Essays* 386).

Echoing Coleridge's definition of the self, Emerson transcends the self-sufficient contemplation of the individual by pointing out the existence of a unifying whole that forms the core of being, transcending time and space.

It is when fully living in the intensity of a sensory perception as well as in the silent, exclusive concentration on one idea that Miriam seems to achieve a momentary merging with Emerson's 'eternal One', that she sees herself as taking part in a dimension of reality that lies beyond ordinary perception. Thus she is reading one of Hypo's letters:

> 'Beyond space and time.' Springing before her mind's eye in their place upon the written page, the words [...] reminded her that indeed she had been transported beyond time and space, that her being, at the moment of reading, had become a timeless being, released from all boundaries, wide as the world and wider, yet still herself (*CH*, 364).

In such *moments* of extra-temporal and extra-spatial rapture a sense of freedom prevails, which - together with her awareness of the ineffable inner 'secret and sacred beauty' (*IN*, 392) - underlines Miriam's deeply felt union with the 'eternal One'. Such experiences of a perfection that is 'beyond space and time' are always clearly marked off as being of short duration,[19] yet they stand out in Miriam's awareness of life as dynamic processes that do not move in space, as 'expansive moments' (*RL*, 282) in which time ceases to be

[19] Some sound takes her back from her silence to the awareness of outer reality; e.g. *IN*, 322: 'Just in front of her a single neat warning tap sounded in the air, touching the quick of her mind. St Pancras clock - striking down the chimney', reminding her most clearly of the incessant flow of time and its chronological measuring. Similarly, a bell that 'buzzed sharply' (*O*, 49) or a door that was opening (*CH*, 310) lead her back from the infinity of her inner experience to an awareness of her room, of 'space'.

perceived chronologically as 'time before' and 'time after'. In this 'endlessness of the passing moment' (*DL*, 196), in the unreflected total experience of the present, Miriam indeed reaches Eliot's 'still point,' 'where past and future are gathered.' Only in the forgetfulness of both place and time, in the total unreflected devotion to the immediate experience of the *Now* does Miriam reach the most profound levels of consciousness. Being intensely aware of this 'still' point within herself,[20] Miriam's experience is, according to Kalamaras's definition, a truly mystical one:

> It carries a perception of the *limited* individual self as completely identified with the *limitless*, expansive self and thus *no longer bound* to the more narrow definitions of conceptual consciousness (84; emphasis added).

And William James defines such an experience as follows:

> We pass into mystical states from out of ordinary consciousness as from a less into a more, as from a smallness into a vastness, and at the same time as from an unrest to a rest. We feel them as reconciling, unifying states. They appeal to the yes-function more than to the no-function in us (*Varieties* 330).

Miriam experiences this vastness, a 'tranquil immensity [that] was everywhere' (*IN*, 373) whenever she is overwhelmed by the 'inexhaustible blissfulness' of solitary silence that makes her realize the 'more', the hidden truth of her inner self. Her process of attaining such a mystical state, her movement in, is perhaps most impressively described in a scene at Tansley Street, where she spends New Year's Eve alone in her cold room. Out of her activities and 'ordinary consciousness' - her keen sensory perception of the room[21] - she passes from 'the outside, where there was nothing to hear' towards an ecstatic moment of insight into 'the calm, steady innermost part of her' (*IN*, 321): She stood

> staring at the sheeny gaslit brown-yellow varnish of the wall-paper above the mantelpiece. There was no thought in the silence, no past or future, nothing but the strange thing for which there were no words, something that was always there as if by appointment, waiting for one to get through to it away from everything in life. It

---

20 *OED XVI* 693 defines 'still' as follows: '1. motionless, not moving from one place, stationary; 2. silent; [...] 4. free from commotion; 5. in mixed sense of 2 & 4. Of places, times, conditions: characterized by *absence of noise and movement*' (emphasis added).

21 Apart from visual and acoustic elements ('the bright light', 'the silence') she is aware of tactile and olfactory sensations too that underline her perception of outer reality: 'She had spent New Year's Eve alone in a *cold* bedroom. [...] She lifted her coat from her knees and stood up. The room *shone*. In her throat and nostrils was the *smell* of dust coming from the floor and carpet and draperies' (*IN*, 320; emphasis added).

> was the thing that was nothing. Yet it seemed the only thing that came near and meant anything at all. It was happiness and realization. It was being suspended, in nothing. It came out of oneself because it only came when one had been a long time alone. It was not oneself. It could not be God. It did not mind what you were or what you had done. [..] But how could it make you so blissful? What was one, what had one done to bring the feeling of goodness and beauty and truth into the patch on the wall and presently make all the look of the distant world and everything in experience sound like music in a dream? She dropped her eyes. From the papered wall, radiance still seemed to flow over her as she stood, defining her brow and hair, shedding a warmth in the cold room. Looking again she found the wall less bright; but within the radius of her motionless eyes everything in the brightly lit corner glowed happily; not drawing her but standing complete and serene, like someone standing at a little distance, expressing agreement (*IN*, 322).

In this scene the four qualities of William James's well-known definition of mystic experience can be identified (cf. *Varieties* 302):

1. *Ineffability*: Miriam's experience goes beyond the limits of verbal description - 'the strange thing for which there were no words' - and even leaves behind the realm of conceptual awareness - 'there was no thought'. In the solitude of her room, but also later on when in society again, her experience cannot be imparted to others; it remains a strong yet self-contained impression, existing, as James says, 'for the individual who has the transport, but for no one else' (321). The 'thing' which 'came only when one had been a long time alone', this mystical consciousness, fills Miriam in similar situations with an 'unexplainable happiness' (*DL*, 224).

2. *Noetic quality*: Entering the depths of her solitary soul, Miriam reaches a more profound state of knowledge, an insight into the truth of her inner life: 'It seemed the only thing that came near and meant anything at all. It was happiness and realization.' It is a revelatory moment, an instant of both exposure and understanding that shows her, however vaguely, a deeper significance of life, her self as part of a larger whole. As we have seen above, these stirring moments of self-awareness enrich her whole being for good; they become, though not overtly referred to, a subliminal 'authority for after-time' (302) as each of them is a revealing landmark of introspection on her lifelong quest for her 'real' self.

3. *Transiency*: As a less sharply marked characteristic, James remarks that 'mystical states cannot be sustained for long' (302). Miriam's illuminations are in fact only short relevatory moments. As soon as her awareness of exterior reality returns, both with her visual perception of the room and with her auditory perception of outdoor noises, her mystical insights lose their power. These states soon 'fade into the light of common day' (302), leaving

a vague feeling of perfection that cannot be put in words. Unlike other intense experiences such as her bee-memory or some musical memories, which stay in her consciousness as concrete, recallable experiences of perfect sensory beauty, these mystical illuminations, however strong their immediate effect on Miriam's consciousness may be, evade such a clear physical and verbal - and thus recallable - fixation in memory. By hinting at some ineffable and transient aspects of experience, Dorothy Richardson reveals the limits of language in rendering what 'reality' ultimately means to the individual. She seems to express Miriam's belief in the existence of a 'gulf between life and the expression of it' (*TR*, 426) that is impossible to be bridged in some verbal form. When she keeps the account of Miriam's mystical insights vague, she acknowledges and preserves the innermost secret of individual consciousness, recognizing what Miriam says elsewhere: 'Nothing can ever be expressed in words' (*TR*, 463).

4. *Passivity*: The last, and least important, peculiarity of mystical experience mentioned by James is a passivity of body and mind, an absence of physical movement as well as a feeling of being 'grasped and held by a superior power,' the mystic's own will being in abeyance (303). In the scene above Miriam does not move - 'she stood staring' - and her mind is not active - 'there was no thought' - but she *is moved* by a superior power - 'It' - that makes her so blissful and makes her perceive everything 'like music in a dream.' This comparison, in fact, contains the core of mystical experience: music can convey ontological *messages* that cannot be completely grasped by means of conceptual thoughts, that therefore remain *ineffable*; a dream, being of relatively short duration, is *transient* and often difficult to remember, and the sleeper is - obviously - *passive*.

Often when Miriam in her solitary, silent contemplations reaches such a mystical state, her sensory awareness of her surroundings recedes to a minimum. Her whole perceptive energy is directed inward to experience an inner sensation that is as vivid a perception of fact as what she through her eyes and ears perceives as 'outward data of consciousness' (James, *Varieties* 338). In fact, her mystical experience leaving her with an increased optimism is a 'gift' to her spirit by means of which facts and the world of the senses 'fall into a new expressiveness and make a new connexion with our active life' (James 338). For a large part of *Pilgrimage* Miriam's mystical perceptions range from lyrical enchantment to some vaguely religious 'healthy-mindedness' that conceives 'good as the essential aspect of being' (James 79). In Emerson's transcendentalism Miriam thus finds a first spiritual vessel for her immediate personal experiences: sharing his view of the individual consciousness as the final authority for being as well as of the immanent divinity in things, she seems to share his idea of the divine soul of the universe being the very soul within the soul of man. Emerson, Dorothy

Richardson's 'earliest close friend' (*WM*, 647), 'a poet, and a mystic' (*DH*, 533), with his poetic insight seems to express the essence of Miriam's spiritual existence. In some of the last novel-chapters of *Pilgrimage* Dorothy Richardson, borrowing images from and making allusions to Emerson's ideas, presents what is 'sacred' to Miriam too: the truthfulness and integrity of the individual mind as the one reality, the immediate presence of the soul, the self, as the centre of life, for, as Emerson says: 'The soul *is*.'[22]

4.2 'The Medium of Temporary Unity:' Silence in Community

> Der Mensch, in dessen Wesen noch das Schweigen ist, bewegt sich vom Schweigen her in die äussere Welt, das Schweigen ist die Mitte des Menschen. Die Bewegung geht dann nicht unmittelbar von einem Menschen zum anderen, sondern vom Schweigen des einen Menschen zum Schweigen des anderen.
>
> (Max Picard, *Die Welt des Schweigens* 59)

> Why can't reality exist in the world? All the things that happen produce friction because they distract people from the reality they are unconsciously looking for. That is why there are everywhere torrents of speech. [...] Silence is reality. Life ought to be lived on a basis of silence, where truth blossoms. Why isn't such an urgent thing known? Life would become like the individual; alive . . . it would show, inside and out, and people would leave off talking so much. Life does show, seen from far off, pouring down into stillness (*DL*, 188).

In accordance with the Romantics, who stressed the importance of solitude, silence and introspection for the complete experience of one's self,[23] Dorothy Richardson's heroine strives to find some form of self-possession in solitary

---

[22] cf. Emerson, 'Self-Reliance' and 'Compensation'. *Essays and Lectures* 261; 299.

[23] cf. Wordsworth, William. *The Prelude (1805)*, IV,l. 388ff, p. 144, emphasis added:

'. . . all was *peace and solitude*,
I look'd not round, nor did the solitude
Speak to my eye; but *it was heard* and felt.
O happy state! what beauteous pictures now
Rose in harmonious imagery - they rose
As from *some distant region of my soul*
And came along like dreams; yet such as left
Obscurely mingled with their passing forms
A consciousness of animal delight,
A self-possession felt in every pause
And every gentle movement of my frame.'

silence, be it in the undisturbed open of nature, or in the sheltering stillness of her solitary room. Whenever Miriam suffers from her mostly self-induced social isolation, whenever she is keenly aware of the abyss between her and the community, she does not aim at bridging this gap by making concessions to her own ways of life, but takes refuge in a positive contemplation of her physical and mental separateness as it entails a heightened sense of individuality. This Wordsworthian delight in solitude appears as a self-protecting strategy which culminates on the very last pages of *Pilgrimage*: Miriam, aspiring to become a writer, revalues her loneliness and cultivates her solitude as the necessary precondition for her creative activity. As Henke (54) has noted, Miriam recognizes that 'only mental solitude gives birth to revelation', that it offers the deep insights that allow her to embark on the project that is to occupy the rest of her author's life:

> Only when I am with others does my sense of isolation return. I shall [...] still feel sure when I am writing, a loneliness that now may encircle the rest of my life. [...] While I write, everything vanishes but what I contemplate. [...] Contemplation is adventure into discovery; reality. [...] Fully to recognize, one must be alone. Away in the furthest reaches of one's being (*MM*, 656f.).

This attitude is Dorothy Richardson's own, as we can see in her interview with Louise Morgan, in which she explains her ideal conditions of work:

> Ideally, everything that favours collaboration between the conscious and the unconscious.
> The best conditions in my experience are winter solitude and inaccessibility. I mean solitude. Servantless, visitorless, and, save for a single agent, tradesmanless. [...] Short of this, the avoidance of anything that breaks the momentum of the unconscious once it is set going (*Everyman*, 22 Oct 1931, 400).

This *writer's* praise of solitude also implies a quest for the introspective stance: only in shutting herself away from society as well as from the world of her immediate senses -'everything vanishes' - can she give free range to the process of unconscious association where she is at last to find her material of writing, the 'reality' of her living self. If we read this 'microscopic self-examination' in solitude (Pykett 110), the super-subtle recording of Miriam's own self-discoveries, as a hermetic system that to quite a large extent excludes the impact of personal relationships, we may indeed understand Woolf's annoyance at 'the cramp and confinement of personality' of many of her contemporary writers, and especially at the concentration on their 'damned egotistical self' that 'ruins and Richardson.'[24] And D. H.

---

24 Woolf, Virginia. 'How it strikes a Contemporary.' *Collected Essays, Vol. Two* 159.

Lawrence's biting comment on the 'awful', 'childish' self-concern of Joyce and Richardson, who 'through thousands and thousands of pages [...] tear themselves to pieces, strip their smallest emotions to the finest threads, till you feel you are sewed inside a wool mattress that is being slowly shaken up,'[25] expresses a - not completely unjustified - feeling of surfeit with the endless descriptions of Miriam Henderson's solipsistic self-absorption.

Yet, if the reader accepts *Pilgrimage* as a grand attempt at rendering an individual's perception of Life, Miriam's concentration on her own self in silence appears as one - major - aspect of Dorothy Richardson's writing. Though silence *does* provide an ideal medium for *self*-discovery, it also appears as a desirable basis for the exploration of relationships at their most profound. Once she feels fully accepted by another person, once she can leave her self-erected walls of solitude to meet her partners on a level of equality and true partnership, Miriam very often seeks their silent company to feel, understand and enjoy the expressive reticence of their silent meeting as it reveals unexpressed facets of their friendship as much as it enhances her own intense sense of self.

It is epecially with single girls and women - Harriett, Grace Broom, 'with whom she had a sort of identity' (*TR*, 455), Amabel, Rachel Mary and Jean - but also with Richard Roscorla and, to a lesser extent, Densley and Shatov, that she overcomes her separateness and achieves a union that is best felt when meeting in silence. In 'wordless communication' (*CH*, 301) she is at unity with the other, which fills both partners with strength: 'Strength that remains; making a link that perhaps, between two people who have ever met in silence, is never broken. [...] Spirits meet and converse and understand each other only in silence' (*MM*, 620f.). *Sharing* a silence for Dorothy Richardson thus is the solution of her dilemma between solitude and society: it means keeping the 'diagonal line' between independence and sympathy that Emerson suggests.[26]

Silence, the 'perfection of social intercourse' (*DH*, 456), provides the ideal meeting-ground exactly because Miriam can express her sympathy for others without giving up a single inch of her sacred independence. In the 'wordless communion' (*DLH*, 245) with Amabel, when they are 'suddenly aware of each other', or in the opening stillness of her crucial meeting with Densley, 'sharing with him an instant of eternity' (*DLH*, 145),[27] Miriam feels

---

[25] Lawrence, D.H. 'Surgery for the Novel - or a Bomb.' *Phoenix* 518.

[26] Emerson, Ralph Waldo: 'Our safety is in the skill with which we keep the diagonal line. Solitude is impracticable and society fatal. We must keep our head in the one and our hands in the other. The conditions are met, if we keep our independence, yet do not lose our sympathy.' in: 'Society and Solitude,' *Complete Prose Works*, 408.

[27] At this same meeting she recognizes that 'any two souls could meet if only sometimes they would be silent together and wait' (*DLH*, 145).

this balance between her and the other. Silence thus becomes a 'Raum der Verbindung' (Bronfen 285), opening up a space of intimate freedom such as Mary Olivier experiences when being silent with her friend Nicholson:

> The silence made everything stand out with a supernatural clearness. [...] Sitting there so still he had the queer effect of creating for both of you a space of your own, more real than the space you had just stepped out of (Sinclair, *Mary Olivier* 343).

Similarly, when meeting Dr van Heber '*in* a radiant silence' (*IN*, 363; emphasis added) Miriam intuitively feels the existence of a deeply attractive bond between their souls swinging in the spatial presence of silence. And even with people whose company she usually shuns she can find such moments of balanced non-verbal understanding; with Miss Holland, for instance, she notices that 'their prolonged silence was speaking. Of course . . . C'est dans le silence que les âmes se révèlent.' (*TR*, 430).

Miriam's ideas about interpersonal silence are fed by her reading Maurice Maeterlinck's *Trésor des Humbles*, a book of essays in which he praises the secret of expressive silences. Maeterlinck, loved by Miriam for his mystical meditations on the individual's everyday life and repeatedly referred to after her reading his work in *Deadlock*,[28] reverences silence as 'l'élément dans lequel se forment les grandes choses' (9), as 'ange des vérités suprêmes' (19); for, according to him, it is in silence only that true life can be lived. Dorothy Richardson's notions about silence thus often sound like mere paraphrases of Maeterlinck's words. When she states that 'silence is reality. Life ought to be lived on a basis of silence, where truth blossoms. Why isn't such an urgent thing known? Life would become like the individual; alive' (*DL*, 188), she echoes what Maeterlinck proclaims as a must:

> [P]our savoir ce qui existe réellement, il faut cultiver le silence entre soi, car ce n'est qu'en lui que s'entr'ouvrent un instant les fleurs inattendues et éternelles, qui changent de forme et de couleur selon l'âme à côté de laquelle on se trouve. Les âmes se pèsent dans le silence, comme l'or et l'argent se pèsent dans l'eau pure, et les paroles que nous prononçons n'ont de sens que grâce au silence où elles baignent' ('Le Silence', *Trésor* 23).

This is again what Miriam in her own words explains to Hypo, who hates silence: 'The test of absolutely everything in life is the quality of the in-between silences. It's only in silence that you can judge of your relationship to a person' (*RL*, 389); or, as Maeterlinck, himself quoting Jean Paul, says: 'Lorsque je veux aimer très tendrement une personne chère et lui pardonner

[28] e.g. *DL*, 68: 'How many people knew that Maeterlinck had explained in words what life was like inside? [... Shatov] must read the chapter on silence and then the piece about the old man by his lamp. That would make everything clear.'

toute chose, je n'ai plus qu'à la regarder quelque temps *en silence*' ('La Vie Profonde', *Trésor* 244).

In the initial phase of her friendship with the extravagant Amabel Miriam experiences moments of intense silent understanding more expressive and satisfying than any words.[29] In their quiet contemplations, in the mutual, mirror-like reflections of two souls that complement each other,[30] Amabel seems to recognize the unconscious processes of Miriam's inner life and reveals them to her, thus establishing a deep, silent bond of comprehensive identification. In Amabel's presence Miriam feels her 'complete' self in a 'quietude of well-being' (*DLH*, 190); her charm opens up Miriam's self-contained reservation, showing her, 'when they were together, somehow between them in the mysterious interplay of their two beings, the *reality* she had known for so long alone, brought out into *life*' (*DLH*, 217; emphasis added). With her, Miriam has found a perfect way of sharing silence:

> No sharing, not even the shared being of a man and a woman [...], could be deeper or more wonderful than this being together, alternating between awareness of the beloved person and delight in every aspect, every word and movement, and a solitude distinguishable from the deepest, coolest, most renewing moments of lonely solitude only in the enhancement it reaped by being shared (*DLH*, 242).[31]

Yet the level of commitment required to sustain this 'inexpressible quality' of their relationship (*MM*, 658), the tender intimacy that knows no secrets, soon becomes too much for Miriam. In their lack of distance, in their merging of personalities, and especially in Amabel's growing possessiveness, Miriam sees her own self threatened. As her independence is at stake, she gladly leaves Amabel in the hands of Michael, freeing herself in rather a cowardly way from the two most intensive and therefore most demanding partnerships of her life.[32]

---

[29] Miriam happily thinks of 'their silences, [...] those moments when they were suddenly intensely aware of each other and the flow of their wordless communion, making the smallest possible movement of the head now this way now that, holding each pose with their eyes wide on each other, expressionless, like birds in a thicket intently watching and listening' (*DLH*, 245).

[30] In a letter to Rose Odle, Veronica Grad, upon whom the character of Amabel was drawn, remembers the very strong ties of her relationship with Dorothy Richardson, speaking of them as 'twins' or 'two halves' of a whole (cf. Hanscombe 1982:184).

[31] cf. also *DH*, 545: In Amabel's company, in the spatial expansion of their shared silence, Miriam feels that 'completeness of being. Side by side, silent, with the whole universe between us, within us, in a way no man and woman, be they never so well mated, can ever have.'

[32] For an excellent analysis of the difficult friendship between Amabel and Miriam see Hanscombe 1982: 133 - 166.

4.3 'My Clue to the Nature of Reality:' The Case of Jean

> [...] a perfect woman, nobly plann'd,
> To warn, to comfort, and command;
> And yet a spirit still, and bright
> With something of angelic light.
>
> (William Wordsworth, 'Perfect Woman,' *Works II* 214)

> [...] the things that cannot be mentioned. Jean lives them, gaily. Lives in a world she sees transfigurable. Already, to her, transfigured. What comes to others only at moments is with her always. . . . Her natural genius. Cultivated.
> Somehow she has mastered the art of incessant prayer? Incessant orientation of her spiritual compass toward the love that is the centre and the gaiety of the universe, and the secret, too, of her deep enjoyment of any and every moment. That is why she never flies into rages and holds me back when I do [...] (*MM*, 579).

What can follow once Miriam is released from the experience of Amabel's embracing, yet almost suffocating relentless intimacy? How can she 'seek those to whom she belonged' (*DH*, 429) if she does not know what she is looking for? Neither an escape abroad, a repetition of her enchanted stay at Oberland, nor the retreat into the lonely quietude of the countryside soon abandoned at the beginning of *Dimple Hill* could possibly satisfy her underlying need for human closeness. Her stay at Dimple Hill, a crucial stage in her mystical awareness of reality to be examined in the following sub-chapter, ends on a note of personal disappointment. At a low point of lonely isolation Miriam is eager to keep 'with perfect sweetness the independence of solitude' (Emerson, 'Self-Reliance' 263) and yet to commit herself, to be solitary and yet not to be alone. She thus, despite her solipsistic tendencies, perseveres in her quest for a truly fulfilling personal relationship: The unconditional devotion to another person in the spirit of silence, the perfection of love, is celebrated in *March Moonlight*, in the portrayal of the enigmatic, sensitive, taciturn character of Jean. According to Hanscombe (1982:126), Miriam's relationship with Jean was Dorothy Richardson's main motivation for the writing of this unfinished novel-chapter; indeed, her strong personality is the only aspect arousing new interest in a book that lives on repetitions, recapitulations and allusions to former novel-chapters.

In body, mind, and soul Jean seems to be the perfectly attractive partner for Miriam. Physically, because her 'oval face' (*MM*, 574) reminds Miriam of both the angelic apparition of Ulrica Hesse she felt so much drawn to in

Hanover and of the seraphic beauty of Amabel;[33] mentally, because of her 'clear intelligence' (*MM*, 574), with which she observes her surroundings in a way akin to Miriam's own analytic power; emotionally, because of her 'gentle heart' (*MM*, 574), her inclination to quietude that comprises a profound understanding of souls. Jean appears as a visiting angel of love promising rest and peace. A 'lover by nature', she at once convinces Miriam of her personal creed: 'I feel so sure that love is in itself the supreme power and will in the end conquer all things' (*MM*, 560).

Thus, 'watching Jean', Miriam 'presently had become aware of the beneficent restfulness of our common silence' (*MM*, 564); their 'intermittent silences, rather than tension-creating searches for fresh material, were fragments of a shared eternity whence, upon an identical rhythm [... they] contemplated whatever had been summoned to stand before [them]' (*MM*, 567). In the stillness of the Alpine winter Miriam discovers the secret of their expressive silences: in their intense *non-verbal* communion of souls she is seized by a feeling of one-ness with Jean, which expresses the unique quality of their friendship.[34] Again, Dorothy Richardson proves to be an attentive reader of Maeterlinck, who writes:

> [E]t s'il vous est donné de descendre un instant en votre âme jusqu'aux profondeurs habitées par les anges, ce qu'avant tout vous vous rappellerez d'un être aimé profondément, ce n'est pas les paroles qu'il a dites ou les gestes qu'il a faits, mais les silences que vous avez vécus ensemble; car c'est la *qualité* de ces silences qui seule a révélé la *qualité* de votre amour et de vos âmes ('Le Silence', *Trésor* 12).

---

33 cf. *PR*, 34: 'Ulrica Hesse had come. Miriam had seen her. There had been three large leather trunks in the hall and a girl with a smooth pure oval of face standing wrapped in dark furs, gazing about her with eyes for which Miriam had no word, liquid - limpid - great-saucers, no - pools . . . great round deeps . . .' Meeting Amabel for the first time, she 'saw only a dim outline, a pale oval face saluting her. [...] Here was "charm," some strange grace and charm that was defying the warning voice within' (*DLH*, 174). On her second meeting, Amabel's silent attraction increases: 'Smoothly draped sheeny dark hair framed the flower-fresh oval face and heightened the "jasmine" white of the column of neck. And this unknown loveliness was already radiating affection, patiently awaiting the fruit of a wondering stare; *wordlessly*, for fear of risking by sound or movement its own full effect' (*DLH*, 187; emphasis added). For a more erotic reading of these relationships see Watts 74.

34 e.g. *MM*, 573: 'I believed, and *silently* at every turn she seemed to confirm my belief that she and I together, because we were together, irradiated our surroundings, she for me, I for her.'
MM, 575: 'our deep happiness, never confessed, *never even alluded to.*'
MM, 577: 'I *don't say much* about our friendship. It is a very precious thing. I am *silent* before the wonder of it. And before your understanding of everything' (emphases added).

Indeed, in Jean's 'immortal love' (*MM*, 584), drawing her to 'an unchanging centre' (*MM*, 566), in the 'incessant orientation of her spiritual compass toward the love that is the centre and the gaiety of the universe, and the secret, too, of her deep enjoyment of any and every moment' (*MM*, 579), Miriam recognizes a spiritual kinship that borders on a total merging of their selves: 'And always our contemplations discovered a truth that left us united, so much one person that in the talk following the arrival of an outsider it seemed, when either spoke, as if it were the other [...]' (*MM*, 570).

For all her claims of equality and unity between the two women, Miriam idealizes her as the 'permanent forgiver' (*MM*, 607), a divine being to be followed on her 'path to freedom' (*MM*, 612), to be adored and invoked: 'Jean. Jean. Jean. My clue to the nature of reality. To know that you exist, is enough [...] With Jean, for me, friendship reaches its centre' (*MM*, 612f.) This retrospective invocation summarizes what for Miriam has become the perfection of human relationships, offering the freedom and commitment necessary to the thriving of any living relationship. Their epiphanic moments in silence, where Jean reveals to Miriam the truth of shared being, appear as the culmination of Miriam's quest: Placing the novel within a tradition of feminine mysticism, as both Stephen Heath and Jean Radford have done, we can read their shared moments as climactical mystical insights into the nature of reality. In the retrospective of writing Miriam intensely remembers the perfection of the shared moment in silence that, though bearing the stamp of transiency, can be enjoyed to the full:

> Was our experience, to her too, a revelation? Leading, as for me it led, to the sudden discovery coming when on that last grey afternoon while side by side we sat gazing in silence at the thawing remains of winter: that in separation we should not be parted? Perhaps she felt me realizing this when simultaneously we turned to each other, laughing and returned, without a word, to the landscape (*MM*, 612f.).

And yet, unlike her long friendship with Amabel, whose intimacy - initially hailed with enthusiasm - has become more and more cumbersome and has eventually induced their alienation, Miriam's relationship to Jean is not more than a holiday 'affair', a quickly formed intimacy that is not put to the test of everyday life. Removed from the *hic et nunc* of Miriam's immediate living present, in the mellow light of both spatial and temporal distance, it appears in its unworldly perfection as a utopian vision of a personal relationship based on silence. Throughout the entire representation of Miriam's immediate sensory reality the two women never meet directly; Jean as a character, in fact, seems a mere creation of the mind, an angelic figure representing Dorothy Richardson's ideas about understanding and love.[35] Yet Jean, internalized, introjected in Miriam's consciousness, assumes an important role in her final development; she has become an inner voice, the arbiter of and guide to Miriam's sense of her self and her surroundings (cf. Hanscombe 1982:128). In the 'language of spiritual revelation' (Watts 74) Dorothy Richardson thus expresses Miriam's final divining of what an ideal relationship might reveal. Through Jean she has learnt that both true individuality and true partnership live on the incessant interplay between closeness and distance:

> If only I could remain always in possession of my whole self, something of Jean-in-me would operate.
> Good that she is gone. How right are the Catholics in separating within their orders those who grow too happy in each other. To give oneself, fully, to God-in-others, one must belong to no one (*MM*, 612).

In its balance of union and separation between the other and herself, in its silent - and therefore infinitely powerful - trust and understanding, Jean's distant friendship shows Miriam a way to self-acceptance that need not - and, in fact, cannot - be bought by isolation and proposes a form of companionship that eventually supports Miriam's identity, her sense of a fulfilled life of her own.

What Miriam sees in Jean as the transfigured perfection of silent, unspoken understanding between individuals is but a concluding comment on a theme developed at length earlier on in *Pilgrimage*. In her London years, after 'years of hoping to meet someone who understood silence' (*RL*, 326) Miriam got in touch with the Quakers. At a meeting of this small religious group, their '*unanimous* unembarrassed stillness' (*DH*, 422; emphasis added) filled her with a 'sense of relief and of home-coming', calling forth emotions not unlike the ones experienced in Jean's silent presence.[36] What is explicitly stated in her relationship to Jean as the aim and fulfillment of community also lies at the core of Dorothy Richardson's depiction of Quaker life in *Revolving Lights* and *Dimple Hill*. In the perfect balance between freedom and security in silent communion with the members of this group, Miriam's experience of life at its most profound reaches an unparalleled intensity.

---

[35] Unlike most other characters in *Pilgrimage*, there is apparently no known prototype for this figure in Dorothy Richardson's own life. Radford (1991:42) suggests that Jean is named for 'John' of the Gospels, the embodiment of human love which most nearly approaches God's love for human beings: 'perfect love.'

[36] cf. *OED XVIII*, 862f: 'unanimous' comes from Latin unanimis = unus + animus = 'one mind'. Thus, already among the Quakers Miriam experiences this unity of minds that is so central in her relationship to Jean.

4.4 'Solitary yet not Alone:' The Quakers' Silence between Society and Solitude

> Only in individuality carried to its full term can we find the basis of unity. Unity amongst Fox and his followers is the fruit and fulfilment of separateness. In order truly to love his neighbour, a man must first love himself. He must achieve singleness of soul, must discover that within him which is of God; that which 'speaks' with him only in the solitude of his inner being. (*GGF*, 9f.)

> And I realized one of the Quaker secrets. Living always remote,drawn away into the depths of the spirit, they see, all the time, freshly. A perpetual Sunday. (*DH*, 491)

Numerous scenes throughout *Pilgrimage* depict the wholesome effect of solitary silence on Miriam. Her awareness of stillness, of the absence of sound, is the most favourable condition for contemplation, for introspection that reaches down to the subconscious depths of the self. In this psychological mysticism Miriam's surface self merges with those depths within her, producing a unification of consciousness that allows her to grasp a reality wider than what is apparent: the more she experiences silence the more she will experience her self and know herself.

In her account of Miriam's close friendships with men and women Dorothy Richardson likewise underlines the importance of silence, the absence of speech, as a means of non-verbal communication. Silence, rightly understood, can transcend the limits of words, reveal unspeakable, hidden sides of one's self to the partner. In the key scenes of these relationships Dorothy Richardson shows that whenever the partners cooperate and produce such meaningful silence, the confidence in the closeness of their friendship, their mutual love and understanding, is enhanced.

Miriam's throwaway remark about becoming a 'Trappist' (*DLH*, 164), however, hints at her longing for a silence that is even more embracing than her enjoying moments of quiet companionship with various friends. It is her wish to join a community whose corporate silence would be the genuine expression of their spiritual condition, to find people who cultivate verbal abstinence in order to leave room for the expression of the unsaid, for the experience of the unspeakable, transcendent, aspects of life. At the height of their affair in *Revolving Lights*, Miriam and Michael Shatov are invited by Dr Oldfield, an American fellow lodger at Mrs Bailey's, to attend a Quaker meeting. It is there in St Martin's Lane, at the centre of the bustle and noise of London life, that Miriam to her surprise discovers a new quality in the shared silence of the Quakers. Waiting *silently* together for the experience of the spirit of God, the participants in the meeting achieve a communion that surpasses both the egocentricity of self-exploration and the exclusiveness of worldly friendship in a spiritual triangle encompassing the self, the community, and the divine. Oppositions and dividing lines seem to be effaced in the contemplative silence that creates in Miriam a feeling of fellowship, of 'being in something alive and positive; at the centre of existence' (*RL*, 327). It is in this initiation to the religious life of Quakerism that she realizes that such an experience of Life at its very core need not be synonymous with *solitary* contemplation; she surmises that the power of shared silence as a means to the attainment of a central spiritual experience - for the Quakers the direct, personal experience of the life-giving, liberating divine light shining within, the 'Inner Light' - by far outdoes her feelings of well-being and happiness associated with solitary silence:

> Being there with others made the sense of [being at the centre of existence] stronger than when it was experienced alone. Like lonely silence, it drove away the sense of enclosure. There had been no stuffiness of congregated humanity; the air, breathed in, had held within it a freshness, spreading coolness and strength through the secret passages of the nerves (*RL*, 327).

What is more, as Penny Brown (204) writes, the atmosphere of silence and 'the tranquil, intense concentration seem to embody the spiritual state towards which Miriam has been groping throughout *Pilgrimage*,' as this immersion into mystical depths of awareness allows those who take part in it to 'move into a stillness at whose pulsating heart was to be found the source of their inmost being' (*DH*, 451).

Miriam's 'pilgrimage' towards a positive experience of the religious dimension is a long one, for her life-story so far has been a story of religious scepticism. From her early experiences in *Pointed Roofs* Miriam, the 'inveterate sceptic' (Henke 53), has opposed the patriarchal point of view of the church which sees woman as 'primarily an appendage to be controlled, guided and managed by man' (*QPP*, 72); she therefore has always distrusted the dominance of male power, of the word, of logic, as masculine ways of expression, as they are celebrated in the services of the instituted churches.[37]

---

[37] *PR*, 73: 'Listening to sermons was wrong . . . people ought to refuse to be preached at by these men. [...] The services might be lovely, if you didn't listen to the words.'

BW, 255, thinking of a vicar's sermon in North London: 'What was it all about? Pompous, pottering, going on and on and on - in the Old Testament. [...] How horribly the words would echo through the great cold church.'

TU, 99: '*All* that has been said and known in the world is in *language*, in words; all we know of Christ is in Jewish words; all the dogmas of religion are words; the meaning of words change with people's thoughts, Then no one *knows* anything for certain. [...] The Bible is not true; it is a culture. Religion is wrong in making word-dogmas out of it [...].'

Her point, similar to Emerson's, is that the church is steeped in forms, rites, dogmas, and verbal explanations which thwart a genuine, immediate access to God - *if* he exists: Miriam's sceptic attitude towards the Christian faith culminates in her confession of being an 'unbeliever' (*HC*, 381), an 'agnostic' (*TU*, 28). Rather than for theological exhortation or intellectual reflection, she thus usually enters a church for the atmosphere, the pure sensory impression of the room, for the feeling of 'the welcome unusual deep quietude' (*CH*, 347) of the building. With Emerson, she likes 'the silent church before the service begins, better than any preaching.'[38] Once retired into 'a quiet pew and ceasing to pretend' (*PR*, 73), she turns to her inner silence to find the seamless unity that the alienating speech of the male preachers deny her.

Despite her critical distance from the established church, she never abandons her spiritual quest, passionately seeking for that reality behind the material, for ultimate Truth. During her London years it is in fiction,[39] in philosophy and in unorthodox forms of faith such as pantheism, Unitarianism or Boehme's mysticism that she - in vain - looks for a form of religious life that would account for the personal, immediate experience of the immanent divine. Not accepting observed revelation, she searches for some form of individual illumination unfettered by tradition or institutional strictures and thus refuses the doctrines of established religion: 'And to what system of religion could she definitely belong? Everywhere was darkness and challenge. Right and wrong, pointing now this way and now that, offered no help' (*DLH*, 251). She 'would never be able completely to experience the emotions of Orthodox Christianity' (*CH*, 348), emotions that in their dull intellectuality would make the soul and its 'kingdom of heaven' within 'a little grey and lonely' (*TR*, 482). What she hopes to find is a more intuitive, mystic form of religion where individual contemplation would eventually 'let you through into the white white brightness' (*TU*, 98), to a Dantean revelation of the divine.

It is with the Quakers that Miriam, the outside observer, recognizes a spiritual kinship, as she is deeply impressed by their silent prayer for the experience of the 'Inner Light'. Her earlier intuition that 'if one were perfectly still, the sense of God was there' (*HC*, 458) seems to be affirmed in their practice of silent worship. After her first contact with the Quakers she, without actually sharing their beliefs, longs for their genuine mystical closeness to God:

Even later in life Miriam holds in derision the falsity of a High Church parson, 'an automaton with an assumed voice and accent, and a mind tethered elsewhere' (*DH*, 423).

[38] Emerson, R.W. 'Self-Reliance,' *Essays and Lectures*, 272.

[39] *TU*, 236f.: *Robert Elsmere*, once 'the answer to my worry about Christ,' is no longer of interest: 'And now I've got beyond *Robert Elsmere* [...]; that's gone.'

> To have been born amongst these people; to know at home and in the church a *shared* religious life. They were in heaven already. Through acting on their belief. Where two or three are gathered together. Nearer than thoughts; nearer than breathing; nearer than hands and feet (*RL*, 326f.).

Alluding to the Bible - Mt 18,20: 'Where two or three are gathered together in my name, there am I in the midst of them' - Miriam recognizes the importance of the community: In their shared silence God's presence penetrates their whole being, mind, soul and body, at once strengthening their spiritual bonds with the Divine. In the 'pure, live atmosphere' of the silent meeting (*RL*, 329), in its inexpressible mystic richness, the Quakers' spiritual quest is consummated. The *unio mystica*, the individual's fusion with God in moments of intensely shared worship is ranked highest among their religious experiences. Their religious culture in fact emphasizes aspects of spiritual life that are the very opposite of those Miriam found despicable in established Christian religion. As Dorothy Richardson writes in another context, the Quaker culture is one which took

> no account of 'persons', 'notions', or 'theories', which put being before 'knowing', intuition before intellection, which dared to trust in and enquire of women, not in name only, but in fact (*GGF*, 12).

Thus, as the entire lifestyle of the Quakers seems to come up to what Miriam in moments of 'mystical quietude' (Powys 20) has imagined as ideal, their company appears even more desirable: She experiences a 'homesickness for daily life with these people who lived from the centre, admitted, in public, that life brims full all the time, away below thoughts and the loud shapes of things that happen' (*RL*, 327).

Observing the women after the service, Miriam idealizes the Quakers as people who, relying on their pre-reflective, intuitive awareness of life at its fullest and most profound, seem to form a desirable contrast to the 'people who moved mostly along the surface levels' of life (*DLH*, 192):

> They looked enviably, deeply, richly alive, on the very edge of the present, representing their faith in their own persons, entirely self-centred and self-controlled; poised and serene and withdrawn, yet not withholding (*RL*, 329).

The memory of this highly impressive encounter with the Quakers as people who *do* understand silence in a most complete sense as an essential part of life attains a fuller significance as Miriam, on her arrival at Dimple Hill, anticipates that in the Roscorla family, a Quaker stronghold, she will find again this deep reverence for silent communion and thus reach 'the richest depth of shared life imaginable upon earth' (*DH*, 430; cf. Brown P. 204).

At Dimple Hill Miriam at last sees the opportunity to live daily life with people 'who lived from the centre'; she hopes 'to plunge immediately on arriving in the house' (*DH*, 441) into the 'deep shared stillness' of this secluded Quaker world which she is to experience as a 'paradise' (cf. Chapter 2.4.4). And, indeed, her expectations seem to be confirmed. The physical act of perception, her atmospheric experience of the 'heavenly' stillness both outdoors and in the house preceding any reflective thought puts her completely at ease:

> Pure morning air came in and stillness, deep country stillness far from the sound of the sea. Yet sounding, even while, as one paused to look, the stillness seemed complete. Offering if, free from an urgent errand, one should step out into it, small near and distant sounds, clear, measuring the height of the sky, making denser the enclosed stillness of this many-roomed, strangely deserted house. Where, at this spell-bound moment, was its life concentrated? (*DH*, 438)

For the largest part of her stay Miriam feels this harmonious union of the sounds of nature and the silences of the house as an organic whole. Whether it is in the 'bourne' of her 'upstairs world' (*DH*, 467) or in the sheltering garden, Miriam invariably enjoys the stillness around her and the sounds breathing the air of silence as an immediate sensory experience offering peace, serenity and happiness. Thus, in the morning stillness of the garden, which is broken only by the cooing of doves 'suggesting peace' (*DH*, 443), or in the 'heart of tranquillity' (*DH*, 538) of her bedroom, listening to the many-voiced sounds of the wind, she senses a 'freshness like water from a spring' in the silence of the waning night - a silence reminiscent of that Christmas stillness at the Brooms', another of her havens, where Miriam experiences this same vitalizing spring of energy in the darkness of her room: there she felt 'nothing but the cool sense of life pouring from some inner source and the deep fresh spaces of darkness all round her' (*IN*, 300f.). And it is this same 'coolness at the heart' of her reality that she recognizes in the stillness of a hot summer evening in London as 'wonderful life, from moment to moment, pure *life*' (*IN*, 405; emphasis original).

This enthusiasm for the momentary perfection of life forms one of the most important themes of *Pilgrimage*. Large parts of Dorothy Richardson's vast book of 'life' are in fact written to capture this deeper, inner, true reality that shines up unexpectedly in moments of contemplative silence. In these parts she expresses, as Pykett (79) calls it, an 'Edwardian vitalism', a belief in the force of Life, 'which was also shared by Lawrence and Forster.' Yet Lawrence's passion and Forster's belief in the connecting power of human relationships go beyond the scope of Miriam's experience of life. While Forster's 'illuminated' heroines Margaret Schlegel and Mrs Moore, like

Miriam all perception and sensitivity, in his well-plotted novels find a way to a deep understanding of other people,[40] Dorothy Richardson in her realistic portrait of Miriam shows her as very often striving in vain for such a concordance of souls. Time and again her outré expectations are thwarted, her initial enthusiasm for other people gives way to a sober detachment. Only with few selected friends - some of whom she is to find in the Quaker family at Dimple Hill - can she overcome her solipsistic tendencies and fully enjoy *sharing* the surprisingly rich beauty of life in community.

In the time leading up to her crisis and withdrawal from London Miriam's awareness of the central importance of 'life' as the source of consciousness, of identity and self-realization was largely covered by the noise and notions of outer reality; but in the vast stillness of Dimple Hill her continual exploration of 'the deep inner reaches of her being' (Thorn 217) loses most of its vagueness to become a centripetal quest for the centre, the spring of life within. In the quiet security of the Roscorla family her whole being is relieved from the noise of the metropolis and from the constrictions of her various social 'traps' in town,[41] in order to turn with an absolute presence of body and mind, of her perception and reflection, to the rural life of Dimple Hill. Eschewing the busy, loud rhythm of urban activities - dictated by the omnipresence of clock-time[42] - she soon appreciates the new rhythm of quietude of these Quaker farmers; in their society she finds an unprecedented completion of shared silence, moments of deep understanding that become endless as time seems to stop flowing: 'After supper, when Richard lifts the great brown Bible on to the table, we shall all feel ourselves quietly together again, free of space and time' (*MM*, 613).

Dorothy Richardson's own deep fascination with the Quaker world of thought is also reflected in her publishing two books on their ideas, *The Quakers Past and Present* (1914) and *Gleanings from the Work of George Fox* (1914), both of which help to illustrate Miriam's religious quest in *Dimple Hill* in non-fictional form. Throughout *Pilgrimage* Dorothy Richardson emphasizes Miriam's commitment to the 'joy of life at first hand' (*MM*, 569), her experience of *immediate* reality rather than theoretical abstraction, together with her incessant search for the truth inside, for the real being. This, in fact, echoes George Fox's essential message, which, according to Dorothy Richardson, is

> to call all men to see their creeds in the light of the *living experience* which had first produced them, to live themselves in that light shining pure and original within each one of them, [...] to refuse to

---

[40] cf. motto of *Howards End*: 'Only connect.'

[41] cf. Chapter 1.4.

[42] e.g. the clock of St Pancras accompanying her London years.

> be put off any longer with 'notions', mere doctrines, derivative testimonies obscuring the *immediate communication of life* to the man himself (*QPP*, 10, emphasis added).

For a Quaker, then, life is founded on an 'immediate inspiration' which can be gained by 'a process of retirement into the innermost region of being, into "the light", "the seed", "the ground of the soul"' (*QPP*, 11). This process is exactly the one Miriam goes through whenever she contemplates her own being. Both the Quakers' and Miriam's mystical quest is a 'journey to the heart of reality' so as to win 'the freedom of the very citadel of Life itself', a journey which is 'a swimming, so to say, against the whole tide of the surface intelligence, and this in no negative sense, no mere sinking into a state of undifferentiated consciousness, but rather [...] a setting forth to seek something already found [...] which has already proclaimed itself in moments of heightened consciousness' (*QPP*, 35).

Silence, bodily and mental, is necessarily the first step in this direction, be it in solitude or in the quiet communion at a meeting. As one of the few 'doctrines' of their faith, the Quakers

> recognise the value of silence not as an end, but as a means towards the attainment of the end; a silence not of listlessness or of vacant musing, but of holy expectation before the Lord, [...] or shall we cease to believe in His silent and immediate working, by His unseen, but not unfelt Spirit, upon our Hearts? (*Book of Christian Discipline*, 31f. and 63)

For, according to them, only in silence, in introversion and contemplation can this holy spirit be felt, can the elusive truth within be grasped. It is a central claim of the Quakers to recognize and respond to truth - calling themselves 'Friends of the Truth' - to the truth which is, in fact, the experience of God who manifests himself in the soul's unity with the divine that exists in every human being.[43] This 'living experience' is not fixed by any doctrines, it is meaningful only to the worshipping individual. The genuinely mystical core of an *individual* faith - which attracted Miriam already in the writings of Jacob Boehme, the great German mystic visionary (*TU*, 283) - eventually accounts for Miriam's lasting fascination with this religious group. She, who on her search for her very own world manages to reconcile her inner visions with outer reality only in mostly solitary moments of epiphanic freedom, admires a Quaker consistency of living in honesty, simplicity and justice, an 'originality' that continues on 'all levels of life' (*QPP*, 23).

Dimple Hill as a whole is suffused with this Quakerly balance of active and contemplative life. The consistent tone of Dorothy Richardson's enthusiasm for this way of living makes *Dimple Hill* one of the most easily

---

[43] cf. Eliade, 'The Quakers.' *Encyclopedia of Religion,* Vol. XII, 132.

accessible novel-chapters of *Pilgrimage*. She succeeds in integrating the more introverted, reflective aspects of, e.g., *Interim* and the sensory joy in nature of *Oberland*, and she delineates Miriam's resocialisation in terms of the quiet optimism encountered with the Quakers. Though only an 'interlude, a peaceful one' (Staley 116), lacking the more intellectual claims of the middle volumes, *Dimple Hill* is very important in representing Miriam's growing confidence in her own way of life. Far from being a superficial holiday account, it portrays Miriam as a woman who learns to listen to her inner voice, to withstand inner and outer conflicts successfully, a woman who faces her reality actively. Even though the existing differences with the Roscorlas are to lead to a certain estrangement, Miriam cherishes the atmosphere of acceptance that forms the basis of their friendship.

With the Roscorla siblings Miriam experiences a deeply-felt communion of souls that touches her innermost being. There is an immediate non-verbal understanding with Miss Roscorla when first looking at Miriam's room:

> They stood side by side, united in silent appreciation. [...] When they turned together to the room's open space, the temporary cessation of audible interchange had produced, rather than the uneasiness that prompts a search for fresh conversational material, a time-expanding satisfaction and the sense, behind them, of an achieved, indefinitely durable past (*DH*, 436).

Radiating an inner strength that is based on her religious conviction, Rachel Mary impresses Miriam as an independent woman who accepts everyone as an individual. In her strong, yet not domineering, presence in the household Rachel Mary represents the ideal woman-to-be, the 'womanly woman' who is perfectly balanced, as she is described in Dorothy Richardson's article 'Women and the Future': The womanly woman

> lives, all her life, in the deep current of eternity, an individual, self-centred. Because she is at one with life, past, present, and future are together in her, unbroken. Because she thinks flowingly, with her feelings, she is relatively indifferent to the fashions of men. [...] Only a complete self, carrying all its goods in its own hands, can go out, perfectly, to others, move freely in any direction. [...] Only completely self-centred consciousness can attain to unselfishness - the celebrated unselfishness of the womanly woman (*GM*, 413).

Miriam thus includes Rachel Mary almost at once in her very special league of female friends who do not need many words to express their mutual understanding and affection. Together with her, Miriam reaches moments of non-verbal intimacy in which she can simply be 'silent. No embarrassment. No need for speech' (*DH*, 523). With her, as so far only with Amabel, she can share a deep understanding of the tacit dimension. In her presence she can drop the mask, abandon her various sexual and social roles, she can be her self and feel a 'fullness of joy; in a new silence' (*DH*, 526). When Rachel Mary smiles at her out of her 'eloquent dark eyes' (*DH*, 442), Miriam feels 'the warm downward plunge into a unity' as the 'fulfilment of the hope' for friendship and understanding cherished for years as the ideal complement to her strong drive towards solitude.

In Miriam's friendships with *men* language plays an essential role. The various encounters with her male friends are to a large extent impregnated with verbose disputations; it is impossible to imagine Shatov explaining his philosophical ideas without the help of language, or Hypo, the 'causeur' and flatterer, being robbed of his tongue! But at Dimple Hill, and especially in her growing friendship with Rachel Mary, Miriam learns to use more direct and intuitive ways of communication than what she comes to regard as the abstraction of words. The use of language is reduced to a minimum: A smile, a touch, a gesture, even the mere sound of a voice to her appear as 'communication more eloquent than the words' actually spoken (*DH*, 506). Revealing more of one's true being, they are 'moments of insight' that far outdo verbal explanations.[44] The sharing of this Quaker distrust in the superficiality of language forms a crucial step on Miriam's way in. Giving preference to such interior ways she tunes in her mind towards the contemplative stillness necessary for what she aims at: the 'direct perception of ultimate reality', the living experience of the very centre of existence (*DH*, 419).

While for Miriam cultivating such non-verbal exchanges has only seemed possible in exceptional moments of intimacy with other women, the Quaker atmosphere of equality removes this gender-borne barrier and she experiences man's capacity for silence in her conversations with the two Roscorla brothers: Alfred, 'this frail, innocent creature' (*DH*, 471), 'who never spoke more than the necessary words [, w]ho knew the deepest truths' (*DH*, 535), whose 'radiance [shining] from within' (*DH*, 445) sheds a peaceful serenity, speaks with 'Quakerly' deliberation, leaving pauses for his answers that even further slow down his speech rhythm. Richard, though more eloquent and more 'worldly' (*DH*, 516) than his brother, is at first sight spotted as being different from 'the average, talkative male'. There is 'a Quaker difference, perceptible in the weightiness of his simple statement' (*DH*, 441) that marks him off as special. When he goes on walks with Miriam, this first impression is confirmed: 'Long intervals of strolling on and on, [...] he seemed to be content to walk in silence' (*DH*, 512). Richard, the 'handsome, battered giant' (*DH*, 441), in his quiet friendliness gives Miriam a 'marvellous sense of support and earthly security' (*DH*, 515). He is best

44 She thus shares Emerson's opinion, who writes: 'Moments of insight of fine personal relation, a smile, a glance - what ample borrowers of eternity they are! Life culminates and concentrates' ('Works and Days', *Complete Prose Works* 446).

remembered for what Dorothy Richardson regards as unusual in men, his gift for quiet contemplation. His gift for silent communication is, as Würzbach (298) writes, the 'central feature' of this eventually rather ambiguous character. Even after Miriam's bitter disappointment about his immature behaviour towards her, she recognizes in their relationship, in their ability to share silence, a profound understanding that still makes it possible for them to be 'drawing strength from each other. Strength that remains' (*MM*, 620). She has learnt to see silent community, shared by people who live their true self, not as strenuous and exhausting, limiting her in her individual freedom, but rather as a profound source of energy, enriching her own personal experience of life. Thus, with all the younger Roscorlas Miriam feels a 'sense of indestructible individuality' (*DH*, 515), for in moments of silent communion 'we are conscious mainly of each other, of something unchanging and trustworthy far away within the personal depths. Such a moment, with man or woman, is a spiritual experience, moving body and soul' (*DH*, 515f.).

Contrary to Miriam's wonted mental reservations about religious gatherings, she even welcomes this 'spiritual experience' as a deep enrichment of her life when she joins a whole group of Quakers in their silent worship. This is impressively shown in the two crucial scenes of *Dimple Hill*, an evening meal (*DH*, 469-475) and a Sunday service (*DH*, 494-505), juxtaposing their worldly and spiritual life respectively; Dorothy Richardson shows them as inseparable parts of the whole that makes up Life, one feeding and enriching the other. The inner, as she puts it elsewhere, is 'not in contradistinction to the outer. [The] abstraction from all externality, the purging of the self' is 'the most practical thing in the world, and ultimately fruitful in life-ends' (*QPP*, 22). The representation of Miriam's temporal participation in this *shared* life based on sincere faith forms an important complement to the recording of what is mainly a self-centred pursuit of *individual* existence, as the two scenes show Miriam's successful acceptance and integration of her religious sensitivity into her more worldly reflections on life.

In the first scene, the Roscorlas start supper by saying grace, 'a moment's immersion within [the] pulsating depths' of stillness (*DH*, 470): from the beginning they have their meal in a relaxed atmosphere of shared silence, a silence that at once forms part of and is nourished by the 'concrete spiritual rhythm' structuring life at Dimple Hill. It is a rhythm that keeps a 'knife-edge balance between two worlds' (*DH*, 470), between language and silence, between active life and contemplation, between physical light and mental illumination, unifying either side in an experience of the present moment where past and future merge in a *shared* mystical experience of the Now:

> She turned her eyes to the light upon the centre of the table. The vanished gloaming, though standing now apart outside the uncurtained window, was still part of the *gathering*, holding in its

> midst, as the leaf-and-petal scented mist stole invisibly in, both the *shared* day and tomorrow waiting beyond a *shared* darkness. But within the depths of the lamplight, moving at the heart of its still radiance, was the core of the *shared* mystery; far away within the visible being of light (*DH*, 470; emphasis added).

The lamp as the focus of attention, as the centre of their visual world,[45] thus assumes a deeper significance. It becomes the representative of that central Light of their shared mystery, uniting this small circle of 'fellow-mystics' for a revelation of a deeper truth and enhancing Miriam's deep joy in community. The 'serene' silence becomes a 'common possession' (*DH*, 473), the expression of their mutual understanding and affection, which is primarily founded on the Roscorlas' religious belief. Psalm 65, the 'farmer's song of triumph' (*DH*, 475), read in the 'deep, vibrant monotone' (*DH*, 474) of Richard's voice, forms the final intensification and natural consummation of their shared silence. The sound born out of this silence is an organic blossoming, a harmonious completion of a well-prepared quietness, just as in the psalm the final 'shout for joy' rises out of the silence prepared by God, who 'stilleth the noise of the seas, the noises of their waves, and the tumult of the people' (Psalm 65:7). In Richard's voice there is a 'power independent of the meaning of the words,' sending 'the hearers down and down into depths within themselves' (*DH*, 474), to a mystical experience, making them share the original emotion of the psalmist, making his praise their own. The words and the mere 'sound of this shared reading' (*DH*, 475) are Quaker ways of expressing the rhythm of Life, giving it both depth and direction.

The Sunday service which Miriam attends with the Roscorla family is a manifestation of this same rhythm, celebrating the Quakers' 'perpetual Sunday', 'drawn away into the depths of the spirit' (*DH*, 491). In the worshippers' attitude, 'inactive and silent, solitary yet not alone' (*DH*, 496) Miriam recognizes an 'Idealzustand' (Bronfen 46), an ideal state of mind for deepest contemplation in the stillness of mind and body. But as she reaches the meeting-room, which 'was utterly still' (*DH*, 497), where everybody expects some divine illumination, her mind and body rebel against a forced 'retreat into stillness'. Miriam's old scepticism against imposed religious experience is about to set in again. Though externally silent, she behind the façade of mute devotion has not reached the inner stillness that might lead to a concentration of her consciousness and to genuine contemplation. As a sign of this discordance between external and internal silence, her body moves on its own accord, breathing so unevenly that she cannot forget the world around her and her state as an 'alien element' (*DH*, 497), a newcomer who

[45] cf. Bachelard 158: 'La lampe du soir, sur la table familiale, est aussi le centre d'un monde, la table éclairée par la lampe est, à elle seule, un petit monde.'

has not yet made the vital experience with God. Once she has willed herself to join the group in their contemplation, her feelings of 'resentment', 'animosity' and 'indifference' (*DH*, 498), however, give way to some expression of affection and longing: To remain always centred,

> operating one's life, operating even its wildest enthusiasms from where everything fell into proportion and clear focus. To re-main always in possession of a power that was not one's own, and that yet one's inmost being immediately recognized as its centre (*DH*, 497).

Her wish for a mystical union with the energizing centre and source of life, for the experience of the presence of God drives her to continue her 'approach to reality' (*DH*, 498). And again she recognizes that only in penetrating the 'layers of a surface being' (*DH*, 498), in leaving behind her physical and mental awareness of herself, in concentrating on the inner state of her soul, will she be able to reach ultimate knowledge:

> Be still and *know*. Still in mind as well as in body. Not meditating, for meditation implies thought. Tranquil, intense concentration that reveals first its own difficulty, the many obstacles, and one's own weakness, and leads presently to contemplation, recognition (*DH*, 498).

In the allusion to Psalm 46, this recognition would be an all-embracing, mystical experience of God that transcends conceptual ideas, a total 'knowledge' that surpasses thought. The complete verse of the psalm thus reads: 'Be still and know that I *am* God' (Psalm 46, verse 10), a recognition of the existence and presence of the Old Testament's 'Yahwe', as the psalmist confirms: 'The Lord of hosts is *with us*' (verse 11, emphasis added).

Once more Dorothy Richardson presents in detail Miriam's spiritual technique, her method of reaching the pathway to an inner reality (cf. *DH*, 498f.). As Radford (1991:41) remarks, her description of this process again could be read as another verbal realization of William James's four-point definition of mysticism. It is significant that this willed entreprise towards 'the living centre' (*DH*, 498), Miriam's strenuous attempt to find herself 'in the presence of God' (*DH*, 500), to approach Reality, first fails. In this act of self-will she is unable to unthink her self, free herself from the impact of reflection. 'Resistance from within' (*DH*, 499) as well as 'distractions' from outside soon bring her back to the world of the senses: There is the visible presence of her fellow-worshippers, there are the sounds of nature from outdoors, there are the voices of the people on the platform: the men's impressive for their complementary ways of 'expressing different features of a common experience' (*DH*, 502), the woman's annoying, expostulating without convincing; they all distract her from her contemplation. In fact, when she is 'up in her mind, open-eyed, everything about her very sharp and clear' (*DH*, 499), she, instead of reaching a state of mystical contemplation, has turned to a stance of analytical observation. Yet Dorothy Richardson's meticulous registering of the processes of Miriam's mind also reveals unexpected turns and insights. When the reader has already accepted Miriam's failure in joining this form of group mysticism and is ready to accompany her on her analysis of her surroundings, Miriam 'closing her eyes to the surrounding twilight' (*DH*, 500) unexpectedly meets with a vision of herself alone in the open. Her inner eye perceives a mental image of perfect sensory intensity: She sees herself surrounded by blades of grass in an 'unlocated meadow', 'as if she were some small field-beast in their midst', herself as part of nature, physically and mentally at one with it.

This vision of a miniature world is one of those experiences of a certain 'fraicheur métaphysique [qui] nous mettent hors du monde, qui nous mettent dans un autre monde [...] dans cet au-delà du monde' (Bachelard 150f.). It takes Miriam out of her surroundings into an experience of otherworldly perfection. In its mixture of memory and anticipation - 'the memory of solitary joy and [...] the certainty of its continuance in the week lying ahead' (*DH*, 500f.) - this moment is a time-expanding experience of the Now, where, to speak again with Eliot ('Burnt Norton' 173), 'in the completion of its partial ecstasy' 'past and future are gathered.' The glimpse of a nook of paradise, an 'unknown field', 'sunlit, showing here and there a nucleus of remembered beauty' offers itself 'as a sufficient representative and bourne' (*DH*, 500).

Can the description of this scene be read as 'representative', as a verbal attempt to render a mystical experience that can never be adequately verbalized, a synecdochical substitution, 'pars pro toto', the visible standing for the bigger invisible, the tangible for the incomprehensible, Creation for its Creator?[46] Shall we read this vision of natural details as a material manifestation of the uncreated Light, an immanental discovery of God's omnipresence, who, in Emerson's words 'reappears with all his parts in every moss and cobweb'?[47] In Transcendentalist terms, nature in all its apparitions hints at God, for nature is a 'vast trope',[48] an emanation of the Divine Mind. Is Miriam's visionary union with nature in the double perspective of worm's-eye and bird's-eye view, expression of her *wish* for or her actual *experience* of that greater union famously described by Emerson: 'I become a transparent eye-ball; I am nothing; I see all; the currents of the Universal Being circulate through me; *I am part and particle of God*'?[49]

---

[46] cf. Augustine, *Confessions*, Book VII, 151ff: 'In an instant of awe, my mind attained to the sight of the God who IS. Then, at last, I caught sight of your invisible nature, as it is known through your creatures. But I had no strength to fix my gaze upon them.'

[47] Emerson, 'Compensation.' *Essays and Lectures* 289.

[48] Emerson, 'Poetry and Imagination.' *Complete Prose Works* 576.

[49] Emerson, 'Nature.' *Essays and Lectures* 10 (emphasis added).

There is no definite answer, as in the final analysis the mystical awareness of the ultimate goal, of God's presence, remains 'ineffable' (Kalamaras 7). Dorothy Richardson touches upon a limit of representation that can only hint at the existence of a reality beyond sensory perception and rational thought. If we understand this vision as the climax of Miriam's mystical contemplation, what George Fox, the first Quaker, said about his divine inspiration is true for her as well: 'I was come up in spirit [...] into the paradise of God. All things were new [...] beyond what words can utter' (*GGF*, 18).

Be it a naturalistic vision, a symbolic perception of a spiritual fact, or a profound mystical experience, Miriam keeps her impression of this moment in shared silence to herself. In the 'unique depth within the depth of Sunday' (*DH*, 500) she seems to realize that her experience reaches onto the other side of silence, into a dimension where language fails. She has made the experience Wittgenstein famously summarized at the end of his *Tractatus*: 'Es gibt allerdings Unaussprechliches. Dies *zeigt* sich. Es ist das Mystische . . . Wovon man nicht sprechen kann, darüber muss man schweigen' (85).

While for the believing Quakers the presence of God is felt in an act of *common* worship, - in this context Matthew 18,20, one of the key sentences of mystical faith, is quoted again[50] - Miriam realizes that her religious experience *is* supported and intensified in the communion with other silent worshippers, but that her vision is essentially a solitary one. For Dorothy Richardson - and also for Miriam - it is certain that divine inspiration can only be grasped in the 'Godward energizing of the *lonely* soul,' in an *individual* quest that is a 'life-process' (*QPP*, 22; emphasis added). Still, in the shared silence of the meeting Miriam reaches

> the misty dawn of a conviction, new and startling and bringing, as it cleared and took shape, a return of the sense of unity with those about her.
>
> I no longer care (*DH*, 504).

Feminism, socialism, doctrines, opinions, 'inspirers of wrath' (*DH*, 504), all the worldly ideas of life she knows *about* lose their power now that she has personally experienced the power of silence, has got to *know* the truth of Quakerism. In her religious quest it is, as she recognized early in her life, 'not dogmas' (*IN*, 355), but only individual faith and the inner preparedness to look for the very centre that might lead to the living meeting with the divine: 'There is a God or a Christ, there is something always there to answer when you turn away to it from everything. Perhaps one would have to remain silent for years, for a lifetime, and in the end begin to understand' (*IN*, 358). It is

---

[50] This time Dorothy Richardson quotes the full verse: 'For where two or three are gathered together in my name, there am I - *in the midst of them*' (*DH*, 498; emphasis original), emphasizing the central position of the divine presence at a Quaker meeting.

Miriam's intensified cultivation of silence that has allowed her to grasp this affirming 'dawn of a conviction': Yes, she has begun to understand.

At the end of her stay at Dimple Hill Miriam's whole attitude to life has become so Quaker-like that Rachel Mary describes her as a 'Friend in all but name' (*DH*, 540) and holiday guests in Vaud immediately identify her as a 'Quakeress' (*MM*, 561). Miriam's quest, whether we call it psychological, philosophical, or religious, in the end is the *same* quest for the Platonic triad of absolute truth, beauty and goodness, for the manifestation of the One, the source of all being, that Dorothy Richardson recognizes in the Quakers' religious seeking.[51] For in their lives 'again there is revealed the fruitfulness of that spirit which believes in and seeks goodness, beauty and truth - these alone, and these in all' (*QPP*, 75). For George Fox and Dorothy Richardson alike, the focus of interest 'is never, except incidentally, the group; never, except incidentally, the family; but the single human soul faced with its individual consciousness, the germ of truth, goodness, beauty, light, love, God, it bears within itself, the seed of God present in all human kind' (*GGF*, 10). To her Fox thus appears as one of 'those in whom the sense of an ultimate and essential goodness, beauty, and truth is the dominant characteristic' (*QPP*, 35), a 'religious genius' who having sought and intuitively found this inner reality, knows with an invulnerable certainty the unity of the divine Being and lives at its fullest the illuminated Life (cf. Underhill 309).

As we have seen, Miriam in rare moments of silent contemplation experiences such 'illuminated', mystical perfection within her reality; it is a radiant consciousness of the 'otherness' of natural things, a sense of reality shining through the phenomenal veil that can 'bring the feeling of goodness and beauty and truth into the patch on the wall and presently make all the look of the distant world and everything in experience sound like music in a dream' (*IN*, 322). Though Miriam lacks the certainty of a converted Quaker - 'It was not oneself. It could not be God' (*IN*, 322) - it is an experience of harmonious completion that breathes divine inspiration. In such moments of insight she catches glimpses of the 'truth hidden below the surfaces of life' (*RL*, 396), of the goodness and beauty of a reality that transcends what is visible. Striving for the union with 'that something within her that was more than herself,' in the 'heart of her being' (*DLH*, 219), Miriam the Mystic seeks a form of 'spiritual holism' (Radford 1991:41) and eventually aspires to the immersion into 'that central peace' (*DLH*, 219) where, just as to Fox, 'the door of Light and Life' (*GGF*, 17) would be opened to her.

---

[51] In Emerson's words: 'Truth, and goodness, and beauty, are but different faces of the same All' ('Nature,' *Essays* 19).

III.

THE EYE AND THE EAR: THE CONCEPT OF UNITY

5. A Union of the Senses? Perceptions of Unity

5.1 'Always Watching and Listening and Feeling:' Polysensory Perception

> Wie hängt Gesicht und Gehör, Farbe und Wort, Duft und Ton zusammen?
> Nicht unter sich in den Gegenständen; aber was sind denn diese Eigenschaften in den Gegenständen? Sie sind bloss sinnliche Empfindungen in uns, und als solche fliessen sie nicht alle in eins? Wir sind Ein denkendes sensorium commune, nur von verschiednen Seiten berührt - Da liegt die Erklärung.
> Allen Sinnen liegt Gefühl zum Grunde, und dies gibt den verschiedenartigsten Sensationen [...] ein inniges, starkes unaussprechliches Band. (Johann Gottfried Herder, 'Abhandlung über den Ursprung der Sprache' 745f.)

> Miriam listened and watched, her eyes and ears eagerly gathering and hoarding visions. (*BW*, 297)

Silence, as we saw in the previous chapter, is an ideal condition for the deepened awareness of the inner reaches of one's self, providing the perfect background for the growth of one's spirituality. This contemplative and reflective 'turn in', this spiritual tendency, helps Miriam to seek her way towards a completion of experience, an encompassing stretching of consciousness until it includes in its span both the world of Being and the world of Becoming, until it simultaneously experiences both the interior, hidden unity in the Eternal Being and its continuously changing outer side of Becoming, that many-coloured and many-voiced way of life which she as an individual constantly follows. This sense of an 'ontological unity' between her fragmentary selves (Radford 1991:119) and the perception of a transcendent reality beyond the world of her senses has appeared as the product of deepened reflection, of the contemplative, abstractive working of Miriam's mind. On the other hand, keeping her 'eyes and ears wide for the sight and sound' of her animate and inanimate environment (*BW*, 300), she shows a strong sense of unity with her surroundings. In moments of perfection, based on a rapturous bodily sensation of completion, this unifying power induces a perception of outer reality at its best: In Amabel's company, 'in a quietude of well-being [...] she felt complete as she was, brooding apart in an intensity of being that flowed refreshingly through all her limbs and went from her in a radiance that seemed to exist for herself alone' (*DLH*, 190). In such moments 'of poise,' in which 'the rhythmic beat of life made itself felt not only physically, but spiritually, imposing its unbounded certainty' (*CH*, 304), Miriam's senses perceive the world of facts in 'experiential intensity' (Watts 22). It is often in the accumulation of different sensory impressions that Miriam's consciousness takes hold of the objective, external reality and turns it into the rich world of her subjective experience. The overpowering presence of stimulating sensations leads to a mental experience of a more-than-real perfection, which is verbalized in words like 'magic' (*PR*, 158; *HC*, 392; *TR*, 498) or 'enchantment' (*O*, 29; *DH*, 514), 'something there were no words for' (*HC*, 392).[1] This primary awareness of external reality, i.e. of anything that exists outside her own body, is a 'spontaneous intuitive perception, neither dependent on nor arising from the operation of the intellect' (Rose 1970:36). What Dorothy Richardson says about her childhood in 'Data for a Spanish Publisher' is true for Miriam too:

> [S]ince things there were, I preferred to *become one with them*, in the child's way of direct apprehension which no subsequent 'knowledge' can either rival or destroy, rather than to stand back and be told, in regard to any of the objects of my self-losing adoration, this and that. These objects were chiefly the garden, as known to me when no one was about, the woods, the sky and sunlight (*JP*, 132; emphasis added).

William James, quoting Griesinger, sees this feeling of a unity with what is around us as a common trait of the *child's* subjective experience, a trait, however, that frequently shows up in adult life as well: In childhood

> we feel ourselves closer to the world of sensible phenomena, we live immediately with them and in them; an intimately vital tie binds us and them together. But with the ripening of reflection this tie is loosened, the warmth of our interest cools, things look differently to us, and we act more as foreigners to the outer world, even though we know it a great deal better. Joy and expansive emotions in general draw it nearer to us again. Everything makes a more lively impression, and with the quick immediate return of this warm receptivity for sense-impressions, joy makes us feel young again ('The Perception of Reality,' *Principles of Psychology II* 927).

[1] An outstanding passage where this experience of 'magic reality' is rendered in condensed intensity is Chapter 8 of *The Trap* (*TR*, 498); one of the shortest of *Pilgrimage*, it convinces in its evocative strength.

In the immediacy of sensory perception, Miriam as a child and as an adult who has kept the child's 'vital ties' with the world of the senses, literally 'in-corporates' and aims at being 'in-corporated' by what is around her, in moments of highest intensity achieving a 'kind of mystical communion with nature and the things of this world' (Kaplan 40f.). James's 'expansive emotions' play a major part in Miriam's perception of external reality. They support both her pre-reflective sense of harmonious unity with her surroundings and her purely sensory perception of outward things unified by the stable working of her consciousness. In a simultaneous cooperation of two or more senses Miriam registers visual, aural, olfactory and tactile sense impressions all at the same time, no longer as independent homomodal sensations, but as parts of a unified *polysensory* perception that calls forth a *single* emotional reaction. In Miriam's consciousness there are underlying interrelations among the separate sense modalities that allow her in such moments of intense emotionality to perceive outward reality as one unified whole. For example, Miriam's impression of the drawing-room at Newlands as being 'light and fragrant and very warm' (*HC*, 357) objectively consists of three separate sensations, a visual, an olfactory and a thermal one, coincidentally perceived at the same time. Yet in her consciousness these separate sensations mingle into one; the three adjectives connote one and the same underlying affective notion of pleasantness. The three sensations thus accumulate and intensify Miriam's happiness, calling forth a unified feeling of complete well-being.

While mere polysensory experience is a common quality of all human perception, Miriam's ability to integrate in her consciousness an incredible multitude of sensory details around her *at once*, as important and interesting parts of her external reality,[2] marks her as a character of outstanding sensory sensitivity. When May Sinclair exclaims that while the reader constantly looks at the outer world through Miriam's senses, 'it is as if you had never seen it so vividly before' (1918:58), she recognizes her as a woman who, by catching the vibration, the form and the sound of a certain moment in its sensuous vividness, can experience the inspiring secret of such a moment: the passion of life at its very core. She is, in Beresford's words, 'one with life'.[3]

Whether to 'see everything simultaneously', 'in terms of life' (*RL* 393), is an essentially 'female' way of perception, as Miriam claims, is hard to prove; but her ideal of a synchronic, synthesizing multiplicity of perception as opposed to a 'male', scientific, dissecting observation of objective facts

---

[2] In 'The Perception of Reality' William James writes: 'The mere fact of appearing as an object at all is not enough to constitute reality. [...] What we need is practical reality, reality for ourselves: and to have that, an object must not only appear, but it must appear both *interesting* and *important*' (924).

[3] 'Introduction' to *Pointed Roofs,* 1921, VIII.

forms the backbone of Dorothy Richardson's idea of gender-based attitudes towards perceiving reality.[4] 'Seeing from inside' (*DL*, 37) and - in contrast to men, who 'have no present' (*RL*, 280) - experiencing the immediate impact of the 'Now, the eternal moment, fully' (*MM*, 635), Miriam recognizes that in the role of a deeply involved participant *and* detached observer of life one 'can have the whole world round one all the time' (*DL*, 20).

Given Miriam's open sensory receptiveness, summarized in her claim that she is 'always watching and listening and feeling' (*RL*, 244), instances of polysensory perception can easily be found throughout *Pilgrimage*. Yet the mere existence of visual, aural and olfactory stimuli (taste and touch being of clearly lesser importance) that might trigger a reaction in Miriam's mind is not enough for Dorothy Richardson - nor for her readers. What she presents us with are sensory data that have been refined and filtered as significant to Miriam's ever-so-subtle consciousness. This consistent representation of an almost incessant stream of perceptions in Miriam's mind, may be impressive as a feat of attentiveness, but it involves the danger of losing much of its fascination because of its inherently repetitive character. In her text Dorothy Richardson thus describes, as Mansfield writes, the sensory impressions on Miriam's mind 'complete in every detail, with nothing taken away from it - and nothing added. This is a rare and interesting gift, but we should hesitate before saying it was a great one' (1919: 309).[5]

What at times may appear as a tedious representation of Miriam's total sensory experience is an important factor of the whole project of *Pilgrimage*. In accordance with William James ('Perception of Reality' 923), Dorothy Richardson recognizes that 'the things of sense [...] are the absolutely real world's nucleus': the attention towards her own senses and towards perceptible things is pre-eminently important for Miriam's perception of reality. Dorothy Richardson's insistence on the sensory quality of Miriam's perceptions shows her belief in its primary function of shaping consciousness.

[4] cf. 'Comments' *Dental Record XXXVI*, 10 (2 Oct 1916), 541-44; reprinted in Hanscombe (1987) 53: Women constituted 'the synthetic principle of human life,' men had a 'mental tendency to departmentalize, to analyze, to separate single things from their flowing environment.'

[5] Staley (106) gives a critical statement that is more differentiated: Dorothy Richardson's 'preoccupation with private sensory awareness tends to restrict Miriam's thoughts to seemingly trivial matters and results in sensory boredom; colors, shapes, reflections, proportions, lines and shades merge within what comes dangerously close to being mere static enclosure without refinement or definition. These images are relieved - if just barely - by the subtle arrangement of reactions by Miriam to this phantasmagoria of images which are apprehended by her senses. Central to an understanding of these minute descriptions of nearly every detail encountered by Miriam's senses is the way in which they blend to form heightened impressions in Miriam's mind which evoke feelings of freedom for thought as well as for a unique awareness of time.'

Similar to Wordsworth, who at the perception of the beauty of his surroundings feels his

> thoughts, link by link
> Enter through ears and eyesight,
> ('How Sweet It Is' 11f. *Poetical Works III*, 21)

Miriam's mental activity is stimulated by the cooperation of her senses, and especially so by the simultaneous perception of vision and sound. Time and again she 'listened and watched, her eyes and ears eagerly gathering and hoarding visions' (*BW*, 297), visions that lead her on to some deepened reflections on life. In the accumulation of sensory data lies the vital basis of all the essential concepts and thoughts in *Pilgrimage*, for, as James puts it: 'Sensations are the stable rock, the terminus a quo and the terminus ad quem of thought' ('Sensation', *Principles of Psychology II* 657).

What Metzger (111) calls 'configurations' or 'distributions' of stimuli, the mind's reactions to a simultaneous stimulation of more than one receptor element, make up some of the most intense moments in *Pilgrimage*. In these configurations Miriam reaches a state of perceiving in the fullest sense: she not only takes account of her surroundings in exceptional completeness but she also recognizes her self taking account of them. Just as the child in the short story 'The Garden'(*JP*,121-125), forging a relationship with the natural world around her, experiences perception, action, and knowledge of herself and her surroundings as an indivisible one (cf. Watts 36), Miriam's consciousness similarly establishes, in Coleridge's words, an 'intimate coalition' between the objective and the subjective, which to her then appear as 'coinstantaneous and one' (145).[6] In the act of perception the outside world thus becomes a living part of her own self; the atmosphere of her surroundings, usually considered as background, becomes the focus of her attention.[7] Thus, what in the text may appear as a disorderly accumulation of sense impressions is in fact Dorothy Richardson's way of representing the immortal moment between taking stock of one's surroundings and becoming involved in them' (*MM*, 561), the moment Miriam feels the atmosphere of her surroundings at its purest and thereby makes them her own.[8]

---

[6] In full, Coleridge writes: 'During the act of knowledge itself, the objective and the subjective are so instantly united that we cannot determine to which of the two the priority belongs. There is here no first and no second; both are coinstantaneous and one' (145).

[7] Powys explains the revelation of 'feminine secrets' in *Pilgrimage* by this very emphasis of the atmosphere: 'Perhaps no writer has ever devoted so much attention to the "atmospheric" aspects of her backgrounds. [All the background details] are part of the very essence of her revelation as to what women, in their subconscious nature, respond to day by day' (12f.).

[8] Powys sees Miriam's 'personalisation' as characteristic of the 'feminine reaction to life': 'One of the most exciting elements [in *Pilgrimage*] is an analysis of [the] mystical

The following polysensory passage out of 'The Role of the Background', a newspaper article emphasizing the atmosphere as a constitutive part of experience, may, as a contrast, throw the quality of more literary passages in *Pilgrimage* into relief. Here Dorothy Richardson merely takes 'stock', enumerating the thermal, tactile, visual, auditory and olfactory stimuli of the atmosphere around her; in a concluding comment she summarizes the emotional reaction of the observer in abstract terms:

> The mere going out into the crystalline air whose touch is electric upon the face, the snow mountains all about one, the sunlit diamond-sprent snow over the valley floor and crisp under one's feet, the frost-bound stillness (broken by the sound of sleigh-bells) that yet is not cold - never the penetrating cold we know in England - and the never-to-be-forgotten characteristic smell of the Swiss village in winter, the smell of burning pine logs . . . all these things are gladness (*Sphere* 22, 226).[9]

By contrast, the passage out of *Oberland* describing Miriam's experience of the same Swiss Alpine winter conveys the Wordsworthian sense of 'something far more interfused',[10] the intimate emotional relationship between Miriam and the 'personalized' circumambient objects of nature.

> The track through the wood [...] narrowed to a winding path that took her in amongst them, into their strange *close fellowship* that left each one a perfect thing apart. Not lonely, nor, for all the high-bulging smoothness of snow in which it stood, cold. It was their secret, pine-breath, that brought *a sense of warm life*; and their close-clustered needles. Out on the mountain-sides they looked black and bleak, striving towards the sun until they were stayed by the upper cold. Seen close, they were *a happy company* bearing light upon the green burnish of their needles and the dull live tints of their rough stems. And very secret; here thought was *sheltered* as in a quiet room (*O*, 72; emphasis added).

In this 'atmosphärische[n], auf die Sinneswahrnehmungen und den Leib bezogene[n] Belebung des gelebten Raumes' (Bronfen 72), in the lively, physical and mental interchange with open and closed space around her,

---

power in women by which they change their natural surroundings and transform their inanimate environments in their instinctive and secret art of self-expression' (17).

9 The description reads like a rather stereotype application of the definition of the word 'atmosphere': 'surrounding mental or moral element; [...] applied to the background *sounds* that evoke a particular mood, impression; [...] the *air* in any particular place as affected in its condition by *heat, cold*, purifying or contaminating influences' (*OED, I* 750; emphasis added).

10 Wordsworth, William. 'Lines Composed a Few Miles Above Tintern Abbey' l. 96. *Poetical Works Volume II*, 262.

Miriam experiences a sense of completion.[11] Bronfen shows that in *Pilgrimage* all forms of physical space have some atmosphere that depends on the

> wahrnehmenden erlebenden Subjekt. [Jeder Raum] kann sowohl Spiegel für die erlebende Figur, Seismograph ihrer Stimmung sein, wie auch als Katalysator bestimmte Stimmungen hervorrufen, und als Filter bestimmte Dinge von ihr abschirmen (54).

This atmospheric, 'konkret nicht benennbare Vitalkraft des Raumes' (76), supports Miriam's polysensory perception towards an ecstatic, awareness of her surroundings, where she can 'see and feel the whole thing from inside' (*TU*, 163); perception and emotion mutually enhance each other in the intense 'intoxication' with her environment. In such 'miracles of perception through which the disparate elements of life coalesce into a single whole' (Henke 54), Miriam experiences a blurring of distinct classes of perception:

> Out in the immense landscape, in the down-pouring brilliance of pure light, thought was visible. Transparent to the mountains who took its measure and judged, yet without wounding, and even while they made it seem of no account, a small intricate buzzing in the presence of mighty, simple statement sounding just out of reach within the air, and invited thoughtless submission to their influence as to a final infinite good that would remain when they were no more seen, there was pathos in their magnificence [...] (*O*, 72).

In the self-effacing act of submission to her surroundings, the borders between exterior and interior reality, between perception and imagination, between observation and emotion are obscured. Miriam's enthusiasm for the beauty of the winter landscape reads like a variation of the experience of Wordsworth's wanderer:

> Sensation, soul and form,
> All melted into him; they swallowed up
> His animal being; in them did he live,
> And by them did he live; they were his life.
> In such access of mind, in such high hour
> Of visitation from the living God,
> Thought was not; in enjoyment it expired.
> ('The Excursion' I, 207-213. *Poetical Works V*, 15)

[11] While her old room at Mrs Bailey's 'had been full at once with the sound and colour of her life' (*TR*, 446), in its *familiarity* directly reflecting her state of being in polysensory intensity, Miriam's immediately emotionalized awareness of *unknown* space can best be seen in her polysensory perception of the interior of churches: in their 'dim cool musty' (*BW*, 310), silent or music-filled, colourful or 'grey' (*CH*, 348) atmosphere they give her a feeling of 'how perfect life is at those moments' (*HC*, 386), they make her want to stay (*PR*, 120) and fill her with a 'profane joy' (*CH*, 348).

Rational analysis is given up for a non-conceptual appreciation of beauty. At the same time, in this moment of coherent perception, 'with thought shut off' (*O*, 72), the mountains become more than what they really are; they assume a transcendent, personalized role as judges of Miriam's mental activities. In her 'submission' to them Miriam again shows signs of the Wordsworthian 'creative sensibility', being likewise a lover of

> [. . .] all the mighty world
> Of eye, and ear, - both what they half create,
> And what perceive; well pleased to recognise
> In nature and the language of the sense
> The anchor of my purest thoughts, the nurse,
> The guide, the guardian, of my heart, and soul
> Of all my moral being.
>
> ('Tintern Abbey,' 105-111. *Poetical Works II*, 262)

The mountains, nature, here become the 'nurse' and guide of *her* being; it is her hope to be 'changed' by the full perception of them, to come back 'refreshed and changed and indifferent' (*O*, 72) - as indeed she will be when coming back to London. The 'background' of nature more than any human relation thus helps her to find a new inner balance again.

Generally, in the coherent perception of her surroundings Miriam reaches a state of mind in which she hovers between (factual) reality and (imaginary) irreality, where things assume an intense inner life of their own. In the very sensory act of perceiving, a transcendent reality shines up, the existence of an *ultra* within the *hic et nunc*. It is this synthesis of the finite and the infinite, an encompassing experience of 'reality' beyond the rational that Miriam summarizes in another context: 'We can move, see, hear, feel somehow *beyond* our immediate selves. We can. We do' (*DLH*, 228; emphasis added).

Time and again the polysensory perception of nature, of the outside world in general, leads to such an expanded experience of the subjective, inner self, a widened consciousness of both her personal emotions and an 'impersonal', 'perfect' timeless present 'beyond'.[12] On a weekend excursion to the sea, 'twilight', 'silence', a 'soft land-breeze carrying the scent of gorse' - visual, acoustic, tactile, and olfactory stimuli *together* - reveal to her 'the afternoon's happiness' and bring to her consciousness the existence of something not immediately perceptible, making her aware of a 'presence beyond' (*TU*, 216), of a transcendence of *space*. Similarly, the 'fresh golden air' or the sound of the sea at Christmas fill her with happiness and transport her beyond the now: her sense impressions 'drowned the present in the sense of seaside summers; [...] the sense of summer was so strong in the bright air that she felt sure, if only she could have always bright screened light in her

[12] cf. *DH*, 449 and 453.

room, summer warmth and summer happiness would last the whole year round' (*DL*, 93-95). The sensory immediacy is thus supported by her wish for a perpetuation of the moment, her awareness of a transcendence of *time* into the future.[13] As we have seen in the repeated descriptions of and allusions to Miriam's bee memory, or in the emphasis on the evocative quality of music, *time* is transcended in a much more important way: the stimulus of *one* sensation can re-create the past in *all* its polysensory immediacy. Apart from light, the 'magic unifier of outer and inner world' (Bucher 148), it is also the sound of music,[14] or a special smell,[15] that has the power to evoke 'the continuous moment that was always and everywhere the same' (*DLH*, 176). Miriam's sensory receptivity combined with her memory, which shows distinct eidetic qualities, helps her to transcend both the intrinsic transitoriness of time and the bound immovability of space.

This 'rare and interesting gift' (Mansfield, 1919:309) of complete recall to a large extent determines Miriam's subjective awareness of reality. Like other women writers of her period,[16] Dorothy Richardson highlights Miriam's sense of the unity of time as vital for her experience of life as a whole: Conscious of the enormous power of sensory perceptions she sees the simultaneity of remembered and immediate sense impressions as a 'knitting together of past and present' (*MM*, 597). Permeated by bodily sensation, the imaginary and the actual interweave and interact in what is to her an overwhelming phenomenal and subjective experience of continuity. Pre-reflectively, she is aware of an underlying identity, a wholeness of Being, which she in a subsequent act of reflection experiences as her *self*, as *I*.[17]

---

[13] cf. *RL*, 339, the sea at Hypo's: a perfect Now in its sensory, mostly visual immediacy, yet expanding in time: 'All waiting for tomorrow, for endless tomorrows' (cf. Chapter 2.3.2).

[14] e.g. *PR*, 44, where the sounds of music bring back the childhood memory of a mill in Devon in polysensory perfection: 'She saw [...] she heard [...] she could feel [...] and sniff [...].'

[15] e.g. *HC*, 392 a 'sweet familiar syrupy distillation' calling up her bee memory; *IN*, 351: the scent of mimosas reminding her of Newlands in spring. Olfactory stimuli are never neutral. They invariably trigger an emotional response in Miriam, enriching her experience of the present moment with mostly visual impressions of the past. The mystery of Miriam's passion for the fragrance of soap, for instance, lies in 'its power of evoking images [pervading] one's best realizations of everyday life' (*O*, 62). Waking up at Flaxman's on a Sunday morning it is the 'faint scent of soap' (*DLH*, 177) that leads her back in memory to images of spring in general and, in particular, to another re-living of her bee-moment in her childhood garden.

[16] cf. Parkin-Gounelas 19: 'Unity between past and present, self and other, is often a principle, both formal and semantic, to be detected in the interstices of women's novels of the Victorian and early Modern periods.'

[17] Rose (1970:32) goes even one step further when she draws a parallel between Miriam, the remembering subject, and Dorothy Richardson, the remembering artist, who

5.2 'Sound made visible:' Aspects of Synaesthesia

Comme de longs échos qui de loin se confondent
Dans une ténébreuse et profonde unité
Vaste comme la nuit et comme la clarté
Les parfums, les couleurs et les sons se répondent.
(Charles Baudelaire, 'Correspondances', 5-8. *Oeuvres I*, 11)

And the wonder of Wagner is that through your ears he makes you see so hugely. (*DLH*, 170)

Can a mental re-enactment of a past experience triggered off by the perception of one sensory stimulus, be it visual, aural or olfactory, be called synaesthesia? Is the vividness of the scenes immediately recalled the sign of a rare gift of coinstantaneous perception in two or more of Miriam's senses, as the term implies?[18]

Cytowyc, a leading neurologist in this field, defines synaesthesia as an involuntary and inevitable joining of two sense impressions, 'in which the real information of one sense is accompanied by a perception in another sense' (1), which is experienced as equally real and vivid, often outside the body instead of imagined in the mind's eye. Thus synaesthesia is a 'product of the brain and not the mind' (2). The triggering of images by musical or fragrant stimuli, therefore, is a case of pure imagination and not interesting to him as a neurologist. From this physiological point of view Bach's music, for instance, making Miriam see 'broad bright morning light running through forest tracery' (*RL*, 347) or the dry fragrance of petal dust calling up 'a fleeting vision of sunlit flowers' (*DH*, 436) are mental processes far too complex to be called synaesthesia.[19] However, Mursell - according to whom

---

in writing her text *lives* in this synchrony of past and present: 'A synthesis occurs of primary experience and its restoration in memory, and of the subjective impression of a remembered experience and its objective expression in art. The resulting "effusion" is a synthesis of the multiple aspects of memory, and becomes itself a new source of creative inspiration.'

[18] cf. *OED XVII*, 467: from Greek συν = together + αισθε = to feel, to perceive.

[19] Despite his 'scientific' approach, Cytowyc is not always very consistent in his argumentation. He thoroughly investigates the most common form of synaesthesia, 'coloured hearing' or 'audition colorée', where sounds take on the accoutrements of sight (cf. Cytowyc 39), yet when he describes the synaesthete of the associative type, who might invariably associate the same colours to the same sounds - in an act of semi-conscious instant recall of former similar situations - the borderline to the mental trigger of memories is not always easy to draw. The simplicity of the images aroused seems to be the major criterion. Thus, according to him, Proust's famous madeleine episode, though the gustatory impression at once calls forth a visual impression, could not be called a synaesthetic experience because of the complexity of the images aroused by the taste of

synaesthesia implies a 'secondary sensation in one sensory field produced by a primary sensation in another field' (23) - and Marks, who defines synaesthesia as a 'stimulation of a single sense [which] arouses a mélange of sensory images' (83), see synaesthesia exactly as such a *mental* response to a bodily impulse, a *reaction* manifesting itself physically again as a different sensory impression. Few people are truly synaesthetic. Rarely do sensory experiences of sight, sound and taste actually arise, secondarily, involuntarily, and inevitably, from appropriate stimuli; also Miriam's sensory perception is devoid of such regular, involuntary cross-modal sensations that would hint at an innate overlapping of two (or more) senses.

Given perception as a largely psychological process that involves the activity of the mind as a filter of physical sensation, Wellek's definition allows us to speak of synaesthesia in Miriam's perception:

> Unter Synaesthesie verstehen wir *jeden* psychologischen Vorgang, in dem verschiedene Sinnesräume miteinander verbunden und in Parallele gesetzt sind, also die Sinnenentsprechungen in jeder erdenklichen Weite des Begriffs. (1929:19)[20]

Whenever such intersensory correspondences occur, Miriam shows a distinct synaesthetic capacity to appreciate the closeness and richness of similarities among visual, auditory and other sensory qualities, a capacity that is strongly aroused in particular by powerful aesthetic experiences. In these rare pinnacles of sensory perception - both real and imagined - but sometimes also in everyday perceptive activities 'a confusion of impressions all joyously claiming the *same* quality' (*DLH*, 267; emphasis added) may set in, implying a unity of the senses that is based on Miriam's underlying sense of coherence. Dorothy Richardson, intent on rendering the complexity of Miriam's subjective awareness of reality as a whole, emphasizes her intermodal

---

the biscuit. To him it is rather a perfect example of instant recall, recreating the past in all its immediate liveliness. Miriam's complex bee memory, aroused by various sensory stimuli, would therefore fall into the same category.

[20] Opera in general and Wagner's musical dramas in particular are sometimes defined as the prototypical synaesthetic works of art of the 19th century (with film as their 20th-century equivalent): this very open understanding of the term 'synaesthesia' simply implies the simultaneity of different sensory impressions that are not necessarily put in parallel - as one conditioning the other - at all: this is what we called 'polysensory perception.' Miriam, by the way, questions the power of Wagner's musical dramas to stimulate eye and ear in an absolutely parallel way, but agrees on the sounds having a truly synaesthetic quality to trigger individual visual impressions:

'There is no possible representation that can compete with the vast scenes this music brings to your mind. I shall see, with the lit stage behind me, instead of the Queen's Hall orchestra in front, much bigger scenes than the stage could hold. *No one can see and hear to perfection at the same moment*. And the wonder of Wagner is that through your ears he makes you see so hugely' (*DLH*, 170; emphasis added).

capacity, mostly in association with her vivid imagination, but also in the 'pure' act of perception of the different sense organs.

Overwhelmed by one sensory impression, Miriam at times actively seeks to grasp its unique power by way of associating synaesthetic correspondences. Yet as long as her reflective intellect exerts its influence on her sensations, these conscious, conceptual rather than perceptual efforts to experience the sensory impression in synaesthetic intensity fail. The working of her abstractive mind prevents a spontaneous transposition of her impression from one sense modality to another.

The immense beauty of Oberland, for instance, eludes the grasp of the eye and calls for a synaesthetic appreciation, which, however, in her conscious summoning forth does not set in: 'She had not eyes enough for seeing. Seeing was not enough. There was sound, *if only one could hear it*, in this still, signalling light' (*O*, 30; emphasis added). The lane leading to Dimple Hill, similarly laden with anticipatory notions of perfection, has 'the enchantment of a sudden plunge from enclosure into air whose scents are *almost* tangible' (*DH*, 514; emphasis added). While the overpowering scent of the azaleas at Newlands make her '*almost* hear the humming of the bees' (*HC*, 392; emphasis added), she also seeks an auditory correspondence when breathing in the 'delicately penetrating incense' of the vines at Dimple Hill, a scent, which has 'become, with the help of stillness and solitude, an *almost* audible emanation' (*DH*, 476; emphasis added). Walking beneath the Waldstrasse lime trees in Hanover, Miriam feels that 'the scent of them *must be visible*' (*PR*, 124; emphasis added); yet there is no visual impression that would really correspond to her olfactory sensation.

However, when she, concentrating on her bodily sensations, lets her imagination roam freely, a strong sensory stimulus can transcend the receptory capacity of its corresponding sense organ, calling forth a cross-modal equivalent: Thus, the visible beauty of the sky at Oberland, the place of her most dramatic raptures, assumes an auditory quality that emphasizes the visual impact: 'Colour was coming from above, was already here in dark brilliance, thundery' (*O*, 29), and causes an emotional response in her consciousness: 'She still longed to glide forever onwards through this *gladness* of light' (*O*, 29; emphasis added). A very rare, in fact the only really synaesthetic experience that involves her gustatory sense is found in her tasting of German food in a German restaurant in London. While the taste of the 'familiar smooth savoury broth' makes her see 'German kitchens, alles rein und sauber, blank poliert' (*DL*, 126), thus triggering off an abstract picture of her German experience, it is in a draught of lager that the gustatory experience calls forth an immediate, both tactile and visual - and therefore truly synaesthetic - reaction, in which Miriam feels spiritual expansion as well: She

> took a long draught of lager. It was still bitter, but the bitterness was only an astringent tang in the strange cool lively frothy tide; a tingling warmth ran through her nerves, expanding to a golden glow that flowed through the room and held her alight within itself, an elastic impalpable bodiless mind (*DL*, 127f.).

In the synaesthetic appreciation of the alcoholic drink she reaches a sense of completion; the expanded physical sensation leads to a liberating expansion of her mind, which helps her to see a new way in her intricate deadlock situation.

> A slight intoxication began it, making it possible to look at things from a distance, in separate wholes and make discoveries about them. It was being somewhere else, and suddenly looking up, out of completion, at distant things, that brought their meanings and the right words (*DL*, 129).

While gustatory and olfactory stimuli play a minor role in Miriam's synaesthetic experiences, sound engendering sight is by far the most productive synaesthetic process in *Pilgrimage*. Be it Mrs Orly's telephone voice, which in Miriam's mind evokes an image of 'her whole self' (*DLH*, 199), be it the familiar nightly bells of St. Pancras whose sound bring 'before her eyes the tree-filled space across' (*CH*, 355): there are many scenes where acoustic impressions are supported by visual responses. Synaesthetic perception in its intensity and expansive drive may help Miriam to overcome the oppositions between her inner and outer realities and (re-)gain emotional stability. Thus, being 'turned out' of Mrs Kronen's drawing-room with an unmistakeable hint at her social inferiority, Miriam feels 'utterly crushed' (*HC*, 415). It is in the synaesthetic, synthesizing experience of Regent Street that she recovers from this humiliation and is reassured of herself:

> Sounds of visible near things streaked and scored with broken light as they moved, led off into untraced distant sounds . . . chiming together. [...] I am part of the dense smooth clean paving stone . . . sunlit; gleaming under dark winter rain; shining under warm summer rain; sending up a fresh stony smell . . . always there (*HC*, 416).

In the merging of visible and auditory impressions she is acutely aware of her body and feels its expansion, which reconciles her with the world: 'She was vast. She could gather up the buildings in her arms and push them away, clearing the sky' (*HC*, 417).[21]

---

[21] Similarly, when visiting Eleanor Dear in hospital, Miriam's synaesthetic perception serves as a reassuring counterpoint to the tense atmosphere bespeaking illness, loneliness and death: 'There was no sound but the strange silent noise of the sunlight and the

Most impressively, perhaps, in *Pilgrimage* it is the power of music that lowers the threshold of sensitivity to other forms of stimulation, especially to the impact of visual elements. The sounds that reach her inmost self evoke a synaesthetic correspondence in the realm of vision, enhancing Miriam's profound emotional reaction. She experiences a 'romantic' unity of perception that - in its lesser form - recalls the synaesthetic sensibility of Keats or Shelley.[22]

It is her consciousness, the 'primary modality' of perception (Marks 252), rather than a real, palpable, sensory impression, that makes her see the sounds. For, as Marks says, music 'generates sight by way of the sine qua non, creative imagination; but it is the imagination itself that gives the impetus, shaping sound into form' (252). This power of her creative imagination can be seen time and again in *Pilgrimage*.[23] The most impressive example of the 'weaving and interweaving' of sound and sight, of a unity of the objectively real music and the 'magic shape' of imaginary, yet subjectively equally real, pictures, is Miriam's playing of a Chopin nocturne in a moment of loneliness at Mrs Bailey's:

> The notes sounded soft and clear and true into her mind, weaving and interweaving the sight of moonlit waters, the sound of summer leaves flickering in the darkness, the trailing of dusk across misty meadows, the stealing of dawn over grass, the faint vision of the Taj Mahal set in dark trees, white Indian moonlight outlining the trees and pouring over the pale façade; over all a hovering haunting consoling voice, pure and clear, in a shape, passing, as the pictures faintly came and cleared and melted and changed upon a vast soft darkness, like a silver thread through everything in the world (*IN*, 333f.).

Miriam's vivid imagination constantly creates images that form a union with the slowly changing music, lifting her out of the distressing and unsettled reality of her early London years into a unified, magic realm that, 'not affected by life or any kind of people' (*IN*, 334), allows her to *feel* her suppressed emotions. She thus hears in Chopin's music what Shelley described as

---

flowers' (*TU*, 253). Sunlight and flowers, symbols of life and happiness, thus catch her attention in unexpected intensity and help her to bear the pains of her visit.

[22] In *Doktor Faustus* Thomas Mann expresses his romantic idea of synaesthesia in similar terms when Kretschmar lectures on the effect of music: 'Ihre mächtigste sinnliche Verwirklichung finde [die Musik] als orchestrale Instrumentalmusik, wo sie denn durch das Ohr alle Sinne zu affizieren scheine und das Genussreich der Klänge mit denen der Farben und Düfte opiatisch verschmelzen lasse' (85).

[23] e.g. *PR*, 44; *RL*, 347; *O*, 35; *DLH*, 170.

> a tone
> Of some world far from ours,
> Where music and moonlight and feeling
> Are one.
>
> ('To Jane: The Keen Stars Were Twinkling' 21-24. *Works* 673.)

At Oberland, similarly, the shape of the tones of the Chopin ballade 'gleaming into sight' (*O*, 36) sets her emotions free and fills her with a happiness that is similar to the immense joy felt at the concert she attends with Shatov, where a little phrase 'spreading coolness within her' catches her on the way 'towards the changeless central zone of her being' (*CH*, 299): it was 'so clear that it seemed *as though*, if she should turn her eyes, *she would see* it left suspended in the air in front of the orchestra, a small festoon of *sound made visible*' (*CH*, 298; emphasis added).[24]

With regard to music, there is a case of unexpected sensory perception that shows yet another aspect of the use of synaesthesia in *Pilgrimage*. Entering Harriett's drawing-room for the first time, Miriam is 'caught' in mostly visual impressions of the room. The black grand piano impresses her neither by its shape or shiny surface nor, what would be the most obvious reason, by its acoustic quality, but the special smell catches her attention:

> She stood breathing in curious odours; faint odours of new wood and fresh upholstery, and the strange strong subdued emanation coming from the black grand piano, a mingling of the smell of aromatic wood with the hard raw bitter tang of metal and the muffled woolly pungency of new felting (*HC*, 448).

Dorothy Richardson uses adjectives relating to tactile, gustatory and even aural sense impressions to verbally grasp and convey the olfactory perception of these 'strange strong crude odours' (*HC*, 449). In the text, there is a fluid transition from psychological synaesthesia, where the cross-modal correspondence is actually perceived by Miriam's creative *mind* as subjective reality, to a more abstract form of synaesthesia, where, on the level of language, a synaesthetic image is used as a means to render a concrete sensory impression by way of metaphorical indirection. Thus, depending on our trust in Miriam's synaesthetic capacities, we can read the passage as a description of her 'real' mental response to the olfactory stimulus, expressing the subjective sensory reality of her consciousness, as an example of intensely felt *psychological* synaesthesia, or we can read the same passage from an 'objective' point of view as an impossible forging of a relationship between features of experience that properly belong to different senses. In what Bachelard calls a 'réalité d'expression' (163), the metaphor aims at expressing the strong - purely olfactory - sensory impression by means of its

---

[24] cf. Chapter 3.1.

synaesthetic equivalents. This '*literary* synaesthesia' (Marks 240) is a means to express nuances of meaning that cannot be fully grasped by the common vocabulary of homomodal experience. By forming such analogical alliances between the senses Dorothy Richardson expands the horizon of meaning and thus verbally reinforces the significance of Miriam's sensory perception. To describe Vereker's voice as 'elegant' (*O*, 79), as 'gently vibrant and sunny' (*O*, 94), is to describe features of auditory experience through the visual mode as well as through the auditory mode itself, hence to rely on fundamental interrelations among the different senses. What - rationally - appears as a violation of common sense, an improper combination of images, is a conscious attempt to explore the 'semantic' power of intersensory connections. A well-applied use of such catachrestic images and similes could add interest to the text, first of all on a linguistic level. In the unusual combinations, the richness of language can further the plurisignificance of the text, alluding to latent meanings and possibly enhancing its literary potential.

On a conceptual level, Dorothy Richardson gives voice to her understanding of perceptual similarities as being based on a common *affective* dimension. In her frequent use of synaesthetic metaphor describing people's voices and eyes, the catachrestic combinations are easily acceptable because of the obvious common connotative quality of the disparate elements. The synaesthetic image with its affective implications consistently expresses Miriam's emotional response to her auditory or visual impression. The rendering of the expressive quality of people's voices or glances is one of the most important means of characterization in *Pilgrimage*, referring as much to the speaker's state of interior excitation as to Miriam's responsive mood. Thus, all the 'colourless' voices heard throughout the novel-sequence imply indifference or boredom both from the speaker's and listener's side;[25] similarly, the 'warm' or 'cold' glances that meet Miriam's eye obviously allude to the relationship between Miriam and her visual partners.[26] While Miriam is most likely to register voices in terms of vision,[27] there are also examples of thermal, gustatory and tactile metaphors, which show Dorothy Richardson's awareness of such intersensory connections.[28]

---

[25] e.g. the 'colourless' voice of the boring American at Oberland (*O*, 69); Mrs Lintoff's 'colourless' voice implying the negative sides of a Jewish life (*RL*, 300); Sissie Bailey's 'shapeless colourless voice' expressing her immaturity as a pupil (*IN*, 340); the 'abrupt, colourless tone' of the idiot's voice hinting at his limited intelligence (*DH*, 453).

[26] e.g. Pastor Lahmann's 'brown warm eyes' implying trust and affection (*PR*, 106); or Sissie Bailey's 'cold haughty eyes' (*CH*, 277) expressing all the disdain against Amabel's extravagance that Miriam feels to exist in Sissie.

[27] e.g. *DLH*, 158: Hypo's voice 'like the blue within the misty grey'; *RL*, 361: Hypo's 'bright' voice; *CH*, 272: Cholmley's voice 'with the glow of a kindly smile in it.'

[28] e.g. thermal: *PR*, 150 / 163: Bertha's voice is 'cold' , 'clean and cool'; *BW*, 252 / 291 Grace Broom's 'hot' voice; *DL*, 22: Shatov's 'warm, deep voice'; gustatory: *TR*, 473:

Despite the frequency of such synaesthetic metaphors, Dorothy Richardson's metaphoric language lacks the freshness and poetic power of a James Joyce or a Virginia Woolf. Almost all her synaesthetic images are 'intrinsic' (Marks 233), expressing relationships that are known, obvious and conventionalized. Her favoured use of adjectives such as 'soft', 'warm', 'bright', which *per se* have cross-modal qualities,[29] does not catch the reader's attention to make him or her aware of any hidden combination that would add to the meaning of the context. Though the mere accumulation of faintly synaesthetic adjectives to describe people, objects and places - one of Dorothy Richardson's most salient stylistic features - may strike the reader as appropriate for a reinforcement of the obvious meaning, her repeated use of such basic adjectives in innumerable combinations does not necessarily have a stimulating effect on the reader's associative mind. Her intrinsic synaesthesia hardly ever shows the fascinating scintillation of paradoxical new images that would allude to some potential hidden meanings. There are just a few instances when Dorothy Richardson tentatively leaves the well-known field of obvious synaesthetic associations: when Miriam perceives the 'harsh and bitter' light of a London street (*CH*, 325) or listens to the huge German at Bonnycliff at the piano, whose playing was 'colourless. Vague and woolly' (*RL*, 381), the combinations in this slightly more 'extrinsic' synaesthetic imagery (Marks 233) are not that salient: they offer unwonted aspects of meaning and therefore rouse the reader's interest.

The analysis of the use of literary synaesthesia in *Pilgrimage* underlines the wide scope of verbal expression, but it also reveals the limited experimental applications of catachrestic metaphors as verbal tools to make the text more thought-provoking, to make it live in multifarious vividness. However, when we appreciate the synaesthetic imagery as stimulating or as a unifying stylistic thread in the text, we will understand its significance for those moments when, in Keats's words, Miriam's

> eyes
> And ears act with that unison of sense
> Which marries sweet sound with the grace of form.
>
> ('Hyperion. AVision [First Version]' *Poetical Works* 250)

In these passages, then, the text oscillates, fascinates, breathing Miriam's whole being, 'full at once with the sound and colour of her life' (*TR*, 446).

Dora Taylor's 'sweet mezzo'; tactile: *PR*, 49 / 59 / 84: Fräulein's 'caustic voice'; *BW*, 230: Trixie Sanderson's 'velvety tone'; *HC*, 371 / 372 / 375: Mrs Staple-Craven's 'thick smooth' voice; *DL*, 90: Gerald's 'smooth polished gentle' voice.

[29] cf. *OED XV*, 927 'soft': 'producing agreeable or pleasant sensations;' used to describe touch, sound, light, colours, air etc.

Conclusion

> Every moment some form grows perfect in hand or face; some tone on the hills or the sea is choicer than the rest; some mood of passion or insight or intellectual excitement is irresistibly real and attractive to us, - for that moment only. Not the fruit of experience, but experience itself, is the end.
>
> (Walter Pater, 'Conclusion' to *Studies in the History of the Renaissance* 188)

> Life what are you - what is life? - . . . perfect reality. (*HC*, 414)

This exploration of the multi-layered aspects of sensory perception in *Pilgrimage* brings under scrutiny the concepts of mind and body, being and becoming, stasis and flux, experience and knowledge, language and silence, as often contrapuntal, always interdependent presences in both Miriam Henderson's life and Dorothy Richardson's narration. Sensory perception - particularly the visual and auditory stimuli that call forth a response in Miriam's consciousness - is a vital basis for all the concepts of mind Dorothy Richardson expatiates upon in her long novel-sequence. Her depiction of one woman's way through life owes much of its attractiveness to the meticulous rendering of Miriam's physical perceptions in carefully selected scenes as they essentially contribute to the central concept of *Pilgrimage*: the representation of Miriam's perception of and reflection on what, for her as an individual, makes up reality.

When Miriam as an adolescent sees life as 'either playing a part all the time in order to be amongst people in the warm, or standing alone with the strange true real feeling -alone with a sort of edge of reality on everything' (*BW*, 320), she perceives it as a strict bifurcation of opposites - society against solitude, warmth against cold, fake against true. It is part of her development to change her attitude towards reality from the separating 'either - or' to an integrative 'as well as;' to find that unity within herself that allows her to see life as a mixture of the two poles, reality as an integrated and accepted, vital part of her self and herself perceiving, reflecting and remembering as an equally vital part of reality.

In our discussion of *Pilgrimage* we have traced four major themes - the journey and the garden, music and silence - as especially attractive representatives of Miriam's extraordinary perceptive gifts and as highly appealing narrative settings for Dorothy Richardson's discussion of essential questions of life. In the preceding chapters we have found numerous instances of Miriam's sense of the splendour of life, of moments when she, in

Pater's words, is 'at the focus where the greatest number of vital forces unite in their purest energy,' where she feels 'that strange perpetual weaving and unweaving of ourselves' (189), being in becoming, becoming in being, as her identity, her self. The paramount importance of sensory impressions in her conception of reality has become obvious as she, throughout *Pilgrimage*, shows an incessant interest in the details of physical life, as she wants to 'be for ever curiously testing new opinions and courting new impressions' (Pater 189).[1] Given her environment as a vital source of stimulation, Miriam, remembering her ecstatic contemplation of a scene at the sea, realizes that

> the registration of impressions was a thing she must either do or lose hold of something essential. [...] It was an experience, perhaps the most important thing in life - far in away from any 'glad mask', a thing belonging to that strange inner life and independent of everybody (*HC*, 431).

Miriam's keen sensory observation of the outside world thus makes her aware of and enriches her most private 'strange true real' inside world of her individual self.

Pilgrimage is in fact a continuous representation of the interwoven aspects of the inside and the outside. Miriam makes a pilgrimage all the way to the centre of her self to meet reality at its fullest and fares out into the utmost regions of sensory awareness in order to find the inmost regions of her soul. It has been a main concern of our discussion to analyze and evaluate Dorothy Richardson's enormous - from a literary point of view not always successful - enterprise of selecting and tracing the patterns of Miriam's mind in this dual process of integrating the objective data of her surroundings into the subjective realm of contemplation and reflection, Miriam's mental condition influencing her receptive faculty and vice versa. We as readers of *Pilgrimage* are interested both in Miriam the perceiver and her subjective behaviour as well as in the object that has attracted her attention, thus in the continuous interplay between subject and object, self

---

[1] Pater's *Renaissance Studies* are alluded to in *Oberland*, when Vereker speaks of the book in a tone suggesting 'warmth [...], lively emphasis [...], his social utmost, for gravity and for joy' (*O*, 53). Dorothy Richardson in fact cherished Pater's *Renaissance Studies*, as can be seen from some comments in her letters: e.g. *WM* 361, letter to John Cowper Powys (15.2.1939): 'This first reading [of *The Pleasures of Literature*], because your writing about Literature is itself such glorious literature, gives me back an experience felt only once, on a first reading of Pater's Renaissance Studies: a breathless response of the whole being to the rhythm, the cadences the - what one must I suppose call the *style* of the material, not only for its own sake, art for arts sake [*sic*], because there's no such thing possible.'

See also *WM* 373, letter to John Cowper Powys (16.3.1939): 'Pater. I, too, love the Imaginary Portraits, especially Denis l'Auxerrois, but for me the Renaissance Studies stand supreme, the quintessence of P. [...].'

and other. Such an intensive investigation of one woman's interrelation with her environment necessarily includes superficial, trivial, dull phases too. When, for instance, the description of a day in the dentist's room gives Miriam's admittedly uninteresting impressions and reflections in meticulous detail, it is part of Dorothy Richardson's realism to convey this sense of dullness of *ten* (!) years of Miriam's working life. Selecting from the multitude of Miriam's sensory impressions, we have chosen for our discussion those that are important *and* interesting as adequate outward correlatives to the inner capacity and spiritual growth of Miriam's consciousness. It is in the continuous interplay of perception and reflection that her quest for selfhood and reality takes place, or in Miriam's own words, 'both ways of approach, the inner and the outer, should exist together in the ideal human being' (*DLH*, 182).

As we have seen in the previous chapters, Miriam's 'intoxication with life' (*DL*, 129) is particularly strong whenever she indulges in a feast of impressions, be it on her journeys, in sunny gardens, in walks through the city, or while listening to music. In the intricate descriptions, in her approach to reality through detail, Dorothy Richardson's own enthusiasm for the wealth of life is apparent. It is here, in the rendering of the immediacy of Miriam's detailed perception, that the text leaves its strongest impact on the reader, for it is, after all, the small things of life that affect us most. Yet this 'celebration of the rich profusion of life' (Thomson, 5), this love for the sensory detail and the subsequent, often unfiltered rendering of Miriam's spontaneous reactions do not make up the whole of *Pilgrimage*. In her attempt 'to produce a feminine equivalent of the current masculine realism' ('Foreword', 9) Dorothy Richardson wanted to depict 'contemplated reality' (10) too, shifting the focus from the outward, objective world of facts to the inward, reflective, subjective world of the individual. By showing the processing of the incessant flood of exterior stimuli in Miriam's active mind, encompassing everything available to an individual's mind from pure sensation to intellectual abstraction, Dorothy Richardson's text presents a sense of reality that clearly embraces more than the 'current masculine realism' of Wells and others. By highlighting the 'secret sacred places' (*IN*, 399) of Miriam's consciousness she gives the reader access to the rich, invisible realm of Miriam's interiority that strives to unify the hugely diverging surface realities in a coherent underlying sense of wholeness.

The first chapter of this analysis - 'The Journey' - has been devoted to the scrutiny of how the description of the outer makes possible the revelation of the inner, felt life (cf. Blake 93). Miriam's role as a restless *viatrix*, observing the moving, changing world around her with a keen eye for both her natural and social surroundings, suggests her unending spiritual quest, her equally open-eyed search for the ultimate direction of the way of her soul. All her 'wanderings' (*TU*, 11), extravert and progressive though they may be, are eventually nothing but voyages '*autour de ma chambre*, meaning *de tout ce que je suis*' (*DLH*, 167; emphasis original), referring to her own self, both developing and stable. Her awareness of outside reality by means of sensory perception thus enhances her awareness of her own self. Dorothy Richardson is at her strongest whenever she catches the moments of intensest communion between Miriam and her environment: the world of her senses and the world of her soul interact, sensation and emotion meet.[2] In the contemplation of outside reality Miriam feels the 'sense of your own unchanging reality come [...] with an amazement and a sweetness' that seizes her whole self (*RL*, 283).

When Miriam realizes something of the underlying unity and continuity, however frail, that makes up the core of her being, she gives voice to Dorothy Richardson's own relentless search for unity behind her fragmentary experience of the world. Perhaps the most adequate outer means to represent Miriam's inner, emotional and spiritual, life is Dorothy Richardson's concept of the garden as analyzed in chapter 2. The garden, both as a real visual presence and as a visionary product of imagination, plays a vital role in the narrative of *Pilgrimage* as it is a highly sensual, stimulating and symbolic place of beauty and happiness. These twin notions, which Miriam consistently associates with her garden contemplations, express the deep bonds between visual perception and emotion most convincingly. Thus we have interpreted her garden views as direct mirrors of her emotional state that comment on her situation especially with regard to interpersonal relationships.

Apart from its visual (over-)presence, the garden as 'collector of memories' (*CH*, 299) represents another dimension of reality: the power of memory, as we have seen, is one of Dorothy Richardson's main concerns in her writings. The persistent presence of the bee-memory (chapter 2.4.1) suggests the availability of the past as a forming constituent of present experience. In the juxtaposition of past and present impressions as equally real and living, Dorothy Richardson aims at a transcendence of time, a synchronicity that for Miriam entails not only an enriched experience of the immediate Now, but also an increased awareness of her own stable self. This intriguing ability to perceive her self in the present and past simultaneously forms the basis of Dorothy Richardson's writing, particularly of her concept of *Pilgrimage*.

For all the sensory power of her impressions the garden assumes yet another function in the reflective working of Miriam's mind. As we have

---

[2] e.g. *DL*, 17: The starlit sky Miriam observes from her window at Tansley Street was 'reaching down into the life that rose faintly in her to meet it, the strange mysterious life, far away below all interference, and always the same.'

argued in chapter 2.4, it appears as a transfigured place of perfection, Miriam's personal paradise that shows obvious allusions to both religious and literary ideas of paradise. It is, I contend, one of the most powerful driving forces of Miriam's pilgrimage to keep up the memory of the lost magic childhood garden, an Edenic place of innocence and security, and at the same time to look out for, to dream of, an equally perfect place of unity and shelter, a lasting home, paradise regained.

We have analyzed this working of memory with regard to visual as well as to auditory processes, as exemplified in the role of music (chapter 3.2.1). The depth and quality of her most intense aural perceptions becomes most obvious in the scenes where music triggers pictures and sounds of the past. The immediacy of the euphonic sounds *per se* in their absorbing beauty enhance Miriam's experience of happiness and shield her - at least temporarily - both from the urban noises and their implications and from the semi-conscious cries of desolation surging up sporadically from unknown depths within herself.

Not many pieces of music Miriam listens to or plays herself are identifiable. Yet, whenever they are, as we have pointed out in the cases of Beethoven, Chopin and Wagner, a special significance can be attributed to them on a textual level. The presence of these explicitly given pieces of music plays an essential part in the structural organization of *Pilgrimage* as a literary work of art. We have argued that in a close reading the apparent shapelessness of the text reveals forms and structural elements that are obviously based on musical concepts (chapter 3.2). Another musical facet that has hardly attracted the critics' attention are the many vocal pieces of music interspersed in *Pilgrimage*. As we have noted in our analysis of the allusive power the myth of the Flying Dutchman has throughout the text (chapter 3.4), their (partly) hidden texts add thematic coherence and support the explicitly described contextual situations, especially with regard to Miriam's relationships.

As a contrast to the extravert beautiful sounds of music, silence, which is a privation of sensuous sounds, appeals by that very fact to an inner activity. Chapter 4 has dealt with Miriam's deep awareness of the absence of sound as an inspiring source for herself and her most intimate relationships. It is in the introvert solitude of reflexion that Miriam recognizes 'the inmost reality' (*IN*, 352); Miriam's mystical awareness is comparable to T. S. Eliot's, when she in the paradoxical turning away from the 'world' and its sounds towards silence 'realizes the whole world' (*RL*, 283). In the silent, mystical communion with her surroundings, especially with nature, 'l'antithèse du *dehors* et du *dedans* est abolie' (Barthes, 1970:220). For encompassing moments of fulfilment she, like Virginia Woolf, discovers: 'That is the whole' ('Sketch of the Past' 71). In her Romantic search for an underlying unity of reality these moments of silent perfection open up another dimension:[3] It has been a major concern of our discussion to throw a clearer light on Miriam's mystical inclination, with a special emphasis on her appreciation of the 'Quakers' approach to reality' (*DH*, 498) in the spirit of silence. Together with Miriam's philosophical 'fathers' Emerson - who 'saw *everything*. The outside as well as the inside things' (*DH*, 417) - and Maeterlinck - who 'had explained in words what life was like inside' (*DL*, 68) - the Quakers' ideas offer her a way out of the binary distinctions of rational analysis towards a non-conceptual, mystical understanding of 'the originality and reality of life *at all levels*' (*QPP*, 23; emphasis added).[4] This, of course, includes the whole field of personal relationships. Miriam's pilgrimage is in some way a series of escapes from and towards relationships, following a pattern of projective expectations and disappointed disillusionment. In her pursuit of reality she very often tries to solve the clash between her own individual needs and wishes and those of her partner(s) by means of argumentative disputes. Deep and lasting friendships, however, as we have seen in the cases of Amabel and, particularly, Jean, are to be based on a form of intersubjective transcendence, in which the boundary between self and other would eventually be blurred. Moments of mystical communion with a partner, however, are only possible when Miriam can relate to her partner from the ground of pre-verbal, intuitive experience (cf. Henke 57). Particularly in her depiction of female friendships Dorothy Richardson articulates a conception of partnership that *lives* from their mutual silences: '*C'est dans le silence que les âmes se révèlent*' (*TR*, 430; emphasis original).

Furthermore, the presence of silence in Dorothy Richardson's narration is supported by her 'writing' of silence: creating a lexicon of silence, a punctuation of the unsaid, metaphors of soundlessness, she marks the presence of silence as an essential part of the whole, of Miriam's way of being. Contrary to traditional - male (?) - worldviews, silence, which to be fully appreciated needs the highest sensory concentration, to her means fullness and life rather than absence and negation.

This fullness of life is also present in the simultaneous perception of different senses. Thus, the last chapter of this study has been devoted to the analysis of Miriam's cooperating senses. In polysensory perception and synaesthesia eyes and ears provide a wealth of impressions that coalesce into

[3] cf. Heath 128: There is always 'the experience, falling into silence, of something different, persistent and elsewhere, another reality.' And Bucher (147) writes: These moments 'culminate in an ecstasy that points to the existence of a different kind of reality, a world behind the surface.'

[4] Miriam finds this distrust of intellectual reflection also in Maeterlinck's *Trésor*: 'Ce que pense la pensée n'a aucune importance à côté de la vérité que nous sommes et qui s'affirme en silence' (126).

a whole, giving her the 'secret clue' to the experience of 'wonderful life, from moment to moment, pure *life*' (*IN*, 405; emphasis original). Though the textual use of synaesthetic images in *Pilgrimage* lacks the creativity of other contemporary works of fiction, the interplay of visual and auditory stimuli forms an important integrative aspect of Miriam's overall perception of the outside world.

Throughout our discussion of *Pilgrimage* we have noted that the text proves receptive to many different sorts of literary influences. Intertextual allusions appear at all stages of the text, revealing more or less explicitly some of the inspiring sources for Dorothy Richardson's writing. It has become one of the most satisfying points of investigation to follow some of these literary traces in so far as they deepen and widen the understanding of Miriam's perception of reality. Allusiveness then results in centripetal connotation and interwoven meanings. Often the purpose of a seemingly irrelevant detail is only recognizable once the context of its literary source is identified. In a surface reading, this device, however uninspired it sometimes appears in the mere rendering of titles of books that have caught Miriam's attention, shows the wide scope of both Miriam's and Dorothy Richardson's literary interest; a thorough investigation of Dorothy Richardson's *tour d'horizon* of Western literature might yield an interesting canon of female reading at the turn of the century. Focusing on a few important writers in more detail, however, we have seen that the host of allusions and quotations emphasize major issues both for the immediate context of the scene and for the overall conception of the text. While the concept of the journey is underlined by the explicit presence of the Bible, of such 'classic' writers as Dante or Bunyan, her idea of the garden as paradise lives from allusions to Genesis, Milton and Dante. In the field of music, some of Wagner's and Schumann's vocal works - among others - appear as intertextual references, whereas Miriam's mystical experiences are supported by her reading of Emerson and Maeterlinck, and by odd allusions to Fox, Boehme or Swedenborg.

Furthermore, we have traced Miriam's strong affinity to the Romantic poets; though their influence on her point of view rather marks a silence in the pages of *Pilgrimage*, Miriam's close relationship with nature, her intense visual perception of natural surroundings, her belief in the power of childhood and memory, and her subjective experiences as an individual self suggest particularly strong parallels to Wordsworth. She in fact is, in Powys's words, '"after" precisely the same thing [...] what Wordsworth himself, indeed, calls quite simply, "the Pleasure which there is in Life itself"' (20). Seeing Dorothy Richardson as a female, urbanized, modern, 'profane' successor to Wordsworth, her literary achievement might be read - rather than being called 'stream-of-consciousness,' which she detested - as a unique voice of Romantic Realism, unifying central issues of both Romanticism and Realism in her writing.

Though a far cry from Joyce's ingenious playfulness or Eliot's subtle adaptations, the manifold intertextual occurrences within Dorothy Richardson's work show that she aims at more than a rendering of sensory impressions. What may become an oppressive burden of her literary past is presented as a multi-coloured presence, a 'bright moving patchwork' (*RL*, 323) of literary reminiscences that support our reading of Miriam's perception of reality in a stimulating way. In the fabric of *Pilgrimage* Miriam's physical, personal *and* cultural background are foregrounded as influential factors in the shaping of her subjective consciousness, each of the allusions forming a more or less strong, more or less shining thread in 'the magic of the woven text' (*RL*, 251).

Tracing parallels to some contemporary writers, we have noted that Dorothy Richardson's text, bound up in the serious business of conveying the unity and continuity of Miriam's consciousness (cf. *WM*, 49), largely lacks the ironic detachment, the structural elegance, the profound simplicity, the poetic brilliance, we may find in Joyce, Mansfield, Sinclair or Woolf. Yet, in the best parts of her writing Dorothy Richardson aspires to the condition Woolf drew for the ideal 'poetic dramatist of the future:'

> One can imagine that he will have extended the scope of his interest so as to dramatize some of those influences which play so large a part in life, yet have so far escaped the novelist - the power of music, the stimulus of sight, the effect on us of the shape of trees or the play of colour, the emotions bred in us by crowds, the obscure terrors and hatreds which come so irrationally in certain places or from certain people, the delight of movement, the intoxication of wine. Every moment is the centre and meeting-place of an extraordinary number of perceptions which have not yet been expressed. Life is always and inevitably much richer than we who try to express it ('The Narrow Bridge of Art,' *Granite and Rainbow* 23).

Looking at life as a kaleidoscope of impressions, as iridescent, subjective 'different sets of realities' (*CH*, 309) that in turns impinge on Miriam's consciousness, Dorothy Richardson consistently presents what happens in Miriam's individual mind. When she fully grasps her immediate, intense perception in a perfect moment, when she gives this moment whole, whatever it includes, her text conveys fascinating insights of sensory perception, reflection, and emotion; she, in May Sinclair's words, 'seizes reality alive' (*The Egoist*, 59). It is in these moments, eventually, that we as readers fully understand Miriam's words: 'Yes, this is my reality' (*CH*, 279).

Bibliography

1. Primary Sources

1.1 Texts by Dorothy Richardson

Pilgrimage. 4 vols. 1915-1938. London: Virago, 1979.

Gleanings from the Works of George Fox. London: Headley Brothers, 1915.

Journey to Paradise. London: Virago, 1989.

The Quakers Past and Present. London: Constable, 1914.

Windows on Modernism. Selected Letters of Dorothy Richardson. Ed. Gloria G. Fromm. Athens (Georgia) and London: The University of Georgia Press, 1995.

'Adventure for Readers.' *Life and Letters Today*, July 1939 (Vol 22, No 23), 45-52.

'Comments by a Layman.' *Dental Record* XXXVI (10), 2 Oct 1916, 541.

'Comments by a Layman.' *Dental Record* XXXVIII (8), 1 August 1918, 350-352.

'Continuous Performance 12: The Cinema in Arcady.' *Close Up* 3 (July 1928), 52-57.

'The Role of the Background.' *Sphere*, Nov 1924 (22), 226.

'Women and the Future.' *Vanity Fair* 22 (1924), 39f., reprinted in: *The Gender of Modernism*. Ed. Bonnie Kime Scott. Bloomington: Indiana University Press, 1990, 413.

1.2 Further Writers

Alighieri, Dante. *The Divine Comedy*. Transl. Charles S. Singleton. Princeton: Princeton University Press, 1973.

Augustine. *The City of God*. 2 vols. Transl. John Healey. London: J.M. Dent, 1947.

Augustine. *Confessions*. Transl. R. S. Pine-Coffin. Harmondsworth: Penguin, 1961.

Baudelaire, Charles. 'Correspondances.' *Oeuvres Complètes,* Vol. 1. Paris: Gallimard, 1975, 11.

Bergson, Henri. *Oeuvres*. Paris: Presses Universitaires de France, 1970.

The Holy Bible. Revised Standard Edition. New York et al: Nelson, 1952.

Blake, William. *William Blake's Writings*. Ed. G. E. Bentley, jr. Oxford: Clarendon Press, 1978.

Brontë, Charlotte. *Jane Eyre*. 1847. London: Everyman's Library, 1991.

Brontë, Charlotte. *Villette*. 1853. London: Everyman's Library, 1992.

Browning, Elizabeth Barrett. *Aurora Leigh*. 1857. London: The Women's Press, 1978.

Bryant, William Cullen. *Poems*. Dessau: Katz Brothers, 1854.

Bunyan, John. *The Pilgrim's Progress*. 1678. Ed. N. H. Keeble. Oxford: Oxford University Press, 1984.

Butler, Samuel. *Alps and Sanctuaries of Piedmont and the Canton Ticino*. 1882. London: Jonathan Cape, 1924.

Byron, Lord. *The Complete Poetical Works, Volume IV*. Ed. Jerome J. McGann. Oxford: Clarendon Press, 1986.

Campbell, Thomas. *The Complete Poetical Works*. Ed. J. L. Robertson. London: Oxford University Press, 1987.

Chamisso, Adelbert von. 'Frauen-Liebe und Leben.' *Sämtliche Werke, Band I*. München: Winkler, 1975, 149-155.

Chopin, Kate. *The Awakening*. 1899. London: Everyman's Library, 1992.

Coleridge, Samuel Taylor. *Biographia Literaria. Or Biographical Sketches of My Literary Life and Opinions*. 1817. Ed. George Watson. London: Dent, 1975.

Darwin, Charles. *Voyage of the Beagle. Charles Darwin's* Journal of Researches. 1839. Ed. Janet Browne and Michael Neve. Harmondsworth: Penguin, 1989.

Eliot, George. *Daniel Deronda*. 1876. London etc.: Blackwood, 1901.

Eliot, George. *The Mill on the Floss*. 1860. Ed. A. S. Byatt. Harmondsworth: Penguin, 1979.

Eliot, T. S. *The Complete Poems and Plays*. London: Faber and Faber, 1969.

Emerson, Ralph Waldo. *Complete Prose Works*. London: Ward & Co., n.y.

Emerson, Ralph Waldo. *Essays and Lectures*. Ed. Joel Porte. New York: The Library of America, 1983.

Forster, E. M. *A Room with a View*. 1908. London: Arnold, 1977.

Forster, E. M. *Howards End*. 1910. London: Everyman's Library, 1991.

Forster, E. M. *Two Cheers for Democracy*. 1951. London: Arnold, 1972.

Freud, Sigmund. 'Das Unbehagen in der Kultur.' *Studienausgabe Band 9: Fragen der Gesellschaft, Ursprünge der Religion.* Frankfurt: Fischer, 1974, 191-270.

Freud, Sigmund. 'Screen Memories.' *The Standard Edition of the Complete Psychological Works of Sigmund Freud, Volume III.* London: The Hogarth Press, 1962, 299-322.

Goethe, Johann Wolfgang von. *Die Faustdichtungen.* Zürich: Artemis, 1950.

Gounod, Charles. *Faust. Opéra en Quatre Actes*. 1859. Leipzig: Peters, 1983.

Haldane, Richard Burdon. *The Pathway to Reality. Gifford Lectures.* London: 1903.

H. D. (Hilda Doolittle). *Collected Poems 1912 - 1944*. Manchester: Carcanet Press, 1984.

Herder, Johann Gottfried. 'Abhandlung über den Ursprung der Sprache.' 1772. *Werke*, Band 1. Frankfurt a. M.: Deutscher Klassiker Verlag, 1985, 695-810.

Homer. *Odyssey*. Transl. A. J. Murray. Cambridge (Mass.): Harvard University Press, 1976.

Hopkins, Gerard Manley. *The Poetical Works*. Ed. Norman H. Mackenzie. Oxford: Clarendon Press, 1990.

Hymns Ancient and Modern for Use in the Services of the Church. Complete Edition. London: William Clowes, n.y.

Ibsen, Henrik. *Brand. Peer Gynt*. 1866/67. (The Oxford Ibsen Volume III). London: Oxford University Press, 1972.

James, Alice. *The Diary of Alice James*. Ed. Leon Edel. London: Rupert Hart-Davis, 1965.

James, Henry. *The Portrait of a Lady*. 1881. London: Everyman's Library, 1991.

James, William. *Principles of Psychology*. 1890. Cambridge (Mass.): Harvard University Press, 1981.

James, William. *The Varieties of Religious Experience*. 1902. Cambridge (Mass): Harvard University Press, 1985.

Jefferies, Richard. *Amaryllis at the Fair*. 1887. Stroud: Allan Sutton, 1992.

Joyce, James. *Dubliners*. 1914. London: Everyman's Library, 1991.

Joyce, James. *A Portrait of the Artist as a Young Man*. 1916. London: Everyman's Library, 1991.

Joyce, James. *Ulysses. The Corrected Text*. Harmondsworth: Penguin, 1986.

Keats, John. *The Poetical Works of John Keats*. London: Hamlyn, 1987.

Lawrence, D. H. *Women in Love*. 1921. Harmondsworth: Penguin, 1986.

Maeterlinck, Maurice. *Le Trésor des Humbles*. 1896. Paris: Mercure de France, 1910.

Mann, Thomas. *Doktor Faustus*. 1947. Zürich: Ex Libris, 1975.

Mansfield, Katherine. *The Garden Party and Other Stories*. London: Everyman's Library, 1991.

Marvell, Andrew. *The Complete Poems*. Ed. George deF. Lord. London: Everyman's Library, 1993.

Meredith, George. *The Egoist*. 1879. New York and London: Norton, 1979.

Milton, John. 'Paradise Lost.' 1667. *The Complete English Poems*. Ed. Gordon Campbell. London: Everyman's Library, 1992.

Ouida. *A Leaf in the Storm*. Berlin: A. Asher, 1872.

The Oxford Book of English Verse 1250 - 1918 (New Edition). Ed. Arthur Quiller-Couch. Oxford: Clarendon Press, 1939.

Pater, Walter. *The Renaissance. Studies in Art and Poetry.* 1893. Ed. Donald L. Hill. Berkeley et al.: University of California Press, 1980.

Proust, Marcel. *A la Recherche du Temps Perdu.* Vol. 1. 1913. Paris: Gallimard, 1919.

Ruskin, John. *The Stones of Venice.* 1851-53. Vol. 9 of *Collected Works.* Ed. E. T. Cook and Alexander Wedderburn. London: Allen, 1903.

Schumann, Robert. *Sämtliche Lieder für eine Singstimme mit Klavierbegleitung.* Leipzig: Peters, n.y.

Shelley, Percy Bysshe. *Poetical Works.* London: Oxford University Press, 1967.

Sinclair, May. *Mary Olivier. A Life.* 1919. London: Virago, 1980.

Tennyson, Alfred Lord. *The Poems of Tennyson.* 3 vols. Ed. Christopher Ricks. Harlow (Essex): Longman, 1987.

Thomas à Kempis. *Of the Imitation of Christ.* London: Humphreys, 1897.

Thomson, James. *Poems and Some Letters.* Ed. Anne Ridler. London: Centaur Press, 1963.

Wagner, Richard. *Der Fliegende Holländer.* 1843. Zürich: Apollo, n.y.

Wells, G. P. (Ed.). *H. G. Wells in Love. Postscript to* An Experiment in Autobiography. London: Faber and Faber, 1984.

Wells, H. G. *Ann Veronica.* 1909. London: Everyman, 1993.

Wittgenstein, Ludwig. 'Tractatus Logico-Philosophicus.' *Werkausgabe.* Band 1. Frankfurt a. M.: Suhrkamp, 1989.

Woolf, Virginia. *Collected Essays.* Vol. 2. London: Hogarth Press, 1972.

Woolf, Virginia. *Collected Essays.* Vol. 4. London: Hogarth Press, 1967.

Woolf, Virginia. *Granite and Rainbow.* London: Hogarth Press, 1958.

Woolf, Virginia. *Mrs Dalloway.* 1925. London: Everyman's Library, 1993.

Woolf, Virginia. *A Room of One's Own.* 1928. London: Bloomsbury Classics, 1993.

Woolf, Virginia. *To the Lighthouse.* 1927. London: Everyman's Library, 1991.

Wordsworth, William. *Descriptive Sketches.* 1793. Ed. E. Birdsall. Ithaca and London: Cornell University Press, 1984.

Wordsworth, William. *The Poems.* Vol. One. Ed. John O. Hayden. Harmondsworth: Penguin, 1977.

Wordsworth, William. *Poetical Works*. 5 vols. Ed. E. de Selincourt. Oxford: Clarendon Press, 1949.

Wordsworth, William. *The Prelude. 1799, 1805, 1850.* Ed. Jonathan Wordsworth et al. New York and London: Norton, 1979.

Yeats, William Butler. *The Poems*. Ed. Daniel Albright. London: Everyman's Library, 1992.

2. Secondary Sources

2.1 Supporting Texts on Dorothy Richardson

Abel, Elizabeth, Marianne Hirsch and Elizabeth Langland, eds. *The Voyage In: Fictions of Female Development.* Hanover, N.H.: University of New England, 1983.

Beach, Joseph Warren. *The Twentieth-century Novel: Studies in Technique*. London: The Century Co., 1932.

Beauman, Nicola. *A Very Great Profession. The Woman's Novel 1914 - 1939.* London: Virago, 1983.

Beresford, J. D. 'Introduction' to *Pointed Roofs* (2nd Impression). London: Duckworth, 1921, v-viii.

Blake, Caesar R. *Dorothy Richardson*. Ann Arbor: University of Michigan Press, 1960.

Bluemel, Kristin. *Experimenting on the Borders of Modernism: Dorothy Richardson's* Pilgrimage. Athens (Georgia) and London: University of Georgia Press, 1997.

Brome, Vincent. 'A Last Meeting with Dorothy Richardson.' *The London Magazine*, June 1959 (Vol 6, No 6), 26-32.

Bronfen, Elisabeth. *Der literarische Raum. Eine Untersuchung am Beispiel von Dorothy M. Richardsons Romanzyklus 'Pilgrimage'*. Tübingen: Niemeyer, 1986.

Brown, Dennis. *The Modernist Self in Twentieth Century English Literature: A Study in Self-Fragmentation.* New York: St. Martin's Press, 1989.

Brown, Penny. *The Poison at the Source. The Female Novel of Self-Development in the Early Twentieth Century.* New York: St. Martin's Press, 1992.

Bryher, Winifred. 'Dawn's Left Hand.' *Close Up* 8/4 (1931), 337f.

Bucher, Urs. *Streams of Consciousness: Dorothy Richardson and James Joyce.* [Diss.] Willisau: Willisauer Bote, 1981.

Fehr, Bernhard. *Von Englands geistigen Beständen.* Frauenfeld: Huber, 1944.

Fleishman, Avrom. *Figures of Autobiography. The Language of Self-Writing in Victorian and Modern England.* Berkeley: University of California Press, 1983.

Friedman, Ellen G. '"Utterly Other Discourse:" The Anticanon of Experimental Women Writers from Dorothy Richardson to Christine Brooke-Rose.' *Modern Fiction Studies*, 1988 (34/3), 353-370.

Fromm, Gloria G. *Dorothy Richardson: A Biography.* Urbana: University of Illinois Press, 1977.

Fromm, Gloria G. 'What are Men to Dorothy Richardson?' *Women and Literature* 1982 (2), 168-188.

Gevirtz, Susan. *Narrative's Journey. The Fiction and Film Writing of Dorothy Richardson.* New York: Lang, 1996.

Glikin, Gloria. 'Dorothy Richardson: The Personal Pilgrimage.' *PMLA* 1963 (78/5), 586-600.

Gregory, Horace. *Dorothy Richardson: An Adventure in Self-Discovery.* New York: Holt, Rinehart and Winston, 1967.

Hanscombe, Gillian E. *The Art of Life: Dorothy Richardson and the Development of Feminist Consciousness.* London: Owen, 1982.

Hanscombe, Gillian E. 'Dorothy Richardson versus the Novvle.' in: *Breaking the Sequence*. Ed. Ellen G. Friedman and Miriam Fuchs. Princeton: Princeton University Press, 1989, 85-98.

Hanscombe, Gillian, and Smyers, Virginia L. *Writing for Their Lives: The Modernist Women 1910 - 1940.* London: The Women's Press, 1987.

Heath, Stephen. 'Writing for Silence: Dorothy Richardson and the Novel.' in: *Teaching the Text*. Ed. Susanne Kappeler. London: Routledge, 1983, 126-147.

Henke, Suzette A. 'Male and Female Consciousness in Dorothy Richardson's *Pilgrimage*.' *Journal of Women's Studies in Literature* 1 (1978), 51-60.

Hyde, Lawrence. 'The Work of Dorothy Richardson.' *Adelphi* 2 (1924), 512-517.

Johnson, R. *Some Contemporary Novelists*. London: L. Parsons, 1920.

Kaplan, Sidney. 'Featureless Freedom or Ironic Submission: Dorothy Richardson and May Sinclair.' *College English* 32 (1970), 914-17.

Kaplan, Sidney J. *Feminine Consciousness in the Modern British Novel*. Urbana: University of Illinois Press, 1975.

Kilian, Eveline. *Momente Innerweltlicher Transzendenz. Die Augenblickserfahrung in Dorothy Richardsons Romanzyklus* Pilgrimage *und ihr Ideengeschichtlicher Kontext*. Tübingen: Niemeyer, 1997.

Knowles, Owen. 'Funerals and Elegies: An Obscure Drama of 1924.' *Conradian* 1986, May 11 (1), 51-56.

Kumar, Shiv K. 'Dorothy Richardson and the Dilemma of "Being vs Becoming."' *Modern Language Notes* LXXIV (June 1959), 495-501.

Kunitz, Stanley J. (Ed.). *Twentieth Century Authors. A Biographical Dictionary of Modern Authors*. New York: H. W. Wilson, 1942.

Kunitz, Stanley J. (Ed). *Twentieth Century Authors. A Biographical Dictionary, First Supplement*. New York: H. W. Wilson, 1955.

Leavis, Q.D. '*Clear Horizon* by Dorothy Richardson.' *Scrutiny* 1968, 81f.

Levy, Anita. 'Gendered Labor: The Female Writer and Dorothy Richardson.' *Novel* 25/ 1 (Fall 91), 50-70.

Loeffelholtz, Mary. *Experimental Lives: Women and Literature 1900 - 1945*. New York: Twayne Publishers, 1992.

McLaurin, Allen. 'Siamese Twins: The Verbal and the Visual in Dorothy Richardson's *Pilgrimage*.' *Trivium* 1983 (May/18), 73-85.

Mansfield, Katherine. 'Dragonflies' (review of *Interim*). *Athenaeum* 9 January, 1920; reprinted in: *Gender of Modernism*. Ed. Bonnie Kime Scott. Bloomington: Indiana University Press, 1990, 310.

Mansfield, Katherine. 'Three Women Novelists' (Review of *The Tunnel*). *Athenaeum* 4 April 1919; reprinted in: *Gender of Modernism*. Ed. Bonnie Kime Scott. Bloomington: Indiana University Press, 1990, 309.

Moers, Ellen. *Literary Women*. Garden City, New York: Anchor Press, 1977.

Morgan, Louise. 'How Writers Work: Dorothy Richardson.' *Everyman* (22 Oct 1931), 400.

Neubert, Albrecht. *Die Stilformen der Erlebten Rede im Neueren Englischen Roman*. Halle: Niemeyer, 1957.

Powys, John Cowper. *Dorothy M. Richardson*. London: Joiner and Steele, 1931.

Pykett, Lyn. *Engendering Fictions. The English Novel in the Early Twentieth Century*. London: Arnold, 1995.

Radford, Jean. 'Coming to Terms. Dorothy Richardson, Modernism and Women.' *News from Nowhere* 1989 (7), 26-36.

Radford, Jean. *Dorothy Richardson*. Hemel Hempstead: Harvester Wheatsheaf, 1991.

Rose, Shirley. 'Dorothy Richardson's Focus on Time.' *English Literature in Transition* 17 (1974), 163-172.

Rose, Shirley. 'Dorothy Richardson's Theory of Literature: The Writer as Pilgrim.' *Criticism* 12 (1970), 20-37.

Rose, Shirley. 'The Unmoving Center: Consciousness in Dorothy Richardson's *Pilgrimage*.' *Contemporary Literature* 10 (1969), 366-382.

Rosenberg, John. *Dorothy Richardson: The Genius They Forgot*. London: Duckworth, 1973.

Schlanger, Judith. 'Dorothy Richardson Ecrivain Célèbre'. *Po&Sie* 1986, 37/2, 81-87.

Scott, Bonnie Kime (Ed.). *The Gender of Modernism*. Bloomington: Indiana University Press, 1990.

Showalter, Elaine. *A Literature of their Own: British Women Novelists from Brontë to Lessing*. London: Virago, 1978.

Sinclair, May. 'The Novels of Dorothy Richardson.' *The Egoist*, April 1918, 57-59.

Smyers, Virginia L. 'Dorothy Miller Richardson. Some Uncollected Authors.' *Book Collector* 27 (1978), 60-70.

Staley, Thomas F. *Dorothy Richardson.* Boston: Twayne Publishers, 1976.

Thomson, George H. *A Reader's Guide to Dorothy Richardson's* Pilgrimage. Greensboro: ELT Press, 1996.

Thorn, Arline R. 'Feminine Time in Dorothy Richardson's *Pilgrimage.*' *International Journal of Women's Studies*, Vol. 1, Nr 2 (March / April 1978), 211-219.

Trickett, Rachel. 'The Living Dead - V: Dorothy Richardson.' *The London Magazine* June 1959 (Vol 6, No 6), 20-25.

Watts, Carol. *Dorothy Richardson.* Plymouth: Northcote House, 1995.

Watts, Carol. 'Releasing Possibility into Form: Cultural Choice and the Woman Writer.' In: *New Feminist Discourses. Critical Essays on Theories and Texts.* Ed. Isabel Armstrong. London: Routledge, 1992, 83-102.

Woolf, Virginia. 'Dorothy Richardson' (Review of *The Tunnel*). *Times Literary Supplement*, 13. 2. 1919. Reprinted in: *The Feminist Critique of Language.* Ed. Deborah Cameron. London: Routledge, 1990, 70-72.

Würzbach, Natascha. 'Subjective Presentation of Characters from Miriam's Experience.' In: *Modes of Narrative: Approaches to American, Canadian and British Fiction.* Würzburg: Könighausen und Neumann, 1990, 278-302.

2.2 Further References

Alcorn, John. *The Nature Novel from Hardy to Lawrence.* New York: Columbia University Press, 1977.

Bachelard, Gaston. *La Poétique de l'Espace.* Paris: Presses Universitaires de France, 1957.

Barthes, Roland. 'Structural Analysis of Narratives.' *Image, Music, Text. Essays Selected and Translated by Stephen Heath.* London: Fontana, 1977.

Barthes, Roland. *S/Z.* Paris: Editions du Seuil, 1970.

Bergsten, Staffan. *Time and Eternity. A Study in the Structure and Symbolism of T. S. Eliot's Four Quartets.* New York: Humanities Press, 1973.

Bigand, Emanuel. 'Contributions of Music to Research in the Field of Auditory Cognition.' *Thinking in Sound. The Cognitive Psychology of Human Audition*. Ed. Stephen McAdams and Emanuel Bigand. Oxford: Clarendon Press, 1993, 231-277.

Bloom, Harold (Ed.). *Edwardian and Georgian Fiction*. New York: Chelsea House Publishers, 1990.

Blothner, Dirk. *Der glückliche Augenblick*. Bonn: Bouvier, 1993.

Boies, Jack J. *The Lost Domain. Avatars of the Earthly Paradise in Western Literature*. Lanham: University Press of America, 1983.

Book of Christian Discipline of the Religious Society of Friends in Great Britain. Ed. Unknown. London: 1883.

Brelèt, Gisèle. 'Music and Silence,' in: *Reflections on Art*. Ed. Susanne K. Langer. New York: Oxford University Press, 1961, 103-121.

Bronowski, Jacob. *The Visionary Eye. Essays in the Arts, Literature and Science*. Cambridge (Mass): The MIT Press, 1981.

Brooks, Peter. *Reading for the Plot*. Oxford: Clarendon Press, 1984.

Brown, Calvin S. *Music and Literature. A Comparison of the Arts*. Athens (Georgia): University of Georgia Press, 1948.

Brown, E. K. *Rhythm in the Novel*. Toronto: University of Toronto Press, 1950.

Brown, Marshall. 'Origins of Modernism: Musical Structures and Narrative Forms.' in: *Music and Text. Critical Inquiries*. Ed. Steven Paul Scher. Cambridge: Cambridge University Press, 1992, 80-89.

Brunel, Pierre (Ed.). *Companion to Literary Myths, Heroes and Archetypes*. London: Routledge, 1992.

Bruss, Elizabeth W. *Autobiographical Acts. The Changing Situation of a Literary Genre*. Baltimore: Johns Hopkins University Press, 1976.

Buckley, J. H. *The Turning Key: Autobiography and the Subjective Impulse Since 1800*. Cambridge (Mass): Harvard University Press, 1984.

Bujic, Bojan. *Music in European Thought 1851 - 1912*. Cambridge: Cambridge University Press, 1988.

Canisius, Claus. *Beethoven. 'Sehnsucht und Unruhe in der Musik.' Aspekte zu Leben und Werk*. München: Piper, 1992.

Christ, Carol P. *Diving Deep and Surfacing: Women Writers on Spiritual Quest*. Boston: Beacon Press, 1984.

Copland, Aaron. *Music and Imagination*. Cambridge (Mass.): Harvard University Press, 1952.

Cosslett, Tess. *Woman to Woman: Female Friendship in Victorian Fiction*. Brighton: Harvester Press, 1988.

Culler, Jonathan. *Structural Poetics. Structuralism, Linguistics and the Study of Literature*. London: Routledge and Kegan Paul, 1975.

Cytowyc, Richard E. *Synesthesia. A Union of the Senses*. New York: Springer, 1989.

Donington, Robert. *Opera and Its Symbols. The Unity of Words, Music, and Staging*. New Haven and London: Yale University Press, 1990.

Eliade, Mircea (Ed.). *Encyclopedia of Religion*. New York: Macmillan, 1987.

Eliot, T. S. 'Introduction.' In: *Revelation*. Ed. J. Baillie and H. Martin. New York: Macmillan, 1937, 1-39.

Elsbree, Langdon. *Ritual Passages and Narrative Structures*. New York: Lang, 1991.

Ford, Ford Madox. *The March of Literature from Confucius to Modern Times*. 1939. London: Allen and Unwyn, 1947.

Forster, E. M. *Aspects of the Novel*. 1927. Harmondsworth: Penguin, 1976.

Friedman, Alan. *The Turn of the Novel: The Transition to Modern Fiction*. New York: Oxford University Press, 1966.

Genette, Gérard. 'Discours du Récit.' *Figures III*. Paris: Editions du Seuil, 1972, 65-282.

Gibson, James J. *The Senses Considered as Perceptual Systems*. Boston: Houghton Mifflin, 1966.

Guetti, James. *Word-Music. The Aesthetic Aspect of Narrative Fiction*. New Brunswick (NJ): Rutgers University Press, 1980.

Gurney, Edmund. *The Power of Sound*. London: 1880.

Harding, James. *Gounod*. London: Allen and Unwin, 1973.

Heil, John. *Perception and Cognition*. Berkeley et al: University of California Press, 1983.

Hensel, Gerhard. 'Das Optische bei Wordsworth.' *Archiv für die Gesamte Psychologie* 76 (1930), 83-192.

Hoffmann, Rosemarie. *Zur Psychologie des Glücksgefühls. Eine empirische Untersuchung*. München, 1981.

Humphrey, Robert. *Stream of Consciousness in the Modern Novel.* London: University of California Press, 1972.

Ihde, Don. *Listening and Voice. A Phenomenology of Sound.* Athens (Ohio): Ohio University Press, 1976.

Jelinek, Estelle. *Women's Autobiography. Essays in Criticism*. Bloomington: Indiana University Press, 1980.

Kalamaras, George. *Reclaiming the Tacit Dimension. Symbolic Form in the Rhetoric of Silence*. New York: State University of New York Press, 1994.

Knapp, Bettina. *Music, Archetype and the Writer. A Jungian View.* University Park: The Pennsylvania State University Press, 1988.

Krasner, James. *The Entangled Eye: Visual Perception and the Representation of Nature in Post-Darwinian Narrative.* Oxford: Oxford University Press, 1992.

Langer, Susanne K. (Ed.). *Reflections on Art. A Source Book of Writings by Artists, Critics and Philosophers*. New York: Oxford University Press, 1961.

Laurence, Patricia Ondek. *The Reading of Silence. Virginia Woolf in the English Tradition.* Stanford (Cal): Stanford University Press, 1991.

Lawrence, D. H. *Phoenix. The Posthumous Papers of D. H. Lawrence*. London: Heinemann, 1936.

Legouis, Emile. 'William Wordsworth.' *Cambridge History of English Literature, Volume 11*. Eds. A. W. Ward and A. R. Waller. Cambridge: Cambridge University Press, 1914, 100ff.

Levine, George. *Darwin and the Novelists: Patterns of Science in Victorian Fiction*. Cambridge: Harvard University Press, 1988.

Lodge, David. 'Thomas Hardy and Cinematographic Form.' *Novel* 7 (1973/74), 246-254.

Luftig, Victor. *Seeing Together. Friendship between the Sexes in English Writing, from Mill to Woolf*. Stanford: California University Press, 1993.

Lukacs, George. *The Theory of the Novel. A Historico-philosophical Essay on the Forms of Great Epic Literature*. London: Merlin Press, 1971.

McClung, William Alexander. *The Architecture of Paradise. Survivals of Eden and Jerusalem.* Berkeley: University of California Press, 1983.

Malamud, Randy. *The Language of Modernism*. Ann Arbor: UMI Research Press, 1989.

Mann, Thomas. 'Richard Wagner und der Ring der Nibelungen.' *Gesammelte Werke, Band 9*. Zürich: Ex Libris, 1975, 502-527.

Marcel, Gabriel. 'Bergsonism and Music,' in: *Reflections on Art*. Ed. Susanne Langer. New York: Oxford University Press, 1961.

Marks, Lawrence E. *The Unity of the Senses. Interrelations among the Modalities*. New York: Academic Press, 1978.

Martin, Timothy. *Joyce and Wagner. A Study in Influence*. Cambridge: Cambridge University Press, 1991.

Meyer, L. B. *Emotion and Meaning in Music*. Chicago: University of Chicago Press, 1956.

Miles, Rosalind. *The Female Form: Women Writers and the Conquest of the Novel*. London: Routledge and Kegan Paul, 1987.

Miles, Rosalind. *The Fiction of Sex. Themes and Functions of Sex Difference in the Modern Novel*. London: Vision Press, 1974.

Moore, Harry T. *Age of the Modern and Other Literary Essays*. Carbondale and Edwardsville: Southern Illinois UP, 1971.

Morris, Paul and Sawyer, Deborah (Eds.). *A Walk in the Garden. Biblical, Iconographical and Literary Images of Eden*. Sheffield: Journal for the Study of the Old Testament Press, 1992.

Mursell, James L. *The Psychology of Music*. Westport (Connecticut): Greenwood Press, 1971.

Musik in Geschichte und Gegenwart, Band I. Ed. Friedrich Blume. Kassel: Bärenreiter, 1951.

The Oxford English Dictionary. 2nd Edition. Oxford: Clarendon Press, 1989.

Parkin-Gounelas, Ruth. *Fictions of the Female Self: Charlotte Brontë, Olive Schreiner, Katherine Mansfield*. Basingstoke, Hampshire: Macmillan, 1991.

Pecora, Vincent P. *Self and Form in Modern Narrative*. Baltimore and London: Johns Hopkins University Press, 1989.

Picard, Max. *Die Welt des Schweigens*. Erlenbach: Rentsch, 1948.

Pratt, A. T. C. *People of the Period*. London: Neville Beeman, 1897.

Pratt, Carroll C. *The Meaning of Music. A Study in Psychological Aesthetics*. New York and London: Johnson Reprint Corporation, 1968.

Reinold, Helmut. 'On the Problem of Musical Hearing.' In: Langer, Susanne K. (Ed.). *Reflections on Art. A Source Book of Writings by Artists, Critics and Philosophers*. New York: Oxford University Press, 1961, 262-297.

Scher, Steven Paul. 'Literature and Music.' In: *Interrelations of Literature*. Ed. Jean-Pierre Barricelli and Joseph Gibaldi. New York: Modern Language Association of America, 1982, 225-250.

Scher, Steven Paul (Ed.). *Music and Text. Critical Inquiries*. Cambridge: Cambridge University Press, 1992.

Schulz, Max F. *Paradise Preserved. Recreations of Eden in 18th- and 19th-Century England*. Cambridge: Cambridge University Press, 1985.

de Selincourt, Basil. 'Music and Duration.' In: *Reflections on Art*. Ed. Susanne Langer. New York: Oxford University Press, 1961.

Showalter, Elaine. *Sexual Anarchy: Gender and Culture at the Fin de Siècle*. New York: Viking, 1990.

Sloboda. J. A. *The Musical Mind. The Cognitive Psychology of Music*. Oxford: Oxford University Press, 1985.

Steiner, George. *Language and Silence*. London: Faber and Faber, 1967.

Stubbs, Patricia. *Women and Fiction: Feminism and the Novel 1880 - 1920*. London: Methuen, 1981.

Trilling, Lionel. 'The Immortality Ode.' *The Liberal Imagination*. London: Secker and Warburg, 1951, 147ff.

Underhill, Evelyn. *Mysticism*. London: Methuen, 1911.

Vinge, Louise. *The Five Senses. Studies in a Literary Tradition*. Lund: Publications of the Royal Society of Letters of Lund, 1975.

Wagner, Richard. 'Ueber Franz Liszts Symphonische Dichtungen.' 1857. In: *Musik zur Sprache gebracht. Musikästhetische Texte aus drei Jahrhunderten*. Ed. Carl Dahlhaus and Michael Zimmermann. Kassel: Bärenreiter, 1984, 306-313.

Waters, Michael. *The Garden in Victorian Literature*. Aldershot: Scolar Press, 1988.

Wellek, Albert. 'Das Doppelempfinden in der Geistesgeschichte.' *Zeitschrift für Aesthetik* 23 (1929), 14-42.

Index

The index is arranged as follows: 1. Index of Dorothy Richardson's Works; 2. Index of Characters in *Pilgrimage*; 3. Index of Places in *Pilgrimage*; 4. Name Index; 5. Subject Index

1. Index of Dorothy Richardson's Works

2. Index of Characters in *Pilgrimage*

3. Index of Places in *Pilgrimage*

4. Name Index

5. Subject Index